Options Trading: 6 in 1:

The Ultimate Guide to Investing and Making a Profit | Successfully Learn How to Get a Passive Income Using the Best Swing and Day Strategies and Maximize Your Earnings

Written by:

Nathan Real

OPTIONS TRADING

The Beginner's Guide for Options Trading to Learn Strategies and Techniques, Making Money in Few Weeks. You Will Find Inside the A-Z Glossary All Technical Terms Used

FOREX TRADING

A Complete Guide About Forex Trading | Including Strategies, Risk Management Techniques and Fundamental Analysis

Stock Market Investing for Beginners

Learn How to Enter the Stock Market | Including the Best Platforms for Trading and Common Mistakes and How to Avoid Them

Day Trading Forex:

The Forex Basics Explained With All Trading Strategies. A Proven Method To Become A Profitable Forex Trader. You Will Find Inside The A-Z Glossary To All Technical Terms Used

Swing Trading

the Beginner's Guide on How to Trade for Profits with the Best Strategies

and Technical Analysis. You will Find Inside the A-Z Glossary to All Technical Terms Used

Stock Trading for Beginners

An Easy Guide to the Stock Market with the Trading Strategy to Achieve Financial Freedom. You Will Find Inside the A-Z Glossary to All Technical Terms Used

Table of Contents

OPTIONS TRADING

The Beginner's Guide for Options Trading to Learn Strategies and Techniques, Making Money in Few Weeks. You Will Find Inside the A-Z Glossary All Technical Terms Used

Written by:

Nathan Real

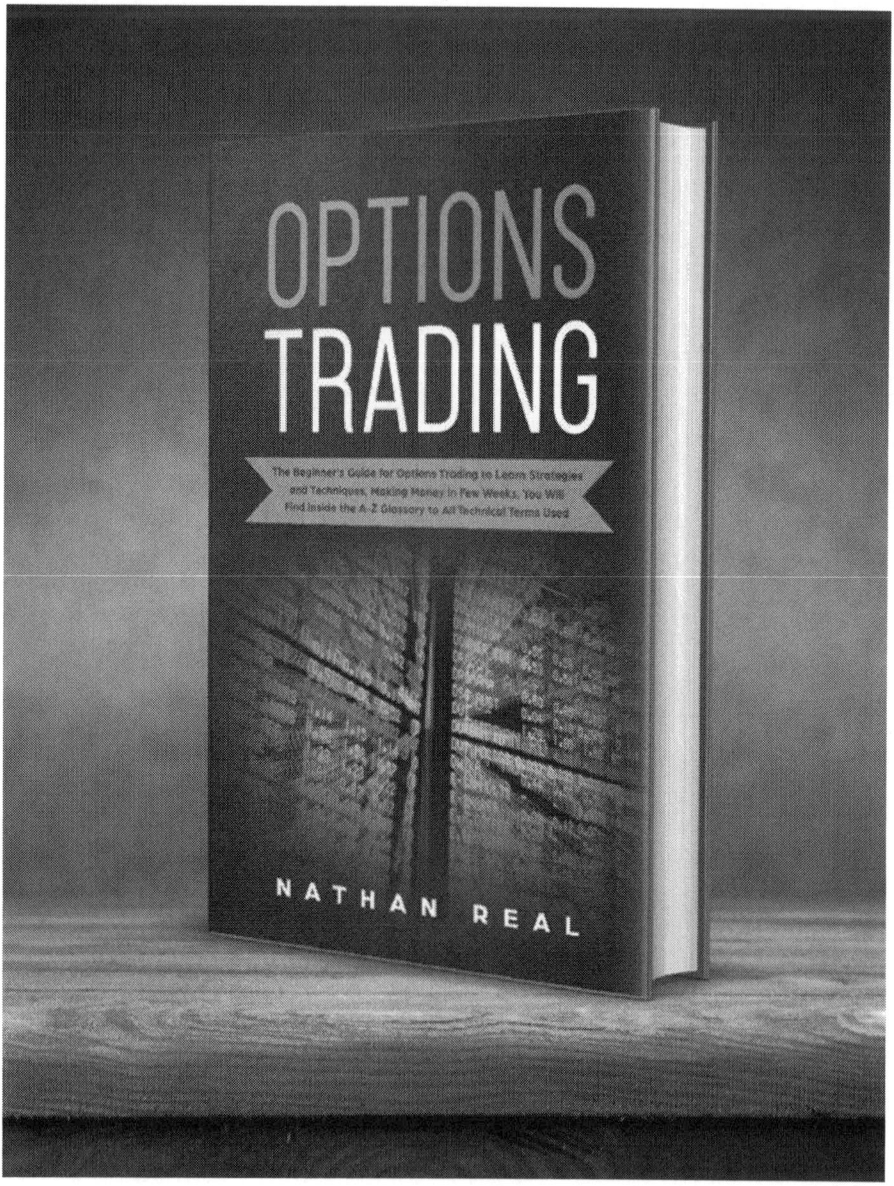
OPTIONS
TRADING
The Beginner's Guide for Options Trading to Learn Strategies and Techniques, Making Money in Few Weeks. You Will Find Inside the A-Z Glossary to All Technical Terms Used
NATHAN REAL

Introduction

Options trading is one of the most lucrative investments in the financial market today. It can help you grow your money over short periods of time, so you need to have a better understanding of how it works.

The options market allows you to trade at relatively lower costs and reduced risk levels. You may also make some passive income from the trade as you enjoy more leverage in terms of the number of shares you can trade.

When you visit the options market, you will be surprised at the wide array of opportunities you will come across. This is because you can make money both from the upward and downward movement of stock prices.

This book highlights the main things you need to understand before and during options trading. When you get to understand the purpose of options trading and how it works, you will be able to trade successfully on your platforms of choice. This will automatically result in better performance—hence more income. You will be able to attain your financial goals faster as you also advance your trading skills.

If you are seeking to gain an in-depth understanding of what options trading entails, then this is the right book for you.

Chapter 1: Options Definition and Function

Apart from the popular financial instruments available on the market today such as stocks and bonds, there are other instruments known as derivatives. A derivative refers to a financial instrument that gets its value from other instruments or assets. One example of these derivatives would be options.

By definition, options are financial instruments derived from an underlying asset such as stocks or bonds. They present you with an opportunity to purchase an underlying security at a specific date and price. In other words, options represent contracts that allow you to buy and sell a certain value of an underlying asset at a particular price. Each contract specifies certain terms about the trade.

How Do They Work?

Options provide you with a very reliable way of investing in stock trading. Just like any other financial transaction, an options agreement or contract is made up of two people—a buyer and a seller. An individual contract represents a number of shares of the underlying security. In most cases, one contract covers 100 shares of stock. The buyer always pays a certain amount against each contract as the premium fee. This amount is always determined by the type of underlying asset as well as the option strike price.

Traders often use options as a form of investment because of the limited number of risks involved in these derivatives. This is because options enable people to protect their real stocks from financial market exposure. However, care must be taken when dealing with options since, like any other trade, it is very easy to lose a large amount of stock within a fraction of time. They involve high profits, but may also result in high risks if not handled well. Despite this, many people consider options as one of the best and most reliable financial instruments on the stock market.

Options as Derivatives

As stated earlier, options are not real stock. They are derivatives whose price is determined by the price of the underlying security. Other examples of derivatives include futures, swaps, forwards, calls, and puts among several others.

Since options only represent a certain asset, the contract entered by a buyer and seller only offers you the ability to trade on the options market. An option call gives you the right to purchase an underlying security at a specific cost and time whereas a put option grants you the capability to sell on the market at a specified period of time and cost.

Each option transaction represents two sides—the buying side and the selling side.

Selling of an option is also known as writing an option. Each side of an option transaction involves its own rewards and risks. When a person buys an option, it is said that they have obtained a long position; when they sell an option, they have a short position. This applies to both call and put transactions.

In options trading, asset owners do not get involved in the transaction. Cash is only exchanged between the parties involved in the options transactions. Most of these transactions happen between investors, brokers, and market makers.

Types of Options

Options come in two major types—put options and call options. Traders choose the kind of option to trade-in depending on whether they want to buy or sell on the options market.

Call Options

The call option options make it possible for you to purchase an underlying asset associated with the option in question. When a call option is in the money, the bid or strike price is less in value than the underlying stock price. Traders always buy a call option when there is a possibility of its stock price to increase beyond the current bid price before the expiration is obtained. When this happens, the trader derives some profit from the call transaction.

Individuals who purchase call options are always known as holders. Once they acquire the option, they can sell it any time before the expiration date. The profit of any option is obtained by subtracting the strike price, premium, and transaction fees from the stock price. The resulting amount is what is called the intrinsic value. This difference is always a negative value when the trader has made a loss and zero value when no profit or loss has been realized.

The maximum amount that a trader can lose from an option is equivalent to its premium. This explains why most people purchase options and not the underlying security.

The call option comprises three components—the strike price, the premium, and the exercise or expiration date. The premium is the amount of money that a trader pays when acquiring a particular option. For instance, a trader may purchase a call option with $55 as the strike price, a $5 premium, and an expiration period of one month; it means that you will pay the seller $5 as the premium. If the expiration date is reached before you exercise the option, you will only pay the $5. If let's say, a week later the price goes up to $70 and you decide to sell your option, you will make a profit of $15 from the transaction less $5 paid as the premium. If the price goes below $55, you make a loss.

Investors may also decide to sell a call option when they are anticipating a decline in the stock price. As the stock price falls to a level that is lower than the strike price, the investor will get some profit from the transaction. The person selling a call is known as the writer of the call. They must sell shares to a buyer at a price determined beforehand.

Put Options

This grants you the ability to write or sell an asset or security at a cost that is already predetermined, also the expiration date. Both call and put options can be used on stocks, commodities, currencies, and indexes as underlying securities. In this case, the strike price becomes the cost by which you sell the option.

A put option allows you to sell a certain asset at a known cost and expiration date. This option can be used on a good number of underlying assets including indexes, currencies, commodities, and stocks. The price at which a trader sells an option is called the strike price.

Traders make a profit from selling a put option when anticipating a decline in the strike price. They make a loss when the value of the stock increases to a level that is beyond the strike price. This indicates that the cost of a put option may rise or fall as time elapses.

The intrinsic value of a put option can be derived by obtaining the difference in the prices of the stock and the option. The resultant value keeps changing as the time value reduces in strength. When a stock option bears a positive intrinsic value, you say that it is in the money. A negative value of this shows that the option has fallen out of the money.

Similar to call options, you do not need to wait for your put options to expire before you exercise them. Since the premium value of an option continues to vary with the price of the shares or the cost of any other underlying asset, you must exercise your options just at the right time to avoid incurring losses in the future.

Options and Stocks

If you have been keen enough then you must have realized that more investors are joining the options market more than the stock market. Stock trading has for a long time been the most popular form of trading on financial markets. You may be wondering if indeed options trading is better than stock trading. One great aspect of options is that they allow you to do more than just trading. Options have several characteristics that cannot be found in other financial instruments. One such characteristic is the use of Greeks, which are mathematical figures that help estimate the risk associated with each option. Traders can use these figures to avoid some trades that seem too risky.

There are several other differences between options and stocks. When you purchase shares of stock from a certain company, you acquire ownership of the percentage of the company. This means that you can sell off the shares anytime you wish to do so. On the other hand, options do not grant you ownership of stocks. They only represent derivatives of the company stocks that are traded on certain predefined terms.

The main reason why investors purchase stocks is to sell them later when the price goes high. They, therefore, wait for the value of a certain stock to decline before making a purchase, then again wait for the price to go up in order to sell the same. When it comes to options, investors use them as a way of generating income and not necessarily as a form of investment. Options traders are never interested in the underlying stock. Most of them trade on short-term engagements. This is why the options market is always filled with almost all kinds of traders. The trader relies on certain changes in the performance of the option to make money.

Another clear difference between stocks and options is the issue of time. Stocks can be traded for as long as decades. They do not have an expiration period. Once you invest in the stock market, it may take you as little as a few days to as much as several years to close your positions and make a profit. However, this can only happen when the company issuing the shares continues to exist. This privilege is missing in the options market since each option has a specific date of expiration.

Most people who invest in stocks always end up with good profits in the long-term. This is because most companies that sell shares keep building their brand portfolio, making it impossible for them to collapse. As the company grows, the share value grows as well. When it comes to options, the value a trader receives at the end of each transaction is very uncertain. Options trading is somehow likened to gambling, which may end in a win or loss. Each trade involves a number of aspects that determine the outcome. It is upon the trader to understand these aspects and apply them accurately in order to realize a profit. Ignoring the rules of trade always results in a loss.

Another great difference between stocks and options is that stocks are always sold in the form of preferred stocks or common stocks while options are traded in the form of contracts. Common stocks are those that cover a percentage of the participation in the profit of the company while preferred stocks are those that pay dividends to the investor. Traders receive these dividends at predefined intervals and amounts. Options contracts, on the other hand, serve as agreements between the buyer and the seller based on certain terms that both have to agree upon.

The pricing of stocks and options also differs. The value of each stock share depends on how the company performs in the long-run, as well as some market factors. On the other hand, the cost of options is determined by an array of factors such as time decay, expiration date as well as the value of the underlying security.

In terms of risk, a stock trader only risks losing their capital if the company underperforms or stops operating. This means that if the company continues to operate, the trader is sure of getting most of their capital back with some profit. In options, the highest value that a trader can lose is equivalent to the amount of capital invested in each position. Since there is an unlimited potential of losing the premium, it means that options trading involves more risk than stock trading. It may take years for a stock investor to lose part of their capital; however, it takes a matter of minutes or hours for an options trader to lose their premium.

The Options Contract

An options contract is an agreement providing you with the authority or right to acquire or give out an asset for a specific amount of money. Basically, an options contract represents 100 shares of stock. Each contract is defined by two categories of people—buyers and sellers. To purchase or sell options, the involved parties must fulfill the rules or formalities stipulated in the contract. In some cases, cash is used to settle contracts instead of shares.

For every contract, the person buying or acquiring a purchase position is the holder, and the seller is known as the writer. An option that is not exercised during the stipulated timeframe expires at the end of this period. One good thing with options is that the loss is often deducted from the money you put in as capital. Once an option expires, you can no longer engage in transactions based on the underlying stock.

The payoff pattern for stocks is almost similar to the one used in stock trading. The contract acts as a form of leverage for each transaction. This is because the holder or writer of each contract only gets control of a small percentage of the underlying security.

This means that traders only get the rights to a tiny portion relating to the stock being traded. During each transaction, businesspeople can keep reinvesting their profits into the same position until the option expires. This gives the trader good leverage during price fluctuations. It is always easy for a trader to exercise an option before its value starts to diminish. This is one way of minimizing the risk of losing all the premium invested in the market.

Options contract provide several details about the market and the trade. Just like any other trade, you are required to make some payment before you start trading. Each contract is governed by a number of terms defined below:

Derivative

We have defined options as forms of other instruments. This is a contract between traders with a value that is dictated by the value of underlying security. For each contract that involves derivatives, involved parties must first agree on the initial cost of the underlying asset. Options are considered derivatives since they only give you the right over a percentage of certain commodities.

Strike Price

This describes the cost or value of an option at any particular time. The strike price can also be referred to as the agreed-upon price. It is the cost of an option agreed upon by the buyer and the seller when making an options contract.

In the case of a call option, the strike price is the value placed as the cost a trader pays to gain rights around the underlying stock. In terms of the put option, the strike price generally implies the cost about which the seller relinquishes the rights to security.

This price does not change during the period of the contract. It is not affected by any market and stock elements. Strike prices are some of the determinants of the profit one can make from the market. If underlying stock prices rise beyond the amount of the strike price, one of the things that will rise is the cost of the option and this is the best time for sellers to close their positions at a profit. When the value of the stock drops below the strike price, buyers can purchase options at this point with the hope that the same price will rise. When there is a variation in regards to the strike price and with relations to the price of the market, this variation is what will be used to calculate the profit.

Expiration

What expiration means is a period when a given options get to an end. When the exercise date is attained, it means that it is no longer available for trading. The difference between the start and end dates of an option is known as its time period. The value of an option often decreases as it approaches the expiration date. In most cases, this date can range from a few hours, days, or even years.

The Underlying Security

This is the asset used to define an options contract. It is the underlying stock upon which you trade your options. It is an essential component of the options market since it enables you to come up with the price and risks associated with certain stocks. It also allows you to choose the right options with the highest profit potential. In most cases, the cost of any option is determined using the worth of the underlying security.

Share

Shares are units of stock belonging to a certain company. Each option represents 100 shares of stock.

Contract Size

The contract size is the number of shares or stocks represented by a given option contract. For example, if a contract covers 100 shares, then 100 is the contract size.

The Premium

We have mentioned this severally before. The premium is the price you need to pay in order to acquire rights on an option. The premium can also be defined as the income that you receive from selling or writing an options contract. It can also refer to the cost of a given contract before it expires. In most cases, the premium is quoted in terms of dollars per share. The premium highlights a combination of three components—the time component, intrinsic component, and implied volatility of the asset.

Traders obtain the intrinsic value from calculations based on subtracting the asset cost from the strike cost. In a call option, this amount is equivalent to the current cost of the stock or security less the strike price. In the case of a put option, this value equals the amount set as the strike price minus the cost of the current stock.

When it comes to the options trading business, what is known as the time value comprises the amount a trader is willing to pay, with the hope that market prices will change in their favor. This time value drops when the option approaches the exercise date. Basically, how much more time is available before the expiration of an option, the higher its time value. When more time is available, it is easy for investors to pay more premium for the option with the hope that its price will change in the future. When there is less time until the expiration of an option, more traders will shy away from investing in the option since very little price change is expected.

The premium, therefore, is an addition between the option time value and the intrinsic value of the option.

Chapter 2: Options Trading

Most people always think of the stock market when they want to invest. Actually, a good number of stock market traders do not understand what options trading is all about. Stock trading has several benefits; however, it may not work for individuals who wish to invest on a short-term basis. Long-term investment strategies such as the buy and hold can help investors increase their wealth significantly, however such strategies do not provide better profits like some short-term ones. This is where more active short-term methods like options trading come in. These are often characterized by more returns.

Options trading has continued to become more and more popular. Basically, it involves the trading of financial derivatives known as options. The concept of options trading is not new. The first options contract was made in 1973 at an Exchange in the Chicago Board. There is a lot of similarity between the options traded today and those used at that time. However, a lot of things have changed in terms of the market size, trading terms, and the volume of exchange carried out every single day. People invest in options for various reasons, which will be discussed later in this chapter.

Options trading is a great way of investing money. Both the wealthy and average people can invest in the business since it does not require a lot of capital to start. Like we mentioned earlier, options are contracts that work within specific time limits.

Trading styles for options do differ from one region to another. This means that options can be categorized as American, European, Barrier, Bermudan, or Exotic options among several others. When trading options, you must be able to tell the style involved to enjoy the necessary gains. American options, for instance, close at the end of every third

Friday of the month of expiry. The price of an option on this date becomes the closing price for the position. One major characteristic of American options is that you can close any moment between start and exercise days. European options, on the other hand, must be exercised on the date of expiration and not before. Positions for these options close on the third Thursday of the expiration month. There are also barrier options, which can only be exercised after the stock value rises beyond a certain level.

Bermudan ones are to be closed anywhere between start and exercise dates while exotic options make use of non-standard exercise procedures.

What Is Involved in Options Trading?

Basically, options trading involves the buying and selling of options contracts in the options market. Traders make a profit by purchasing contracts at relatively low costs and selling the same at higher costs.

When you buy a call option, it is like you are betting that the share price will rise in the future. For instance, if you purchase a call option for company X for $1500, you are indicating your certainty that the cost of the asset will shoot upwards beyond this purchase price for you to make a profit. Every time you purchase a put option, you are anticipating a decline in the cost of the underlying security. In stock market terms, you are expecting a bearish outcome on the stock.

Options trading is more flexible than stock trading. This is because options are derived from a wide array of underlying securities. This gives traders more variety in terms of the scope involved in the trade. Investors use the price of options to determine price movements of stocks, commodities, foreign currencies, and indices. This presents a lot of profit-making opportunities that may not be present in the stock market. More versatility is also realized in the numerous types of options and orders that traders can place on the market.

Stock traders only have two ways through which they can make a profit—that is long positions and short positions. However, in options trading, investors get spoilt for choice since positions can be executed in several diverse ways and combinations.

Purchasing Options

Purchasing an options contract is just similar to purchasing stock. Investors buy options by selecting what they wish to buy, stating the amount then placing a buy to open order either directly or indirectly through a broker. If the value of the option goes up, you can sell it or exercise it depending on what works for you. One serious advantage of options trading is that you can make money from price increases and also from price declines. If you anticipate a rise in the prices, you can buy a call option and if you anticipate a drop in the prices, you can purchase a put option.

When you decide to buy an option, you will get several contracts on the same underlying stock. This will be in terms of the types of calls and puts available for the same stock. For instance, you may find an option for company selling at $100 for each share, and find several others for the same company selling at different premiums.

Buying a Call Option

Let us assume that you want to purchase a call option for company A with an exercise cost of $60, a premium of $10, and an expiration date of one month. 7 days later, the stock price increases to $75. This means that you will make some $15 from the transaction. However, since you had already paid a premium of $10 to place the order, your profit will be $15 less $10 which comes to $5. This is as illustrated below.

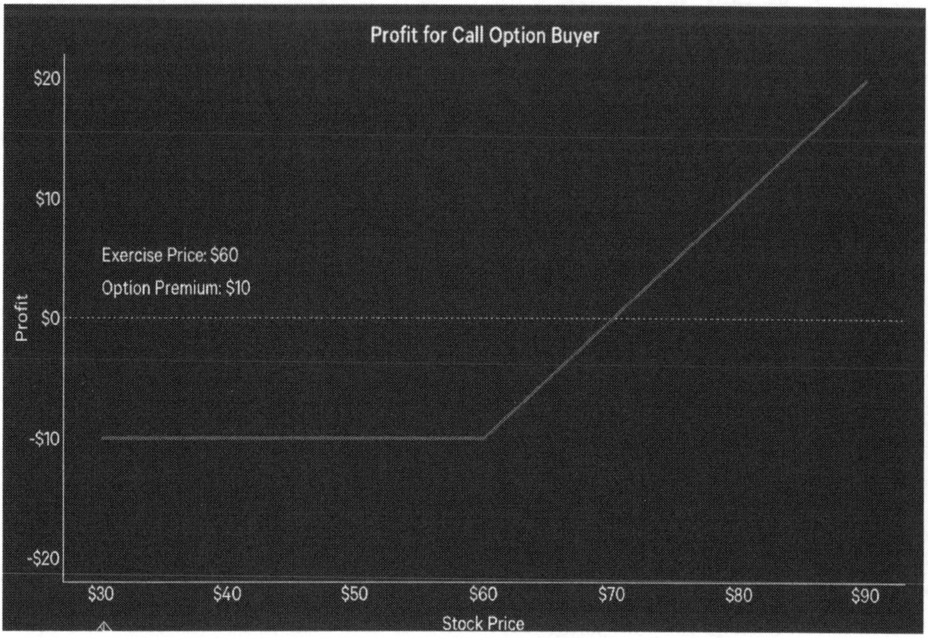

Figure 1: Buying a Call

If the price of stock declines to, say, $50 per share and you decide to let the option expire on its own. You will get an outlay of -$10, which is equivalent to the premium you paid for the order.

Buying a Put Option

Let us also assume that you are purchasing a put option from company A for $45, a premium rate of $15, and an expiration of one month. After one week, the price drops from $45 to $25. If you exercise the option at this point, you will get a difference of $20. Your profit at their point will be $20 less than the premium that is $5.

Selling Options

Writing or selling of contracts occurs in two ways. The first one is when you have pre-bought contracts that you want to release at a profit; similarly, in a position when you do not want to suffer more losses, then you can place a sell to close order on the options market. You can raise this order if the price of the option has gone up and you want to get some profit from this change, or if the option price is constantly falling and you want to close the position before you incur more losses. The second way is through opening short positions. This is what is known as the writing of options because the strategy involves creating new contracts for the options market. When a buyer agrees to your contract, you will be obliged to sell the underlying security associated with the contract to them.

The process of writing options is often completed using the sell to open order. The seller receives a payment that is equivalent to the strike price as soon as they place this order. Using such orders may sometimes be riskier than engaging in ordinary buying and selling, but it may also come with higher returns in terms of profit. Most investors place the sell-to-open order when they are certain that the buyer will not close a contract early enough as they seek to generate some income.

Selling Calls

This involves allowing the buyer to make purchases against an asset or underlying equity. The market prices and other factors may force a seller to give away some equity with the price agreed on earlier as the strike price. When the investor selling a call option also turns out to be the one owning the underlying equity, the process gets the name "writing a covered call." If the person selling the same option turns out not to be the one owning the stock, then the process gets referred to as "writing a naked call."

Selling a Put Option

Besides buying put options, you may also sell them at a profit. Investors who sell put options do so with the hope that the options will lose value in the future. When a trader sells a put option to the buyer, they have some authority to acquire the equity involved in the trade at a predefined cost if the option is exercised. For the seller to make a profit, the cost of the equity should remain either as it is or goes higher beyond the current strike cost. In case the cost remains under the strike cost, the involved seller makes a loss while the buyer makes a profit from the trade.

When it comes to options trading, profit is made from selling, buying, and writing options, not necessarily by exercising them. The point at which a trader exercises a contract depends on the strategies used in the trade as well as the need to acquire underlying security. This means that you can make a profit both from exercising options and from just buying and selling them.

Expiration

One aspect that governs options is their expiration capability. At the end of each expiration period, the trader realizes a profit or loss. The reason why most traders try to learn and apply as many strategies as possible to each trade is that they want to realize profits for each contract. Most traders always feel frustrated when a contract ends without yielding any profit.

The profit of an option is determined by its intrinsic as well as time value. This is why it is important to consider the expiration period of any contract before investing in it. Some options may seem promising in terms of profits but end up at a loss because of the short expiration period. Options also do exist only for the period of time that the underlying stock is available on the market for trading. Once a company stops listing its stock on the market, the options related to this particular stock will cease to trade as well.

The more an investor holds onto options, the more its value decreases. Unlike stocks, options tend to expire faster, and as the expiration date nears, the possibility of making profits from the trade also diminishes. Professional traders always ensure that they get more out of an open contract before it gets too late.

The Volatility of the Options Market

In the options market, the term volatility describes the way the cost of a specific equity fluctuates over a period of time. Highly volatile options are often derived from highly volatile stocks; these carry more risks. Options with low volatility are always a featureless risk. In the options market, those stocks that feature high volatility always cost more than those with low volatility. It is not easy to identify certain stocks in terms of their volatility levels since it is easier for some low volatility stocks to become highly volatile and vice versa. Volatility is of two types—implied or historic.

The historical type of volatility is alternatively called statistical volatility. It measures price fluctuations based on predetermined time frames. It helps you to determine how the price of a particular option fluctuates over a period of time, say one year. A rise in historical volatility increases the cost of the equity in question. When this amount drops, the price of equity also goes back to normal. By understanding the changes in options prices over time, investors can make informed decisions on when and how to invest in a particular type of option. For instance, if the historical volatility of a particular option for 6 months is 25% and the volatility over the last 5 days is 50% it means that the stock has a volatility that is higher than normal.

Implied volatility, on the other hand, refers to the estimation of a particular stock or future volatility of the option based on some market factors. It is also known as projected volatility and is mostly used by traders who want to determine the future prices of certain options. This type of volatility is often derived from the cost of a given option. Traders make use of the price as well as the historical performance of an option to determine its future price trends.

In case you are purchasing an option that has a high potential to generate profit, the premium of such an option may be higher than other options. This is because you can easily sell the option at a profit. Such positions are claimed to be in the money. Another trade may be "at the money" indicating that the cost is similar to the price of the equity. There is another one that can get "out of the money," which means that the cost of trading the option is way higher than the value of the equity. An option like this one is not good since it is almost impossible for you to get some profit from it.

Once a call option gets in the money, it indicates that the cost of the equity has shot higher than the strike cost. When a put option gets in the money, the cost of the underlying equity is far below the strike cost. If there is still a wide time gap between the beginning and end of a trade transaction, more time is available for a trader to make a profit.

Benefits of Options Trading

One major reason why people invest in options is the level of risk involved and the returns realized. By now, you must have noticed the huge difference between trading with options and trading directly with stocks. Options can be traded in combination with other financial instruments to leverage profits. The trade is easily carried out and, in most cases, the profits are very good.

Options are considered by many people as a great alternative to stock trading. They do not cost much and help secure your underlying assets during the trade. Let us look at some of the major advantages that options have over other investment tools.

Options Involve Lower Costs

We have already mentioned the fact that options have a high potential for generating large profits for small capital investments. Most people trade-in options as an alternative to other forms of investment for this particular reason. Even those with very little capital can gain significant profit from the trade so long as they apply the right knowledge and strategies.

This means that traders can open an option position with the same potential as a stock position using lower amounts of capital. Let us say for example, that you wish to purchase 100 shares of stock at $80 for each share. This means that you will need to raise $8000 to make this purchase. However, if you were to buy the same shares using two call options, each with a premium of $20, then you will need half of the total capital for the same value of the stock. This is because each call represents 100 shares. Two calls will represent 200 shares, multiplying this by $20 per share comes to $4000.

The low costs of trading options are quite advantageous because they give investors the potential to raise large amounts of income over a short period of time. This advantage is absent in a number of financial instruments, especially those that are long-term since large amounts of cash must be invested in such instruments to generate income.

Options Are Associated With Reduced Risk Levels

Each financial investment tool bears a number of risks and this also applies to options trading. For most of these tools, it is always assumed that the higher the risk, the higher the returns. However, this is not true with options since there is a high balance between the risk and reward of each transaction. On most occasions, the risk of a trade is very little compared to the reward realized. Some market factors make it possible for traders to make a profit at very low risks. One great advantage of the options market is that you get to choose the kind of strategy you want to use in your transactions by first determining the amount of risk you are willing to expose your investment. You can always balance various strategies and market factors to balance or lower the risk involved in each position. The more you understand the basics of options trading, the more you will know how to minimize the risks involved in the trade.

The success of each trade always depends on the trader's ability to mitigate risks. If you do not understand how to measure risks and work around them, it may be difficult for you to generate profit from some transactions. Although there is still a high risk of losing your capital when trading options, this risk is relatively low compared to the risk of trading stocks or underlying securities. The only amount you may lose from trading options is the premium amount. If you analyze your contracts correctly and stick to the rules of trade all the way, you will always make some profit from options trading.

The strategies used in assessing options help investors to calculate the risk involved in certain contracts before putting their money in any of these contracts. This makes it easy for traders to estimate the expected profits and losses in good time. With such information, you can easily delve into the trade with confidence knowing what you should expect from the market. By using the right trading styles and sticking to the right strategies, you can easily reduce losses and make the most out of each trading period.

In a nutshell, it is in order to say that options feature limited risks and unlimited profits. When the cost of an option has not favored you by the time of expiration, you can allow it to expire worthlessly, but you will lose your premium. This is why, just like any other form of investment, it is advisable that you only invest what you can afford to lose. The level of risk involved depends on your level of expertise and commitment. If you become careless in your trades, the risks may increase and you may end up losing each time.

Options Help You to Generate Passive Income

The options market involves the use of several strategies. Some of these strategies can help you generate some passive income from the trade. For instance, the covered call strategy allows you to purchase stock, then earn some cash selling calls from the same stock to investors. This way, you are still the owner of the stock, but making some returns from the stock at the same time.

Other strategies assist you in making maximum use of market factors such as volatility and time decay. Options spread and combination strategies also assist you in gaining more from the market. As you trade, you may keep growing your stock from the returns. If you add more shares to a stock that pays dividends, you will be able to grow your income significantly.

Options Provide Leverage for Your Investment

For each option contract that you start, you either purchase or sell 100 shares of stock. This means that you can gain control over a large number of shares without utilizing large amounts of capital. This is because the amount you need to trade an option is far much less than the exact price of the shares. By spending less on each contract, you will be able to enter more positions and trade in large amounts of underlying stocks within a shorter period of time. As a result, you will multiply your profits faster and this will translate faster growth of your investments.

Buying an options contract does not give you any right to the underlying shares. You only gain access to a small percentage of the underlying security. If the other party decides to exercise the contract before expiration, there is very little and, in some cases, nothing to lose. Since the value of an option is affected by several other factors besides the value of the underlying asset, it is very easy to make good money from positions even at the time that the cost of the underlying equity has not made any significant change. This explains the reason why the options market has both small as well as more established investors.

Options Offer More Flexibility and Versatility

Options trading is very flexible. This is one of the many factors that make investors flood the options market. The contracts always feature the most versatile terms and the strategies involved in the trade are quite diverse. Traders can comfortably apply a combination of strategies on a single contract to make the best in terms of capital.

Options are also bought and sold depending on a wide array of underlying assets.

Besides understanding the direction, which prices may take, you can also get to find out how the prices of foreign currencies, indices, and commodities can change in the future. This helps you to know the type of underlying security you need to go for to ensure that you get quick profits.

With the many strategies in place, it becomes very easy to determine the kind of opportunities to invest in. For instance, if you are skilled in determining changes in the foreign exchange market, you can easily apply this skill in the options market to determine how the market is going to change over time. One great strategy that ensures flexibility of options trading is the use of spreads. You can significantly reduce the cost of trading by incorporating certain spreads and combinations. These not only reduce the risk of entering certain positions but also enable you to make a profit from price changes in more than one direction. In uncertain trades, you can use these strategies to hedge certain positions as a way of minimizing losses.

You may also use options to create synthetic trade positions, which offer you several opportunities that help you to attain your profit goals. These positions are commonly used by experts and provide a great alternative to the normal strategies used in options trading.

Flexibility in options trading is also enhanced by how people use their time. When it comes to options, it is not a must for you to spend all day watching the market for you to gain profit. Options allow you to create your contracts based on predicted price movements. This is totally different from the buy and holds strategies used in other investment tools. If you invest in an option contract with a high probability of success, it is not a must that you spend time monitoring the trade. You can define stop-loss orders to ensure that a contract position closes as soon as the direction of the market changes.

Besides all this, you also have the opportunity to dictate the duration of each contract. You can, therefore, trade on a daily, weekly, monthly, or even annual basis depending on the amount of time you have. For instance, if you have more time within the day, you can take up daily positions.

The benefits listed above explain why options trading has been appealing to a good number of investors. The process is quite simple and a lot of profit can be made within a short time period. When you balance your contracts properly, you can easily reduce risks in your overall portfolio. For example, you may decide to combine selling stock and buying a put option at the same time. This will grant you an advantage when the stock price goes up, and limit losses in case of the stock price decreases.

When coming up with a trading plan for the options market, you must beware of every aspect involved in the market. First, you must understand what account you need to be able to trade, as well as the amount of capital required as premium. With a good plan, you will be able to trade successfully and keep improving with time.

Chapter 3: Options Trading Fundamentals

Options trading offers you an investment opportunity that cannot be compared to any other. However, before venturing into the trade, it is useful to gain a deeper understanding of the rules and fundamentals of this business. You must know exactly how the trade works because this will serve as a foundation for all your contracts. When you are equipped with the right information, it becomes easy for you to make a huge fortune from stock options.

Because options are governed by time limits, most people have a misconception that the trade is associated with a large number of risks. This is however not true since the trade has remained profitable to individuals who spend their time understanding and applying the necessary techniques.

The same way business people create a plan is the same way every trader should have a plan before starting to trade. You should base the plan on the knowledge you have about the options market as well as the strategies involved in each trade. The plan should consist of things such as:

- Your level of risk tolerance
- Intended portfolio size
- Trading times
- Stop-loss definitions
- Types of stocks to trade-in
- Profit targets
- Premium amounts

People get into the options market for different reasons. However, it is risky to start trading without any knowledge about the business. Doing this will automatically result in the loss of your capital. This chapter discusses the fundamental aspects of options trading that you must acquaint yourself with before beginning to trade.

Options Trading Systems

This refers to a tool or method used to create buy and sell signals on the options market. An options trading system utilizes several stock analysis techniques to generate signals that help you establish the right styles, strategies, and time for buying and selling options. Most of these systems are derived from a number of trading strategies and utilize both technical and fundamental analysis to predict market trends.

Technical analysis is one of the methods used to determine the price of options through analyzing the previous performance of the options. Fundamental analysis, on the other hand, utilizes market research information as well as stock-related factors to determine the price of options. Most option trading systems use these two methods as well as other factors such as the volatility of an option and time decay to define trading patterns.

The system helps you to meet all the criteria required before entering any contract. After you meet the necessary requirements for the trade, it generates a signal that tells you whether to enter, remain, or exit the market. Without the right procedures and information, the options market can become quite complex. It is almost impossible to carry out trade on the options market without a trading system. Besides regulating your performance, the system also prevents you from making emotional decisions that may lead to loss of capital.

Basically, a good trading system will give you leverage on the market. You can easily use the system to control various contracts covering thousands of shares at the same time. You will easily identify those signals that can help you make a profit, thus avoiding those that are fake. Most trading systems operate using some of the best strategies on the market. They will, therefore, help you hedge your investment and this will ensure that you do not lose much in case the market becomes uncertain.

One great advantage of options trading systems is that any trader can develop one. For you to succeed in options trading, you must be able to create a system that makes use of the different types of strategies available on the options market. You can incorporate these strategies one by one until you are satisfied with the resultant system. Remember, the more strategies you incorporate the more prepared you are for the dynamic nature of the options market. Most investors start with a plan before coming up with a system that helps meet these plans. It is always advisable that you start with a basic system then continue building on it until you are sure that it can give you 100% success on the platform.

In case you wish to create a trading system, here are some important steps you should follow:

Choose a strategy—select a strategy that meets your trading needs for you to start. For instance, the best way to start is by purchasing calls and puts. You can get a strategy that helps you to achieve this then use it to come up with your system.

Start trading—as soon as you define your strategy, you can start taking some basic contracts. Do not go for complicated ones since your strategy may not be able to handle these. You can begin with one or two contracts and keep increasing the number as your system grows. Keep a record of your transactions as this will enable you to analyze your performance and determine the changes you need to make on the system.

Evaluate the system—check out your failures and successes and use these to improve on your system. How frequently you evaluate your system depends on the frequency of your trades. If you are an aggressive trader, then you will need to do this more often so that you do not miss out on some important trends. As you do this, make a comparison between your wins and your losses. List the factors associated with each win and those associated with every loss. Together with this, be sure to analyze your mistakes so that you avoid them in the future.

Make the necessary adjustments—if you spot a weakness in your system, try and adjust it before making any more trades. This is how most investors improve their performance in the options market. If you keep justifying your weaknesses, you will be unable to make the right adjustments and this will always result in losses. Study market changes and keep updating your system to meet these changes.

Learn—every trading system you create must keep changing to meet the standards of the market. You must always be ready to learn new strategies and skills that will contribute to the growth of your system. The more you study, the better you become in options trading.

The Use of Option Spreads

Options spread allow you to open two options positions that are opposite to each other. They are used by traders to reduce the risk involved in the options market. The spreads make it possible for you to buy and sell options derived from the same asset at the same time. These two options always feature different strike prices and expiration dates.

The option positions created are always derived from the same class of stock. Their work is to limit the potential upside and downside of each contract. One advantage of using spreads is that they also reduce the cost of trading as compared with single positions.

Traders can create several types of spreads to fulfill various purposes. A good number of options trading strategies make use of option spreads. As a trader, you need to understand each spread and where it can be applied to the options market. These can be grouped into three basic categories—there are diagonal spreads, then horizontal spreads, and lastly vertical spreads.

Spreads that are called vertical spreads normally come from the same underlying security class, and also similar dates for expiring. The only difference between these spreads is the strike price.

Those spreads considered horizontal can also be called calendar spreads. These are made using options that feature the same strike prices and underlying securities but different expiration periods.

The third class, diagonal spreads are those that use options that share the same underlying security but have different expiration dates and strike prices. Examples of vertical spreads include bull, bear, as well as butterfly spreads. Diagonal spreads include covered calls.

Using Orders in Options Trading

When investing in the options market, you will always be required to place an order with an options broker. There are different types of orders that you can use to control how you purchase and sell options. Basically, an options order comprises several parameters that dictate how the order works. These determine whether a trader should open or close a position, and also whether to buy or sell a contract. For every order that you use, you must choose its timing and how it is filled. You may decide to automatically enter into positions or exit positions using a number of orders. Let us have a look at some of the orders that you can use when trading options.

Buy to Open

This is one of the most common orders placed by investors. You are supposed to use this order if you want to purchase a call or put option or if you want to buy a combination of these two. The buy to open order is common when investors are positive that the price of a particular contract will increase before its expiration. For instance, if a call option for a company X is being traded at $2 and its put option is selling at $1.90, you may decide to purchase the call and put it simultaneously to maximize the profit.

Sell to Open

This type of order is commonly used by traders who wish to sell their positions. If you are anticipating a decrease in the price of a particular option, you may wish to take advantage of this move by opening a sell-to-open order in an attempt to short-sell the option. You may also use this order to sell a put option contract if there is a possibility of the price of the contract going up.

Buy to Close

This order is used when you want to close an already existing short option position. For instance, if you have opened a sell-to open position, you can end it using the buy-to-close order. This is the same as purchasing a position that you once sold to another trader. This kind of options order can be applied in a number of circumstances. For instance, if the value of an option has declined, you can use the order to buy it back at a profit. Alternatively, if you sell a position and the value of the underlying security keeps going up, you may use this order to close the position as a way of preventing further loss.

Sell to Close

You can use this order to close a long position that is already in existence. For instance, if you previously entered a buy to open position, you can end it using the sell to close order. This order is mostly used by individuals who wish to realize profit after the price of the options contract goes up. It can also be used to stop further loss when the price of a contract continues to fall.

Filling Orders

When placing any type of order, you must go through an options broker who will assist you to execute the option. Besides telling the broker the kind of option you want to make; you must also inform them of how the order will be filled. Each order can be filled depending on the kind of filling order you want to use. There are two types of filling orders—market orders and limit orders.

Limit orders are used when you want the broker to fill your order at a cost that is less than the amount you have specified. This means that your order will not be processed until it meets the certain parameters that you have specified. This type of order hinders you from purchasing options at a price that is higher than what you can afford to pay. In case you are selling an option, the order also prevents you from selling the contract that has a cost, which is significantly below what you expected.

Other orders are such as market orders, which, on the other hand, allow the broker to fill your order at any cost without being governed by the price you quote. Such orders are often used when dealing with contracts that feature stable prices and high liquidity. Market orders are not ideal for use with options that are highly volatile since you may end up spending more costs than expected when buying options, and receiving very little when selling options. This results in reduced profits.

Timing Order

A timing order is used to add time parameters to any order you place. Timing orders specify some important parameters that the broker uses when establishing the best orders for you. Some of the timing orders include all or none, day order, GTC, IOC, and MOC. The all or none order, also known as AON is applied to those orders that must be filled in entirety. This means that if you are seeking to purchase 100 options yet the broker can only get 95 then this order will not be applied. The order will remain open until all your requirements have been met before it expires. The day to execute the order must be agreed in advance. In case the order is not filled for that day, it automatically becomes canceled.

The fill or kill order, or FOK order is almost similar to the AON. The only difference is that the AON order remains open until it is fulfilled, while the FOK order cancels automatically if the conditions of trade cannot be met at the time that the order is opened. The GTC or good until canceled order is one that remains open until the broker cancels it.

Exit Orders

Another class of orders is the exit options orders which you can use to limit losses when trading in options. These are useful when you have several contracts open at the same time to the extent that you cannot close all of them manually. You can set up exit orders to help you close some of these automatically. Some exit orders used on the options market today include stop orders, limit stop orders, trailing stop orders, and contingent orders.

Stop orders are used to close a certain contract once a specified position has been attained. For instance, if you have several contacts, you can set a stop order at a given price level. This means that when a contract attains that price, the system automatically sells it at a profit.

The limit stop order is one that changes into a limit order as soon as the contract attains a certain price level while the trailing stop order is one whose stop charge is based on the fluctuations in the cost of the contract entered. Investors and market analysts normally denote this change as a number or percentage. For instance, a trailing order for a certain option may be activated as soon as the option price falls by 10% from its highest price. There are other orders known as contingent orders. These are used to exit positions depending on a customized set of parameters. For instance, you may create an order that requires the broker to sell your option as soon as its price goes up by a specific percentage.

Orders can also be used in combination. This is quite common in more advanced trading strategies. There are two specific types of combination orders. One is the One Trigger Other or OTO order. For this type, a primary order triggers a secondary order as soon as it is filled. The second type is the Once Cancel Other or OCO order. This means that one order gets canceled as soon as the other one gets filled.

Pricing of Options

As you get into the business of trading options, you must first seek to understand how they are priced and some of the factors that determine the pricing. This is because the price of options goes beyond the value assigned to the underlying security. Individuals can easily make estimations of the price of a particular contract if they have information about the elements that contribute to its price changes. For each value that you come across when trading options, several calculations may have been made to obtain it.

Several models have been established to help investors determine the price of options. One such model is the Black Scholes model that helps traders to value their investments with so much ease. The model helps you to generate the value of an option by combining several attributes associated with the contract such as volatility, expiration date, and interest rates. It utilizes a number of assumptions that affect how the price is calculated.

One of the assumptions is that the market and interest rates do not change during the contracts trading period. The model also assumes that the investor earns no dividend on the underlying stock and that there are no transaction costs involved in the trade. It also views volatility as a constant figure throughout the transaction.

Despite all these assumptions, most traders rely on this model to price their options and predict any trends in the options market. The model works using a Brownian motion formula as quoted below:

$$\text{Theoretical option price} = pN(d_1) - se^{-rt}N(d_2)$$

$$\text{where } d_1 = \frac{\ln\left(\frac{p}{s}\right) + \left(r + \frac{v^2}{2}\right)t}{v\sqrt{t}}$$

$$d_2 = d_1 - v\sqrt{t}$$

The variables are:

p = stock price

s = striking price

t = time remaining until expiration, expressed as a percent of a year

r = current risk-free interest rate

v = volatility measured by annual standard deviation

ln = natural logarithm

$N(x)$ = cumulative normal density function

Figure 2: Black Scholes formula

This model determines the price of an option from six variables. These are the type of option, its cost of trade or strike cost, cost of equity, rate of interest, levels of volatility, and the time value of a contract. Based on this formula, the time left for an option to expire greatly impacts the profit that an investor makes from the trade. It also indicates that earning releases, financial news, and rumors about the options market can impact the price of an option significantly. Positive news increases prices while negative news causes a decline in the options prices.

Besides this model, several other factors are used to determine the price of an option. We look at some of the basic ones.

The Equity

This is the initial determinant factor of options pricing. When the cost of the equity changes, automatically the cost of the options contract changes as well. The alterations that a stock price undergoes also impact the closing cost of any position. When you buy or sell and the underlying equity goes up, the cost applied to the relative option also increases. If it happens that the stock price decreases, then the cost of trading the related option decreases as well. The amount of value attached to underlying equity is dictated by a wide array of factors. One of these factors is the level of supply and demand; others include the volume of the stock as well as the reputation of the company that lists the stock on the market.

Stock Volatility

Volatility has become a widely known component because of the role it plays in the stock market. It can be defined as the rate at which the value of a particular option keeps changing either upward or downward.

This is one of the most common elements that affect prices in the options market. In simple terms, volatility refers to the rate at which price options change, either in a positive or negative way. High volatility often results in high prices while low volatility causes low option prices. Both historical volatility and implied volatility are used to establish the price of options. However, you must note that volatility is not a figure and can only be estimated.

Expiration Period

The value of an option is greatly affected by how much time there is before the option gets to expire. As an option approaches expiration, its time value goes down and this may cause a decrease in the pricing since fewer people are interested in investing in the option at this point. When the period between the current time and the expiration time is too huge, the option still has the potential to change course and this considerably large amount of time available may make a demand increase, causing a rise in the prices. Time is thus a major component impacting the ultimate cost of buying and selling contracts.

Strike Prices

Describes the cost agreed upon by options buyers and sellers when generating an options contract. Factoring in the class of options in question, profit can be received when the underlying security value of an option goes above or falls below the strike price. As mentioned earlier, two categories of options are transacted on the options market—puts as well as calls. The cost of an option is also determined by the type. Purchasing an option or selling it can cause the value of an option to decrease or increase since this affects the liquidity of the option. Taking this example, the cost of a certain option may option drops drastically, and many buyers will rush to purchase it. This means that the demand for the said option will become high. As a result, the number of shares associated with the option may decrease, resulting in a drastic increase in the prices of the same option within a short period of time.

Interest Rates

Although the effect of interest rates on the price of an option is quite small, it is still important to note it down. High interests always result in high costs for call options and lower costs for put options.

Besides these, there is also the place of dividends in affecting options prices. Generally, options do not attract dividends since they only represent an underlying stock. However, when dividends are released, the price of options may be indirectly affected. In most cases, an increase in the number of dividends causes an increase in the price of put options and a decrease in the price of call options. This is because dividends affect the value of the underlying stock, which in turn affects the value of the associated options.

Aside from these basic factors, there is also an array of more advanced factors that can affect the value of an option either directly or indirectly. These are either fundamental factors or technical factors.

Fundamental factors are those that revolve around the basis and the profit ratio of an option.

The earnings ratio of a particular option is the profit realized from trading the option.

The earning base, on the other hand, is determined by the company selling the stock.

Technical factors are external conditions that impact the supply and demand of an option is the underlying security. These include factors such as market sentiments, inflation, market trends, and pricing news.

Options Trading Signals

Trading signals are very popular in the options market. These are used by both beginners as well as experienced traders. If you are a beginner, signals can help you understand the trading process faster and if you are an experienced trader, these help you to place and manage higher volumes of trade. They also help you to understand how the market behaves and what you should expect to happen on the market in the future.

Trading signals are effective when it comes to increasing your profit. They help you to reduce the time you need to spend evaluating the market. Although these are helpful, they come with an extra expense since you must pay subscription fees to signal providers for you to enjoy the services. The success rate of the signals also differs from one provider to the other. Because these are only available through third-party companies, it is important to understand how they work as this will enable you to select those that are most reliable.

When it comes to the options market, signals can be generated either by human experts or by software applications. They often use a set of market parameters to determine the most likely price movement of a particular stock. These market parameters may be in the form of chart patterns, technical indicators, and many others. Options signals that are generated by human beings mostly make use of fundamental factors to predict price changes. Once generated, these are sent to the trader as information that can be used to determine the direction of trade. The trader uses this information to establish the right time and strategy to use for trading.

Basically, options trading is carried out on online platforms, which give traders access to a large number of global markets. Different platforms always feature different underlying securities and this means that the platform you choose is essential when it comes to determining the success of your trade. It is upon you to establish your needs then identify a platform that enables you to meet your investment needs. When selecting a platform, check out the range of financial instruments available since you want to have a market that has as many choices as possible. Doing this will increase your trading opportunities significantly and you will have better alternatives each time one instrument fails to deliver success.

Chapter 4: Getting Started in Options Trading

Getting started in the options market can be difficult, especially if you have not mastered the right trading styles and strategies. A lot of changes take place on the market and there is a lot that you need to learn even as you try the business out. One great advantage of this type of trading is that information is readily available. Most successful traders that have been in the business long enough admit that the first step towards becoming an expert in options trading is getting good resource materials. These are helpful to you because they give you an idea of what goes on in the options market and how you need to find the right trading tools. This chapter outlines everything that you need to start buying and selling options.

Options Trading Accounts

Once you have acquired the right knowledge about options trading, the next step is identifying the right trading account. Once you get an account, you can start placing your orders and having a broker execute them for you.

Basically, two types of accounts can be used in options trading—a margin account and a cash account. When opening an account, the broker will always ask you the type of account you wish to have. A cash account allows you to use the cash in your account as premium while a margin account lets you use your stock and long-term options to borrow funds from brokers for use as premium. Below are steps you need to take when opening an options brokerage account:

Establish the type of account you need—this can either be a cash or margin account. The type of account you select will be determined by your investment objectives, terms of operating the account as well as the amount of capital you have. If you have enough cash for the trade, the broker will definitely open a cash account for you. However, if you have some underlying stocks but do not have enough cash, you may need to consider getting an account that has margin privileges. With such an account, you will be able to borrow money for purchasing your options and return this later. In this case, the stock you have will serve as the collateral.

Identify any additional costs—some accounts come with additional charges such as maintenance and support charges. Each also comes with standard commissions for brokers. You must go through these charges to understand how much you will be required to pay in total to start transacting. For instance, some brokers often charge an amount of $0.75 for each contract they order for you besides the standard commission charges. You need to find out if such charges apply before creating the account.

Check the list of services—the cost of an account is not enough when determining what suits you. Although it is good to find an account that costs less. It is important to consider other factors, as well as these, also determine the worth of any options trading account. For instance, you must find out if the account will give you adequate access to research information. Some good brokerage accounts offer traders a wide array of stock ratings as well as links to third-party information about options trading. Find out if the account you are choosing provides this information. Also, check out some of the trading platforms supported by the brokerage account. Some brokerage firms will allow you to test some accounts before committing yourself. It is good to check the kind of platforms that the account supports for versatility purposes.

Choose a brokerage company—once you have the details about different firms, make an informed decision by weighing the advantages and disadvantages of each firm. This will help you select the best firm for you and once you are done with this, you can create the account. Most of the trading accounts can be created online, although you may need to provide copies of some of your identification documents.

Deposit funds—with a trading account ready, you can then deposit some funds into it to start trading. As you add money to your account, have the broker's minimum in mind since each account may have a different minimum amount.

Basically, there is always a minimum amount of capital required when opening an options trading account. This amount depends on the type of account you want to create as well as the rules of the brokerage company you engage.

With an account, you are now ready to start trading. Here is a systematic guide on how you should carry out your first options trade:

1. Log into your trading account.
2. Find the trade or order page in the trading account.
3. Check out the list of market quotes available and choose one that involves options.
4. Select the strike price and expiration month.
5. Define whether it is a call or put option.
6. Specify the amount number of contracts you wish to trade.
7. Set the desired premium.
8. Set orders for your contracts.
9. Confirm your options and submit.

Creating a brokerage account for options trading does not necessarily mean that you may start buying and selling options. You must wait until your account is approved by the brokerage firm you choose before you can start trading. There are typical scales that these firms use to rate you before approval is granted. These include access to covered calls, spreads, uncovered calls, and puts and buying calls and puts. The level of your approval is determined by a number of factors. One factor is your trading objectives. They would assess whether you are seeking to maintain your capital or you just want to increase your income levels.

Another factor is your experience in the options market. The more experienced you are the higher you rate on the five scales above. This means that the firm will expose you to more trading opportunities than a person who is average or lacks trading skills altogether. Your expertise will be determined by the number of trades you have completed successfully in the past. One last factor will be risk tolerance, that is, whether you can withstand certain levels of losses. Information that will be required in this case is whether you are employed if you have invested all your savings in the trade, as well as your net worth. Brokers will use this information to determine the trading level that suits you.

Setting an Option Plan

An options trading plan outlines the terms and conditions you need to fulfill when trading in the options market. It is important to come up with an options trading plan before starting to trade because it will help you identify and implement some of the options investment strategies successfully. Having a plan before you start investing will help you avoid those contracts that are not so promising in terms of profit. Some of the components that should define your options trading plan include:

Intended initial investment—this is the amount you intend to invest as your first premium. It is important to list this because you do not want to end up straining in your personal endeavors. One great thing with options trading is that you can invest small amounts of capital and still make some good profit. When getting started, it is recommended that you do not put large amounts of cash on the market since this may expose you to a wide array of risks. As time goes by and you understand how the market operates, you can increase your deposits gradually in order to increase your profits.

Risk capital—it is also essential that you define your risk tolerance levels. This is the amount of capital you can lose without it affecting your standard of living. Most plans only include the amount a person is willing to invest but fail to include the amount a person is ready to lose. By defining your risk capital, you will easily determine when it is the right time to quit the trade. When you lose an amount that is equivalent to the risk capital, you can either decide to reinvest some more or quit the trade.

Trading strategies—when it comes to options trading, each position is always unique. Therefore, not all strategies work for everybody. When coming up with your trading plan, you will need to identify those strategies that will work for your plan. These strategies will help govern your selling and buying decisions. If for instance, you are a person that understands the principle of defensive investing, you may not need to include some strategies in your plan since you can control yourself. However, if you are a trader that needs to operate under strict rules, then you will need to include every strategy you intend to use in your trading plan. It is always better to outline everything than to risk leaving some important steps out and then making mistakes while trading.

Stop-loss orders—these must also form part of your plan. Although options are associated with very small risks, it is not good to assume that you will not lose any money. Therefore, you must be able to implement risk management techniques such as stop-loss orders to ensure that you do not lose any of your investments beyond a certain percentage.

Market analysis—how do you intend to study market trends? How will you establish winning contracts and how do you intend to differentiate them from those contracts that are worthless? Technical analysis is the foundation of each effective trading plan. This helps you to determine market directions and why such directions take place. It is a powerful aspect that enables traders to enter into some positions and exit others.

Trading goals—these help you accomplish your trading needs. A good trading plan is one that defines realistic and achievable goals in terms of profit, risk, and reward. For instance, you should be able to define the minimum risk/reward ratio that is acceptable to you. Most traders only take up positions whose profit is three times greater than the risk or more.

Entry and exit rules—each trade has an entry point and an exit point. Most traders use all their efforts to determine which positions to acquire but they fail to determine how they will exit such positions. For each trade that you enter, you must always define an exit point. Exits are actually more important than entry points because they determine whether you will close a position at a profit or loss.

Finding an Options Broker

Options brokers play a vital role in ensuring that you succeed in the trade. They provide the best in terms of information, support, and tools required for you to trade effectively. They also protect you from entering into unnecessary orders and teach you how to control your investments to ensure a minimum loss.

Options brokers also assist you to make the right decisions when it comes to investing in the options market. You may select brokers from two categories—discount-based or full-service-based.

Full-based type of brokers are also called traditional brokers. These offer you a wide range of trading services at high costs. Part of their services includes offering you trading advice and helping you manage your investments. Discount brokers, on the other hand, do not provide you with investment information. They also do not take part in your investment decisions, allowing you to make all the decisions relating to your account. The only work that discounted brokers do on your behalf is processing orders.

Therefore, they charge significantly fewer amounts than full-service brokers do.

If you are a new trader that wants to be guided through the trading process, you may need to get a full-service broker. However, if you are an expert in options trading and you are confident about your expertise, you can consider getting a discount broker since you can carry out most of the tasks on your own.

Getting the right broker is an essential part of options trading. How skilled and experienced the broker is will determine if your orders succeed or fail. You may find one who offers the best commissions but does not have all the tools you need for the trade. Let us look at some of the other factors you should consider when choosing an options broker:

Availability—when choosing the best broker, you must first understand the availability of their brokerage platform. The responsiveness and availability of the trading account are some of the most crucial components for online trading. It does not make sense to get a brokerage account that charges low commissions yet the site is overwhelmed with high traffic. This means that you will be losing on some contracts due to site unavailability. The responsiveness of a platform determines how timely you become in your transactions. Just like any other aggressive form of trading, time is so much essential when it comes to options trading. Therefore, you need a brokerage account that is available 24/7 because markets keep changing every second and you do not want to miss out on any opportunity to make a good profit.

Quality of transactions—a good broker is one that guarantees you the best buying and selling price for each contract. Most brokers are skilled in negotiating contracts and you must settle for one who can negotiate on your behalf. You should always get the best ask price when purchasing options and the best bid price when selling your options.

Convenient tools—since the options trading process is somewhat complicated, especially for beginners, you should endeavor to get a trading account with an interface that is easy to use. Simple trading and order placing interfaces will help you avoid certain errors that can make you incur more costs. For instance, you may need to get brokerage firms that provide single-screen order forms for some of the most complicated options trading strategies like condors, covered calls, and butterflies.

Brokerage fees and commissions—some of the options trading brokers are often complex when it comes to calculating commissions and fees. For most brokerage accounts, the fees section always has two types of charges—the per-contract fee and the per-trade fee. The per-trade fee is always a minimum fee that the broker charges for each transaction and the per-contract fee is charged for each contract involved in a trade. Others also charge the option assignment fee, which is charged each time you sell an option or when your option is exercised by a buyer. The exercise fee is charged when you exercise either a call or put option.

These fees vary with different brokerages and if you are not careful, they can reduce your payoffs and profits significantly. In case you want to invest in options, you must be able to understand how much of your payoffs and profits will be claimed by the broker.

Once you have considered the other factors mentioned, you must ensure that you get a broker that charges realistic commissions. After you have mastered the trade, you can start accomplishing some tasks by yourself to minimize the commissions. That is why you must continue studying platforms and trading styles even if you have a good broker who can do everything for you. It is more fulfilling and rewarding to trade as an individual than engaging in the services of a broker. In the ultimate end, your wish is to get something good as profit from each transaction.

The trading platform—what trading platforms does the broker offer? The trading platform you use greatly determines how much you will make from your investments. It should enable you to analyze the options market, set up simple trades, and compare various market parameters before placing an order. This only means that you need a platform that will provide you with information such as performance graphs, risk profiles, and the volatility information of your options of interest. It should also be flexible enough to allow you to switch between different information areas with ease. A good broker is one that offers you such a platform.

Routing of orders—order routing is what gives you leverage when it comes to getting the best fill process. A broker who gives you theoretical knowledge about the market is good, however, you need one that practically delivers when it comes to order routing. Basically, a broker should ensure that your orders are sent to a large number of exchanges and that they assist you to get the best deals in terms of price and market liquidity. A broker should also ensure that your orders are processed at faster speeds so that you do not miss some deals. Some brokers do this in real-time, while others take time to process your orders. You should determine this before deciding to settle for a particular broker.

Support—once in a while, you will need support and guidance on how you should place your orders. You want someone who will verify whether your analysis and predictions are correct. Your broker should be available to guide you when the need arises. The best brokerage firms are those that offer active, ongoing support and education to you as a trader. As you continue engaging the services of such firms, you should also continue to grow in your trading skills and abilities.

Option Trading Mentors

Mentors are great people that help you acquire experience easily. Just like any other business, you also need a mentor in options trading. This is a person who will assist you to acquire knowledge about the investment by transferring to you what they have learned with time. Although research books can provide you with all the information you need about options trading, these cannot replace the need for mentorship.

When identifying a mentor, you want to get someone who is more experienced in the trade than yourself. However, you must first understand what you want. Before you start engaging some experts, have an idea of what you want to achieve. This is because options have several functions in different setups. Define your goals and narrow them down into effective strategies. Are you in the trade to generate income from your own stocks? Do you want to trade options as a way of protecting your stock portfolio or are you just seeking a way to make more profit? These are some of the questions you need to ask yourself beforehand.

Once you have set your objectives, define clear strategies that can help you achieve your goal.

Trading Platforms

Options trading platforms come in several varieties. These are offered by brokerage firms to help you trade at any level you want. Some platforms only feature basic components, while others contain more advanced features such as trade and market analytics as well as pricing tools. These are available as web-based applications or as standalone programs. The decision to use any of these lies with the investor. However, most web-based platforms are often less responsive and not easy to customize. They are often accessible through the broker's website. Standalone platforms tend to be more flexible and contain more in terms of tools and charts. You can easily customize these to a layout and screen that suits your trading needs.

Choosing the right options trading platform that suits your needs is very important because it can make your trading experience more productive and less time-consuming. However, with the wide array of platforms available on the market, selecting one that is good can become a tedious exercise. This is because some platforms are more advertised than others. However, there are a number of things that professional investors look for when choosing a good options trading platform. Here are some of them.

Price per trade—this is always the first consideration that investors make when they need to choose a trading platform. The price per trade refers to the amount of cash you will pay for each transaction that you complete on the platform. If you are an active trader, then you will realize how important this is each time you have to part with some fees and commissions. You must check out platforms that charge less for each trade you complete.

Monthly fees—some platforms charge investors a monthly service fee. This is always in the form of inactivity and maintenance fees. You need a platform that charges zero monthly maintenance fees as this will ensure that your investment returns remain at a maximum.

Faster execution—this is another priority for investors and traders. If you need an account that completes your trades faster, then you must choose a platform that allows you to do this with ease. This is quite important when the options you want to trade in represent fast-moving assets. In this case, the difference between getting a profit and losing your investment lies in how fast your orders are processed. Therefore, the execution speed of transactions should be a top priority for you if you want to succeed in your trades.

Besides the speed, you also want to get a platform that brings added value to you. For instance, some platforms always offer value promotions for their clients. Like when you open an account, you are given $1000 free. Others provide 24/7 user support while some even offer free research tools. Some platforms also feature demo accounts that allow you to learn the trade before you can start placing orders through your real account.

Functionality—investors always possess different levels of knowledge and expertise. You want to ensure that the trading platform you get has all the features you need to succeed in your transactions. For instance, novice traders only need a few basic features to get started. But if you are a professional trader, you want features that allow you to analyze market trends, predict pricing and compare trade information between exchanges. The user interface should be easy to use and not confusing to you.

Learning resources—options trading is a learning process. If you are an experienced trader, you may not need a platform that offers educational resources. However, if you are a beginner, it is important to check out if the choice of platform you make offers you this option.

Resources can be in the form of tutorials, articles, or the latest market insights.

Besides using a broker, you may decide to invest in the options market directly. With a good options trading platform, it is easier for you to invest in several securities at the same time without needing assistance. Most investors prefer trading platforms to brokerage firms because of the discounts offered by such platforms. Since there is a reduction in the costs involved in these platforms, traders are assured of high profits and low commissions.

Trading through an online platform is also faster than using traditional brokerage accounts. They enable you to complete your transactions faster and also reduce the amount of paperwork that is often exchanged between the trader and the broker. In a nutshell, the trading platform you select depends greatly on how you wish to trade. Some platforms may be geared towards more aggressive trading while others may tend towards long-term trading. Whichever platform you choose, the most important thing is to put your predictor cap on all the time. You must always be able to predict option price movements by establishing whether they will go up or down. This will help you apply the right strategy at the right time. You must also be able to predict how much the prices change as this will ensure that you set the right strike prices. Lastly, you should establish how long it may take for these movements to take place. You can do this by studying historical price patterns including the expiration dates.

Chapter 5: Options Repair and Trading Methodologies

The trading of options offers tremendous investment opportunities with great income potential. The secret to obtaining the best in terms of monetary benefits lies in using the right strategy.

There are several trading and position repair strategies that you can use in the options market. Traders choose these based on the type of trade and the anticipated direction of prices. Options strategies enable you to continuously improve your trades. They are often defined at the planning stage of the trade since they determine the motion of your contracts. They also help you to establish whether an option will move vertically, horizontally, or diagonally.

When it comes to the options market, no single strategy fits all trading positions. Sometimes, it may be important for you to customize a unique strategy based on your trading goals since you are the only person that understands what you expect from each of your trades. To identify the right strategy, you must first understand the basics of options trading. Basically, most strategies only use a combination of the four major trades—the long and short call, and the long and short put. Understanding these major trades will help you customize a more effective strategy for your trading needs.

In case you do not have enough knowledge about your trades, it is recommended that you select a strategy that is neutral, or non-directional. In this case, the possibility of you making a profit will largely depend on other factors such as the volatility of the stock. Traders who often get into options trading without the understanding of the strategies struggle with their investment.

Options trading strategies can be divided into two categories—trading strategies and repair strategies. Trading strategies are the basic ones used to manage contracts as a way of maximizing profits. Repair strategies are those which are applied to a losing trade to counter the loss.

Basic Options Trading Strategies

The Covered Call

When it comes to buying and selling calls, you may decide to purchase a naked call or structure this into a covered or buy-write call. The covered call is one of the most popular strategies used in options because it minimizes the risk involved in trades and also helps you to generate more income. For you to execute this strategy, an investor holds a long position on given security then sells call options from the same security.

Since the covered call is a neutral options trading strategy, it does not generate large returns in income. Options participants make good use of this technique any time they possess a neutral view of the market or a particular option.

Covered calls feature both long and short positions in a single trade. It is used when an investor wishes to hold onto the stock for a long period of time yet does not anticipate a cost change in upcoming times. Therefore, a covered call hedges long-term stock positions and allows you to earn income from the premium you get from selling the call option. In most cases, the maximum amount of profit that you can receive from a covered call is normally equivalent to the divergence between the strike cost associated with the short position and the cost of equity and premium. The highest amounts of losses are often equated with the divergence between the costs of the underlying security less premium.

To use this strategy, you will have to purchase the equity involved then generate a call option on the stock that you purchase.

The Bull Call

This strategy allows you to buy more than one call at the same price then sell these at higher strike prices. In this strategy, the value of the equity, as well as its expiration date, are the same.

The bull call spread is often used to make a profit from small increments in stock prices. It features two strike prices that are used to limit losses and cap gains. Majorly, investors raise call options to make a profit from the increase in stock prices. Whenever the contract closes before its expiration time, the investor gets forced to purchase associated equities at the predefined strike price in stock trading but this does not apply in options trading. The bull strategy allows you to pay the premium for a call option in advance. If in any case, the cost of the commodity seems closer to the strike cost, then the premium might be higher. In case the cost of the equity falls below striking costs, the trader holding this equity will lose a significant amount when the option expires. Else, in case the cost of the equity appreciates over the strike cost, a buyer may decide to buy the shares but this is not a guarantee.

The bull call spread strategy seeks to reduce the cost of call options. One drawback of this strategy is that it not only limits the risks but also caps the amount of gain you can get from the trade. Therefore, it is advisable that you only use this strategy when you are certain about the amount of money set as the strike price shooting significantly, especially when trading in highly volatile stocks.

Applying this strategy basically involves the following three steps.

- Selecting an asset whose value may appreciate in the next few days, weeks, or months.
- Acquiring call contracts at a cost that fairly is more than the current cost of the underlying equity. Specify an expiration date and make payments of the initial capital.
- At the same time, write another call contract with a strike cost slightly higher beyond the one used in the first option. Ensure that the expiration date of the second option matches the first one.

The second option will generate some premium for you if the price moves in the anticipated direction. You can then use the premium to offset the amount you used as a premium for the first call.

The Long Straddle

This strategy applies when you buy a call and put an option at the same time. The two options are always derived from the same underlying assets. They also share an expiration date and strike price. You can use this strategy when you are certain that the amount charged on the security might increase or fall beyond certain ranges that are considered normal. The long straddle ensures that you get unlimited profits from trade while keeping the losses to the minimum.

A modification of this type of strategy is when you acquire a put contract that is termed as out of the money, then also acquire a call contract that is also out of the money concurrently, with similar expiration and similar equity or base stock. Traders employ this method each time they are expecting large changes in the underlying commodity but very unsure about the direction of this movement. This is known as the long strangle strategy. Most investors use this in the place of the long straddle strategy because it limits losses more and the options always cost less since they are out of the money.

The Married Put

In this strategy, you buy an asset or security then also buy options that represent the shares you have bought. This then creates a platform for trading shares with pre-estimated strike charges. This strategy is often employed by people who wish to minimize the downside risk of owning a certain stock.

The married put works similar to an insurance policy. It specifies the lowest price that a given option can reach in case the prices reduce significantly. A good example of this is when you purchase 100 shares from a certain stock company, then open a put position on the same shares. This allows you to raise the potential upside on each trade while cutting down the bad effects on the downside. One disadvantage of this strategy is that if the stock value does not fall, you will lose an investment that is equivalent to the premium paid for the position.

The Bear Put Spread

This is also a vertical kind of strategy that allows you to buy more than one put option at the same time. The intention of using this strategy is to purchase the options at a specific strike price then exercise them at a relatively lower price. The options you use in this strategy must come from the same underlying security. They should also bear the same expiration date. The bear put strategy is the direct opposite of the bull call spread. It is often applied to markets where the value of the underlying security is expected to decrease. It also limits the gains and losses of each options contract.

The Protective Collar Strategy

This is accomplished through buying a put contract that is way out of the money, then starting a sell contract for a call option which is considered as out of the money also, concurrently. These two options are traded using the same expiration date and underlying security. Investors employ it when they have made good gains from a long stock position.

The protective collar reduces the downside risk of trading a particular option while allowing you to sell your shares at higher costs.

The Long Call Butterfly Spread

Most of the strategies we have discussed only combine two contract positions and feature two strike prices. The long call butterfly strategy is unique in the sense that it features three different strike prices. It combines the bull and bear strategies and the options used are of the same expiration dates. These are also derived from the same underlying security.

One example of this strategy is when you make a purchase of a call contract that seems in the money at a significantly small strike amount, sell double call options that are at the money, and buy one call option that is out of the money. This results in a good net profit and is known as a call fly. The long call butterfly spread strategy is mostly used by investors who anticipate very little change in the stock price before the expiration.

The Iron Condor Strategy

This is also another strategy that combines the bear call and bull put strategies. It is derived through selling one put contract, which is considered out of the money than buying a single put option, which is also termed to be out of the money with relatively low strike costs. It also entails selling a single call contract and purchasing another call contract at strike costs that are quite high. These four spreads share similar underlying security; they have a similar exercise date with the same size of the spread.

The iron condor allows traders to earn some premium from this setup. It is commonly used in stocks that have low volatility. Traders love this strategy because it creates a high possibility of generating good premium amounts. Maximum returns are obtained as the trading gap increases. As the stock value moves away from the strike prices, the loss also increases.

This strategy can be combined with the butterfly spread to form an iron butterfly strategy where you sell a put option that is at the money, get a put contract, which is out of the money, write a call contract that has at the money characteristics then also buy one call contract that is out of the money. This strategy is different from the ordinary butterfly spread because it utilizes both put and call options. Each option performs a specific task in the contract. For instance, the call option that is out of the money shields the contract against an unlimited downside, while the put option that has out of the money shields the contract from short strike cost. Profits obtained from this kind of strategy depends on the strike prices set by the investor for each option.

Options Trading Repair Strategies

Basically, when traders are faced with a substantial loss in a contract, they only have few decisions to make which often do not divert the loss completely. The trader may decide to sell the option at a loss, hold onto an option position with the hope that prices improve in the future, or add more premium to the existing trade to increase chances of making a profit.

Holding onto the position and hoping that they improve can be risky since it may take a long time for the prices to change and things may even become worse. Doubling down your investment can also be risky since you may throw in more money only to end up with more losses. Luckily, there is a strategy that you can use to repair your positions without increasing the risk of further loss. This is known as the repair strategy.

This strategy is often built from losing positions that are already in existence. It involves purchasing certain options and selling others in an attempt to raise premium amounts that can minimize or offset the loss. The strategy used fits short and long calls simultaneously.

Long positions are often associated with smaller amounts of risk and high-profit potentials. However, the losses incurred from such positions are always too big and sometimes too difficult to recover. Most inexperienced options traders allow long positions to expire on their own and, in most cases, there is no profit received. Allowing options to expire worthlessly is quite risky and may result in account destruction. This is where the repair strategy comes in.

Being a successful options trader not only involves making a profit but also being able to repair positions that have gone wrong. To do this, you need the right techniques and strategies that can help you to return back to the right track. Every trader needs to include a repair strategy in their trading plan. This includes outlining a list of "what ifs" and customizing strategies that can help curb the items listed down. Most traders ignore this at the beginning of their investment and sometimes incorporate the strategies when it is already too late to recover any premiums. In a nutshell, it is important to understand that the kind of profit you make from options trading partly depends on how well you manage your losing trades.

Let Us Look at an Example—The Long Call

Most traders enter into a call and put option positions only to realize later that it was a wrong move. For instance, you may enter a long call that is out of the money, and then the prices begin to decrease. If you do not take any action to counter the drop in prices, you will experience some unrealistic losses on your investment. The basic action you will think of is to average the loss by buying more options, but if the prices continue to fall then you will continue to lose.

One strategy that you can use to bring the breakeven point lower, in this case, is by the use of a bull call spread discussed above. You can start by placing an order to sell two calls at a specific price and, at the same time, buying a call at a higher price. The net result from these options will be the premium obtained from selling the call options less the premium paid in purchasing the third call. If the resultant figure is positive, then this is the amount that will be used to offset the loss. This can be done repeatedly until the option expires. Another strategy that you may apply here is the butterfly spread. In this case, you will sell two call options at a smaller price than another call at a relatively higher price, which is still smaller than the premium of the sold calls combined. The maximum profit you can gain from this is equal to the premium you receive from the two short calls less what you pay for the long call.

Note that you can combine more than one strategy to improve the effectiveness of recovering your investment. When used correctly, these strategies can assist you to convert looming losses into good profits. For instance, you can combine a bull-call spread and a butterfly spread on a single options contract to increase the overall gain.

Generally, the repair strategy seeks to convert losing positions into winning positions. However, you must be careful since some strategies that you apply on losing positions may incur more risks and if the price movement does not favor you, you may end up increasing your losses instead.

Besides, long call positions going sour, some short call options may also decline and cause you to lose part of your investment. You, therefore, need to apply recovery strategies on these as well. You need to understand which strategy to apply in each circumstance and define the level of risk involved in each.

You must also understand when you need to let go of some trades since some are quite complex and cannot guarantee you of any change even if you attempt to recover them. With such positions, it is good to close them to save some amount of investment, or before you lose everything on such contracts.

Alternatively, you may also consider opening synthetic short positions. A synthetic short position combines a short call and a long put as a way of generating profit. In most cases, the payoff received from this combination may be large enough to cancel part of your losses.

For instance, you may want to get repair methodologies that help you recover a covered option call that has gone wrong. In this case, you may look for diagonal, vertical, or horizontal spreads that can help resolve the situation. Vertically, you may consider ordering a call with an amount either higher or lower than the present strike cost depending on the direction of decline. Horizontally, you may start a position that has the same strike price but different expiration periods to see if you can make some profit from it. Lastly, you may enter favorable positions that feature a different expiration and strike price from the existent position as a way of generating profit. You can even set up multiple positions of such kind to maximize returns. The resultant profits can then be used to counter the effects of the losing covered call position.

Options Trading Tips: Tricks and Risks Involved in Options Trading

Options trading is one area of investment in the stock market. It is not a high-risk investment process where high costs are involved. Depending on some changes in market elements based on specific equity, an option estimated value can either rise or fall, until their maturity date.

The good thing about investing in options is that it is totally different from buying assets and stocks directly. Hence, one can withdraw from the transaction or agreement at any point. Simply buying or selling options does not always mean that the investor has to go through with the buying and selling of the options. Due to such a setup, it is determined that options are derivative tools whose costs are dependent on other things like the equity involved, estimated cost of the market, and other securities.

Buying an option involves an investor purchasing share during a time that is in the future. A put option allows the trader to sell or write shares of equity at a later or future time.

Call Option

This is whereby there is a binding agreement allowing the investor to purchase a certain number of shares belonging to security for a specified period. This means the trader can be able to buy a certain amount of shares at a future time.

In the case of purchasing a call position, the exercise amount of equity, for instance, is calculated based on the present estimated cost of that equity. An example is when a share of the asset is set at $1000; if the strike cost is higher than this amount then the contract becomes out of the money. If this same cost is lower than the amount of equity, then the market is in the money.

The trader buys some stock and hopes the prices will go up shortly, so they can buy the stock and sell them immediately hence making a profit.

Put Option

On the other hand, the put option is a case where the investor receives authority to sell a given number of shares for a certain cost and specific time frame. It merely gives the trader the right to transfer shares to a buyer either before or during the time that the contract ends.

Just like with the call contract, the cost of money received after selling equity is what is known as the strike, and the premium is that amount that the buyer gives to the seller when sealing the contract.

These options operate the same way as to call options, what differs is that there is a drop in the cost of the equity, in this case, it does not arise.

Pros of Options Trading

Does Not Require a Lot of Initial Financial Commitment

The price an investor or trader uses to buy an option is always way below the amount you would pay when dealing with the equity directly. An options trader pays less money to transact what other forms of trade would cost more. Yet the benefits are similar to the ones made by those who engage in direct stock trading.

The Downside Is Largely Regulated

As a trader acquires a put or call contract, it is not a must for them to continue to the end of the contract. In case the market takes an uncertain direction, the trader is always free to terminate the contract early enough to avoid incurring significant losses.

Options Are Flexible for Traders

Investors always have several benefits or strategic moves they can work with before an option contract expires. These include:

- Letting go of the option and purchasing the equity shares as an addition to what they already own.
- Letting go of the contract, purchasing the equity shares, and then selling either some or all.
- Writing contracts, which are in the money to some investors on the options market.
- Generating some returns from any cash spent on contracts with out-of-the-money attributes through raising contracts to other investors way before expiration.

Fixing Stock Prices

It gives investors the right to determine the direction that equity costs take within certain times, as long as they know it will be beneficial to them. Depending on the type of option they chose to use, there is always a guarantee that traders will be able to engage in the buying and selling of equities at a set cost price before any contract reaches the expiry.

Cons of Trading Options

High Levels of Loss

The option buyer has an advantage when it comes to this trade, but not the seller. Options sellers have high chances of incurring in huge losses that are more than the contract amounts. This is because investors who write calls must end up buying or selling the shares when the contract expires even if the market has turned out to be unfavorable to them. This means, in case of prices going against their expectations, they still got no chance but to go through the losses.

Short-Term Trading Arrangement

Most investors concentrate on capitalizing on major price movements that must take place within short periods in case they want to make some profit. This means they have a very limited time to make two basic assumptions—either selecting the right moment to purchase a contract and then determining when to close it or simply closing positions and getting away from them right before the expiry date is reached. Whichever option the investor chooses will determine if they make a loss or profit from the trade.

Aggregate Requirements

Before engaging in this business, a trader must be able to attain a list of requirements. They first need to get approval to trade from a broker by providing information about their financial status. This information may include the previous experience in the trade and whether you understand some of the risks involved in the trade. Based on this information, the broker decides whether to award the trader an account and at what level should the trader be allowed to transact. There is also an amount that the trader must be able to raise to start trading. This is a global requirement that cannot change, although the starting amount differs depending on the platform used and the region of trade.

Additional Transaction Costs

Some of the trading strategies need the investor to have a margin account that may serve as collateral for loans and other money needs. Collateral amounts also differ from one broker to another and sometimes there are some hidden charges involved that the trader is not aware of. Interest rates for some margin loans may be significantly high, meaning that the trader cannot make good amounts of profits for each subsequent trade.

It is always advisable to get into options trading with a great understanding of how the system works, its procedure, and what you might find yourself against. There are several well-known strategies available that lower the risk level and can maximize your profit. With some effort, a new trader or beginner trader can learn how to take advantage of the flexible offers. Below is a breakdown of some of the strategies one can start with to get to a win-win situation:

Strategic Tips to Options Trading

One strategy of dealing with this is buying a naked call option. This strategy is quite popular as it makes income and also minimizes the issue of getting into long stocks without a clear plan. The main issue, in this case, is that traders should at all-time manage to sell shares at favorable costs. This cost is what is called the short strike.

This works by an investor purchasing equity or underlying security using the normal process of selling the same shares by starting a call contract on them. The call covers your stock; in case the price of the equity increases, the short call counters this using a long position. Traders use this when they have open anticipation in regards to the direction the market costs might take.

Example:

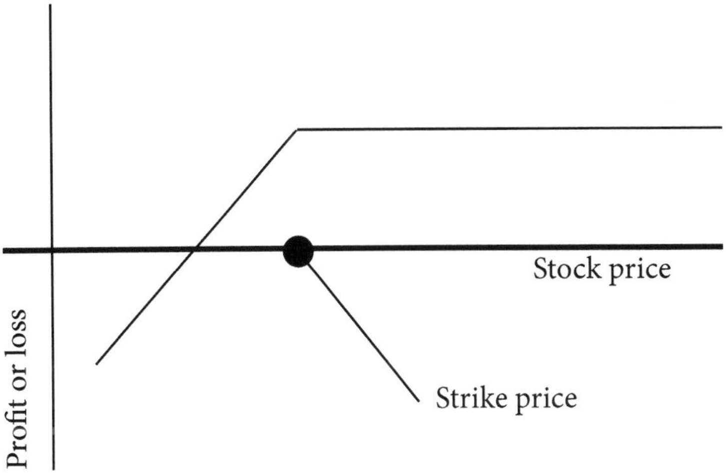

In the diagram above, the cost of the underlying equity rises but the loss from this call is slightly covered through the long position created. As the cost of the equity crosses the strike amount, the trader recovers back the premium amount issued, while selling the call allows them to sell the stock at a higher price.

When it comes to the bull call spread strategy, the trader concurrently buys calls with a specified strike amount; then makes a sell with a similar amount of calls, but at a strike amount higher than the previous one. This is mostly used when an investor is more exposed to the business and knows or expects there will be a rise in the price of the asset. They then limit their upside on the trade, but they end up using less premium than that which is used in naked calls.

For such things to work out, investors always have to ensure that the price of equity keeps rising so that they can make a profit off the two calls.

Another tip lies in using the protective collar strategy, which is created through buying a contract that is out of the money then selling the same kind of contract based on similar equity. This one is common in investors who take a long position that has gone through some great gains. This combination of the two options allows investors to have downside protection, as they also enjoy the potential of getting to sell some shares at favorable costs.

When it comes to the long straddle, the trader purchases both a call and put contract at the same time. This is accomplished using the same cost and exercise date. Investors apply this kind of strategy when there is a positive feeling that the cost of the underlying equity will either increase or decrease with a magnitude that is beyond normal. In this case, the investor is not quite sure of the direction that the market will take. Doing this grants the investor an opportunity to make the most gains from any change in direction. The maximum amount that can be lost in this case is equivalent to the combined premium of the two options. The highest amount of profit is attained when the equity prices change largely but only in one direction.

In terms of the naked puts, traders create this by coming up with an out-of-the-money sell contract where some premium is taken from the buyer. In this case, two things can happen, the option may expire as worthless or it may generate a profit.

Helpful Tips on Options Trading

To successfully trade options, an investor needs to have some knowledge and experience in the field. Some traders have done it for a long time and expertise to make a kill. With constant practice and lots of information on trading, one can become an expert. As it is said, Rome was not built in a day, so challenges are expected for anyone new to the trade.

Assess Your Options

Trading options is more complex than most people think, as it is more than just buying and selling a stock. It involves so many details. Just to mention one example, you must obligatorily get familiar with the trading argot: calls, puts, premiums, etc.

When planning to invest, you have to consider the following:

Individual goal—what do you plan to achieve in the long run? Are you investing in the future? Or are you working on a short-term scheme?

Risk constraints—are you able to take the risks that come with online trading? Do you have other sources of income apart from the trading? What happens when you lose your whole investment?

Time value—the time value of an option is the value that is attributed to the time until that contract expired. As an investor, would you be interested in investing more time or not? The longer the time invested in most options, the higher the value.

Tax constraints—trading, just like any other genuine business, has to go through tax. Is this something you have considered as an investor?

Liquidity needs—when planning to invest, it has always to be money you can put away for a while. Will you, at some point, need your money back hence pull out of the contract? This most of the time ends up leading to a loss.

Knowing the answers to the above questions can help one know if they are ready to invest or not. It is vital to know what kind of investor you are, and what might or might not work for you.

Using Volatility to Your Advantage

Most investors don't pay attention to volatility; however, it has a great impact on options trading. It is important to know about the implied volatility and the historical volatility. The implied volatility is what creates an expectation of the future market prices. On the other hand, historical volatility comes in when measuring the present state of an asset.

You can position yourself as an investor for success by getting familiar with how both types of volatility affect the overall cost of an asset. When buying an option, you must take care if the current implied volatility is closer to, or on a higher point, of its past value. Similarly, when selling an option, you must check if the current implied volatility is near, or at a lower point, of its past value.

One way to determine if the price of the options contracts is high is by evaluating the implied volatility against their past price ranges. In this case, the straddle strategy is the one designed to capitalize on this, as it is about expectations for higher implied volatility and a relatively large move in either direction.

Work With Dividends

Most new options traders fall prey to focusing only on their expectations for the direction in which the underlying stock will move. As much as this is very important, the impact of dividends on options is another one of the areas you need to familiarize yourself with, mostly when selling options.

Before getting into any options trade business, first, find out if the stock pays any dividend. If it does pay, then you will have to take time to examine if that is considered in the money or close to it as expiration time approaches. If the dividend offered is of more value than the time value of the stock, then you know that the stock could be assigned. This means the owner of the option can exercise the option in order to earn the dividend, which would force you to sell the stock even before expiration.

As an investor, you can manage this risk by waiting first to see if the stock is assigned, or just close the position and roll it out to a later month to avoid the owner assigning it.

Manage Risk

How you position yourself when dealing with options can be of great benefit in the number of risks you will run into. It is always helpful for an investor to assess the options they are getting into and work on alternative exits in case things go against their expectations. When an options trade is already open, the trader has several choices to make throughout the life of the contract to safeguard their investment. This may include closing out the trade, letting the options go to expiry, or rolling it out if one is still willing to be in the position.

Ways to Manage Risk

Using your trading plan—have a trading plan laid out so as you can have clear guidelines and parameters for the options trading activity. This helps you to manage well both your money and the risk. Follow your plan and only use money set aside for options trading. This means you can avoid making big mistakes because of the fear of losing money. This is called using "scared" money.

Also, as you trade, stick to understanding the amount of risk highlighted in your pre-trade plan. In case you want to be making transactions that involve less risk, you mustn't do it at one-point start, exposing yourself to high level risk trading. This always leads to emotional breakdowns for some traders, especially in cases of huge losses.

Tips Related to the Use of Options Spreads

These are great and very essential tools for any trader. Some of the powerful trading strategies discussed in this book make use of spreads. This helps minimizes the risk of losing your investment in the options market. You may apply this to your transactions to minimize the costs required when entering positions and also to reduce the amount of cash that you may lose as you engage in the trade. The use of spreads allows you to enter into some positions that can bring you great gains since these positions are run concurrently. Here are some of the tips you may apply to your trade when using spreads.

Closeout a trade—this involves taking an offsetting position. For example, if you had purchased a call option, you can go ahead to sell an identical option to effectively close the trade out.

Let the option expire—this is when you let an option contract reach its expiration date without being exercised and it is possible if you purchase or sell a call or put.

Rolling out an option—this option involves closing out an option that is about to expire and simultaneously purchasing a similar trade with a later expiration date. This works well especially when you are anticipating the market to make a huge move in one direction shortly.

Assignment—you can decide on this by selling an option, which means you might have to receive or deliver shares of the underlying stock.

Managing Risk Through Diversification

This is another way most investors use that is great for risk management. Diversification helps one in coming up with a wonderful portfolio that ensures you generate some income from your capital. The idea behind this is that you can easily "spread" your investments amongst diverse industries and companies to balance your equity portfolio and also increases the chances of you making profits. If one trade fails, there are high chances that another one will work out.

You can come up with such diversification by combining more than one strategy and using contracts that work on different ranges and equities. This gives you a larger platform for making profits in different ways and is not entirely dependent on one particular outcome from one trade.

Using Option Orders

Another easy tip to minimize your trading risk is through the use of options orders. There are main four order types that investors use in the market as below:

Buy to open orders—this is where one places a "but to open." order to purchase a specific options contract when they want to open a position and go long in a specific options contract. This order would be used when you feel the options contract will go up in value, of that they would likely want to exercise the option.

Buy to close orders—this is used to purchase an options contract, but it is mostly used to close a previously opened position rather than opening a new one. If an investor has short-sold an option and wanted to close the position, they then place a buy-to-close order on the options contract.

Sell to open orders—here, the order is used to open positions on options contracts by short selling them. If an investor feels like a certain options contract is likely to fall, they take advantage by short selling the options contract using a sell to open order.

Sell to close orders—this is one of the most used orders in options trading. It is used to close positions that one has opened through a buy to open order. If you had bought a specific options contract and wanted to sell the contract after it has gained some value, you will have to use the sell to close order to sell the contract and gain the profit.

By using the above limit orders, an investor can easily set the equity and the charges at which the orders may get processed. This also helps them avoid buying and selling at prices that are not favorable to them.

Apart from the four above, there are other types of orders you can use to close and open options positions to help in risk management. There are market orders that need to be processed at the best available cost during the execution time. There also orders one can automate exiting positions by locking some of the little profit made already as a way of cutting losses on a position that has changed direction significantly.

These tips are helpful to avoid scenarios where one gets to miss out on profits by holding certain positions long enough or incurring in some great risks of losing the little cash made already. If you mastered the use of orders well, you can limit the risks involved in each trade.

Chapter 6: Options Trading Updates

In this chapter, we will be looking for new ways of trading options. Ratio charts is one of a new way to trade options.

Ratio Charts

A ratio chart shows the price of one security valued in terms of the other security. In other words, take the price of one security and divide it by the price of the second security to get the ratio. The actual value is not usually as important as the technical trend of the ratio. This type of chart is quite useful in uncovering trends between two assets and when they may change. It can also be useful in debunking myths about perceived relationships between assets. One of these myths is that the Chinese market is highly correlated to U.S. equity markets. There are many so-called expert opinions as to why this is so. Some say it has to do with the use of Chinese labor to manufacture goods for U.S. companies. Others point to the Chinese housing market and its use of raw materials from the United States. Still, others make reference to the size of the population of China and the growth of its middle class as a potential market for U.S. goods. These are all good theories and may hold some merit.

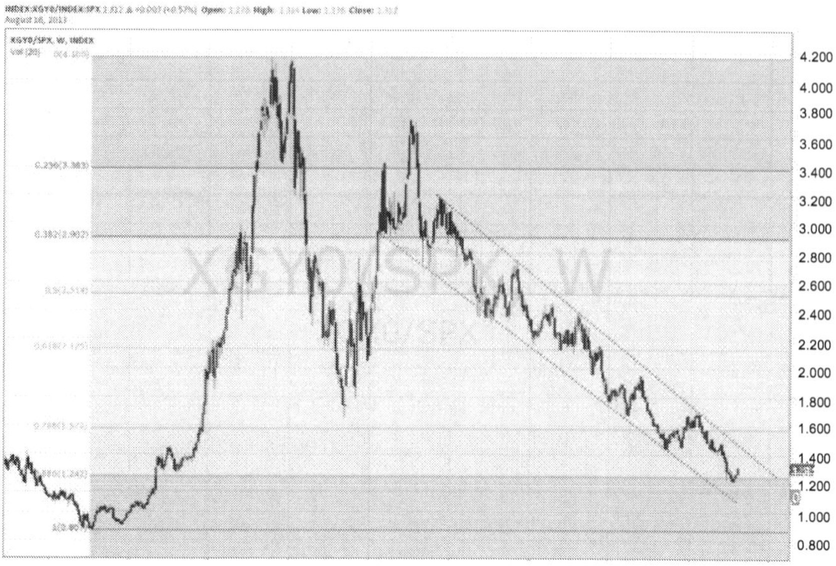

This chart shows a clear down trending channel continuing from late 2009 through to late 2013. As of this writing, the ratio has retracted 88.6 percent of the entire run-up it saw from 2006 to 2008. Nothing continues forever, and trends can change on a dime, so making sweeping statements about correlations can be dangerous. But this chart looks to be heading lower toward a full retracement. So, what has happened during this time? The U.S. market has recovered from the financial crisis lows to new all-time highs. Yet the ratio chart shows that all during that time, the Chinese market has been ceding ground to the U.S. market. Clearly, for a four-year period, these markets were not positively correlated but inversely correlated. Armed with that knowledge, it will likely be important when this trend changes. I wonder if, at that point, the expert opinions will be that these markets are always inversely correlated.

Significant Market Ratios

Every trader has additional measures that are used to monitor the health of a trend. For me, aside from seeing a visual of the aforementioned influencers, it is also useful to look at many ratios involving them.

The S&P 500 Versus Emerging Markets

The ratio that looks at the flow of funds between the S&P 500 and emerging markets is a very good indicator of the global risk appetite. When the ratio is rising, there is relative strength in the S&P 500 compared to emerging markets. A trend like this can occur when emerging markets experience a recession or other shock to their economies. It can also happen when the U.S. economy is perceived to be growing more strongly than those of emerging countries. In this trend, the S&P 500 looks to continue strong. But oddly, even if the flow is favoring emerging markets, this can be good for the U.S. market. Especially deep into a trend, it can show that the appetite for risk is growing, which can signal that the strength in the U.S. market can continue. Trends in both directions can be good for U.S. stocks. This ratio really emphasizes the importance of the change in trend over the trend itself.

U.S. Treasuries Versus Junk Bonds

U.S. Treasuries versus high-yield ("junk") bonds is another measure of risk appetite, but mainly within the U.S. economy. As investors and traders take on more risks, there is a flow into high-yield bonds from U.S. Treasuries. A trend lower in U.S. Treasury prices compared to high-yield bond prices is an indication of acceptance of more risk in the bond market. It is not a direct one-for-one correlation between high-yield bond prices and U.S. equity prices, but high-yield bonds can be a good proxy for equities in terms of the amount of risk-taking in the broad marketplace. This is a very good measure of the direction of risk appetite in fixed income securities.

S&P 500 versus U.S. Treasuries

The S&P 500 versus U.S. Treasury securities is another measure of risk appetite within the U.S. marketplace. As discussed earlier, these two markets are usually perceived to be negatively correlated. So, a flow from one to the other can indicate either the addition of risk or a flight to safety that may not be as obvious in the individual charts. That is a good short-term view. In the longer term, though, as discussed in the previous section, bond prices and stocks have tended to move in the same direction. This ratio's current trend persisting is a non-event, but a change is often triggered by some sort of shock and becomes important. If the trend changes, keep watching.

Silver to Gold Ratio

The silver to gold ratio stands as a good proxy for the direction of the S&P 500. From the chart given below, it is easy to see that the correlation between this ratio and the S&P 500 was very strong until the end of 2011. Prior to that, for more than 10 years, the direction of this ratio could be used to identify the direction of the S&P 500. The magnitudes of the moves were not precise, but knowing the direction is 70 percent of the game. Many traders follow it to look for clues, based on this correlation, as to when the S&P 500 might turn before the change shows up in stock prices. Sadly, it looks as if this relationship has run its course, with the correlation flipping 180 degrees in 2012 to an inverse correlation. Again, it was the change that mattered. As the correlation flipped, the S&P 500 started its long uptrend, with gold reversing its 15-year uptrend.

Rising and Falling Three Methods

Maybe the most boringly named pair of patterns, these were certainly not coined by someone seeking favor from the emperor. The Rising and Falling Three Methods patterns are different from all of the previous patterns in that they signal a continuation of a trend, not the start of a new trend or a reversal. These are typically five-candle patterns, with a long candle in the direction of the trend, followed by three small body candles where the entire real body remains inside the real body of the previously mentioned long candle; then the fifth candle is another long candle in the direction of the trend that makes a new higher high or lower low. A long candle, three smaller consolidating candles, and another long candle resuming the pattern make up the formation. I picture these as a sandwich with the two long candles as the bread and the three interior candles, maybe as the turkey, a slice of cheese, and a tomato (or an onion if that suits you better).

The Rising Three Methods is illustrated in the chart given below in the (light gray) box. Notice that it happened in the middle of the trend when it looked like a consolidation might occur. It might also be interpreted and a bull flag or a consolidating channel. Finally, I should point out that there were four interior candles and not three. There is a key point on this to put a candle or maybe two or subtract one. How many is too many, you ask? Again, you will know it when you see it. We are not looking for a quadruple-decker sandwich, just lunch before the next move higher. Finally, notice that the run continued for $12 after the pattern was completed, despite having already moved $26 into the pattern. Just because a stock has had a long run does not mean it cannot have another run equally long or even longer than the first run. In the chart below, we can see that the average was high (long light gray stick) after several highs (short light gray sticks) but then it suddenly went significantly low (long dark grey stick).

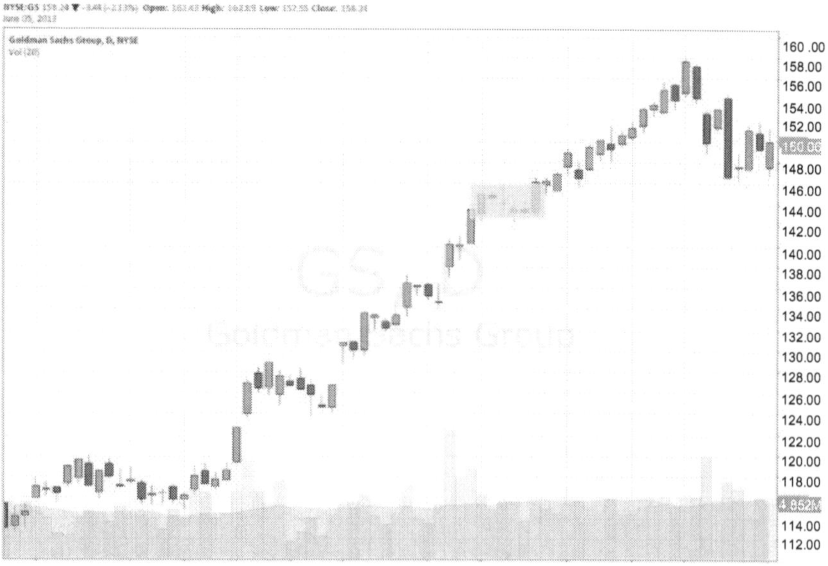

Rising Three: Long sticks indicating price average in an option, from the lowest (dark) to the highest (light)

The Falling Three Methods is similar but in the opposite direction. So, there is a long down (light or dark grey) candle followed by three candles with small real bodies and then another long down (light or dark grey) candle to a new lower low. The chart of Foot Locker in next figure shows this pattern in a not so tidy way. You can see the first long (light or dark grey) candle indicating an average (light gray meaning a rise, dark grey a low). but then the next three candles jump around and look like they could be Hammer reversal candles. But each conforms to the Falling Three Methods by maintaining the real body within the long first candle. The long (light or dark grey) candle following to confirm the pattern and continued downside is also unlike what you might see in a textbook. This is not a neat sandwich visual, but one that is mangled or falling apart—like you packed it in your luggage and brought it on a trip, only to find it smushed when you are ready to eat it. All the pieces are there, and it tastes great, but it does not look very good. But like the sandwich, it is the taste that matters, not the looks. Nonetheless, it is a Falling Three Methods, and the trend continued lower for another $3.

Although these are continuation patterns, they can also be interpreted as a change in the trend if you can expand to thinking of the trend in three options: up, down, or sideways. The trend moves from one direction to sideways and back to that same direction again. In this way, the trend change can signal a new entry if you missed the initial entry at the beginning of the trend.

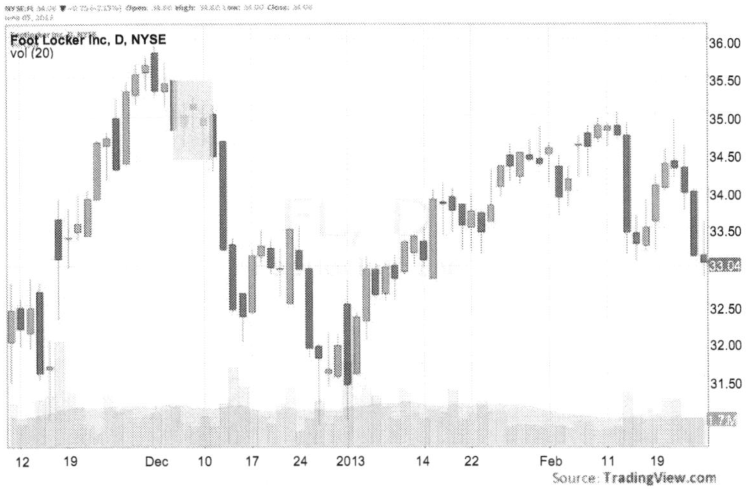

Falling Three: Long sticks indicating price average in an option, from the lowest (dark) to the highest (light)

The picture above shows how prices can change and it is a guide for traders taking important, fast decisions that can be translated in huge losses or significant profits. The small sticks indicate a rise (light gray) or a fall in the price (dark gray). Long sticks indicate the average (light gray meaning a high average) from the minimum to the maximum. In this case, this stock could have a good high price average between 32-34. But finally, after reaching a price of around 35, it returned to a low average of 33-34, as indicated by the final long dark grey stick.

The Elements

The one option that would be the gateway to the whole phase is your first choice in creating an options trading setup. It's the premium call or put you choose to buy or sell. A first choice would be referred to as the driver since it is used to assess the trade's profitability. No matter what else is going on in the economy, you want to be long or short on the call or put choice. It could be obvious, such as the at-the-money (ATM) call with a near-month expiry, or it might be less obvious, such as the 3-month-out call 15% over market price. The most critical choice is picking a chart. It stems from your initial involvement in trading the product, which was ignited by your study of the chart and the opportunity for a change.

If the element has been found, the stock's trading setup may be used to evaluate the best alternative or options to reduce the trade's expense and offer further control. These are alluded to as financing alternatives since they are used to finance or compensate for the exchange. They cut the price. This is where the experience of the Part III variations comes in handy. When the chart indicates a fast 10% jump on a breakout versus a slow increase over the next 3 weeks or a stabilization with a possibility of a move either up or down, understanding which combination of options is better will make this aspect of the phase simpler. What is the explanation for this?

Take a stock like State Street, which has a predicted $8 shift in the map. If the August 70 call, which was provided at $1.55, is your driver, you must decide if the funding choice would be clear.

Call spread, or will it be a fast August 62.5 placed for 55 cents to save a third of the cost? Or both, in order to save more than half of the driver's cost? The spread leads to a reward-to-risk ratio of more than 3:1. However, by growing the expense by more than 25%, the put selling would not cap the upside benefit opportunity and suits the requirements of a financing alternative. It also requires margin and the probability of owning the stock in the case of a substantial drop in price— further risk.

However, there are more possibilities. Since the July options in this chart have only seven trading days remaining, the trader can choose to sell the July 70 calls for 75 cents. This leaves the exchange uncapped and offers you the option of exchanging the July 70 short call for an August 75 call at a later date. It also opens up the option of offering a shorter-dated July 65 put for 40 cents, a higher strike than the August 62.5 put previously possible but with slightly less time for the stock to decline in price. Reviewing the trade-off between the gain of financing and handling the risk, either eliminated or introduced in selling options to finance the trade, maybe the most difficult aspect. Without the advantage of retrospect, it's difficult to tell which solution will be the better.

In this scenario, I'd go for a July/August 70 call Calendar spread and offer the July 65 placed for a net cost of 40 cents, or just 26% of the driver's cost. If the July 70 call expires useless in seven days, it offers an uncapped trade into August with a chance below 65 for just seven days in a rising sector with a portfolio that has broken out. At that moment, the greatest danger seems to be the prospect of needing to buy back the short July 70 call if it goes in-the-money (ITM). When picking these July strikes, I found that the 65 strikes on the put side and the 67.5 strikes on the call side have a higher open interest, which may prevent the stock from going too rapidly higher. If the price increases past 70 before the expiration date in July, I can always buy the July 70 calls and sell the August 75 calls, turning the trade to a call spread with a short July put. This conversion would almost definitely be free if the price increases steadily since the July option depreciates quickly than the intrinsic value, while the August option depreciates more slowly in relation to the price movement compared to the intrinsic value. Over time, you'll get more used to this aspect of the protocol.

Once you've settled on the driver and financing choices, you'll need to determine the danger that exists in the transaction. Before you are able to execute, you will need to pick a danger limiter if appropriate. The downside danger in the July/August 70 call Calendar selling the July 65 put is a potential $65 in the contract. If it falls during market hours, simply buy back the short put to reduce the chance. However, if it persists after the close, you would be denied redress. The stock is unlikely to gap down to zero, but a 10% decline is not unthinkable. And you can typically defend yourself for very little capital. A long July 60 put for 11 cents, or a long July 62.5 put for 18 cents are two alternatives in this situation. Based on your study, you can infer that no security is needed to mitigate harm. If you decided to purchase State Street at 64, for instance, the quick 65 puts might be a reasonable place to start. Switching from a hunt for a mix that will drive income at an appropriate debt level and capital outlay to an emphasis on risk control will often result in a significant redesign of the trading structure. If the chance of a missed breakout at 65 for seven days is too high, you might sell a July/August 62.5 put Calendar to cover the downside for seven days and then carry on the 62.5 risk moving forward.

In this discussion of the driver, financing choices, and danger limiter, there is a lot to take in. Before going on to the next part, I recommend that you read it a couple of times and make notes on the map to help you grasp the dynamics.

Position Sizing and Stop Losses

It's more for risk control when it comes to position sizing. Risk management is the first goal as an options broker. There is no capital left to take care of without adequate risk control. So, what part does position sizing play in this? It's the crux of the dilemma. This achieves a successful combination between danger and reward. If you have so many choice roles, you risk getting wiped out easily, and if you have too few, you restrict your prospects. So, how can you choose the right size? There is no one-size-fits-all solution to deciding this, much as there is no one-size-fits-all approach to determining stock market schemes. What you can bear in mind is that, among other aspects, the sizing requirements would defend against a crisis but still allowing for performance.

The Process Starts with Goals

One obvious (two-part) aim is to stop a disaster but also allowing for progress. But isn't it a bit vague? Protecting against a crisis involves not placing too much money at risk and trying your best to recognize where the crisis may originate. The first is a mechanical item. The second section is focused on experience and mastery of the subjects covered earlier in the book. As we discovered in the first section of the book, a top-down technical observer would first analyze the pattern and then the trend's influencers to decide what could alter it. There is a clear tailwind for both equities; for example, whenever Sample 500 is rising when the US Dollar Index and Treasuries are declining. However, if the currency increases and Treasuries increase with it, equity values can be jeopardized.

Examine the stock's individual threats next. A swing trader's threats involve the stock's liquidity, which relates to the number of securities exchanged and the usual spread, as well as whether or not there are options to hedge and how liquid they are. A stock with strong visibility and tight spreads in both the stock and the options will look better than one with a major change opportunity but no way to hedge. This research, coupled with a technical evaluation of possible support and resistance thresholds, contributes to a calculation of how much danger a transaction involves.

A stock in an uptrend in a sector that is trending higher, with good liquidity and encouragement from Intermarket influencers, can be exchanged with more faith than a stock that is trending against the market.

Of course, there is some art and calculation involved in this method. It is inevitable. Sizing a deal becomes mechanical with this study in mind, and it depends on balancing four factors: portfolio and trade risk tolerance, time period, technical triggers, and liquidity.

1. Portfolio and trade risk tolerance. This is simply how much of your portfolio you are willing to lose on any given trade and then on the portfolio in total. You can try to control all sorts of risks, but if an overnight gap or halt comes into play, what is your pain threshold? Look at this as a percentage of your portfolio. It may be bigger if you trade infrequently and smaller if you are more active or have many positions. I look to limit the total capital or margin used for a trade to 5 to 7.5 percent of the portfolio, so that is the maximum that a stock trade can lose. But then use a stop loss on each position to measure a worst-case expected move on a stock trade that will limit a loss to far less. For trading breakouts, it is usually a lot less, as the breakout level is a natural stop loss.

For options, it is a similar story. You also do not want to have a margin from a short option that can destroy your portfolio. I use a limit of 7.5 percent of the portfolio here as well, and for ease of calculation, I assume that margin is taken at 10 percent of the short option strike. Long options and options spreads can be very cheap, and that would allow for very large positions using 7.5 percent of capital, so I limit them further to 2 percent of capital. This is not the only way to do it, but it works for me.

2. Time frame. What time frame do you trade? Are you a day trader or a swing trader; a position trader or an investor? For our purposes, we are assuming a swing trader, someone who will hold positions for a few days up to a couple of weeks on average. Your time frame may be different for different trades, and that is okay. Whatever your time frame is will influence your risk on the position and, therefore, your position size. This will be crucial for determining where to set your entry and stops. For example, day traders have the risk of a halt in stock but do not have overnight gap risk, so they might use bigger position limits. A long-term holding may have a wider stop and thus a smaller size.

3. Technical triggers. From your own review of the chart of any particular stock, where are the triggers to enter and exit? How far apart are they? And on what time frame do they work? This will determine how much money you can risk per share. Two stocks with the same price and all other factors equal will have different stops based on support and resistance levels nearby and therefore may also have different sized trades. If you can lose $1 in stock before your trade is invalidated compared to $2 in the other stock, it makes sense for the trade with a wider loss potential to be smaller. Strikes on the option come into play in this area as well.

4. Liquidity. You never want to have a position that is more than 5 percent of the recent average daily volume. Unless you are Carl Icahn or Bill Ackman, who frequently have large positions, this becomes important when trading a thinly traded stock or, if you have a large portfolio, when trading a very low-priced stock. Being a large percentage of the daily volume is a problem only when you are trying to exit fast. You are never trying to exit fast when the stock is moving in your direction, only when it is going against you. And that is always when you are being stopped, not when you are making money. You do not want to be in a position where your desire to sell is depressing the price further.

Frequently Asked Questions

These are sets of answers to the questions that are commonly asked about options, how they are traded, and some of the strategies involved. The purpose of these questions is to help you with any of the concerns you may have on options trading. Let us look at some of them.

How Does Options Trading Work?

Basically, when seeking to understand how options work, it is important to first get the fact that these instruments are derived from other financial instruments; therefore, their prices are determined by the price of the underlying asset. Options are often traded online as well as in standalone exchanges. The process of buying and selling a particular option is often outlined in the options contract which gives a trader the right to either buy or sell options. The buyer always has the right while the seller has the obligation over a contract.

What Are the Types of Options?

Options are generally divided into two types—there is the call option, then the put option. Call options permit the trader to buy a contract while put options permit the trader to sell a contract.

What Are Options Moving Averages?

These are averages used to determine options trends. They are very similar to the averages used on a day-to-day basis. They assist traders to establish trends in the options market and in the price of underlying securities. Moving averages are forms of technical indicators, commonly used in the technical analysis of financial instruments. There are two major forms of averages—simple and exponential moving averages. These two types operate using similar procedures except that exponential averages keep building on previous data exponentially. These are considered more effective when establishing market and price trends than simple moving averages.

Is There Any Difference Between Options and Futures?

Options and futures belong to a class of financial instruments known as derivatives. The difference between options and futures comes in at the obligations that bind the parties involved in the trade. In a futures contract, the seller and buyer all must meet the requirements of a contract on a given date while in options, parties only get the right, not the obligation to execute contracts. Also, futures contracts give buyers an unlimited amount of profit or loss while in options trading the buyer can only make unlimited profits since the loss is often limited.

What Is the Strike Price of an Option?

This commonly used term is also called the purchase price. It is the amount traders give to acquire ownership of the underlying security of a certain option. For call options, it is the price a trader pays when purchasing a contract; in the case of a put option, this refers to the amount the seller receives from selling an option.

What if an Option Expires "Out of the Money"?

In case this occurs, two possibilities will happen—the buyer may lose their premium and the seller may get a profit if it is a call option, or the buyer incurs losses and the seller earns some profit in case of a put option.

How Do People Settle Contracts?

Contracts get settled in the form of cash. This is done daily either before or during the expiration period.

What Is the Purpose of Options Contract Adjustments?

These are changes in the terms stipulated in an options contract basing on some changes that take place in the underlying security. For instance, factors such as splits, mergers, and acquisitions can trigger adjustments in option contracts. These adjustments occur each time there is a significant change that affects the value of the underlying stock.

What Is Meant by Covered Calls?

Covered calls are those options transacted by a trader who is still the owner of the underlying instrument for the option.

What About Naked Options?

These are options you trade-in without being the owner of the underlying instrument.

Is There a Difference Between Squaring an Option Off and Exercising It?

Yes, there is. Squaring an option off involves opening a position that is exactly the opposite of your existing positions. Exercising an option, on the other hand, entails closing an existing position as a way of gaining some profit or minimizing losses from it. Exercising of options can take place anytime during the transaction or at the end of a contract.

What Rights Do Stock Buyers Have That Differentiate Them From Options Buyers?

Stock traders always have several rights that may not be applicable to option trading. When you trade-in stocks, you become the owner of a percentage of the company's shares. This gives you a right to acquire dividends on calculated intervals and also allows you to determine the management of the company since you get to receive some voting rights. You also gain a right to some capital when you want to trade on certain exchanges.

Things are different in options trading; you do not receive any rights since all the terms of the trade are restricted to what is stipulated in the option contract.

How Do Index Options Work?

Index options are those contracts whose underlying asset is the index. Basically, an index option has a group of stocks as the underlying security and each of these stocks is weighted based on certain attributes or calculations within the index tool. Most index options feature an expiry cycle that three months.

Conclusion

Options trading provides a unique way through which investors can make money. While there are a few risks involved here and there, these are normally at a minimum. This means that you can make good money from trading options.

Adequate research and understanding of when to enter or exit positions are just some of the factors that make you succeed in the trade. If you are not sure of what to do on the options market, it is good that you engage the services of a broker. The information in this book ensures that you understand how easy it is to buy and sell options. Now that you have gone through it, you are well equipped and therefore can start trading without any fear of losing your investment.

Options trading is a process that comprises several steps. From placing orders, to entering positions then finally exercising your contracts, you must always be sure of what needs to be done to avoid making serious mistakes. The basis of options trading lies in understanding what it entails. Options are derivatives of other financial investment tools. They are commonly used by investors who do not want to put their stocks on the market directly. You must beware of every process involved in selling and buying calls and puts. Let us go through a recap of some of the things learned from this wonderful book.

An option is a kind of financial contract that allows you to trade on equities indirectly at a specific price and time period.

The cost of each option contract is always a derivative of the cost of the underlying capital. An option represents this asset and people who trade options do not trade directly with the underlying asset.

A call option allows you to buy shares with a specified amount as the exercise cost. A put option gives you the opportunity to sell shares at specified amounts as the exercise price.

The options market is made up of four types of traders:

- The buyer of a call
- The buyer of a put
- The seller of a call
- The seller of a put

The process of closing a position or options contract is known as exercising an option while the cost of each option is its premium.

When it comes to options trading, how you understand and apply the strategies outlined in chapter 5 and the tips in chapter 6 determine how far you go in the trade. This is especially important if you are just starting the investment. Engaging in options trading without the right knowledge is a very risky affair. This book helps you appreciate the principles applied in the options market. It also assists you in understanding the benefits and methods you need to use to choose the right trading platform.

Of course, determination and patience are key factors when it comes to options trading. You must be able to come up with a winning plan that will shield you from making emotional investments.

Finally, you must always see options trading like any other business where you will make either profit or losses as each day passes. Avoid entering into positions just because they look promising. When you lose, understand that it was bound to happen, and continue improving on your strategies to avoid this from happening in the future.

Thank you for reading this book.

If you enjoyed it, please visit the site where you purchased it and write a brief review. Your feedback is important to me and will help other readers decide whether to read the book too.

Thank you!

—Nathan Real

FOREX TRADING

A Complete Guide About Forex Trading | Including Strategies, Risk Management Techniques and Fundamental Analysis

Written by:

Nathan Real

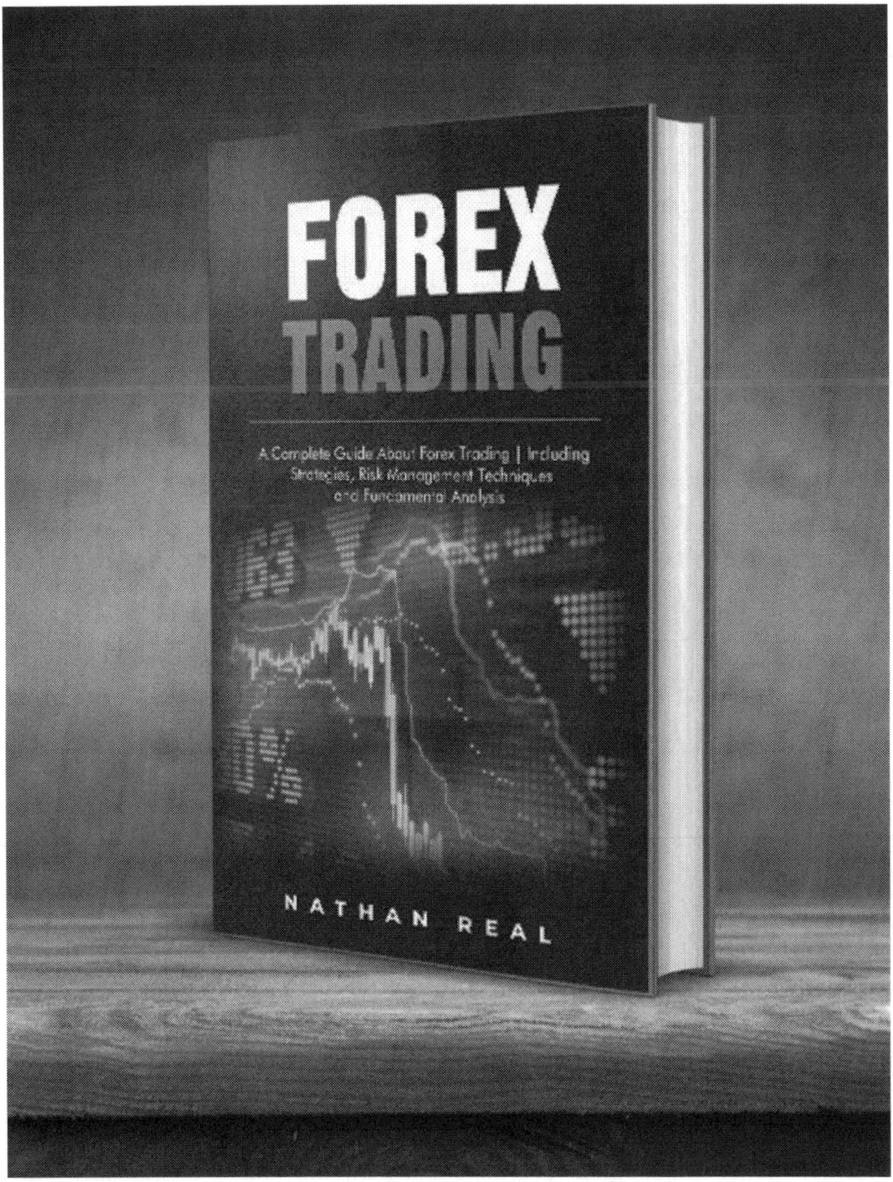
FOREX
TRADING
A Complete Guide About Forex Trading | Including Strategies, Risk Management Techniques and Fundamental Analysis
NATHAN REAL

Introduction

Forex is also called foreign exchange, currency trading or FX. It is an internationally competitive system in which all the currencies of the world are transacted. The Forex market is the world's biggest liquid market, with an estimated daily volume of more than $5 trillion in exchange. Not even any of the consolidated capital markets around the globe come near to this. Through looking at Forex trading more closely, you could find some interesting trading opportunities inaccessible to other assets.

Forex, or foreign exchange, may be described as a network of buyers and sellers that trade currency at a negotiated price among them. It's the way people, firms, and central banks change one currency into another.

Although a lot of foreign exchange is conducted for practical reasons, most of the currency trading is performed in order to make a profit. The sum of currency exchanged per day results in very unpredictable market fluctuations in certain currencies. It is this uncertainty that may render Forex so enticing to traders: making high returns more possible, but still increasing the risk.

If you have ever flown abroad, you probably made a trade to Forex. Take a ride to France and convert to Euros your Pounds. The Forex exchange rate among the two currencies — which is based on demand and supply — decides how many Euros you find for your pounds when you do it. Plus, the exchange rate keeps on changing continuously.

On Monday, a single Pound could bring you 1.191 Euros. You might get 1.200 Euros on Tuesday. It does not sound like a huge deal, especially this slight adjustment. You need to consider it on a larger scale than that. A big multinational corporation will need to compensate workers abroad. Imagine what it will mean in the end if, as in the previous case, swapping one currency for another will cost you more based on when you do it? Just a few pennies rapidly add up. In both situations, before the Forex exchange rate is more attractive, you — as a visitor or business holder — may want to keep your currency.

Much like commodities, money may be exchanged depending on what you believe it's worth it (or where it is headed). However, the primary distinction in Forex is what you can trade just as comfortably upwards or downwards. If you think the value of a currency would rise, you should purchase it. If you believe it's going to go down, so you should sell it. Locating a buyer when you are selling and a supplier when you are purchasing is much simpler than in most markets with such a wide demand. You will listen in the news report that China is degrading its currency to lure more international business into their state. If you think this pattern would persist, sell Chinese currency against the other currency, let's say, the U.S. dollar, you might create a Forex profit. The higher the earnings, the further the Chinese currency devalues compared to the U.S. dollar. If the value of the Chinese currency rises when you have your sale place open, your losses escalate, and you need to get rid of this trade.

Both Forex transactions require two currencies since you bet on a currency's worth against another. Consider EUR / USD, the world's highly traded currency pair. The pioneer currency in the pair, Euro, is the base, and Dollar, the counter. As you look at a listed price on your program, that cost is how much 1 euro in US dollars is worth. You still have two prices, since the purchase price is one, and the selling price is one. The distinction between the 2 is circulated. If you press on sell or buy, the first currency in the set is bought or sold.

Let's presume you believe the value of the Euro would climb against the US dollar. Your set will be EUR / USD. As the EUR is first, because you believe it's going to rise, you purchase EUR / USD. If you believe the Euro is going to decline in value versus the US dollar, you should be selling EUR / USD.

If the buying price for EUR / USD is 0.7065 and the selling rate is 0.7064, so the spread is 0.44 pips. If the trade shifts in your support (or not in favor of you), so you can make a loss (or profit) on your trade until you cover the spread.

If you quote values to the one-hundredths of the cents, how do you make some meaningful go back on your asset when you trade Forex? The solution to that is leverage.

While you trade Forex, the initial currency in the set is essentially borrowed to purchase or sell the other currency. Along with a USD 5 trillion per day market, liquidity is so large that liquidity suppliers — the major banks, basically — leverage you to trade. To trade on leverage, you basically place aside the margin needed for your scale of trade. For example, if you sell 200 ratio 1 leverage, you will trade $2,000 in the market, whereas putting aside just $10 in the margin in your trading account. For a ratio of 50:1, the same scale of trade will also need just about £40 in the margin. This allows you even more exposure, thus holding your investment in the capital down.

But leverage not only enhances the opportunity for profit. It will also raise the losses that can outweigh the funds invested. You can often begin trading with reduced leverage ratios while you're new to Forex before you feel secure in the market.

Proper preparation is necessary for an environment as volatile as the Forex. If you're a seasoned market operator or new to currency trading, staying ready is key to continuous profit-making.

That is far better said than achieved, of course. It's important that on-the-job training never ceases to ensure you have the greatest shot at Forex success. In the fast-paced, a few areas to remain successful are the Forex environment, cultivating sound trading activities, attending technical webinars, and maintaining the business education.

If your aim is to become a Forex trader that is reliably successful, then your learning must never end. As the adage says, practice makes perfect; whereas for the active traders, ' success is always difficult; it should be normal to be trained for each session.

Forex is the world's biggest market for capital. With a daily turnover of more than $5 trillion, the Forex is a global trading platform where investors, speculators, and liquidity suppliers from around the globe trade.

It's essential to create an educational base for those fresh to the international currency exchange before getting in with both the feet. Comprehending the Forex's fundamental points is a crucial part of keeping up to speed as fast as possible. You must be able to interpret a quote, calculate the leverage and place the orders on the market.

Unless you play the lottery, it's not an accident if you win. It requires willingness, determination, and aptitude to learn every discipline. It's no different from becoming a successful Forex trader. Your path to the marketplace is most possibly lost until it starts without the desire, will and know-how.

Luckily, a few of the variations between good traders and money-losers are no longer a mystery. Studying the behavior of individuals shows there are three places where popular traders succeed. Since there's no "holy grail" for lucrative Forex trading, building up good risk and reward routines, leveraging, and timing is a perfect way to improve your results. Studying their best techniques and market tactics allows a person to understand how successful traders handle the Forex.

We will discuss in detail successful trading strategies, trading techniques, and trading types to help our readers learn and master effective Forex trading skills.

CHAPTER 1: History of Forex Trading

Unlike financial markets, whose origins can be traced to centuries, the Forex market is a comparatively new market as we understand it today. Undoubtedly, in its most intrinsic sense, where people convert one currency to another for financial gains, Forex has been around from the time nations began to mint currencies. Nevertheless, the modern Forex markets are a truly modern creation. Subsequent to the accord at Bretton Woods in 1971, a number of pivotal currencies were given permission to float randomly against one another. Since the rates of individual currencies tend to change, thus provoking the need for foreign exchange trading and services.

Although investment and commercial banks do the majority of transactions on behalf of their clients in the Forex markets, yet veteran and individual investors can capitalize on available speculative opportunities for trading one currency against another.

Origin of Forex Trading

Forex trading that involves exchanging fiat currency is centuries-old–that dates to Babylonian times. The Forex market today is one of the world's largest, most liquid, and available markets, and it has been created by several major global events, such as Bretton Woods Agreement and the gold level.

Understanding the background of Forex trading and the major historical events that created the market is important for Forex traders. It is because similar events could probably happen again in distinct but similar forms – affecting the landscape of trading. History is prone to replicate itself.

1.1 Where It All Started

The barter scheme is the ancient trading tool that started around 6000BC, initiated by tribes from Mesopotamia. Products were traded for other products in the barter-system. The mechanism then developed, and items such as spices and salt became a common means of trade. Ships would move, in the earliest form of foreign exchange, to barter for these products. Eventually, the first gold coins were created as early as the 6th century BC, and they served as a currency, since they had the essential characteristics such as portability, longevity, divisibility, uniformity, restricted availability, and suitability.

Gold coins were generally recognized as a means of trade, but since they were large, they became inefficient. Countries in the 1800s introduced the gold standard. The gold standard ensured every sum of paper money would be redeemed by the government for its worth of gold. This served well until World War I, when European countries were pressured to abandon the gold standard to publish more currency for the war.

At this point and during the early 1900s, the foreign-exchange business was protected by the gold standard. Countries worked together, and the currency they earned could be changed into gold. However, during the world wars, the gold standard was unable to hold on.

1.2 Major Events That Have Made the Forex Market

We've seen significant events throughout history that have profoundly affected the Forex trading system. Here are some features:

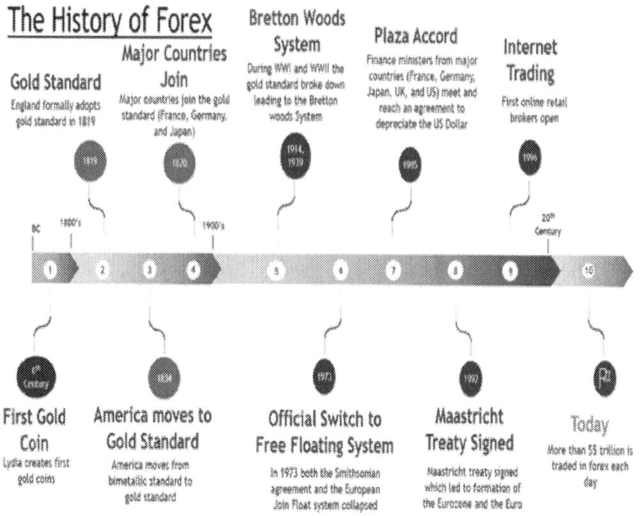

1.3 The Bretton Forests System 1944 – 1971

The initial major restructuring in the foreign-exchange marketplace, the Bretton Woods System, happened at the last of World War II. In the United Nations Political and Financial meeting in Bretton Woods, the United States, NH, France, and Great Britain agreed to develop a modern worldwide economic mandate. The location was selected because the United States was the only state that had remained untouched by war at that time. Any of Europe's large countries had been in dumps. After the stock market collapse of 1929, WWII bounded the dollar from a failed currency to a standard currency against that most of the other international currencies were equated.

The Bretton Woods Contract was designed to establish a secure atmosphere from which world economies would rebound. It attempted this by the development of a flexible, secured foreign exchange market. A flexible secured exchange rate is a mechanism of exchange rates in which a currency is attached to another currency. Other countries would then 'fix' their exchange cost to the dollar. The dollar was being indexed to gold, and at that point, the US had the world's largest gold reserves. And other nations would be transacting in the US Dollar (that is how the dollar became the reserve currency of the world as well).

Eventually, the Bretton Woods contract refused to limit gold to the U.S. dollar, and there was not adequate gold to back up the volume of U.S. dollars in demand owing to rising government spending and lending. President Richard M. Nixon dismissed the Bretton Woods regime in 1971, which rapidly contributed to the US dollar's free-floating against other global currencies.

1.4 The Beginning of the Free-Floating System

The Smithsonian Agreement came in December 1971, after the Bretton Woods Agreement, which was similar but allowed for a greater currency fluctuation band. The US pegged the dollar to gold at $38 / ounce, depreciating the dollar as a result. Under the Smithsonian agreement, other major currencies could fluctuate against the US dollar by 2.25 percent, and the US dollar was tied to gold.

In 1972, the European community attempted to shift from its dependence on the U.S. Dollar. West Germany, Italy, the Netherlands, France, Luxemburg, and Belgium, then made the European Joint Float. Both agreements made mistakes like the Bretton Woods Contract and collapsed in 1973. The consequence of these problems was an official transfer to the free-floating method.

1.5 The Plaza Accord

The dollar had significantly improved against the other global currencies throughout the early 1980s. This was challenging for exporters, and a shortfall of 3.5 percent of GDP was consequently generated by the U.S. current account. Paul Volcker, in reaction to the stagflation that started in the early 80s, increased interest rates that caused a powerful U.S. dollar (and reduced inflation) at the cost of the competitiveness of the U.S. industry in the global market.

The U.S. dollar's weight crushed third-world nations under obligation and shut down American factories because they are not able to compete with foreign challengers. In 1985, the G-5 sent delegates to what was meant to be a confidential conference in New York City at the Plaza Hotel, of the world's most strong economies – the U.S., Great Britain, France, West Germany, and Japan. The meeting's news leaked, imposing the G-5 to make a report which encouraged non-dollar currencies' appreciation. That became famous as the "Plaza Accord," and its impacts caused the dollar to fall precipitously.

It didn't take very long for the traders to understand the profitable opportunities in this modern currency-trading environment. Although there were still higher degrees of fluctuation amid government intervention, and where there is fluctuation, there is revenue. This became apparent a bit over time after Bretton Woods' crash.

1.6 Establishment of the Euro

After the end of WWII, Europe entered many treaties, the main objectives of which were to bring countries in the area close together. Out of these treaties, one was regarded as the important effective treaty of the 1992 treaty, which is now mentioned as the Maastricht Treaty. Maastricht Treaty is the name of the Dutch city where the meeting was conducted. The Treaty formed the European Union (EU), developed the euro currency, and integrated a coherent whole that involved foreign rule and security initiatives. The pact has been changed numerous times, but the existence of the euro has provided European banks and corporations the distinct advantage of reducing currency threat in an ever-globalized environment.

1.7 Internet Trading

The currency markets became more complex and quicker than ever in the 1990s when capital – and the way people interpreted it and used it – shifted. An individual sitting at home alone might discover, by pressing a button, a correct price that would take an army of brokers, traders, and telephones only a few years ago. These communication advances occurred at a period when past divides gave way to globalization and capitalism (the collapse of the Soviet Union and the Berlin Wall).

Everything improved for Forex. Currencies historically shut down could be sold in totalitarian political regimes. Emerging economies, including those in Southeast Asia, also exploded, drawing foreign money and currency.

Since 1944, the past record of Forex markets provides a perfect picture of a free market in motion. Economic dynamics have produced an unmatched liquidity market position. Spreads have declined significantly among trustworthy users, with intensified online competition. Individuals that trade vast volumes also have access to similar electronic communications networks as foreign banks and retailers do.

1.8 When Forex Became Popular

In 1982, retail customers traded the first currency pairs, followed later that year, with more currency pairs becoming available. By 1987, the largest proportion of trades in the world were by the United Kingdom, followed by the United States. It was in 1991 that Iran amended its oil-to-foreign exchange arrangements with other nations.

Previously, Forex was an activity carried out by educated business people or those who learned about trading at universities. Things started to shift with the advent of the internet, and Forex's universe opened to more and more investors seeking to make money off this highly common investment tool.

The Forex market remained open around the clock. It never sleeps as a decentralized market. You can trade anytime you like, 24 hours a day, seven days a week. Improvements in technology have done a lot to develop Forex's success and usability.

Besides, the tradable currency pairs have risen, more traders have joined the market, and in the last decade, in particular, Forex has been the phenomena that it is today, and this shows no indication of stopping.

1.9 The Story Today with Forex

Forex now represents the world's largest and most active liquid market. With too many currencies to pick from like majors, minors, and exotics or new pairs, customers have more options now, and you can make the trading experience a more enjoyable one.

With links to educational services and analytical methods, like social media, by both brokers and other third parties, more insight is accessible now to enhance techniques and awareness. Thanks to major technical developments, smartphones empower everyone to get a piece of the action, and you don't have to be a committed investor with plenty of capital to get started.

You will open an account, use the demo platform to familiarize yourself with the software and trading, and then start investing when and where you want to in your option of pairs. Instead of being tied to a computer for trade at specific times, you can now take it with you wherever you go and use a myriad of apps to either trade or help you with your business.

Choose from a multitude of brokers who offer different incentives to open an account and place trades on the move when and where it suits you.

Today the Forex market is the world's biggest market. There's more than $5 trillion traded regularly on the Forex market. Forex's future is shrouded in uncertainty and is ever-changing, giving Forex traders everlasting opportunities.

To be competitive in an evolving market, Forex traders need to stay ahead of the curve. Daily news and analysis on foreign exchange usually keep traders up-to-date with the latest Forex happenings.

In Forex, typically, one currency is converted into another. It is one of the world's most heavily traded markets, with an estimated trading amount of $5 trillion a day.

CHAPTER 2: The World of Forex Trading

The Foreign Exchange Market is the center of the movement of currency around the globe. The Forex Market helps companies, businesses, financial firms, states, private investors, and speculators to trade just about everything in the currency of the assets they wish to trade. The money between countries couldn't move without Forex Market. It is the 'glue' or 'foundation' that helps for the international exchange of currency. Therefore, it is the largest financial market in the world. According to the Bank of International Settlements, the latest forecasts placed regular turnover, for 2016, at USD5 Trillion. Some forecasts suggested it would cross USD10 Trillion by this year, that is, 2020. As the most active financial market throughout the world, foreign exchange gives anyone that can leverage its intrinsic volatility a range of opportunities.

2.1 Functions of the Forex Market

The Forex Market is an excellent avenue for international trade. The Forex market is a platform where businesses and individuals transact in foreign currencies to their own.

Business Transactions

Consider the example of the Australian national airline, Qantas. The Australian national airline wants to acquire a plane from the American aircraft maker Boeing. The trading currency of Qantas is the Australian Dollar (AUD), and Boeing's is the US Dollar (USD). Qantas would turn AUD into US Currency. So to enable the payment, it will contact its branch. In the Forex marketplace, their bank will turn their AUD into USD to pay Boeing for their product.

Individual Transactions

That will be a transaction equivalent to a person going on holiday from the UK to the USA. They would need to translate UK Pounds (GBP) to US Dollars (USD) to enable them to purchase goods and services when in the US.

These two players are a significant part of the Forex business. Yet it, what's known as Capital Market Trading, is by far the greatest proportion of the actual Forex Sector turnover.

Capital Market Transactions

Capital markets, usually referred to as the financial markets, comprise sectors such as real estate, shares, treasury bonds (fixed income), derivatives and commodities (oil, gold, silver and copper). Markets, including Bonds and Equities, are present in both countries exchanging stocks. U.S. Equities and European Equities are the prime examples of financial markets. To encourage investment managers to sell immediately, let's assume European Equities that are in Euros and buy U.S. Equities. To encourage the transition in asset distribution, it is necessary to convert from EUR to USD. It is exchanged through what's known as the Spot Forex Market, which is effectively an instant currency exchange. Other forms to enable you to 'order your rate' in advance are Currency Forwards, Futures, and Options.

But as you can see, money is moving across the globe continuously. It is this global capital movement that makes the Forex market so big, and knowing the movement of foreign money is crucial to the Forex market success.

2.2 Participants of Forex Market

Those that use the Forex Sector are quite varied from institutions, governments to individual buyers such as retail traders. The Forex sector started to develop in 1978 when, in conjunction with 'Supply and Demand,' the worldwide currencies could 'float.' Originally, it was the sole domain of banks and central banks, but over the years, various laws, legislation, and technological changes took place. This removed credit risk because, in recent years, the Forex market opened to virtually everyone, and thus the Forex market boom. While all transactions are still going through the largest FX banks like Citigroup, and Deutsche Bank, UBS is known as the 'Sell Side,' that is, they are selling the financial products of Forex to the 'Buy Side.' Participants in "Buy Side" are the ones who buy FX products.

The buy-side participants in order of importance

Listed below are the buy-side participants in order of their importance:

Corporations

These are mainly big corporations like Boeing that get involved in cross-border transactions.

Investment Bankers and Managers

This group is comprised of institutional investors like Pension Funds, Insurance Companies; Mutual Funds Exchange Traded Funds (ETF's), Proprietary Trading Firms, Hedge Funds, Commodity Trading Advisors (CTA's), and the banks' Proprietary Traders.

Governments

You cannot exclude the Governments from this list as they also need the FX Market to allow them to buy and sell medical equipment, military equipment, and other such goods.

Central Banks

Although central banks do not typically use the FX market, they can interfere in order to allow them to control and sustain the monetary policy. Why are there separate categories for government and central banks? Central banks are responsible for regulating the monetary policies without any external intervention, but when enforcing monetary policy, they operate independently.

Therefore, from the above-market players, it can be seen that the Forex market is competitive and provides an incredibly volatile environment providing prospects for Forex traders daily.

2.3 Infrastructure of Forex Market

It is imperative to know about most of the participants, as it is the key to understand the movement in the Forex market.

Non-Centralized Market – Over the Counter

The Forex market is a business that is not centralized. The Forex Business is an Over the Counter (OTC) system, unlike stocks purchased and sold via a central exchange such as the New York Stock Exchange. This ensures that transfers pass through the main banks known as the Interbank. It also implies that there is no way to see trading volumes occurring at any given moment. The Bank of International Settlements undertakes a survey of participating central banks every three years to track the developments in the Forex market and to report on the activity in the Forex market.

Interbank

The Forex industry has been virtually an uncontrolled market ever since the fall of the Bretton Woods Arrangement in 1974. It is also self-regulated when serving its consumers with the banks dealing with each other in a competitive price environment.

2.4 How Do Forex Markets Work?

In comparison to stock or securities, in an over the counter (OTC) system, Forex trade takes place not on exchanges but clearly among two parties. A multinational system of banks operates the Forex market, spread among four main Forex trading centers in various time zones: New York, London, Sydney, and Tokyo. You may trade Forex 24 hours per day because there is no central place. There are three different kinds of Forex markets:

Spot forex market

The raw exchange of a currency set takes place at the precise point the trade is resolved – that is, 'on the spot' – or in a short interval of time in the Spot Forex market.

Forward forex market

An agreement is negotiated in the market in forwarding Forex to buy or sell a fixed volume of a currency at a particular price. Such a contract is usually negotiated in the future dates at a specified date.

Future Forex market

A deal is negotiated in the Future Forex market to purchase or sell a specified sum of a defined currency at a fixed date and price in the future. A future deal is officially binding, unlike forwards.

Many traders wondering about Forex rates would not intend to have the currency supplied to them. Instead, they create forecasts of exchange rates to take advantage of market price fluctuations.

Quote and Base currency

The first currency mentioned in a Forex pair is a base currency, whereas the second currency is considered the quote currency. Forex trade often means selling one currency to purchase another; that is why it is mentioned in the pairs-the price of a Forex pair is how much one unit of the main currency is valued in the quote currency.

Every currency in a set is mentioned in a 3-letter code, which appears to consist of 2 letters reflecting the country and one that stands for the currency itself. GBP / USD, for example, is a pair of currencies that imply the purchase of the Great British pound and sale of the U.S. dollar.

Thus, in the case below, the base currency is GBP, and the quote currency is USD. If GBP / USD trade at 1.353, so one-pound worth $1.353.

As the pound increases against the dollar, one pound would be worth more dollars, and the price of the pair will rise. If it decreases, the price of the pair will decrease. Or if you think a pair's base currency is expected to increase against the quote currency, you should purchase the pair. If you believe it's going to decline, then you should sell the set (short). Most providers divide the pairs into the following groups for simplicity and clarity:

Major pairs

Major pairs are composed of 7 currencies that constitute 80% of global forex trading. These include USD/JPY, EUR/USD, GBP/USD, USD/CAD USD/CHF, and AUD/USD.

GBP / USD
Base currency, or the currency you are buying when you trade the forex pair
Quote currency, or the currency you are selling when you trade the forex pair

Minor pairs

Minor pairs are usually traded less frequently in the Forex market. They also show international currencies against each other rather than against the US dollar. These include EUR/CHF, EUR/GBP, GBP/JPY.

Exotics

The exotic category constitutes a global currency against a tiny economy or a developing one. This category includes USD/PLN, EUR/CZK, GBP/MXN (Sterling vs. Mexican peso).

Regional pairs

In this category, pairs are categorized by region, for example, Australasia or Scandinavia. These may include AUD/NZD (Australian dollar vs. New Zealand dollar), EUR/NOK (Euro vs. Norwegian krona), AUD/SGD.

What pushes the forex market?

The Forex market consists of currencies from across the world that can render forecasts of exchange rates challenging since there are several variables that may lead to price fluctuations. Like other financial markets, however, Forex is driven primarily by demand and supply trends, and it is essential to get an insight into the factors that cause price volatility here.

Central banks

Trade is regulated by central banks, which will implement steps that would have a major impact on the price of their currency. For example, quantitative easing means adding more capital into an economy, which can trigger the price of the currency to decline.

Latest reports

Commercial banks and other buyers here want to inject their investments into strong-looking economies. So, if any good news reaches the markets for a specific country, it will stimulate speculation and boost demand for the currency of that county.

If the currency provides a parallel rise, the imbalance between demand and supply will trigger the price to rise. Similarly, any bad news will drive down demand and reduce the price of a currency. Therefore, currencies appear to indicate the economic health reported in the country they serve.

Market sentiment

Market perception may also play a significant role in moving currency rates and is mostly in response to the news. If traders think a currency is moving in a specific direction, they are going to trade accordingly and can encourage other people to follow suit, resulting in an increase or decrease in demand.

Economic data

For two reasons, economic data is vital to currency price movements – It provides an example of the way an economy operates and provides insight into what the central bank could do next.

Consider, for example, the case of Eurozone inflation that has increased above the level of 2 percent, which the European Central Bank (ECB) tries to sustain. The ECB's key policy tool for fighting increasing inflation is to raise European interest rates – so the traders could start purchasing the euro in expectation of rising rates. With more traders demanding Euros, the price could rise for EUR / USD.

Credit ratings

Investors would want to optimize a market's profit, thus reducing their risk. But they may even watch credit ratings when determining where to invest, alongside interest rates and economic results.

A country's credit rating is an objective measure of its probability of repaying its debts. A nation with a higher credit rating is perceived as an investment region better than one with a lower credit rating. Once credit ratings are improved and downgraded, this also falls into a special view. A nation with an improved credit rating may see price rises in its currency and vice versa.

2.5 Trading in the Forex market

There are a lot of various ways you can trade Forex; however, they all operate the same way: purchasing one currency while selling the other at the same time. Many Forex traders have historically been conducted through a Forex broker, but then with the rise of online trading, you can get the benefit of Forex market fluctuations utilizing derivatives such as CFD trading.

CFDs are leveraged goods that allow you to open a place for just a small percentage of the total trade value. You don't gain control of the asset as compared to non-leveraged goods; you take a stance about whether you believe the price would grow or decline in value.

While leveraged investments will magnify your earnings, if the market turns against you, they will magnify losses too.

How to trade Forex

When you understand how to trade Forex, it's not difficult to watch why it's such a famous market amongst the traders. You will discover that there are many various currency pairs to trade-from mains in developing currencies to exotics-24 hours per day. Let us learn how to use a Forex broker to trade Forex, how the Forex market functions, and watch an instance of a Forex transaction.

A step-by-step guide to Forex trading

It can seem daunting to learn how to trade any market, so we have broken Forex trading down into some easy methods to help you get started:

Deciding between trading Forex CFDs and trading Forex through a broker

There is so much Forex trading among the main financial and banks institutions, buying and selling large quantities of currency every day. However, there are two main ways to get involved for individual traders who don't have the way to make billions of dollars in Forex trades: Forex CFDs or Forex trading through a broker.

Know about Forex CFD

A Forex CFD is a deal in which you choose to swap the difference in the A currency pair's price from when you open the place to when you shut it. Place a lengthy position, and if the Forex market rises in price, you'll make a return. If it declines in value, you'll get a loss. Start a short position, and the reverse is valid. Forex is only one of the markets you can trade with CFDs.

Know about Forex trading via a broker

Forex trading through a broker-or even through a bank-operates in a way that is somewhat like CFD trading. You speculate on currency pair price fluctuations without necessarily taking control of the currencies themselves. If you feel the price of a currency pair is going down, you should go short rather than long. However, if you transact Forex through a broker, you will not have contact with other markets.

Discover how the Forex market performs

When you intend to trade currencies, one of the first items to understand is how the Forex sector works; it is somewhat distinct from exchange-based mechanisms such as securities or futures.

In place of purchasing and selling currency at a centralized platform, Forex is acquired and exchanged via a banking network. This is considered a market of over the counter. It functions because certain banks operate as market makers – providing a bid rate to purchase a specific currency pair and selling a Forex pair with a quote amount.

Trading through Forex suppliers

Many retail traders aren't going to purchase and sell Forex quickly from one of the big banks – they're going to use a Forex dealer. Forex exchange companies work with the banks on behalf of you, seeking the best deals possible and contributing to their own spread of the business.

Any companies would let you personally connect with the order books of market leaders. This is known as direct market access, or DMA, which ensures experienced traders may sell and buy Forex without the spread – in its place, they trade at currency providers' rates and a variable fee.

Open an account

If you wish to trade Forex with CFDs, you will need to have an account with a leveraged trading company. You will create an account within minutes, and there is no need to attach funds before you plan to locate a company.

Create a trading plan

It is very important to build a trading plan if you're fresh in the markets. A trading plan makes it easier to remove emotion from your decision-making process, it also provides a building for opening and closing positions. Also, you might need to consider using a Forex trading policy, which directs how you get market opportunities.

When you have selected a specific Forex trading approach, it's time to implement that strategy. Using your preferred tools for strategic assessment of the markets, you require to transact to determine what your initial trade should be.

Even if you like to be a solely technical trader, you also must show interest in any improvements that may contribute to market volatility. For example, future economic developments could well resonate across the Forex markets – something the technical analysis may not consider.

Select the Forex trading platform

You can choose from various trading platforms, such as your web browser or one of your mobile apps, depending on your needs and the one that can give you a smarter and quicker approach to trade Forex.

With custom alerts, interactive charts, and risk management tools, each of the Forex trading policies can be customized to fit your trading style and choices.

Open, supervise and close your first position

You may start trading after you have decided on your platform. Simply open your selected market ticket for the deal. You will look at both a listed purchase price and a retail price. You can also choose the scope of your position and combine any hurdles or boundaries that will shut your trade as soon as it reaches a specific level. Hit buy to start a long position or sell for opening a short position.

You can observe the profit or loss of your position within the dealing platform's 'open positions' section.

Once you have chosen to shut down your position, just make the parallel trade to when you started it. Now let's examine some of the examples of Forex trades and their potential results.

Forex trading example-Trading a GBP/USD CFD

GBP / USD has a 1.35540 selling price and a 1.35560 purchase price. You assume the pound would get worth against the U.S. dollar, anticipating the Bank of England will lower interest rates, so you choose to sell five regular lots at 1.35540.

Any contract is equivalent to the pair's base currency of 100,000. In this scenario, selling a single standard GBP / USD contract will be equal to swapping £ 100,000 for $135,540, so the overall stake will be worth $677,700 (£500,000).

CFDs are a leveraged product because you don't have to place the maximum value on your position. Typically, a transaction of this scale on GBP / USD has a boundary limit of 0.50 percent, meaning the margin will be 0.50 percent of the trade's overall value, which is $3,388.50 (£2,500).

If your guess is correct

As you guess, the pound starts falling. When the purchase price reaches 1.35440, you decide to shut down your position.

To calculate your profit, you multiply by its size the difference between the closing and the opening price of your position. 1.3554 – 1.3544 = 10 points, multiplied by five CFDs to arrive at a profit of $500.00 (minus overnight fees). The other way is that your $677,700.00 is worth £ 500,369.17 ($677,70/1.3544), then your profit is £369.17 (£500,369.17-£ 500,000.00).

Calculating profit from your FX CFD

1.35540 – 1.35440 = 10 points. You then multiply it by five CFDs to get a profit of $500.00.

You must keep in mind that you just need to pay overnight funds. Overnight funding changes are applied if your status is held overnight. Commission charges are charged only if you're trading FX directly.

If your prediction is wrong

On the contrary, GBP/USD starts to rise. You immediately plan to minimize your losses and reverse your trade when the buy price reaches 1.35700.

Your position moved 16 points against you. This translates into a loss of $800.00.

Calculating loss from your FX CFD

1.35540 – 1.35700 = -16 points. Then you multiply it by $50.00 to arrive at a loss figure of $800.00.

2.6 Forex for Hedging

Companies conducting business with other markets are at risk as they purchase or offer products and services outside their home sector because of volatility in currency prices. Foreign exchange markets provide a form of currency risk hedging by specifying a rate at which the trade will be made.

To achieve this, a trader can, in advance, buy or sell currencies in the forward or swap markets, which locks at an exchange rate. Imagine, for instance, that a business is preparing to market US-made blenders in Europe while the euro-dollar exchange rate, which is at (EUR / USD) is €1 to $1 parity.

The blender requires $100 to make, and the U.S. Corporation intends to market it for €150—which is comparable with other blenders produced in Europe. If this scheme works, the organization will earn a profit of $50 because even the exchange rate for EUR / USD is stable. Unfortunately, the USD continues to increase in value over the euro when the EUR / USD exchange rate reaches 0.80, so purchasing €1.00 currently costs $0.80.

The challenge confronting the business is that although producing the blender only costs $100, the business will only market the commodity at a fair price of € 150, which, when retranslated into dollars, is just $120 (€150 X 0,80 = $120). A stronger dollar produced a far lower profit than anticipated.

This possibility may have been minimized by the blender industry shortening the Euro and purchasing the USD while the currencies were on parity. Thus, whenever the dollar goes up in value, trading gains would outweigh the decreased benefit from blenders' sales. If the value of the USD drops, the more advantageous exchange rate will boost the benefit from the selling of blenders, which reduces the trade losses.

Such hedging may be achieved in the futures market for currencies. The benefit for a trader is that a central authority is standardizing and clearing futures contracts. Currency futures, though, could be less competitive than forwarding contracts, which are unregulated and globally operate within the interbank framework.

2.7 Forex for Speculation

Factors such as interest rates, capital flows, travel, economic growth, and geopolitical instability influence currency supply and demand, generating regular turbulence on the Forex markets. There is a possibility to benefit from developments that will raise or decrease the value of one currency over another. A prediction that one currency is going to weaken is basically the same as predicting the other currency in the pair is going to improve when currencies are exchanged as pairs.

Imagine a broker anticipating interest rates to increase in the U.S. as opposed to Australia when the exchange rate between the two currencies (AUD / USD) is 0.71 (it requires $0.71 to purchase $1.00 AUD). The trader claims higher U.S. interest rates would boost demand for U.S. dollars, and thus the AUD / USD exchange rate would decline, so purchasing an AUD would take less, stronger USD.

Assume the trader is correct, and interest rates increase, reducing the AUD / USD exchange rate to 0.50. That means purchasing $1.00 AUD needs $0.50 USD. Had the creditor gone short in the AUD and long in the USD, he or she may have profited from the fluctuations in the value.

Currency as an Asset Class

Currencies are granted two distinct features as an asset class:

- You will gain from the difference in interest rates of two currencies
- You can reap the benefits of exchange rate changes

By purchasing the currency with the higher interest rate and short-selling the currency with the lower interest rate, an investor will benefit from the disparity of two interest rates in two separate economies. Before the financial crash of 2008, short selling in the Japanese yen (JPY) and purchasing British pounds (GBP) was very popular, since the interest rate gap was very high. Sometimes this strategy is termed a "carry trade."

Why We Can Trade Currencies

Before the internet, currency dealing was very complicated for common investors. Much of the currency traders were big international firms, hedge funds, or high-net-worth individuals because Forex trading demanded a lot of money. A retail market focused on individual traders has developed with the aid of the internet, offering convenient access to the foreign exchange markets, either through the banks themselves or by brokers allowing a secondary market. Many online brokers or dealers give quite significant leverage to individual traders who have a limited account balance between managing a large trade.

2.8 Pros and Challenges of Trading Forex

Given below are the pros and challenges of Forex trading:

Pros

The Forex markets are the biggest in the world in terms of the regular volume of trade and hence deliver the most liquidity. In certain market environments, this allows it easy to enter and exit a trade in each of the major currencies for a tiny spread within a fraction of a second.

The Forex business is conducted 24 hours a day, five days a week — starts in Australia every day and finishes in New York. Sydney, Hong Kong, Singapore, Tokyo, Frankfurt, Paris, London, and New York are the main centers.

Challenges

Banks, brokers, and dealers in the Forex markets have a high amount of leverage, which implies traders may manage big positions with their comparatively little capital. Leverage inside the 100:1 range is a high ratio in Forex, but not rare. An investor needs to consider the use of the leverage and the threats posed to an account by leveraging. Significant amounts of leverage have caused numerous dealers to inadvertently become insolvent.

Productively exchanging currency needs knowledge of economic dynamics and measures. A currency trader has to equip himself with a clear understanding of the different economies of the various countries and their underlying fundamentals that cause fluctuations in currency values.

2.9 Critical Information

To start Forex trading, you'll need to make sure your trading account carries enough money. There is no defined cap as compared to the capital exchange. This suggests that the needed capital will vary depending on the priorities and type of trading, but traders are also advised not to gamble more than 1 percent of their accounts for each transaction. For example, if you have $10,000 in your account, you can decide not to gamble more than $100 on a single trade.

If you've decided how much money you have at your hands, you'll need to start planning the remainder of your Forex trading plan – which could include when you intend to get out of Forex trading, the time you're able to devote to investing, studying the markets you need to trade, your risk control policy and your trading strategy.

If you're totally latest to trading or have successfully operated other markets, Forex price uncertainty is a rather special phenomenon that requires time to learn. However, if someone improves their exchange expertise, builds a Forex trading plan, and gathers market trading experience, he will be able to trade Forex.

A Forex trading approach should take into consideration the trading style ideally tailored to your objectives and the time available. Day trading, for example, is a technique involving opening and closing positions during a single trading day and taking the benefit of minor fluctuations in a currency pair's price. Position trading, on the other hand, is the practice of keeping positions open over extended periods of time to take benefit of big market fluctuations. Both have varying time commitments and demand the strategies required for performance.

The essence of the Forex market is very unpredictable, so a currency pair exhibiting large price fluctuations in one week may not display the same volatile price behavior the next week. However, the bulk of Forex trading volume is focused on a handful of Forex set, including EUR / USD, UDS / JPY, GBP / USD, AUD / USD, and USD / CHF – since most traders are drawn by these pairs, they always witness the most price fluctuations.

2.10 Beware of the Associated Risks

Be aware of the risks associated with Forex trading and understand how these risks can be mitigated.

Loss risks from investing in CFDs can be significant, and the cost of your investments can change. CFDs are challenging tools and present a higher chance of quick loss of money due to leverage. You must consider if you get to know how this product performs and if you can manage to lose a huge loss of money.

Currencies can be dangerous and difficult to sell. There are contrasting degrees of rule and regulation on the interbank market, and Forex devices are not standardized. Forex trading is practically completely unregulated in several parts of the world.

The interbank market consists of banks that trade around the globe with each other. Banks must recognize and acknowledge sovereign credit risks risk themselves, and internal processes have been established to protect themselves as safe as feasible. Such regulations are imposed by the industry for the safety of each contributing bank.

The market pricing mechanism is based on demand and supply as the competition is rendered by one of the participating banks making bids and deals for a specific currency. As there are such big flows of trade within the scheme, rogue traders have difficulty influencing the cost of a currency. This system aids in creating market transparency for investors who have access to interbank trading.

Some small-scale retailers trade with comparatively small and semi-unregulated Forex dealers who may (and sometimes) re-quote rates and sometimes deal with their own clients. There may be certain governmental and industrial regulation, depending on where the dealer exists, but those precautions lack consistency around the world.

Some trade investors should spend some time researching a forex trader to see if it is circulated in the U.K. or the U.S. (there is more oversight for dealers in the U.S. and UK) or in a state with lax regulations and supervision. It is also a great idea to get out what sort of account safeguards are offered in the event of a market downfall or if the supplier is insolvent.

In the Forex market, for traders — especially those with limited funds — day trading or swing trading in small amounts is easier than other markets. Long-term fundamentals-based trading or a carry trade can be profitable for those with longer-term horizons and bigger funds. A focus on understanding the macroeconomic fundamentals that drive currency values and technical, analytical experience may help new Forex traders become more profitable.

Why Forex?

Forex can be a desirable market for several reasons, even for learners who have not enough experience. The Forex market is available, which requires only a little deposit of cash to help traders start trading. The market is also open 24 hours a day / 5 days a week (it is closed on weekends for a small period). That means that at any point of the day, traders can enter the market even when other extra centralized markets are shut.

Forex traders often incur a basic selling charge, which is calculated by spreading between currency offers and asking rates, and selling is also regulated by simpler tax laws. Finally, traders will predict their stop-loss and sell exit rates before joining each deal, ensuring they have greater leverage of how much risk they want to take on.

Like some other forms of financial-market trading, for beginning traders, Forex trading may seem complex, abstract, and intimidating. The underlying activity involved, however, —trading one national currency for another — is simple.

Forex trading used to be the exclusive territory of large market operators, but now it is accessible to the public, and there are plenty of resources available to help beginning traders succeed.

Forex trading involves a certain threat, and traders should be conscious of that before they jump into the market. Major financial institutions and banks are still doing the largest part of Forex trading around the world. These units usually have more supplies than individual traders in terms of information, leverage, and technology. Consequently, retail Forex traders often get themselves under the pressure of market activities, which they may have less or no control power.

In addition, in certain price volatility situations, traders may also be subjected to the "risk of execution," which takes place when market requests cannot fill up for the same price as asked.

2.11 How to Initiate

Although the Forex market may be complicated and can take some research for traders to get acquainted with it and trade effectively, it is reasonably easy to get started in Forex trading.

Aspiring traders fresh to the business must:

- Open an account with a Forex broker
- Use the broker trading tools and fix a trading app on their computer or mobile phone.
- Must deposit £50 into the trading account before initiating trading

Traders would have links to live market fluctuations once they have set up their accounts, submit orders, and build up trading policies. Currencies are sold in pairs, but if a dealer purchases one currency, he sells another at the same time. Many currency pairs are accessible for trading, including some big currencies and a variety of currencies that are less known or small.

Demo Account

Trading the Forex market must be preceded by the opening of a demo trading account by the new beginners so that they could evaluate the profits and risks and do better later. Most brokers provide this service, so the traders may get accustomed to the business world of trading and Forex.

Demo accounts can enable traders to watch current market conditions and to practice trading tactics and transactions so that they can transact without needing to place some capital on the line. You will then go live with an actual trading account once they feel sure they are ready to start.

Read the latest news

Many seasoned traders use technological market research, but some are acquainted with the fundamental issues that influence the currencies they transact. It is a better idea to know the governments and national rules which regulate the currency that you'd like to exchange. This can also involve getting the schedule of main releases of results, such as knowledge regarding national trade, interest rate decisions, and balance of payments.

Risk-Reward Ratio

One important thumb rule that can serve as a guideline for traders to mitigate their vulnerability is to do business with a "risk-reward ratio" in mind. That implies that they can establish a stop-loss before entering a buying or sell order for a given quantity of risk and a maximum value (or benefit maximum) at a defined level of revenue that is a multiple of the amount of their risk.

Usually, the ratios can differ from 1-1 to 1-5 (or more), depending on the risk profile of the trader. For newcomers, the adage of "let go your profits" is what might be counter-intuitive. This suggests that they may try to ensure that they will get adequate value on any trade to guarantee that their net business operation is lucrative, minus any charges, expense, or tax rate.

However, what sometimes occurs in Forex dealing is that traders are "stopped out," which suggests that their stop losses are activated, and they cash out their trades at a loss before they can make a profit. These are a few explanations of why traders want to research the market world in which they are investing carefully and come up with a convincing trading plan before putting down money on a transaction.

Automation

The Forex market is particularly well-suited with automated trading, which is another cause that it has invited an increasing number of contributors. Many brokerage trading platforms permit for trades, which will automatically take impact when specific price or market situations occur.

Thus, trades may be left unsupervised because the trading account manager is occupied with other tasks. Works with electronic trading needs traders to spend some time knowing about the trading functions and techniques on the platform they plan to use.

Forex is a fast-moving, open market with the ability for rewards along with the losses beyond early investments, even for new traders. Forex trading isn't harder than trading in other markets. However, the Forex market presents its own specific conditions, behavior patterns, and challenges that learners should be informed of before they set up.

2.12 Bottom Line-Is Forex Trading Easy or Difficult?

People often ask about whether trading in Forex is easy or difficult. The response to this relies on one thing and just one thing, which is preparation and commitment.

You need to dedicate time and effort to be successful in any field. It's not very different to trade in Forex. Therefore, it depends on you to respond about whether Forex trading is simple or difficult.

Understanding that Forex trading isn't for everyone is also important. Now we'll discuss some of the principles you need to learn whether Forex trading is right for you and what it requires to thrive in the Forex markets.

If you can spend time to put it into practice to learn about the currency markets, your interest can rise over time.

Why do most Forex traders fail?

Most Forex traders are losing because they see Forex trading as a path to easily get wealthy. It includes an aspect of greed, which sets away from the idea of hard work and learning.

Forex traders say owning a trading scheme is enough to make profits for them. Sadly, that's not the case. Traders have ambitious goals, too. For starters, several Forex traders assume or expect 20 percent or more returns. In the capital sector, this is unheard of and is typically synonymous with Ponzi schemes. Forex trading is no different from equity investing or derivatives investing. There is one approach that must be practiced.

What steps can you take to be successful in trading Forex?

Above everything, you need a clear knowledge of the financial markets. That requires paying tremendous attention to fundamental research. Most traders are only seeking to understand the mechanics of the technical study. They assume this is what they need to trade in the Forex market.

While you're just trading in intraday markets, the truth remains that fundamentals dominate the markets. Therefore, it will help you to resolve this by integrating your Forex technical, analytical abilities with fundamental insight.

It is just as essential to have a trading strategy. Without a plan in sight, Forex trade can't move that far ahead. You could only wind up wasting a lot of money.

Only when you know the basics and the technical analysis really well will you have a strong trading strategy.

How to practice Forex trading?

Although studying is important, it's important to practice what you read, too. Many Forex brokers already offer a free account of demo trading. You will decide for yourself, with actual trading requirements, how nice your trading is.

Conclusion

Let us get back to the issue of whether Forex trading is simple or challenging; the response is both. Actually, Forex trading is challenging if the main goal is to earn money rapidly. With that mentality, even before you start to deal, you have set yourself up for failure.

Forex trading is also simple if you are able to commit your time and resources to become a successful businessman. Forex dealing is no different than any trade, too. It can take time and, in many instances, years to master the art of Forex trading.

Everything said and done, however, note that Forex trading is unpredictable. You'll still run the risk of wasting your money, no matter how successful you're. Loss-taking is part of Forex dealing. The key is to make sure you lose less and gain more.

CHAPTER 3: Fundamental and Technical Analysis Based Forex Trading

The fluctuating fortunes of life are calibrated as highs and lows on the graph of your life. While you can't possibly eliminate the occurrence of failures or lows, nevertheless, you can control and manage the frequency and impact of these apparently non-charming yet experience-centric events.

3.1 Price Behavior in Financial Markets

Prices in Capital and Forex Markets of the world do not depict a stereotype or lackluster behavior. For prices do not move in a straight line and are susceptible to frequent changes. These price changes transpire even in as much short time-span as a second. Price changes give a wavy appearance to prices when these are plotted on the graph.

The premise behind all investment decisions is to generate money in a smart and efficient manner while keeping the risk factors to the minimum. You, as a prudent investor, have to make a decision to select the best investment opportunity from the available options. You, being the investor, will be guided in your quest by researching for answers to different critical questions such as:

- What investment option offers the most secure return with regard to Investment Time?
- Where is that particular investment option currently in its Business Cycle?
- When is the best time for committing the Investment Amount?

Prices, as mentioned above, do not move in a straight line, and the price activity is shaped by scores of factors stemming from changes in political and industrial policies to frequent shifts in international business supply and demand factors.

This standard operating procedure is usually also followed in the Capital and Commodity Markets with the addition of another crucial factor that attempts to seek and investigate the reasons behind such an investment decision. Succinctly, an investment decision in stocks or commodities revolves around the three W's.

3.2 What to Buy or Trade

Once you have arrived at an investment or trading decision, the next rational step is to set off for a comparative analysis of different available investment options based on their liquidity. Liquidity is an attribute of an investment or trading option, which makes it easily accessible both during the buying and selling process. This first step will assist you in unraveling the best performing investment or trading option based on its past and current performance.

3.3 Why to Buy or Trade

The ensuing step should be to perform a threadbare analysis of investment options based on earning potential, market competitiveness versus exclusivity, price, behavior, etc.

3.4 When to Buy or Trade

Finally, a decision has to be made on the investment time. Prices move in a wave-like pattern. This wave-like pattern owes its formation to the crest and troughs, which appear on a graph as a result of respective highs and lows attained during a particular time span. These highs and lows are materialized because of the respective bullish and bearish spells in the stocks and commodities. This is because all business cycles follow a cyclical movement of Growth (Expansion), Peak (Top), Decline (Contraction), Recession (Trough), and then back to Expansion.

If you commit your investment in an astronomically performing stock or commodity at the peak of the business cycle, then you should be ready to be flushed out from the market bare-handed as peaks do not remain intact for a long period of time and stun the investors by the sharp downturn. Thus the timing of investment is the most critical factor which must be worked out in an astute manner. An investment or trading decision, no matter how smart, could result in the wiping of funds if not exquisitely timed.

Besides the above-mentioned factors, you ought to address and define the following in your investment or trading plan:

3.5 Risk Factor

Investments must be guarded by defining the maximum amount to be put at stake, lest the market behaves against the worked-out plan. Objectively defined Risk Factors help in determining and place logical stop loss levels in the electronically operated markets and protect the erosion of major investment or trading capital.

3.6 Profit Objective

All investments are made in pursuit of profit. The profit objective has to be ascertained at the time of investment or trading decision to help you exit successfully from the market.

Fundamental Analysis vs. Technical Analysis

There are two techniques or methods which guide an investor or trader in his decision-making process in the Capital and Commodity markets:

Fundamental Analysis

This involves the study and analysis of all those factors which can contribute to any positive or negative change in the future price of a stock or currency. These could be supply, demand, competitiveness, industry standards, management techniques, government policies, balance sheets, income statements, etc. The aim of fundamental analysis is to determine the intrinsic value of a stock or a currency. The intrinsic value is used to gauge whether a stock or currency is overpriced or underpriced. It is worth mentioning that this technique is mostly employed in capital markets and has little or no utility when it comes to making trading decisions in commodity markets as these markets are highly speculative in nature and are impacted and influenced by frequently changing international conditions and scenarios.

Although technical analysis includes poring through maps to find patterns or developments, fundamental analysis involves poring through news headlines and economic data statements. And random tweets from a certain world leader will shake the Forex market nowadays, too.

Fundamental analysis is a way to look at the Forex market by examining fiscal, social, and political factors that could influence currency prices. That makes a whole lot of sense if you think about it. Much as in your Economics 101 class, the amount, or in our case, the currency exchange rate, is decided by the supply and demand. It's convenient to use supply and demand as an indication of where price may be going. The challenging part includes analyzing many of the conditions influencing supply and demand.

In other terms, to decide whose economy is booming like a Taylor Swift single and whose economy rocks, you must look at various aspects. You have to consider when and how such developments, such as a rise in the unemployment rate, impact the economy and monetary policy in a nation that eventually influences the demand level of its currency. The concept behind this sort of research is that if the present or potential economic situation of a nation is positive, it can boost its currency. The more an economic system of a nation is developed, the more international businesses and investors participate in that region. This adds to the need to buy the currency from another nation in order to acquire certain things. This is what fundamental analysis is all about.

Let's say, for instance, the U.S. dollar is now gaining strength because the U.S. economy is improving. As the economy gets better, there may be a need to raise interest rates to regulate growth and inflation. Higher interest rates make the financial assets denominated in dollars more attractive. Traders and investors must first buy some greenbacks in order to get their hands on those lovely assets. That increases currency demand. As a consequence, the value of the U.S. dollar against other currencies with lower demand will most likely increase. You'll also need to learn about which economic data points tend to drive currency prices and why. You would know who the Fed Chairman is and how the economy is portrayed in retail sales numbers. You're going to spit out global interest rates like lyrics on songs.

It is essential to understand how economic, financial and political news will impact currency exchange rates in order to be able to utilize fundamental analysis. This requires a good understanding of geopolitics and macroeconomics. But such fancy-sounding words don't need to scare you. For now, simply know that fundamental analysis is a way to analyze a currency's potential moves through the strength or weakness of the economic outlook of that country.

Using Fundamental Analysis for placing

Using fundamental research in addition to technical research may be an efficient way of financial transactions. It's crucial to note that fundamental analysis lets you recognize what drives the markets, and technical analysis will help you timing the trades and choosing the correct price levels to initiate the trades.

This takes us to the issue of how to plan your trades using simple research and how to integrate it with your technical trading, which is what you can discover in this section of the book.

The fundamental analysis starts with the economic calendar

The first step in fundamental research is to have a preview of the economic developments to come. It is usually better to commence the fundamental research at the beginning of the week, looking at all the activities expected for the next five-day trading cycle. This means you will also concentrate on the particular currencies where major activities are expected.

The first move is to sort out the low effect activities, beginning with the weekly Forex economic calendar. Much of the activities on the economic calendar are divided into large, medium, and low-impact affairs. But even the low-impact incidents will drive the markets dramatically in certain situations. Therefore, often review all the weekly events scheduled and then sort out those that are less significant.

Now that you've narrowed the list down to the key factors that could influence the markets, the next move is to narrow down the list more and concentrate on particular currency pairs you're confident in trading.

For example, if EURUSD is your priority for the week ahead, then philter the economic calendar focused on Eurozone- and U.S.-related high or medium impact events.

The resulting collection of economic activities now offers you a wide description of what to consider during the week.

To summarize:

- Schedule your trades over the weekend, beginning with the weekly economic calendar

- Select developments depending on their potential effect on the market and then concentrate on the currency pairs you wish to exchange
- Verify that external incidents do not influence the currencies in question
- Please remember the precise duration of the releases

Making use of charts to augment the fundamentals

The next step is to take a look at the charts, start your basic analysis, preferably from a weekly time frame, and scale down to the preferred shorter time frame of your choice.

Usually, the weekly and daily time frames give you a comprehensive picture of price trends as well as any potential reversals that might be on the horizon (candlestick patterns or indicator confluence).

Based on your approach to technical analysis (whether using indicators or simply taking price action), the next step is to chart the potential levels of support and resistance where prices are likely to pull back during a trend.

Analyze the market's expectations

The next step, which is the final phase, is knowing what the needs of the consumer are. Do not confuse this move with the data points foreseen or anticipated.

In comparison to the forecasted figures of economists, the markets appear to factor in their own expectations or place simply how the economic announcement would impact asset values. Reading through the relevant papers on financial websites, such as CNBC, Bloomberg, or Reuters Finance, is the easiest way to gather knowledge.

Generally speaking, the bigger an incident is predicted to be, the sooner the investors start talking about it. It is important to gather this knowledge since it demonstrates how the markets are positioned in the case.

For instance, if U.S. GDP is projected to grow by 0.90 percent in a quarter and the markets anticipate seeing an improvement or a beat on the forecasts, it is very obvious that the markets have already priced in a bullish scenario. This implies the negative costs are higher in the event that the final result slips behind the forecasts.

Now, when you add this knowledge with the technical levels on your graph, it becomes even simpler to trade on the right level and in the trend direction.

Fundamental analysis: A practical example

Now that you have all the requisite details, the next move is to wait before the event occurs. Rather than purchasing or selling immediately on the consequences of the case, it's better to wait a bit before determining what to do.

If you find that rates have dropped to a degree of support and the momentum is rising, long positions are advantageous and vice versa at levels of resistance.

Often verify when initiating a transaction that there are no additional events coming up in a specific period of time in the currency in question, since this may result in the investment going sideways.

EURUSD trading based on fundamental and technical analysis

Feb 15, 2016 - Feb 20, 2016 — Up Next — Today

Date	7:33	Currency	Impact		Detail	Actual	Forecast	Previous	Graph
Mon Feb 15	14:00	EUR		ECB President Draghi Speaks					
Tue Feb 16	10:00	EUR		German ZEW Economic Sentiment		1.0	0.1	10.2	
Wed Feb 17	13:30	USD		Building Permits		1.20M	1.21M	1.20M	
		USD		PPI m/m		0.1%	-0.2%	-0.2%	
	19:00	USD		FOMC Meeting Minutes					
Thu Feb 18	13:30	USD		Philly Fed Manufacturing Index		-2.8	-2.9	-3.5	
		USD		Unemployment Claims		262K	275K	269K	
	16:00	USD		Crude Oil Inventories		2.1M	3.2M	-0.8M	
Fri Feb 19	13:30	USD		CPI m/m		0.0%	-0.1%	-0.1%	
		USD		Core CPI m/m		0.3%	0.2%	0.1%	

The above picture displays the compilation of economic activities linked to the Euro and the U.S. Dollar during the week of February between the 15th and 19th of the said month.

Notice that there are planned lots of activities between Monday and Friday. From the list above, we will narrow down the calendar further to display only the most important events that will influence the currency pair.

Feb 15, 2016 - Feb 20, 2016

Date	7:26	Currency	Impact		Detail	Actual	Forecast	Previous	Graph
Mon Feb 15	14:00	EUR		ECB President Draghi Speaks					
Wed Feb 17	13:30	USD		PPI m/m		0.1%	-0.2%	-0.2%	
	19:00	USD		FOMC Meeting Minutes					
Fri Feb 19	13:30	USD		CPI m/m		0.0%	-0.1%	-0.1%	
		USD		Core CPI m/m		0.3%	0.2%	0.1%	

The filtered calendar now features a speech by ECB President Mario Draghi accompanied by a briefing on the US Consumer Prices Index, minutes of the US FOMC meeting, and reports on US inflation.

The following chart illustrates how the above helped set up a EURUSD trade focused on the degree of support and resistance from technical analysis, and then used the fundamental analysis to trade.

EURUSD was trading lower subsequent to dovish comments from ECB president Mario Draghi-after the help and resistance levels had been plotted.

U.S. PPI also exceeded forecasts, increasing by 0.10%, which made the euro further decline compared to the dollar. The minutes of the FOMC meeting saw a minor bullish close, but EURUSD was still trading below the next level of support at 1.1107 by then.

By the time the US CPI data came out late Friday, EURUSD had hit the support level, saw a bit of stabilization, and started to drop, dipping to approximately 1.0949 – 1.0932, the next support.

The example above illustrates how fundamental research can not only help you grasp what affects the markets; it also adds confidence to your technical trading, something that is lacking when used in isolation.

Trading Contracts for Difference (CFDs) entails a considerable risk of failure that does not suit all participants. Before you plan to exchange Contracts for Difference (CFDs), you can evaluate your market priorities, degree of maturity, and risk perception with caution. You may lose all of your savings. But you can not spend funds you can't afford to risk. Please ensure you are completely informed of the risks and take sufficient measures to handle the risk.

3.7 Technical Analysis

Technical analysis is an art that capitalizes on the study of price charts (minute-based, hourly, daily, weekly, monthly or yearly). The underlying basis of this technique is that all markets trend. Why? This is because the prices during their daily undulation-and-fluctuation-phase hit or attain certain highs and lows. These highs and lows of any stock or commodity are then plotted on a chart. You will notice later in this book that the prices, after being plotted, never surface up in a helter-skelter manner on a graph chart.

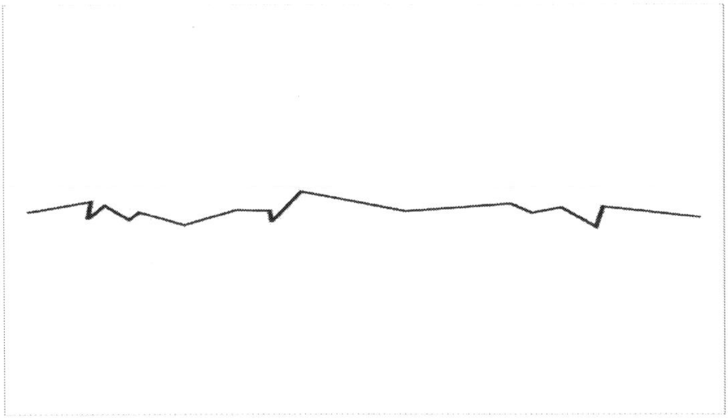

These prices, when plotted, take the form of a wave. This wavy form is a classic result of prominent crests (highs) and troughs (lows). Eventually, these highs and lows create identifiable points on the chart. These points can be easily joined by a line, which is then studied and analyzed for the identification of future price trends and forecasting of price targets. Besides, this technique helps you to timely identify the buying or selling opportunities and thus offers excellent opening and exit points.

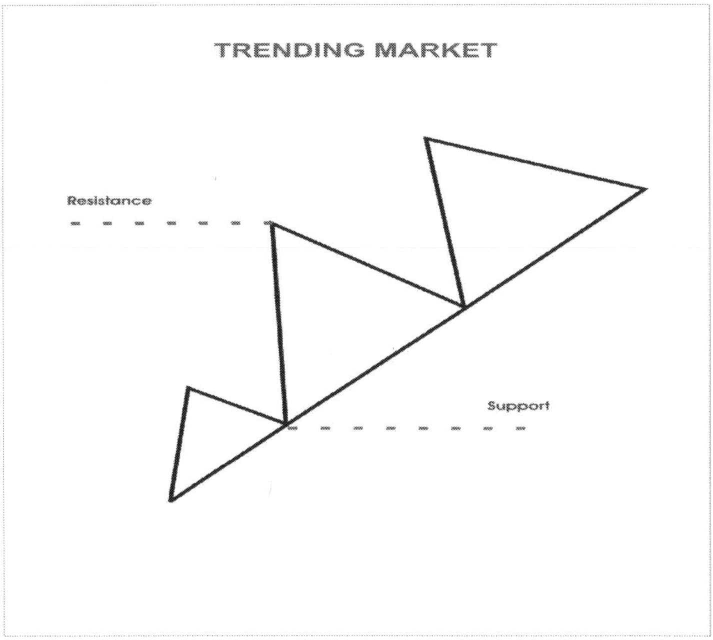

Any market is always in any of the three typical phases:

- Trending phase- Primary/Secondary Bullish
- Trending phase- Primary/Secondary Bearish
- Consolidation Phase

It is generally the trending phase that offers phenomenal returns. It is the dream of every investor and trader to capitalize on an investment opportunity with unprecedented profit potential. This, generally, is true about unleashing a trend that is about to unfold in the form of a string of enormous magnitude.

3.8 Pioneers of Technical Analysis

We shall briefly review the work and contribution of renowned personalities towards the development and creation of a fabulous technique of Technical Analysis.

Charles Henry Dow

Dow is accredited with the invention of the Dow Jones Industrial Index. Besides, he also has the honor of establishing the renowned "The Wall Street Journal," which has now become a financial benchmark for all financial papers.

Dow would record the highs and lows of the Index on a daily, weekly, and monthly basis as he did not have the liberty and facility of recording short-term data on the lines as is being conveniently carried out by modern electronic trading software.

Assumptions of Dow Theory

Charles Dow advocated three primary tenets of his theory for analysis of market price and for making future projections or forecasts. The following critical points deserve the attention of market participants before we elaborate on Dow's assumptions:

The proposed market behavior is subject to variations and hence does not hold true under all market conditions.

These assumptions are interpretations of the market reality, which are frequently experienced by traders, and thus can be banked on for trading decisions.

Human psychology plays a dominant role in determining prices. As such, the way humans think, act, and react tends to remain uniform and exhibits conformity in identical conditions. The markets portray similar behavior, as does human psychology.

Market Prices Progress in three trends

The first assumption states prices progress in three forms simultaneously. These forms are described as Primary, Secondary, and Minor trends of the price movement. The prior knowledge of the kind or trend of the market price assists a trader to work out a realistic profit-objective and evade early market exit.

Price discounts all

"Price discounts all" means that the market price at which buyers and sellers concur to enter into a trade is a price that has weathered the brunt of all relevant (positive or negative) information presently available to market participants. This information could vary from new economic fundamental data to new developing events, stories, regional conflicts, central banks' initiatives, and policies, etc. Besides, this final price is also reflective of the current emotional and financial status of the participants. Any new information or contradictory information is efficiently "discounted" by the market participants, and the final price tends to portray the current information level and sentiment status of the participants.

History repeats itself

Technical analysis is described as the study and analysis of past price trends to predict and forecast future price movements and trends. Technical analysis of charts is an art used to identify patterns in price movements. These price patterns are then used to predict future market behavior and price targets.

You must understand and remember that the market is not just a number of shares of different companies exhibiting different price movements. In reality, a market is a collection of human beings who, based on their knowledge, perception, and financial strength, are responsible for the movement of the price in different directions. It is the demand or supply emanating from the people that make the market depict a specific behavior or trend. This essentially moves the price!

You will be wrong in your assessment if you think that the reasons behind a positive movement in the currency price can only be attributed to economic or political factors. The price goes up because news is conceived positively by the market participants, and consequently, they jump in with their funds to buy that currency. The human beings demand stoked by specific factors propels upward movement in prices. This is a very critical concept in your understanding of technical analysis.

Human psychology remains more or less constant and tends to react to similar situations identically. The study and analysis of the past market behavior at turning points are incredibly beneficial and advantageous in the identification of specific price patterns for the development of an understanding of the market's most probable future reaction. Hence, technical analysis is based on the assumption that people will continue to make the same mistakes that they made in the past. Human relationships are incredibly complicated. The markets, as explained above, are a reflection of people in action, never duplicating their performance exactly. Still, the recurrence of similar characteristics is sufficient to enable market watchers to identify major junction or turning points.

Technical analysis banks on the study of market action, which in turn is contingent upon the study of human psychology. Different chart patterns have established their authenticity as a result of the review of their effectiveness in all types of markets. These patterns continue to appear on charts with a regular frequency, depending on the particular trend of the market. These patterns reveal the bullish or bearish psychology of the market participants. The past utility of these price patterns in generating excellent trading profits makes them viable and tenable for future decision making. Hence the key to understanding the future lies in the study of the past or that future is a mere mirror image of the past.

Market Trend and Types

- Dow Theory helps in:
- Identifying the existence of a trend
- Deciphering the direction of the trend
- Classifying the phase of the trend

A trend can be identified by merely joining the two points with the help of a line and then extending that line to see if it meets other points to establish its validity.

If the market is registering higher highs and lows, then the upward slanting line is drawn, which reflects the positive or bullish trend in the market. On the contrary, if the market is making lower highs and lows, then a downward slanting line tells about the negative or bearish trend of the market.

Movement of prices from a trough or bottom to crest or a peak is categorized as a rally, while the downside movement from a peak to bottom is defined as a sell-off in the market. The diagram below demonstrates the upward and downward trends with associated rallies and sell-offs, and vice versa.

A market trend is characterized by the presence of three intermittent trends or phases:

Major or Primary Trend or Phase

The core job of a technical analyst is to identify the major direction or long-term trend of the market with the help of different price patterns and tools. This is typically the most critical aspect of technical analysis because it enables the trader to ensure the optimal ride of the wavelength, which translates into the maximization of trade profit. The long term trend usually lasts for one to three years with some variations.

Secondary Trend or Phase

Sell-off or corrections, or retracements in the primary trend defines the secondary trend of the market. If the underlying trend is bullish, then any erosion in prices marked by price movement in the opposite direction of the prime trend is classified as a market correction or retracement in the prime trend.

On the contrary, markets in primary bearish or downward trend shall exhibit upward corrective or secondary bullish trends. The secondary trend comparatively has a short time span of three weeks to three months. The technical analyst makes use of the Fibonacci retracement tool to work out the correction or retracement in a given market.

Fibonacci Retracement

Fibonacci identified the sequence of numbers that were translated into mathematical relationships and subsequently converted into ratios. These ratios are applied to calculate the approximate length of corrective waves. Fibonacci retracement works by applying the following ratios/percentages to the value arrived at by measuring the distance between a peak or crest and a trough or bottom:

- 23.6% or 0.236
- 33% or 0.382
- 50% or 0.50
- 61.8% or .618 or 66%

100% (sometimes the markets retrace the total length of the preceding wave)

The identification of retracement levels facilitates the identification of support and resistance levels. This is usually done by drawing horizontal lines at each peak or retracement level. An efficient trader shall use these support and resistance levels to maximize trade profits by astutely defining his entry and exit points.

Minor or Consolidative Trend or Phase

The last phase is characterized by the development of minor trends resulting from small corrections within the secondary trend. The direction of prices during the minor trend is always against the direction of the secondary trend.

This is typically one of the most tedious phases, and ignorant and hasty traders tend to lose a lot of money in this phase because of choppy price behavior.

However, a technical analyst who is aware of the bigger picture either avoids trading during this phase of the market or keeps his financial commitment minimal. This is because excessive trading in this phase can result in distraction, and you can ultimately be deprived of enjoying the lucrative monetary benefits of major trends.

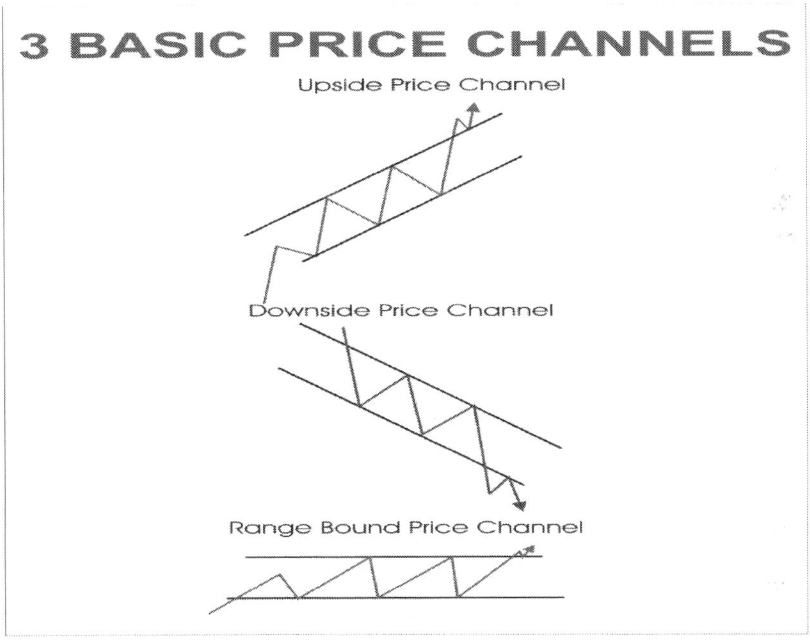

How does a Trend Unfold

Generally, the bullish market is marked by the initiation of the accumulation phase. The well-informed investors, also called smart money, after having sensed that the market is bottomed out and entails excellent profit potential at depressed price levels, start committing their funds into the market.

The accumulation phase is ensured by the participation of the general public. Prime factors leading to public participation are a switch in general sentiment from negative to positive and improving fundamental economic conditions. Usually, the public participation phase initiates after the culmination of a bearish trend. It becomes identifiable by the inability of the prices to post a new low due to diminishing selling pressure. This phase witnesses maximum participation of technical analysts, retail traders, and investors who failed to invest their funds at the lows of the market either because of fear or lack of sufficient supporting information. The prices are pushed higher and higher, complementing the trend's progress; there is buying euphoria; sentiment is extremely positive, and profits exponential. This phase is the longest of all phases in terms of time and wave-length.

Informed investors enter into the market with a defined profit-objective and corresponding exit level or range. Informed investors start to liquidate their positions near or around the levels mentioned above, thus reducing their overall stake in the market. Their positions are often bought by less-informed traders or emotional market participants. These are typically the people who were initially fearful of entering the market and are forced into late buying because of past regrets. The market's top is identified by the absence of new highs, loss of upward momentum, increased participation of the general public, and failure of the market to post new highs in response to positive fundamental news.

The initiation of a downward trend is preceded by the off-loading of stocks from the informed investor during the phase, which is referred to as the distribution phase. A critical sign of this phase is a sharp spike in the prices near the highs, which is followed by a sharp decline to the levels from which the prices initially rose. Hence the traders might get trapped into this phase by construing it as a consolidative phase.

An important indication of the impending downward trend is when the market not only fails to make a new high but also penetrates the previously attained high during the downward corrective phase. In the process, prices even exceed the previous low, which usually acts as a support level for all downward price movements. The combination of all these factors alludes to the market reversal or initiation of a downward trend.

Eventually, this paves the way for another public participation phase. The dampening sentiment, discouraging fundamental news from the economic front, and gloomy business conditions all contribute to the strengthening of downside momentum. Thus the downward trend grips the market with full fervor. As sellers outnumber the buyers, the prices start making lower highs and lower lows, leading to fast price erosion. Traders, less-informed investors, and late entrants book their losses, and technical traders tend to reverse their positions at this juncture and take short positions in the market.

Panic selling by the general public stoked by sheer despair results in the culmination of downside. Prices usually take a nosedive and sometimes crash due to extreme sell-off triggered by adverse news. At the end of the bearish phase, negative bearish sentiments engulf the market, news about unfavorable business and economic conditions are rampant, and market participants' cynicism is at its peak. Buyers transform into short-sellers as they anticipate further erosion in the market. It is usually at this critical juncture that the elusive smart money starts penetrating the market, and another new market trend begins to develop.

Correlation between Volume and Market Trend

Burgeoning volumes support the movement of prices in a trend, thus corroborating the trend's direction. Any price movement that is not complemented by a burst of activity with increasing volumes is to be taken as a false signal during the analysis and identification of a trend's direction. Usually, thinly traded markets that typically exhibit abnormal price movements are a trap set for emotional or novice traders. The market's upward or downside momentum can be gauged by analyzing the correlation between volume and price movement. In other words, increasing volumes confirm the validity and continuation of the trend.

Conversely, if the trading volume is low and price movement is abnormally high, then this should be seen as the conclusion of trend and a signal of imminent change in the market's direction.

The premise behind this is that for a trend's continuation, the majority of traded money must move with the market.

Bullish and Bearish Chart Patterns

The market, during its way up or down, carves out specific patterns and formations. These patterns have different implications for the market trend, depending on the direction and phase of the market they appear. Usually, these formations can be categorized into three categories on the basis of their implications:

- Bullish formations
- Bearish formations
- Consolidative formations

If you are a smart trader and have enough expertise, then you should be able to interpret these formations keeping in view the following important considerations:

Bullish and bearish formations can appear in both bullish and bearish markets.

Bearish formations in bullish markets are more commonly treated as corrections in overbought markets.

Bullish formations in bearish markets are viewed as upward corrections in oversold markets.

Some of these patterns portray a trend-reversal, while others are continuation patterns. Besides, trend reversal patterns can transform into continuation patterns and vice versa.

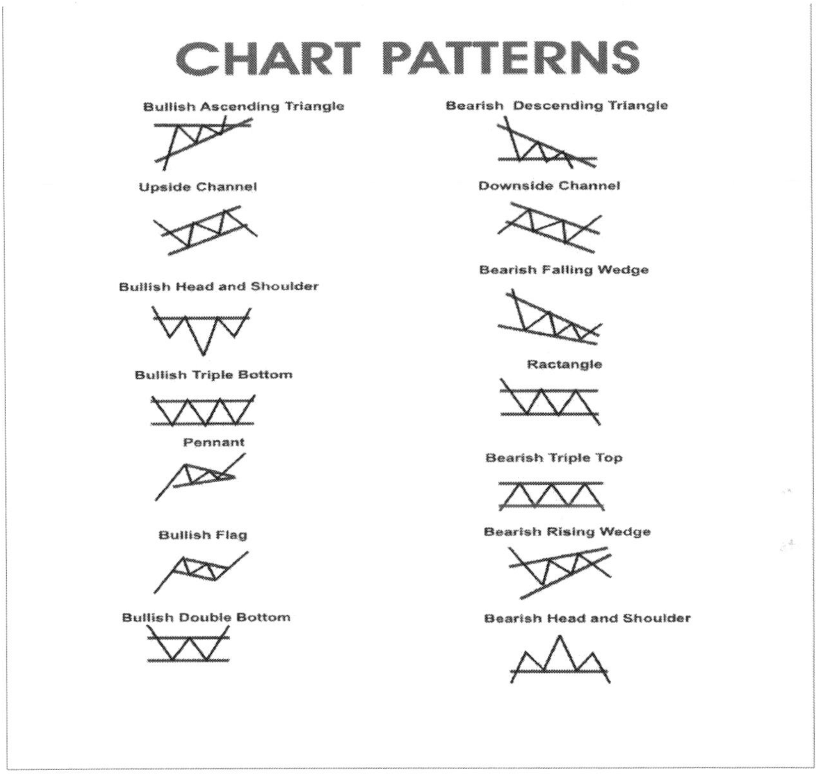
CHART PATTERNS
Bullish Ascending Triangle
Bearish Descending Triangle
Upside Channel
Downside Channel
Bearish Falling Wedge
Bullish Head and Shoulder
Ractangle
Bullish Triple Bottom
Pennant
Bearish Triple Top
Bullish Flag
Bearish Rising Wedge
Bullish Double Bottom
Bearish Head and Shoulder

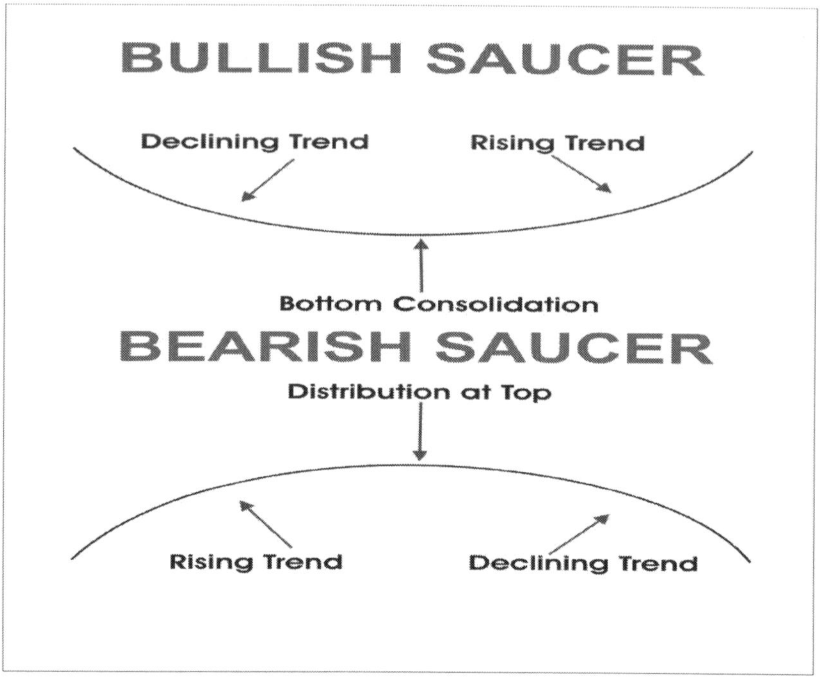

Contrary Opinion Theory

You cannot become a profitable trader unless you equip yourself with the requisite trading arsenal. In other words, you should have sound knowledge of all the concepts and theories relevant to the trading markets. Surprisingly, you can sometimes benefit by playing against the generally considered opinion of the market players. The underlying principle of this theory is that since the majority of the public is a loser, so you must not do what the losers are doing. The contrary opinion is a theory by which a trader tries to analyze and comprehend popular opinion and then act contrary to it. The opinion must be widely held and have considerable influence on the majority of people. The concept is quite simple: If the market is in an overbought condition, meaning that all the bulls have already committed their funds into the market, and there are no bulls left to buy, then the market shall fall of its weight. Your belief is strengthened when bullish news fails to give upside momentum to the market up. It is at this point when all of the bulls look to exit the market. Since there will be no cushion of new buyers to soften the decline, consequently, the market shall come thrashing down. The same holds for a market in which "all the bears" have already sold.

Even the astute traders attach great importance to behaving in a contrarian manner. The reason behind the success of the theory of contrary opinion is that it helps in staying aloof from the crowd's psychology. If we can create mechanisms that help us disregard or distrust our impulses and emotions, then the odds that a rational thought process will prevail improves dramatically.

Another reason contributing to the success of the contrary opinion theory is that it is usually challenging for the crowd to anticipate a change in trend as they are merely followers or laggards. The general public expects trends to remain intact for an indefinite period. History is replete with examples of the traders who entered the market after a lengthy period of extended gains but were later proved wrong by the market's subsequent action.

A contrary opinion is also a useful tool in assessing the market's residual buying potential. A thriving market is in absolute control of bulls; therefore, one can easily deduce from this that there is an apparent dearth of buyers, with fresh funds, in an extremely bullish market, especially around its top. Since only pumping of additional funds can catalyze an upward price action, but in this case, prices cannot be pushed higher because there are no funds left. However, if the sentiment is mixed and skepticism abounds, then new participants can be lured into investing in the market.

But a trader must not get blindfolded by this principle, for if the majority of the crowd will start applying the contrary opinion; then, the market is also expected to move in the direction contrary to the perceived judgment of the majority. The timing of the trade is also of the essence in the application of the contrary opinion.

3.9 Ralph Nelson Elliott- Theory of Waves

The credit for developing the Wave Theory goes to Ralph Nelson Elliott. Before the Elliot Wave Theory, there was a pervasive misconception of "helter-skelter stock market movement" in the financial world. However, Elliot found a systematic movement akin to the Dow's wave-like movement in the stock markets. Besides, he believed that markets behaved thematically and repetitively. We will briefly discuss the principles of Elliot Wave Theory and its applications to capital and commodity markets.

Elliot Waves for Predicting Future Market Behavior

Elliott's theory has a stunning resemblance with the Dow Theory, as both have supporting evidence about the movement of prices in waves. Another exciting feature of Elliot's discovery is that that these waves tend to repeat in the future and hence can be used to predict future market behavior.

The Elliott Wave Theory Explained

The Theory says that a typical bullish market advances with the help of 5 waves. Waves 1, 3, and 5 depict rallies in a primary bull market, whereas waves 2 and 4 are corrective waves within the bull trend. These corrective waves help a bullish market rectify its overbought status and attain a level where the force of both buyers and sellers exhibit a state of equilibrium, thus galvanizing the market to scale new highs with renewed vigor in the direction of the existing trend.

Collectively, waves 1,2,3,4, and 5 are called Impulse Waves.

A typical precondition for the validity and subsequent identification of the impulse wave theory is, though, there are exceptions in that the bottom of wave four must not overlap with the top of wave 1.

Waves 1 and Wave 5 usually cover the same distance and hence are of equal length.

Wave 3 is the most extended wave amongst the advancing waves.

Length of wave 5 in bullish markets, where wave 1 and wave 3 are of equal length, is measured by multiplying the total distance covered between wave 1 and wave 3 by the Fibonacci factor of 1.618.

The 5-way movement in the direction of the primary trend is ensured by the 3-wave movement, represented as A, B, and C in the diagram, in the direction opposite to the primary market trend.

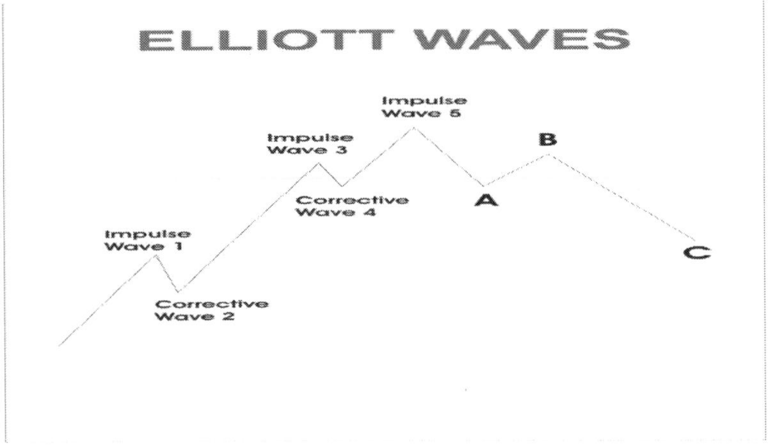

The 3-wave retracement of impulse waves further breaks down into three distinct price movements. Waves A and C split into 5 minor waves, each with progress in the direction of the main correction, whereas wave B divides into three small waves in a direction against that of the main correction.

The future predictability feature of Elliot Theory is derived from the fact that the basic 5-3 pattern is perennial in nature and remains constant with variations in the time span of each wave.

The combined 5-3 move of impulse and corrective waves subsequently become a part of a larger trend, which again takes the form of a 5-3 combination. Thus the first 5 impulse waves take on the form of wave 1 of the impulse waves of the next bigger wave, and the 3 corrective waves become corrective wave 2 of the same. Hence Elliot waves are composed of trends and countertrends, as shown in the diagram.

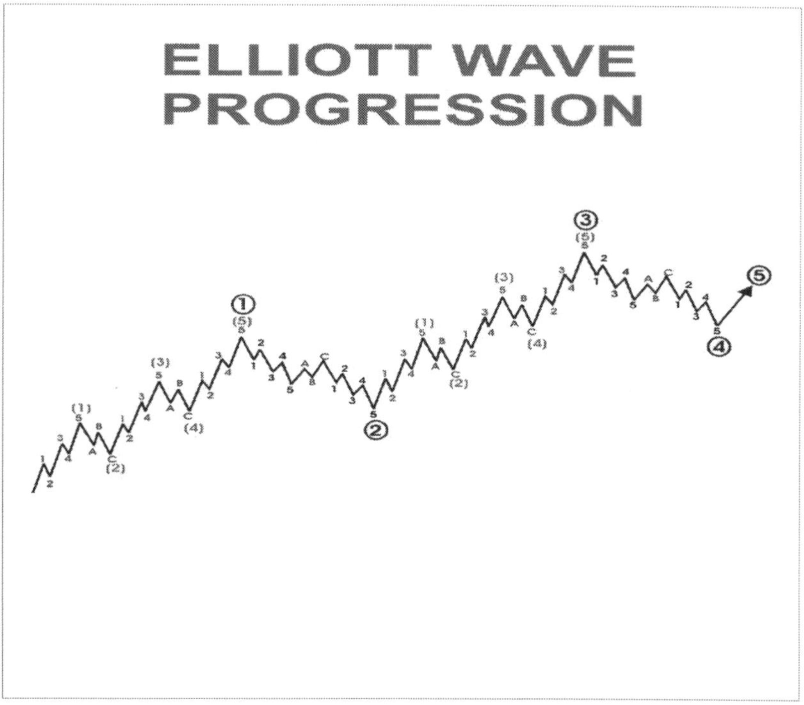

Wave Degrees

The hierarchy and time frame of Nine degrees of waves, from largest to smallest, as identified by Elliott, are:

- Super Cycle waves constitute Grand Supercycle, which extends to centuries

- Cycle waves constitute Super Cycle waves, which extend to 40-70 years
- Primary waves constitute Cycle waves, which extend from one year to many years
- Intermediate waves constitute Primary waves, which can extend from months to few years
- Minor waves constitute Intermediate waves, which can extend from weeks to months
- Minute waves constitute Minor waves, which can extend over several weeks
- Minuette waves constitute Minute waves, which can extend over several days
- Sub-Minuette waves constitute Minuette waves, which can extend over several hours
- Sub-Minuette waves can extend over several minutes

The critical job of a technical trader making use of Elliot wave theory is not only to identify an ascending impulse wave; instead, he has to spot its sequence or position in the trend correctly. Once the trend and position of the impulse wave have been identified, a trader can then apply it for taking long and short positions in the market. Besides, it will also help the trader to multiply his profits by enjoying the downside of the market through short positions in the negative trending market.

3.10 Japanese Candlesticks

Japanese Candlesticks provide an accurate graphical representation of price actions. In contrast to bar charts, a single candlestick is potent enough to help a trader assess the current supply and demand level of any stock or commodity at any given time. The interpretation of candlesticks is made based on positive and negative closing prices at any given time.

Bullish Candle

The metric for a positive closing is the opening price. If prices open lower and close higher, then such a scenario is construed as a positive one and is graphically represented as a hollow white or green candle on the price chart.

Bearish Candle

Conversely, markets opening higher and closing lower are represented as black candles denoting the negative closing at any given time.

Besides, there are three components of a candlestick:

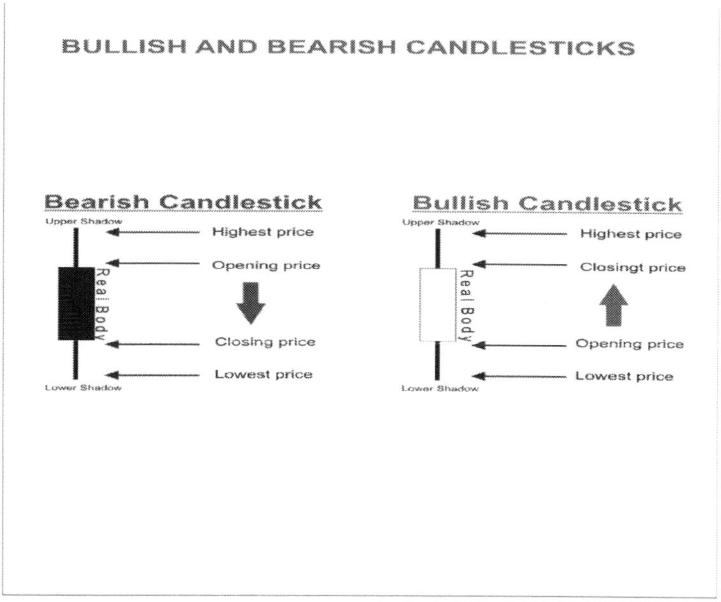

Real Body

The central portion, hollow or black, depicting the distance between the open and the close of the traded commodity or security, is called the Real Body of the candlestick.

Upper Shadow

In a bullish candle, the upper shadow can be seen as a vertical line between the high and the close of any given period. On the contrary, for a black candle, this line starts from the day top and extends to the open level.

Lower Shadow

In a bullish candle, the lower shadow is typically the vertical line between the low and the open of any stock or commodity. Conversely, it is the distance between the low and close recorded for a particular period.

Benefits of Japanese Candlesticks over Bar Charts

Although Japanese candlesticks and bar charts provide the same information, however, candlesticks have added advantage over bar charts as:

- Candlesticks are eye-catching
- Help gauge supply and demand through real body's color analysis
- Shadows help assess the upside or downside pressure or support and resistance range

Famous Candlestick Patterns and Interpretations

Japanese Candlesticks formations are identifiable and interpretable. We are briefly describing some of the critical patterns with their bullish and bearish implications.

Doji

A Doji is formed when prices open and close at or around the same level. However, the length of shadows may vary and thus subject to different interpretations.

A typical Doji appears at or near the market top. It also reflects at a pause in the ongoing trend, thus signaling either the continuation of trend or trend reversal. It also hints at the indecision between the buyers and the sellers.

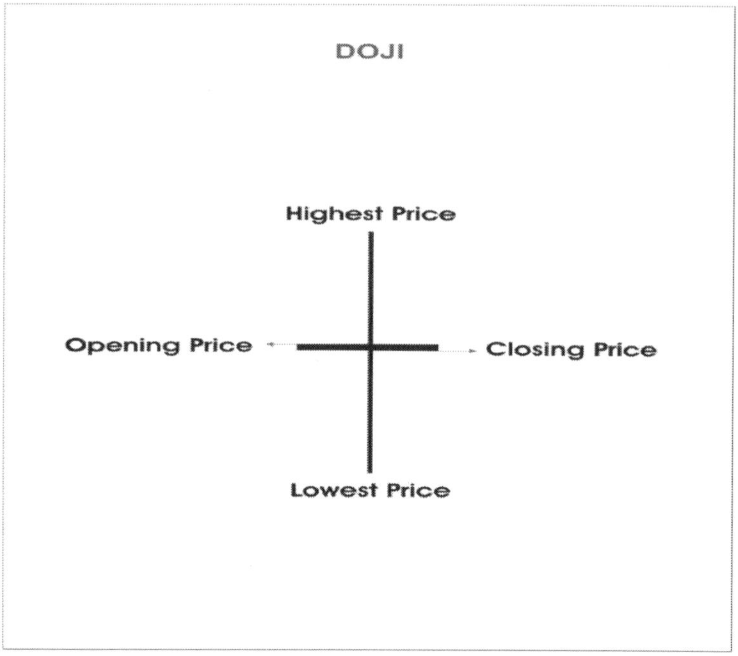

Gravestone Doji

This pattern derives its name from the gravestone because of its stunning resemblance to the same. It is formed when the prices open and close at the day or trading period low.

Since gravestone Doji is a bearish reversal pattern, so it tells the trader beforehand of future decline in prices, which can be capitalized on for offloading of holdings along with initiating short positions.

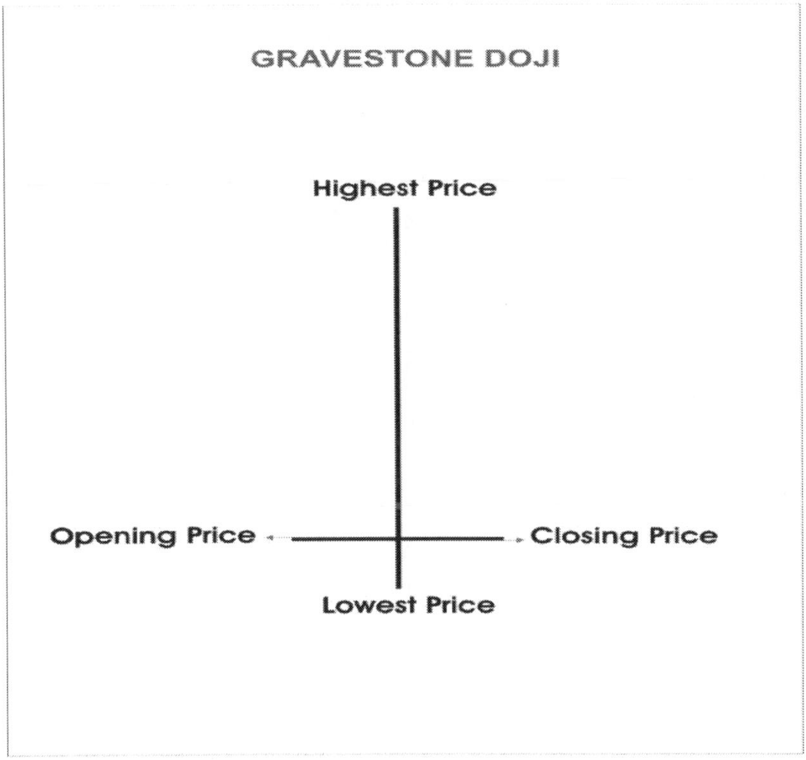

Dragonfly Doji

Contrary to gravestone Doji, the prices in a dragonfly Doji open and close at the trading period highest point.

Dragonfly Doji has a long lower shadow, and it indicates an imminent trend reversal in the preceding trend.

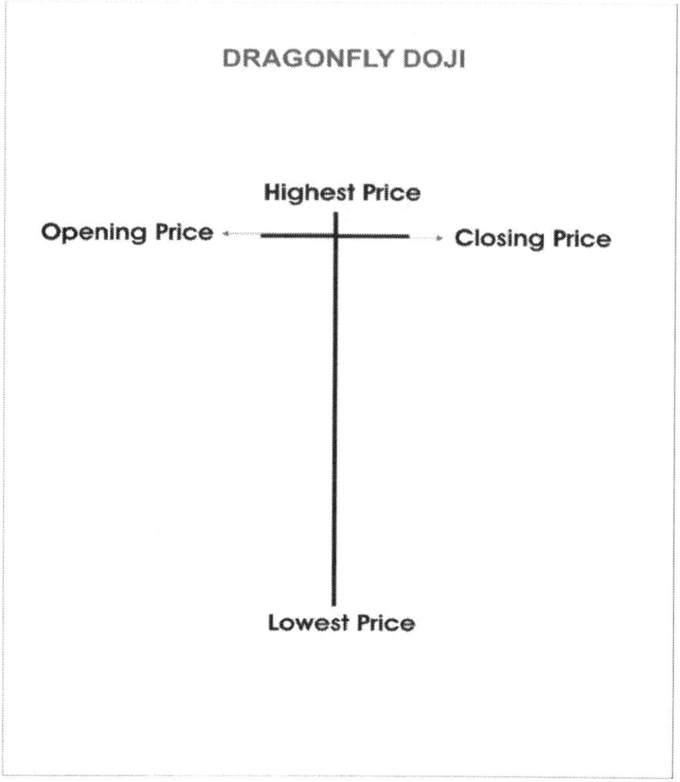

Bearish Engulfing Pattern

It is a twosome candlestick pattern consisting of one white and one black candlestick. The formation of a large black candlestick takes place after the appearance of the small white or hollow candlestick on the charts. The large black candlestick is large enough to engulf the preceding white candlestick. Besides, the long black candlestick also closes below the lower shadow of the preceding white candlestick.

It is a bearish pattern, usually appearing at the top of a market trend. Thus it portends a downtrend in prices or a price reversal.

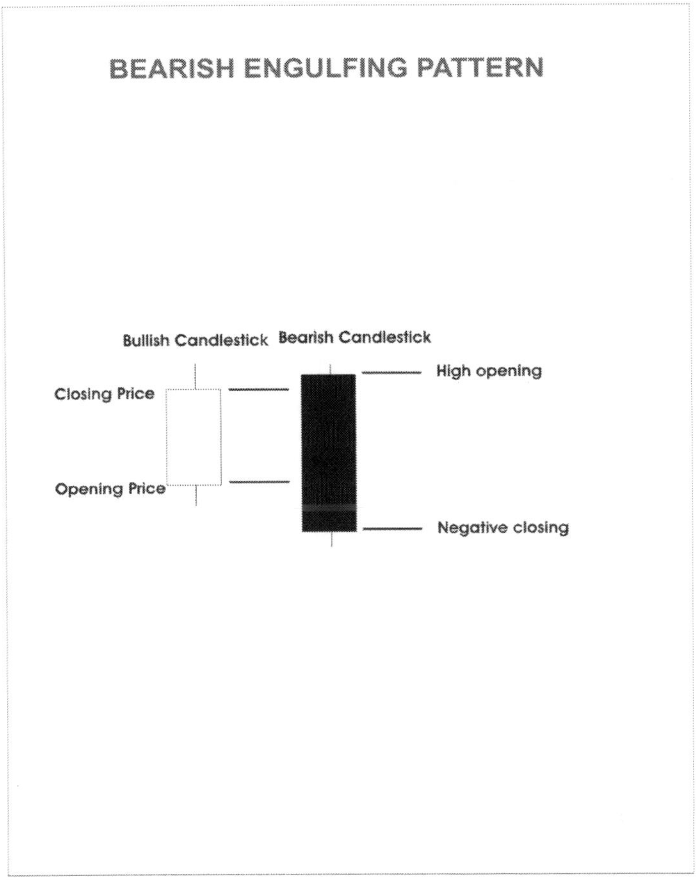

Bullish Engulfing Pattern

This pattern is also created by the formation of two back to back candlesticks. In contrast to a bearish engulfing pattern, a small black candlestick precedes the formation of a large white candlestick. The large white candlestick is large and engulfs the preceding black candlestick. Besides, the large white candlestick also posts a closing above the upper shadow of the previous black candlestick.

This bullish pattern usually occurs near or at the market bottom. Besides signaling the end of a bearish trend, it also hints at the start of a new bull trend in the prices.

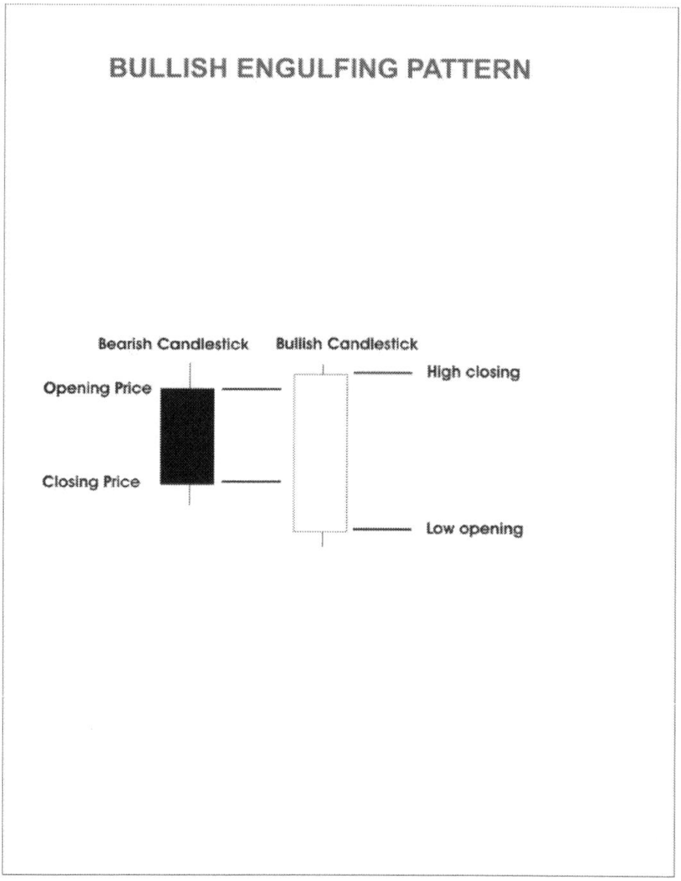

Hammer

A hammer is formed when prices after trading significantly lower than the opening price jump back to close above the opening level. Consequently, a white candlestick with a small body and long lower shadow is formed, reflecting the inability of bears to drag the prices lower. The size of the long lower shadow is almost double the size of the real body.

A hammer usually appears at or near the market bottom and signals a reversal in a bearish trend. Trend reversal is confirmed with the formation of a strong white candlestick the very next day. Bullish white candlestick's closing above the previous day hammer validates the reversal in trend from bearish to bullish.

A candlesticks trader will usually close short positions and will take new long positions after the appearance of a confirmation candlestick pattern.

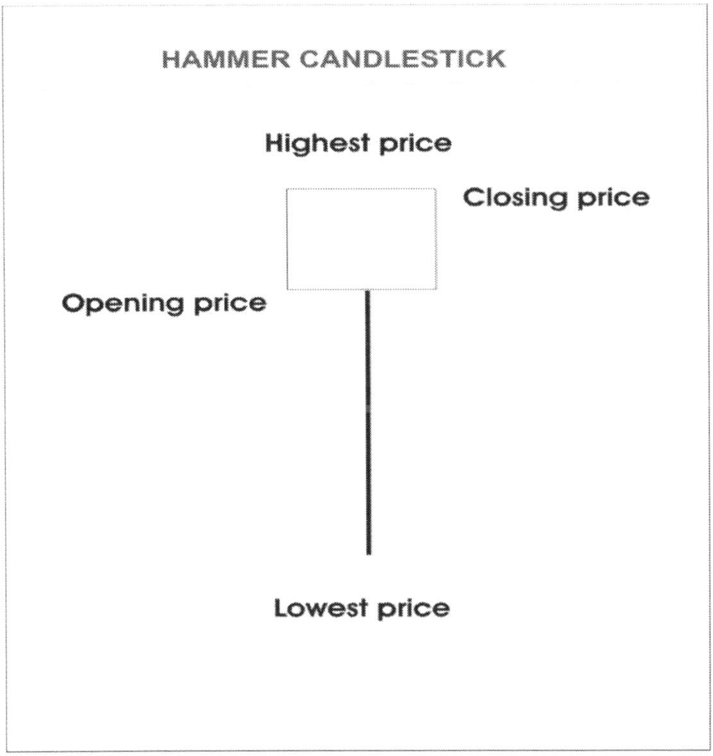

Hangman

It is almost the mirror image of a hammer with the difference that it has a small black body, and it usually appears at or near the top of a bull market. Hangman has minimal or no upper shadow.

The long lower shadow indicates that bears were able to make inroads into the market, but bulls managed to push the prices up to close around the top. It reflects a significant dent in the bull market and the weakening of bulls' control.

A candlesticks trader will usually close long positions and will take new short positions after the appearance of a confirmation candlestick pattern.

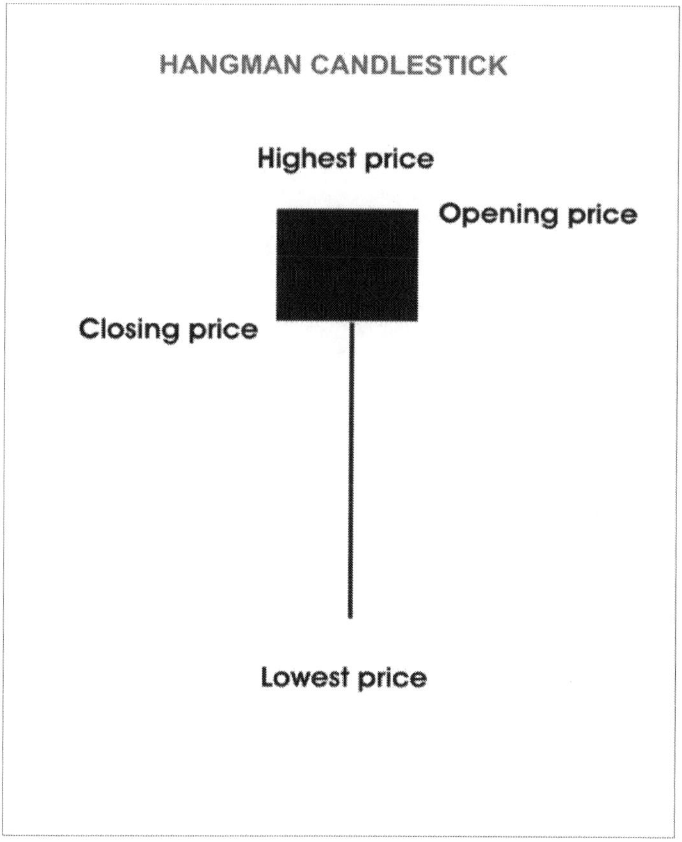
HANGMAN CANDLESTICK
Highest price
Opening price
Closing price
Lowest price

CHAPTER 4: Major Currencies and Currency Pairs in the Forex Market

Although the foreign exchange sector is sometimes referred to as the game of a banker, currencies may also be a perfect way to diversify a portfolio that may have entered a little bit of a rut. It's a sector that can deliver enormous prospects as other global markets also fall into the doldrums.

Get to know a little bit about forex and the dynamics behind it will also allow substantial contributions to the arsenal of any broker, portfolio manager, or investor. Have a look at 8 currencies each investor or trader should recognize, along with their respective nations' central banks.

4.1 Essential Information About the Forex Market and Major Currencies

The crucial and important details about the hot currencies exchanged in the Forex market are described below.

The U.S. dollar is the home currency of the strongest economy in the country, often referred to as the greenback.

The European Central Bank is entitled to issue euro banknotes as it sees fit, while policymakers can intervene with bank failures or machine failures.

The Bank of Japan administers monetary control, currency-issuing, cash market activities and data / economic research.

The Bank of England shall have a Board of Directors or an agent named by the Monarch. It also has a Monetary Policy Committee, which is chaired by the bank governor.

The Swiss franc, the Canadian dollar, the Australian and New Zealand dollars, and the South African rand supplement the list of top currencies that are tradable.

U.S. Dollar (USD)

Established by the Federal Reserve Act in 1913, the Federal Reserve System — also recognized as the Fed — is the primary U.S. banking body. The structure itself is governed by a board of governors and a chairman, with the focus on the Federal Open Market Committee (FOMC)'s branch. The FOMC regulates free-market activities and monetary or interest rate decisions.

The present committee consists of 5 of the 12 founding presidents of the Federal Reserve Bank and 7 Federal Reserve Board members, with the Federal Reserve Bank President of New York remaining on the committee always. And if there are twelve active participants, as the committee meets every six weeks, non-members — that includes multiple Fed Bank chairmen — are encouraged to express their opinions on the present economic condition.

Also named the greenback, the U.S. dollar is the home currency of the world's biggest country, the U.S. As with any of the currency, economic indicators, like the gross domestic product (GDP) and statistics on production and jobs benefit the dollar.

The US dollar, however, is still highly affected by the central bank and the interest-rate decision announcements. The dollar is a currency competing against the other big currencies, notably the Japanese yen, euro, and British pound.

While the foreign exchange sector is sometimes advertised as a game of a banker, currencies may also be a perfect diversification for a portfolio that might have entered a little bit of a rut.

European Euro (EUR)

The European Central Bank has its offices in Frankfurt, Germany, and is the central bank of Eurozone's 19 member countries. The ECB has a central part responsible for implementing monetary policy choices in a comparable manner to the FOMC, the Executive Board, which consists of four members and a president and vice president.

The ECB's policy representatives are picked on the basis that 4 of the positions are allocated for four of the system's five main countries, including Germany, Italy, France, Spain, and the Netherlands. It is to guarantee that in the event of a transition of policy, the main countries will always be properly reflected. The Board meets almost every week.

The ECB still retains the power to print money as it looks appropriate, in addition to maintaining authority over monetary policy. Like the Federal Reserve, politicians may intervene in periods of bank defaults or system errors. The ECB varies from the FED in a significant region: Instead of increasing wages and preserving long-term concern rate stability, the ECB is aiming for a prime price stabilization principle, with secondary commitments to general economic policies. Consequently, policymakers will concentrate on consumer inflation as they make crucial interest-rate choices.

The monetary structure is very ambiguous, but the currency isn't. The euro (EUR) appears to be a weaker currency against the US dollar relative to its counterparts (i.e., the Australian dollar or British pound). The base currency will trade between 70 and 80 pips on a typical day — or percentages in point — with more extreme fluctuations reaching marginally higher, at 100 pips wide daily.

Another factor for trade is time. Since the FX market is available 24/7, forex traders need to prepare the FX trading plans strategically. Trading of Euro-based pairs may be used during the U.S. and London sessions' overlap — which takes place from 8 a.m. till midday EST.

Japanese Yen (JPY)

The Bank of Japan, founded back in 1882, acts as the central bank for the world's third-biggest economy. It controls monetary strategy and currency-issuing, activities on the money market and economic/data research. The principal monetary policy board seeks to strive for economic prosperity, continually sharing opinions with the ruling administration, and at the same time striving for its own freedom and openness. Meeting on monetary policy takes place 8 times a year, the governor heads a group of 9 decision-makers with two deputy governors.

The Japanese yen (JPY) continues to exchange under the name of a part of carry-trade. The currency is matched against top-yielding currencies, with a low-interest rate, particularly the New Zealand and the British pound, and

Australian dollars. Consequently, the fundamental factor continues to be quite volatile, forcing FX traders to take longer-term technical perspectives. Normal regular ranges are between 70 and 140 pips, with peaks far over 200 pips. To exchange this currency with a bit of a crunch, you will need to concentrate on the London and U.S. time crossover (8 a.m. to noon EST).

British Pound (GBP)

The Bank of England, as the UK's central bank, acts as the fiscal counterpart to the Federal Reserve System. The Court of Directors is also a controlling board named by the Government, consisting of five administrative officers and as many as nine others, including the chair and vice-chair. There is also a Monetary Policy Committee (MPC), chaired by the bank's governor and consisting of nine members, four of which are named by the Exchequer's Chancellor.

The MPC, which determines policies at least eight times a year, focuses on interest rates and wider monetary policy, along with primary concerns for overall economic market stability. The MPC thus already has a user price inflation target set at two percent. If this criterion is breached, it is the duty of the governor to inform the Chancellor of Exchequer by mail, one of which received as in 2007 as the Index of Consumer Prices (CPI) for the UK increased significantly to 3.1%. This letter's publication appears to be a forerunner for markets since it raises the risk of contractionary monetary policy.

A bit more competitive than the yen, the British pound (GBP)—also often stated as a pound sterling or cable — manages, during the day, to trade a broader range. It's not uncommon to look at the pound trade as thinly as 20 pips with movements that can cover 100 to 150 pips. Swings in prominent cross currencies aim to establish a flexible nature for this major, with traders focused on pairs like the Japanese yen / British pound and the Swiss franc / British pound. Consequently, the currency is the most unpredictable during both U.S. and London times, with limited fluctuations throughout Asian timings (8 p.m. to 4 a.m. EST).

Swiss Franc (CHF)

It is often dubbed the currency of the banker. Unlike all other global central banks, the Swiss National Bank is regarded as a private and publicly held governing body. The conviction derives from the reality that, under specific legislation, the Swiss National Bank is legally a company. This results in the sovereign cantons or states of Switzerland and other public authorities control far more than half of the governing organization. It is this structure that underlines the strategies of financial and economic security set by the SNB board of directors. Monetary policy judgments, smaller than other regulatory bodies, are made by three main bank heads who operate on a quarterly basis. The Board of Governors sets the range (± 25 basis points) of where the concern rate may reside.

There is a fascinating partnership between the Swiss Franc and the Euro. Like the pound, in neither of the individual hearings, the Swiss franc (CHF) undergoes major movements. Therefore, go for this specific currency to move within the regular average range of 45 pips a day. For this currency, the high-frequency rate is typically matched for the London session (3 a.m. to noon EST).

Canadian Dollar (CAD)

The Bank of Canada, founded by the Bank of Canada Act 1934, acts as the central bank recommended to concentrate on the objectives of stable and low inflation, a secure and safe currency, financial strength, public debt, and useful management of government funds. The central bank of Canada operating separately draws parallels with the Swiss National Bank, and it is often viewed as a company, with the finance minister owning stocks directly. Given the proximity of desires of the government, it is the duty of the governor to foster market stability at the length of an arm from the present administration, while at the same time acknowledging the needs of the community. With an inflationary target of 2 percent, when it comes to some market fluctuations, the BoC has continued to stay a little more hawkish than accommodative.

Keeping in line with other currencies, the Canadian dollar (CAD), often named the loonie, appears to exchange between 50 and 100 pips on similar regular ranges. Often currency and product rates shift together, and a special feature of the CAD is its correlation with crude oil. The state remains a big commodity exporter, and therefore, this currency is used by many investors and traders as either a buffer against existing commodity prices or sheer speculation, tracking signs from the oil markets.

Australian/New Zealand Dollar (AUD/NZD)

The Reserve Bank of Australia has constantly maintained economic growth and price stability as the cornerstones of its long-run agenda while providing one of the highest interest rates in the main global markets. The bank's board, led by the governor, is comprised of 6 members-at-large, additionally a deputy governor and the treasury secretary. They work closely to achieve inflation between 2% and 3% when meeting eleven times a year. Similarly, New Zealand's Reserve Bank seeks to encourage controlling inflation, aiming to establish a pricing base.

Since the Australian AUD and New Zealand NZD dollars deliver the strongest returns of the seven global currencies on certain markets, both currencies have become the target of carrying traders. Consequently, these pairs will encounter uncertainty when there is a deleveraging impact. Or else the currencies appear to move between 70 and 80 pips on identical averages. Both currencies still retain commodity-related ties, most especially gold and silver.

South African Rand (ZAR)

The South African Reserve Bank, historically based on the Bank of England of the United Kingdom, serves as the monetary body for South Africa. In certain cases, the SARB is often regarded as a trustee, a clearing agent, and a main keeper of gold, carrying on significant duties close to those of other central banks. The central bank is in control, above all, of achieving and preserving market stability. This often involves interference as the situation begins on the foreign exchange markets.

The South African Rand (ZAR) average regular range may be as large as several thousand pips, deemed reasonably unpredictable. But do not let yourself be misled by the regular wide range. The fluctuations are equal to a typical day in the British currency when converted into dollar pips, which makes the currency a good pair to trade against the dollar (U.S.) — especially when considering the carry opportunity.

Traders also recognize the relationship between the currency and platinum and gold. Since the country is a global boss when it comes to shipping of both metals, a close link between crude oil and CAD is only normal to see. Consequently, think about the commodities markets generate openings while there is limited economic data.

4.2 What are the Main Currency Pairs?

The main pairs are the 4 currency pairs most actively traded on the Forex market. The USD / JPY, EUR / USD, USD / CHF, GBP / USD, are the four big pairs.

These four main sets are deliverable currencies, which belong to the currency group of the G-10. Although these currencies make a large amount of quantity related to economic dealings, these are often some of the most actively exchanged pairs for dangerous reasons, even by traders.

The EUR / USD, GBP / USD, USD / JPY, and USD / CHF are the four main currency pairs.

Global currencies and commodity currency pairs are some of the most extensively exchanged sets in the world: USD / CAD, NZD / USD, and AUD / USD.

The EUR / USD is the world's most actively traded currency pair and is famous for speculators because of its daily high volume.

Understanding the main pairs

Most regard the big pairs as the driving force behind the global Forex market, as they are the most actively traded. Even Though it is generally believed that the main sets consist of just four pairs, others claim that the pairs of AUD / USD, USD / CAD, and NZD / USD may also be counted as majors. These three sets, however, can also be found in the "commodity pairs" category.

The 5 currencies are representing the main sets — U.S. Dollar, the euro, the Japanese yen, the Swiss franc. And the British pound – are all among the top 7 currencies that are heavily exchanged.

The USD/ EUR is the most actively exchanged currency pair in the world, responsible for over 20 percent of all Forex traders.

The JPY/ USD is a distant 2nd position, followed by the USD / GBP and the CHF / USD, with a limited portion of the global Forex sector.

Trading amounts in the AUD / USD, USD / CAD, and NZD / USD would sometimes outweigh those in the CHF / USD and often the USD / GBP owing to their commodity-based economies.

Why you should trade the main pairs

Volume generates and attracts the volume. It is because more volume spans appear to widen among the bid and ask range, which implies the majors prefer to have narrower spreads than the exotic sets. The main pairs are rather voluminous. Therefore, they seem to draw the best traders, which appears to hold the volume large.

High turnover also indicates that traders with large position sizes will go in and out of the market easily. It could be more challenging to buy or sell a big position in lower volume pairs without allowing the cost to change substantially.

Large volume often implies more customers involved in purchasing or selling at a given moment. That implies less risk of slippage when it occurs. It is not to suggest that major slippage cannot take place in big pairs, it does, but it is uncommon than in exotic pairs that are thinly exchanged.

How are the prices of the big pairs be determined?

The major pair of currencies are free-floating currencies. That implies the big pairs' prices are dictated by demand and supply for the currencies in question. Central banks may move in to regulate the market, but usually only where there is a need to avoid the market from too much rising or dropping as it may trigger economic damage.

Demand and Supply are influenced by fundamental or economic conditions in each region, interest rates, potential market/currency projections, and existing positions.

4.3 Understanding Forex Quotes

In terms of another currency, a Forex quote is the price of one currency. These quotes often contain pairs of currencies, so you purchase one currency while selling another. For instance, when examining the EUR / USD currency pair, the cost of one euro would cost $1.1404. Brokers would usually list two values for each currency pair and, in normal market circumstances, collect the difference (spread) between the two.

The following paragraphs elaborate on the numerous facets of a Forex quote. Throughout this portion, the same quote is used to hold the figures accurately. This example is presented below:

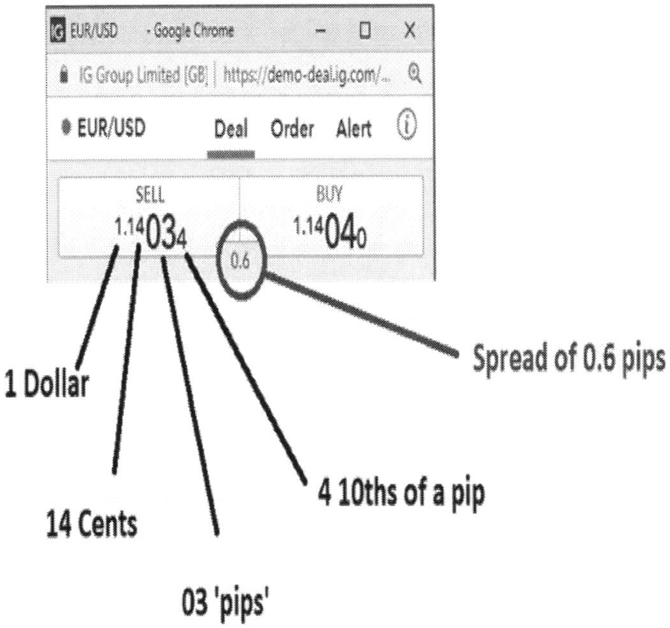

Understanding Forex Quote Basics

Traders should be conscious of the following basics of a Forex quote to interpret the currency pairs correctly:

ISO code: The International Organization for Standardization (ISO) establishes, releases, and extends universal norms to global currencies. Which means the currency of each nation is abbreviated to three characters. For instance, the euro is reduced to EUR and the US dollar to USD.

Base currency and variable currency: Forex quotes indicate two currencies, the first showing base currency and the second representing variable currency. The first currency's price is still expressed in 2nd currency units. In keeping with the earlier illustration of EUR / USD, it is obvious that one euro would cost one dollar, 14 cents and 04 pips. This is rare since you can't easily carry one-cent fractions, but this is a common element of the foreign exchange sector.

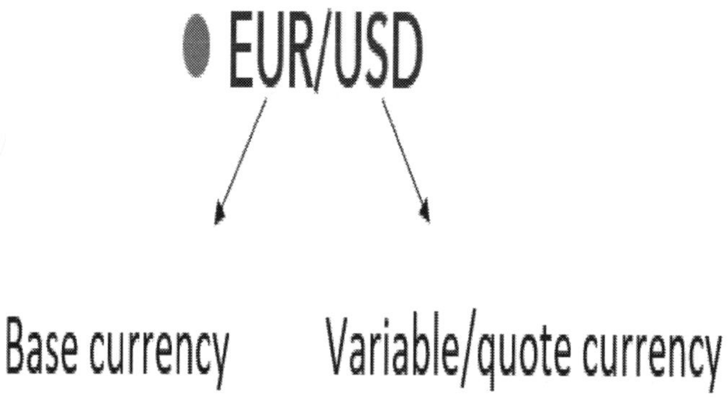

Bid and ask price

In the forex market, a currency pair will always quote two different prices:

The price of the Bid (Sell) is the price at which traders can sell currency, and the price of the ask (BUY) is the price at which traders can purchase currency. This can sound complicated since it is just normal to think about "bid" from the point of view of purchasing, but just know the bid / ask language is from the viewpoint of the broker.

Traders will still be looking to purchase Forex when the price is down and sell as the price rises or to sell Forex in expectation of potential currency depreciation and buy it back at a lesser price.

Spreads

Usually, the price to purchase currency is higher than the price to sell the currency. This disparity is called the spread, which is where the broker makes money to carry out the market. Owing to its large trading volume and liquidity spreads appear to be narrower (less) for major currency pairs. The EUR / USD is the most commonly exchanged currency pair, so it's no wonder the spread is 0.6 pips in this case.

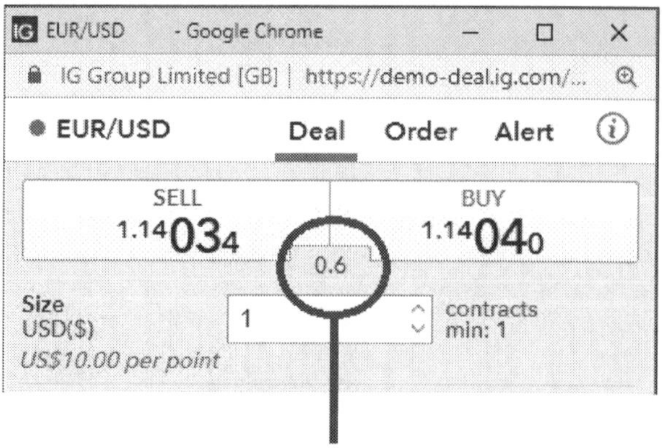

$1.1404_0 - 1.1403_4 = 0.6$ pips

Direct Vs. Indirect Quotes

Quotes are always shown with the "home currency" in mind, that is, the country in which you live. A direct quote for U.S. traders seeking to purchase Euros would read EUR / USD and be meaningful to U.S. people, as the quote is in U.S. Dollars. This specific quote, in terms of their home currency, which is 1.1404, would provide U.S. people with the price of one Euro.

The indirect quote is basically the actual currency vice versa (1 / direct quote = 0.8769). In terms of foreign currency, it indicates the worth of one unit of the domestic currency. Indirect quotes may be useful for converting purchases of foreign exchange overseas into domestic currency.

CHAPTER 5: Trading Strategies and Risk Management Techniques for the Beginners

A Forex trading strategy describes a method utilized by a Forex dealer to decide whether to purchase or sell a pair of currencies. Traders may use different Forex techniques like technical analysis or fundamental analysis. A successful Forex trading approach enables a trader to assess the demand and conduct trades efficiently using solid risk management strategies.

5.1 Forex Strategies

Forex tactics may be separated into a distinct organizational framework that will help traders identify the approach that is most appropriate. The diagram below shows how the general framework and the interaction between the Forex strategies fit under each strategy.

Venn Diagram Showing How the Different Forex Strategies Are Related

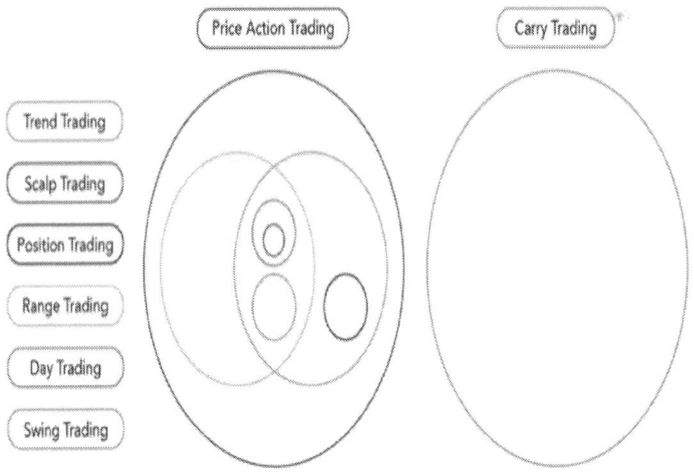

5.2 Effective Forex trading strategies

Forex trading demands that several considerations be placed together to devise a trading plan that works for you. There are numerous methods that can be implemented, but it's important to learn and be happy with the approach. And trader has specific priorities and tools that must be taken into account when choosing an effective strategy.

There are three parameters that can be used by traders to evaluate various strategies about their suitability:

- Time resource required
- Frequency of trading opportunities
- Target price

We have set them out in a bubble map to conveniently evaluate the Forex strategies on the three parameters. 'Risk-Reward Ratio' is on the vertical axis, with tactics at the top of the graph providing a greater reward for the risk incurred in each transaction. Position Trading is usually the technique with the largest risk-reward ratio. The time commitment on the horizontal axis is what reflects how much time it requires to continuously track the transactions. Scalp trading is the tactic that requires the most in terms of your time capital, owing to the large volume of trades being regularly placed.

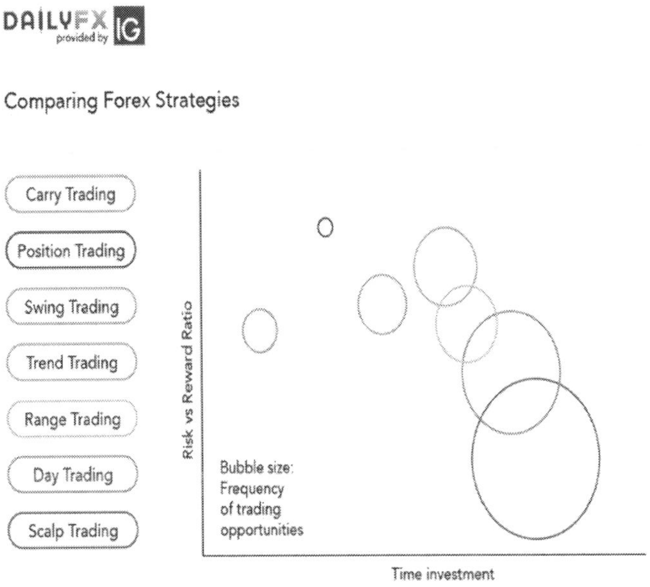

5.3 Price Action Trading

Trading of price action includes the analysis of past prices in order to devise plans for strategic trading. Price action may be used either as a stand-alone strategy or coupled with an indicator. Fundamentals are seldom used; nevertheless, the use of global developments as a substantiating element is not unheard of. As illustrated above, there are several other strategies that fall within the price action class.

Length of trade

Price action trading can be used with different time periods, namely long-term, medium-term and short-term. The flexibility and option of using multiple time frames for analysis make price action trading favored by many traders.

Entry/Exit points

You can work out support and resistance levels using different techniques. These levels are then utilized for working out entry/exit points:

- Fibonacci retracement

- Making use of Candle Sticks
- Trend identification
- Indicators
- Oscillators

There's a range, pattern, day, scalping, swing, and position trading inside the price action. These strategies conform to numerous types of trading criteria, which will be described below. The illustrations demonstrate various methods for trading these strategies to illustrate how flexible trading can be, as well as a range of tailor-made options for traders to select from.

5.4 Range Trading Strategy

Range trading requires finding points of support and resistance from which traders place positions at certain main levels. Without significant volatility and no discernible direction, this approach performs effectively in the market. The main technique associated with this approach is technical analysis.

Length of trade

As range-bound techniques will function for any time period, there is no fixed duration per transaction. Risk control is an important part of this process since breakouts can occur. A range trader would therefore want to close some existing range-bound positions.

Entry/Exit points

Oscillators are often widely employed as timing devices. A few of the more common oscillators are the Relative Strength Index (RSI), Commodity Channel Index (CCI), and stochastic. Market behavior is often used in combination with oscillators to further verify signals or breakouts for range-bound markets.

Over the last few years, USD / JPY has experienced a protracted period of range-bound price action. The above chart shows a simple band of support and resistance, which traders use as points of entry/exit. The RSI oscillator displays the timing of entry/exit points, as shown by the shaded blue and red boxes-blue: overbought and red: oversold.

However, range trading will contribute to lucrative risk-reward ratios; this is accompanied by long time investment per transaction. The pros and cons below match your objectives with the amount of money you have as a dealer.

Pros

The pros of subject trading strategy are:

- A significant number of trading opportunities
- Favorable risk-to-reward ratio

Cons

The cons of subject trading strategy are:

- Requires lengthy periods of time investment
- Required a lot of work using technical analysis

5.5 Trend Trading Strategy

Trend trading is a basic Forex technique used by several traders of all levels of experience. The trend trading approach aims to produce favorable gains by capturing a bullish trend in the markets.

Length of trade

In general, trend trading takes place across the mid to long-term spectrum, as trends fluctuate in length themselves. Multiple time frame analysis may be implemented in trend trading, much as in price action.

Entry/Exit points

Typically, entry points are determined by an oscillator (CCI, RSI, etc.), and exit points are measured on the basis of a favorable risk-reward ratio. Traders will either match or surpass the distance using stop level distances to preserve a favorable risk-reward ratio, e.g., If 50 pips away are used as a stop-loss level, then the profit objective would be set at 50 pips or more away from the entry stage.

In the simple example above, EUR/USD manifests an upward trend corroborated by higher highs and higher lows. The opposite would be true for a negative declining price action.

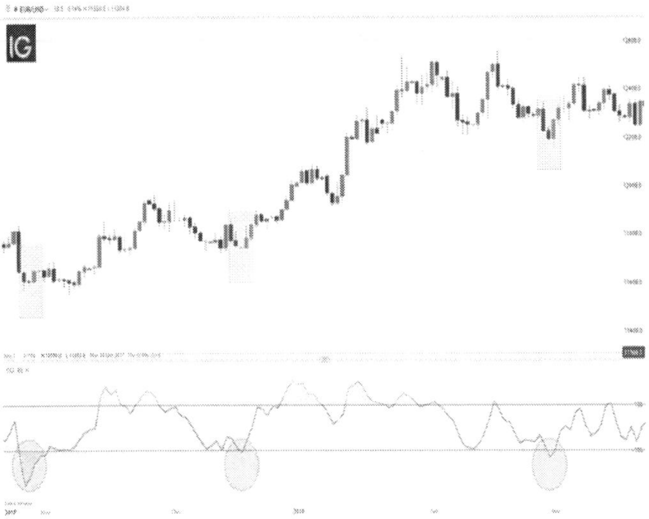

When you see a strong market pattern, trade-in trend direction, the solid uptrend in EUR / USD, for the example above.

Using the (CCI) as a metric to time entries, note how prices reacted with a rally any time CCI dipped under -100 (highlighted in blue). Not all trades would operate that way, but since the pattern is being pursued, each dip has prompted additional buyers to join the market and to drive higher rates. In conclusion, for a successful trend-trading strategy, finding a strong pattern is critical.

So many factors to remember, pattern trading may be relatively labor-intensive. The list of pros and cons will help you decide if trend trading is for you.

Pros

The pros of subject trading strategy are:

- A significant number of trading opportunities
- Lucrative risk-to-reward ratio

Cons

The cons of subject trading strategy are:

- Requires lengthy periods of time investment
- A good understanding of technical analysis

5.6 Position Trading

Position trading is a long-term approach mainly based on basic factors but technical approaches such as Elliot Wave Theory. In this approach, smaller minor market movements would not be included, as they do not impact the larger market view. This technique can be used from stocks to Forex in all markets.

Length of trade

As described above, position trades have a long-term outlook reserved for the more persevering trader (weeks, months, or even years!). In predicting potential trades, knowing how external conditions influence economies or thorough technical predispositions is important.

Entry/Exit points

Thanks to the comprehensive market view, the main thresholds on longer time span charts (weekly / monthly) provide useful knowledge for position traders. Entry and exit points may be measured similarly to the other methods using the technical analysis.

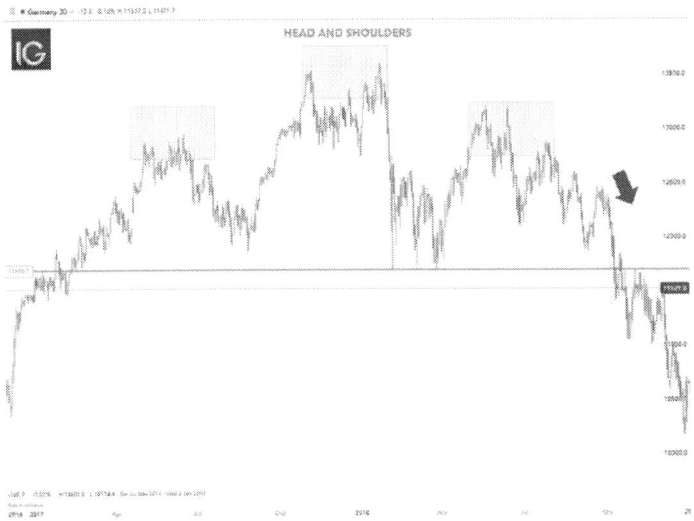

The Germany 30 map above illustrates an average trend of two years of head and shoulders trailing the right-hand side, which aligns with a possible dropping below the neckline (horizontal red line). In this selected case, Germany's 30's downward fall played out both technically and fundamentally, as expected. Germany and the US / China trade war affecting the automotive sector went through a technological contraction at the end of 2018. Brexit talks would not improve matters, since the chance for the UK to depart the EU would most definitely also have a detrimental effect on the German economy. In this case, knowing technical patterns as well as having clear fundamental foundations permitted a powerful trade concept to be developed by mixing technical and fundamental analyses.

Pros

The pros of subject trading strategy are:

- Does not require too much time investment
- Positive risk-to-reward ratio

Cons

The cons of subject trading strategy are:

- Minimal trading opportunities

- Requires strong appreciation of technical and fundamental analysis

5.7 Day Trading Strategy

Day trading is a strategy that can help you to trade financial instruments during the time limits of a particular trading day. This means that all positions are closed before the market close. You can go for a single trade or multiple trades throughout the day.

Length of trade

Trading times range from very short-term (minutes) or (hours). However, the trade has to be closed and opened within the day of trading.

Entry/Exit points

As shown in the example below, traders will try to enter points when the price penetrates in the direction of the pattern (blue circle) via the 8-period EMA and exits using a risk-reward ratio of 1:1.

The above chart demonstrates a typical day trading system utilizing moving averages to define the long trend in this case, as the price is above the MA lines (red and black). Entry points with stop levels placed at the previous price break are outlined in blue. Taking profit levels would be the equivalent of stop distance in trend direction.

While adopting this approach, the pros and cons mentioned below should be contemplated. Trading on a day requires a lot of time and money with little gain, as seen by the illustration above of EUR / USD.

Pros

The pros of subject trading strategy are:

- Significant trading opportunities
- Moderate risk-to-reward ratio

Cons

The cons of subject trading strategy are:

- It is extremely time-intensive
- Should have a sound understanding of the application of technical analysis

5.8 Forex Scalping Strategy

In Forex, scalping is a generic word used to characterize the practice of regularly taking small gains. This is done by day-long opening and closure of several positions. This may be accomplished manually or by an algorithm that uses predefined rules on when / where to enter and exit positions. The most liquid Forex pairs are favored, as spreads are usually smaller, allowing the strategy's short-term function appropriately.

Length of trade

Scalping constitutes short-term trades with comparatively less return. It usually operates on smaller time frame charts (30 min – 1min).

Entry/Exit points

Like other strategic techniques, it steps one to recognize the trend. Often scalpers use metrics such as the moving average for trend evaluation. Using these main trend levels on longer time frames helps the trader see the larger picture. These levels build bands of support and resistance. Scalping within this band can then be tried using oscillators such as the RSI on smaller time frames. Stops are put a few pips away to prevent big trading moves. Another valuable instrument that the trader can use to enter / exit trades is the MACD indicator.

A typical example of a scalping technique can be seen in the EUR / USD 10 minute chart shown above. The Moving Average (price over 200 MA) supports the long-term pattern. Afterward, the narrower time period is used to aim at entry/exit locations. The red rectangle in the trader's bias (long) shows the timing of entry points. Traders may often use the MACD to close long positions as the MACD (blue line) crosses the signal line (red line) indicated by the blue rectangles.

Traders, therefore, use the same principle for setting up their algorithms without the trader's manual execution.

Use this realistic illustration of scalp trading to pick a suitable trading approach that better fits you, along with using the list of pros and cons listed below.

Pros

The pros of subject trading strategy are:

- Offers a significant number of trading opportunities compared to all Forex strategies

Cons

The cons of subject trading strategy are:

- It requires a lot of time investment
- Should have a sound understanding of the application of technical analysis
- Lowest risk-to-reward ratio

5.9 Swing Trading

Swing trading is a speculative strategy. In swing trading strategy, traders try to capitalize on range-bound as well as trending markets. Traders can enter long and short positions by picking 'tops' and 'bottoms.'

Length of trade

Swing trades are generally categorized as medium-term positions. It is because these positions are usually held for a few hours to a few days. Longer-term trends are considered the best for swing traders, as traders can take advantage of multiple entries and exit points during the unfolding of the trend.

Entry/Exit points

Similar to the range-bound technique, oscillators and indicators may be used to pick suitable locations and times for entry/exit. The main distinction is that swing trading extends to trend- and range-bound markets as well.

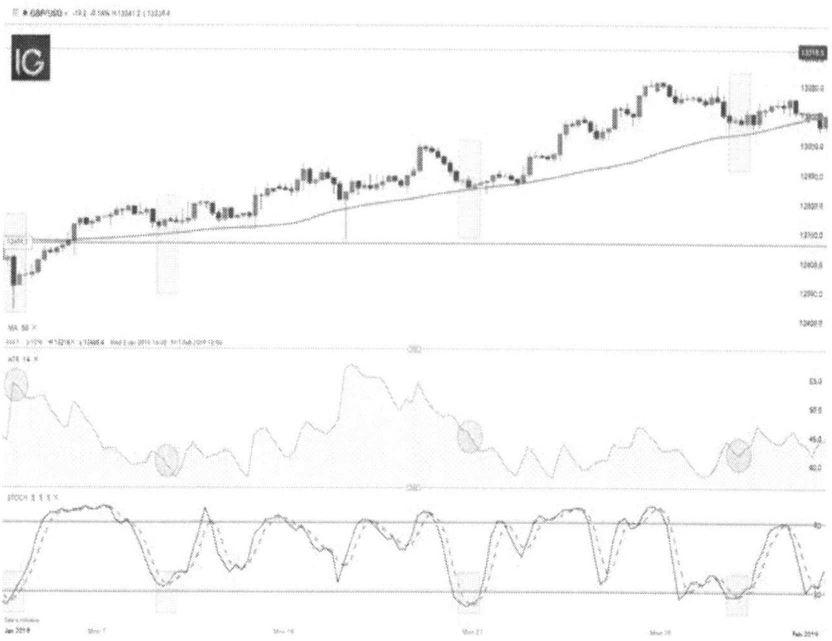

In the above illustration, a mixture of stochastic oscillator, ATR predictor, and the moving average is used to demonstrate a standard swing trade technique. Initially, the upward pattern was established using the 50-day moving average (price above the MA line). In the case of an uptrend, traders would refer to the old adage of 'buy low, sell big' to take long positions.

The stochastics are then used to classify entry points by checking for over-sold indications outlined on stochastic and chart by the blue rectangles. Risk assessment is the final stage during which the ATR offers an indication of stop level. The red circles show the ATR number. This figure represents the approximate number of pips away, which should be set to the top level. For instance, if the ATR reads 41.8 (reflected in the last reading of the ATR), the trader will aim to place the 41.8 pips to stop away from the entry. At DailyFX, we suggest that you trad with a favorable risk-reward ratio of at least 1:2. This will involve putting at least 83.6 (41.8 x 2) pips away or higher on a take benefit basis (limit).

Consider the following collection of pros and cons to decide whether this approach will fit your trading style.

Pros

The pros of subject trading strategy are:

- It offers significant trading opportunities
- Medium risk-to-reward ratio

Cons

The cons of subject trading strategy are:

- Must have a strong grip on technical analysis
- It requires a lot of time investment

5.10 Carry Trade Strategy

Borrowing one currency at a cheaper cost is usually done in carrying trade transactions. It is then accompanied by the transaction at a higher yield rate in another currency. Ultimately, that will end in a good carry trade. Primarily this technique is seen in the Forex market.

Length of trade

Carry trades are based on interest rate fluctuations between the associated currencies. Hence, trade duration supports the medium to long-term (weeks, months, and possibly years).

Entry/Exit points

Strong trend markets operate well for carrying trades because this approach requires a longer period of time. Confirmation of the pattern should be the first move before trading (higher highs and higher lows and vice versa)-see Illustration 1 above. A carry-trade has two facets, namely exchange rate risk and interest rate risk. Thus, the beginning of a cycle is the best time to profit completely on the fluctuation of the exchange rate, and thus the optimal moment to open the positions. With respect to the interest rate variable, everything would be the same regardless of the trend since the trader would always earn the interest rate difference if the first currency named has a higher interest rate relative to the second currency called, e.g., AUD/JPY.

Consider the following pros and cons, and see if the Forex strategy suits your trading style.

Pros

The pros of subject trading strategy are:

- Does not require a high time investment
- Moderate risk-to-reward ratio

Cons

The cons of subject trading strategy are:

- Must have a good understanding of the Forex market
- Less frequent trading opportunities

5.11 Forex Strategies: The Bottom line

It may be helpful to measure how much time commitment is needed behind the monitor when deciding a trading approach to follow. One should also take into consideration the risk-reward ratio and regularity of the overall trading opportunities. Based on personal characteristics, each trading technique can appeal to different traders. In the end, balancing the style of trading with the required approach would enable traders to take the first move in the right direction.

5.12 Forex Risk Management Tips

Managing Forex risk is one of the most discussed trading issues. On the one side, traders want to minimize the size of their possible losses, but on the other side, traders still want to prosper from making any transaction allowing the maximum potential profit. And there's a widespread perception that you ought to take more chances in order to earn the best returns.

In Forex, the reason many traders lose money is not just inexperience-it's bad risk management. The Forex business is highly volatile because of its uncertainty. Therefore, risk control in Forex is a non-negotiable aspect of performance for both rookies and seasoned traders alike. It is here where the issue emerges about effective risk control.

The critical step to Forex risk management depends on understanding Forex risk

Forex trading risk is generally the risk of loss that may befall a trader during trading. These risks might include:

Market risk

This is the chance that the financial market would behave differently than you might predict, which the most prevalent danger of Forex exchange is. You'll lose money if you think the U.S. dollar would climb against the Euro and purchase the EURUSD currency pair just for it to decline.

Leverage risk

Since most Forex traders use leverage to enable trades that are far greater than their deposit amount, in some situations, much more capital will be lost than you originally deposited.

Interest rate risk

The interest rate of an economy may influence the value of the currency of that country, suggesting traders could be at risk of sudden interest rate adjustments.

Liquidity risk

Some currencies are generally more liquid. This means they are getting more supply and demand, and transactions can be completed very easily. For currencies in which there is less demand, there may be a pause between opening or closing a deal on your trading platform and completing the transaction. This may imply that the transaction is not conducted at the expected price, and as a result, you are making a lower profit (or even losing money).

Forex risk management tips

We have compiled a list of risk management tips, which will help you reduce your Forex risk irrespective of whether you're a new trader or a pro:

- Before entering the Forex market, it is incumbent upon you to educate yourself about the different types of Forex risk. It is also imperative to know of different trading styles, techniques, and trading strategies
- You must not commit all your investment in a single trade. You also need to safeguard your investment by using the risk-management technique of stop-loss
- You come to the market to generate additional revenue streams for your family. You must not risk more than you can afford to lose
- Leverage offers you an opportunity to multiply your profits with limited amounts. However, you must not make excessive use of leverage
- Your profit targets should be realistic and rational. Irrational profit expectations can ruin your trade and be detrimental to you
- Letting your profits run is a good strategy, but you must learn to realize profits by closing profitable trades
- You must start with a sound Forex trading strategy
- You should prepare yourself for the worst, as the Forex market is very unpredictable and extremely volatile
- You must not let your emotions take control of your Forex transactions and need to take effective measures for managing Forex risk
- You should be ready to switch your positions the time you discover that your initial analysis and subsequent trade was wrong

5.13 Best time to trade in the Forex market

Most Forex traders enter the market hard for the first time. They watch numerous economic calendars and transact voraciously on any data update, seeing the 24-hour-a-day, five-day-a-week foreign exchange sector as a comfortable place to transact throughout the day. Not only does this tactic easily deplete a trader's savings, but even the most successful trader will burn out. Unlike Wall Street, which operates on daily business hours, the Forex sector works on four different parts of the world's usual business hours and their corresponding time zones, which ensures trade continues all day and night.

Then what's the substitute for being up the entire night? If traders are willing to develop an awareness of trading hours and set reasonable targets, they would have a much better probability of generating money within a workable timeline. The forex market runs on the normal business hours of four different parts of the world and their respective time zones.

• The U.S./London market overlaps (8 a.m. to noon EST) provide the largest trade frequency and are an ideal fit for trading opportunities.

• The gap between the Sydney / Tokyo markets (2 a.m. to 4 a.m.) is not as extreme as the variance between the USA and London, but also provides opportunities.

5.14 Choosing your Broker

Now we will discuss the attributes that you should look up for when picking a forex broker.

Security

The first and foremost attribute a successful broker ought to have is a strong safety rating. After all, you won't turn over thousands of dollars to somebody who only says he's legal, right?

Fortunately, it is not really hard to verify a forex broker's reputation. Globally, there are enforcement bodies that distinguish the trustworthy from the dishonest.

Before even contemplating placing your money in a broker, make sure the broker is a part of the regulatory bodies.

Transaction Costs

No matter what type of currency dealer you are, like it or not, the trading costs will still be yours. You would have to pay either the spread or a fee each time you start a trade, so it's just reasonable to search for the lowest and most reasonable prices.

Even for a more reputable broker, you can need to abandon tiny transactions.

Ensure that you know if tight spreads are required for your style of trading, and then check your options. It's just about having the right mix between low transaction rates and security.

Deposit and Withdrawal

Good forex brokers would encourage you to deposit cash without any trouble and withdraw your money.

Trading Platform

Most trading operation in online forex dealing is performed via the trading platform of the brokers. That means your broker's trading platform needs to be user-friendly and secure.

Still, search what the trading platform has to deliver while searching for a broker.

A good trading platform must offer a news feed. What about the charting and technical methods that are simple to use? Can it give you all the details you need to deal with properly?

Implementation

It is important that your dealer fills you up with your orders at the best available price.

Under regular market circumstances (e.g., usual liquidity, no big press reports, or unexpected events), there is actually no excuse for the broker not to fill you up at or above the market cost you see as you click on the "sell" or "buy" key.

Customer Service

Brokers aren't flawless, but you ought to choose a broker who you can quickly contact in case of issues.

Conclusion

There was a barter system in the very beginning, i.e., exchanging of commodities with each other according to specific requirements. But its apparent shortcomings contributed to the creation of networks of trade, which were largely embraced. Metal coins entered into the scenario accordingly.

However, during the Middle Ages, the paper form of governmental IOUs demanded authorization of democratic administrations.

Before the First World War, several central banks went on with convertibility to gold to sustain their currencies. Although this also contributed to global turmoil owing to crippling inflation. This was because of increasing paper money availability and little gold coverage. For this purpose, Forex regulations were introduced to safeguard the national interest.

The United States subsequently adopted the Bretton Woods Treaty after World War II. As a result, this arrangement culminated in a regime of set exchange rates that restored, to a degree, the gold standard and regulated the dollar at USD 35 / oz, too.

The other popular currencies were all fixed to the dollar and, therefore, made binding. However, owing to its drawbacks, the rescinding of the Bretton Woods Deal contributed to the free flow of currencies and, thereby, to the development of the Forex sector.

Forex is commonly regarded as the foreign exchange market. Here the brokerage companies and banks are associated with an electronic network. This network helps them to convert the countries' currencies worldwide. It is the world's biggest and the world's chief liquid financial market. The regular dollar value of money trades approaches $5 trillion in the money market. Even also the overall value of all U.S. equities and futures markets fails to hit this level.

The Forex is often viewed as controlled by central banks of the country, as well as commercial and investment banks. This is why private investors favor currency exchange deals. Access to them through various technological developments such as the Internet is fast.

Currencies that are commonly exchanged include the U.S. Dollar, British Pound, Swiss Franc, Japanese Yen, Canadian Dollar, and Australian Dollar. Trade of Forex is conducted round the clock with constant access to traders around the world for five days a week. The emphasis is not on any specific position or sale like it is for the stock or futures markets. Transactions take place over a telephone line or over an electronic network between two parties involved.

The last few decades have seen Forex trade grow into the world's largest industry. By now, all the capital exchange controls have been put off in a number of countries. It also culminated in the markets becoming independent from settling Forex prices according to their perceived values.

Forex trading has gained popularity due to a variety of factors. The most notable involves liquidity accessibility, maximum profitability all day round the clock, and extremely low trading costs. In general, trade here is conducted on a margin basis.

Trading is done using 2 currencies concurrently. But there are still two sides to trade, i.e., long (bought) and short (sold). Trade currency is not necessarily, however, more commonly, with the maximum value.

Spot and forward trades are primary Forex trading functions. This means that if no other action is taken, then within two business days, trading will be concluded.

Another main aspect of the Forex sector is interest rate differentials. Multiple interest rates are paid out by various currencies.

There are other fundamentals of Forex trade as well, but one thing is certain – the growth of Forex has rendered every other financial sector much smaller now. The Forex market, in addition, gives its players enormous lucrative trading prospects.

Stock Market Investing for Beginners

Learn How to Enter the Stock Market | Including the Best Platforms for Trading and Common Mistakes and How to Avoid Them

Written by:

Nathan Real

STOCK MARKET
INVESTING
FOR BEGINNERS
NATHAN REAL

Introduction

Have you ever asked yourself, "What is stock?" Do you ever wonder what it feels like in investing your excess cash or savings to the stock market? Have you ever tried to become a shareholder of a company, well-known or not? Have you tried to browse what it would be like when you invested or purchased stocks in a stock market? Do you even know what the basics of stocks are? Well, this would probably help you as a guide in your beginner's journey in the stock market.

Stocks are said to be the shares held by the shareholders, the holder of the stock certificate who has a claim to be a part of the corporation's assets and earnings. History has proven that investing in stocks has been one of the most effective and efficient way for individuals to build wealth and raise their passive income. Investing in stock is complex. Hence, stocks are still misunderstood by some people. There are factors that must be taken into consideration before investing in stocks, such as the company where to invest and what type of stocks to buy. Thus, stocks usually have two types: the common stock and the preferred stock. When people talk about stocks, they are generally referring to the common stock. In fact, the great majority of stock is issued in this form. It represents a claim on profits (dividends) and confers voting rights. On the other hand, preferred stock usually doesn't come with the voting rights. Also, they are given a guaranteed fixed dividend unlike with the common stocks, which give variable dividends that varies along the profits or earnings of the corporation for a period.

Investing is risky. You need to enrich your investment strategy and be tactical in order to maintain your investment and attain your desired goals. Therefore, investing is truly about "working smarter, not harder."

Chapter 1: Entering the Stock Market

One of the most interesting realms of finance is capital exchange. There are hundreds of inventories accessible for trade from across the globe. For both budgets, there are sufficient inventories. There are shares that pay just a few bucks a share, and other high-end stocks valued tens of billions of dollars.

Capital exchange is a huge market in which billions of dollars are exchanged every day. People of all walks of life trade in stocks in terms of improving profit. Some people work for short sales or other options that rely on the dropping value of the stock. Business variety is one of the main strengths, and there is enough for all to be involved in.

Knowing how to navigate the stock market needs a professional and performing well. Only the strongest and most experienced traders would be able to reliably identify products that are most likely to perform at their peak.

This guide would clarify how the equity market operates and how value stocks may be found.

Difference between Stocks and Options

Trading stocks and options are amongst the best opportunities for investment. Many investment companies offer investors both of those services. What are the dissimilarities between those two opportunities to invest?

In a particular company, the stock is a portion of ownership-how much of anything you own at a particular time. You could own as many stock shares in a firm as you could afford.

An option is not a form of real ownership, but a right to choose and trade a certain investment. You have the right, with an option, to buy or sell a specific stock to a certain value within a given period of time.

Derivative and Intrinsic Values

The intrinsic value of stock refers to the real value of an asset or enterprise. The value is related to how much trust people have in a business and how well that team is growing. Due to news reports or other articles concerning the stock, it may also change in value.

An option is focused on the economic value—a security value at a given time. The value of an option is affected by the stock price, and it simply adjusts to the stock changes.

Long or Short-Term?

There are no specific guidelines about how long an option or stock needs to be kept. Options also have an expiration date. That is, an alternative must be pursued within a specified timeframe. You will specify the exact time limit for the expiry of the contract, authorizing you to perform a transaction or selling at a certain cost at that point. You can hold a running option for as long as you like. Any ideas last an hour. Others may stay for a couple of days or even weeks. Knowing the correct time to pick an alternative is crucial to your plan.

Stocks are special in that as much as you find appropriate, you may keep them. Day traders also sell stocks in the course of a day many times. This is important when contemplating the long-term value-increase ability of a stock. For example, at the beginning of 2014, Home Depot (NYSE: HD) saw its stock traded at about $80.

The same stock was worth a little more than $185 in 2018. Day-traders also profit within a day from shifts in the valuation of a stock. The same Home Depot inventory could start at $185 on a normal day and then go up to $188, drop to $186, and then up again to $188 at the last hour of the day.

What about Dividend Stocks?

Dividend stocks are securities that pay dividends to shareholders, and the prices of such dividends can differ. If their prices begin to grow and the business stays successful, you'd be more likely to make a return from stocks. Shares of dividends can be valuable as long as you accept their efficiency. You'd need to study how often shares you need to buy if you want to take advantage of a dividend portfolio. You'll later hear about a calculation to use in this guide to decide what you'd have to pay on an inventory to have a dollar in dividend payments; this formula will impact the size of the spot you'd like to purchase.

Who Could Benefit from Day-Trading?

There are several groups of individuals who should have benefited more from day trading:

- Those who want better returns over shorter durations can get more from the day-trading phase. It is independent of whether one is trading in options or stocks.

- Anybody who likes to be the master of their life would enjoy day-trading. You will operate similarly to your own timetable for this while selling at a rate where you are relaxed.

- You don't have to be heavily trained to be a decent day-trader. Getting some experience does benefit, which you can read earlier in this part.

- Day traders will operate on any assets they like. Trading websites promote the discovery of exclusive products and opportunities for them. When combined with prescreening software, making the correct options becomes simpler for the day traders.

- People will be enthusiastic, like day-trading, if they want an interesting job atmosphere. In a day trader's job, there really is a boring moment.

What Problems Persist with Day Trading?

As fun as becoming a day-trader may be, you should be mindful of any issues.

- There's still a chance to lose money on a deal. Those losses may also be largely based on how a product travels. This might be severe if they don't put the correct stop-loss instructions.

- Before you can finally start trading, you will have to buy the necessary supplies. In this chapter, these products are discussed later.

- It may be overwhelming to someone not completely trained or able to tackle any of the involving trades. You have to be able to rapidly conduct transactions. The real chance for a transaction may also be incredibly limited.

- Most day-traders can operate from 9:30 am to 4 pm Eastern Time, mostly during the entire daily trading day. Any traders could swap far past those hours.

- Making a profit entails difficulty. While you can make different minor trades now and then, once you are willing to purchase bigger positions, it is far simpler for you to earn money.

What Does It Take to be a Great Day Trader?

Anyone might be a successful day trader as long as that individual is very well trained and experienced. To make the best of day trading operations, you must have the necessary skills to:

- Successful buyers understand how to recognize the success of securities and can detect those trends of exchange.

- People will know the history of the company whose inventories they regard. Even the overall profits and other internal considerations inside a company may have a strong effect on a stock market feeling.

- Analysis competencies are important to all traders. Traders ought to be able to recognize certain products and how they're changing.

- The strongest traders would stay centered on the specific stocks into which they plan to buy. People also find it convenient to lose count of the products they have available in the market.

- You will have to properly regulate your feelings. Being upset over any exchange is really simple, not going as far as one would have thought. A brilliant day-trader knows what to expect. An investor may look for what is going into a portfolio when checking for contingency plans to avoid future losses lower than they should be.

What You Need for Trading

You'll hear what you should do to win the investment market all through this tutorial. You'll need to get the necessary tools available for trade purposes to make this effective. There are some items you're going to really need that are built to keep track of the competition while still being able to perform well.

Enough Money for Trades

To get started, a sensible budget for day trading will need to be set. You should determine how much money you are prepared to spend on your trades. More specifically, you ought to consider what you're prepared to sacrifice. There's always a chance all your trades might be duds. You should plan your budget on the assumption you are not actually making a profit. Playing the financial markets is about finding ways to make money in the process without spending too much.

To make business on the exchange, you'll need a minimum capital of $25,000. This is enough capital to help you make several trades without leverage or spreads being needed. In some trades, you might still be able to use leverage or margins, though that is a purely unnecessary solution.

U.S exchanges and securities Commission or SEC states that, if you plan on trading, you need to have $26,000 or more in equity:

1. Anyone who trades four to five times in 5 business days will need $25,000 in equity or more. The SEC perceives day-trading as a process on the same day on which you purchase and sell things.

2. You will have this volume of money available if your portfolio's day-trades equal at least 6 % of your overall trading operation for the next five business days.

If you can, add more than the $26,000 required to your day-trading account. A bit of extra money lets you work with a buffer. This ensures some freedom in handling whatever trades you wish to complete in the future.

Sensible Strategies

Build a plan with your trades that you can use. Your plan could be focused on such factors as:

- If you get interested in a transaction
- How to stay out of this deal
- The cumulative danger you are at in every transaction
- An overview of how good stock performs
- As you can learn in this tutorial, your financial strategy can contain several techniques in your trading plans, depending on

what you find, depending on your analysis, and common sense in general.

Online Resources

To support you handle your transactions, you may have to use professional online tools. There're numerous trading sites that can help you find available commodities, help you conduct transactions, and others that show all the specifics of how commodities travel. You must be presented with historical details from one of those services.

Even a portfolio screener is important to your progress in investing. It allows you to get product statistics depending on unique requirements. You are actually applying different parameters to the software and only making the best choices.

A Strong Mindset

The most critical thing you require is a strong attitude for day-trading. You need to be emotionally prepared to deal and able to consider what might happen, and be ready to react quickly when anything unforeseen occurs. If it's the price that unexpectedly dipped or an opportunity that arrives at the right moment, you need to know when and how to play the stock market and when to keep out. You will need to develop a mentality based on a plan and sticking with it during the whole investing phase. It is possible to lose sight of what you do while you are trading. You could run across some successful trades you didn't intend to see, and maybe you're not completely equipped to make such trades. Perhaps worse, you may feel like dumping a plan because it doesn't succeed over and over again. Don't shirk the plan. Being stubborn and oblivious is important to help you remain focused.

Proper Education

And if you are not allowed to obtain a trade degree in the industry, you should at least have the necessary experience. It's better to take benefit of an educational curriculum that shows you how to make trades and what's open.

If you read this document, of course, then the chances are that you already grasp the many points about online trading. There are numerous online trading institutions that will provide you with knowledge about how the business operates. Companies such as the Internet Trading School, TradePro School, Market Whisper, Day-Trading Academy, champion's Edge Trading, and several other organizations with their own web programs. These applications can also be used by even folks who understand about trading to clear up any doubt one may have on how to exchange properly. You will use them in this tutorial to learn the techniques you'll be thinking about.

Chapter 2: How to Choose the Right Stock for You?

It's crazy how many stocks there are, and you can find stocks from every part of the world easily in any area. The first approach is to know what securities to invest in. It is important to know how to select a warehouse. There are lots of factors to remember when determining which stocks are right for you. These points are important for evaluating any methods you intend to use to invest.

Choose Field Stocks You Understand

The first tip for locating a stock is to search for stock details in an area you have particular expertise about. Investing in stocks is better because you recognize the demand in which stock is sold, the variables affecting the sector, and the uncertainty the stock of interest may be facing.

As long as Home Depot is concerned, you should be aware that the stock is powered by the building and home renovation sector. You will also recognize that the industry includes rivalry in the U.S. and Canada with Lowe's, True Value, Home Appliances, and several other firms. Investigate the Warehouse at Home and the rivalry. Your market experience will make you feel more secure about the product you are buying.

The National Market

The New York Stock Exchange and NASDAQ comprise the vast majority of the worldwide trading volume. That doesn't suggest you ought to confine yourself to just two platforms. You can transact products from numerous markets across the world as well. These include the Shanghai Stock Exchange, the Japan Stock Exchange, Euronext, and the London Stock Exchange. The economy of one nation may also be drastically different from another. E.g., there may be a bull market in Canada where the trading of the TMX Group is located or in

Germany where people are trading on the Deutsche Borse. A bear market in India, meanwhile, could trigger India's Bombay Stock Exchange and National Stock Exchange to fall in value. So it's best to stay with stocks based on markets that you're comfortable with. Analysis markets outside of the NYSE or NASDAQ would be appropriate. Just because an American stock is doing well, that doesn't mean every other market in the world will do the same. The economies in the U.S. are simpler to evaluate.

Do You Know the Company?

You ought to study the business you intend to invest in. It contains the following things to know:

- What the company does.
- Where it stands.
- The manufacturing sector.
- Any other business rivals.
- Updates what is being achieved by the company; this involves big news reports.

Take SandRidge Resources, Inc. (NYSE: SD), for example. If you hear about SandRidge? The chances are you will not be acquainted with the business unless you hear about the Oklahoma City natural gas and petroleum sector, even whether you live near the company headquarters.

You may be more conscious of Yum! Products, Inc. (NYSE: YUM). This corporation is an agency running fast-food franchises KFC, Pizza Hut, and Taco Bell. You might have easier access to knowledge on what Yum! The brand is doing since the company itself is so famous all around the world.

You have the luxury of investing in businesses you're not acquainted with, but you can do as much homework as possible on the company and how the business works, and how it has developed through the years. Check the website of that company, and read its financial results. Make sure that you have enough details and don't fail to locate data in a warehouse. Having as much knowledge as possible about a business is critical to your success in the sector.

Review Price Trends

The next thing to remember is how the valuation of a stock is increasing. And the stock has its own pattern on how it can go up or down over time.

One reason to remember is how, over the years, Sears Holdings (NASDAQ: SHLD) has undergone a downward trend in its portfolio. In 2004, Sears Shares saw a significant boost in its market valuation as the stock rose from $20 to $110 over the span of a year. Soon afterward, in 2006, the price fell to $80. In the late part of 2015, the stock exchanged about $20. Since then, the stock had been falling, and two years later also dropped below the $5 level.

Price patterns may be useful, but you can remember how long such patterns have been taking place and whether any major improvements have occurred. The Sears Holdings case is only one of a variety of instances of how market patterns will change. Only because a stock is dropping in value doesn't mean it will continue to go down. There is a possibility the supply might be going back up. Positive economic reports or stronger market confidence among investors may trigger this to happen.

Work with Moving Averages

A smart way to track market patterns is to take a peek at the moving average of a stock. That refers to a set of stock market averages over a prolonged period of time.

You might, for example, set a 14-day moving average to see if the valuation of a stock is increasing. That calls for the following:

1. Take from each of the last 14 days the selling price of one volume.

2. Put all 14 of those values, so they come together.

3. Break the number by 14.

4. This shows you the total moving average.

5. Produce as many moveable averages as possible for stretches of 14 days. For, e.g., you might match the moving average for March 1-14 with the average for March 2-15, March 3-16, etc.

By using as many statistical averages as practicable, you will get an understanding of how the valuation of a stock varies. Fast-moving averages favor day traders. A combination of short and long-term averages can be used when appropriate. That will offer you an understanding of how the economy and the prices of individual stocks shift. Looking at how a stock might change in a short period of time is crucial to your trading success, particularly if you are attempting to do brief trading as a day trader.

Revenue and Debt Relationship

Revenues and loans are a justification for themselves. Such specifics can be contained in a stock's official SEC records.

Clearly, a company that receives more money would do better work. It will have ample funds to compensate its workers, finance numerous activities, and offset any of the costs or loans. While the profits of the company are important, the loans it retains may be crippling. This includes costs to acquire new properties, loans, or handle different workers ' wages. Debts, such as monthly debit fees and interest rates, can be ongoing. They can also be one-time payments for materials that are needed for operating needs. It would be risky to invest in a company that carries a lot of debt. This may be a major challenge stopping an organization from reflecting on its overall development.

Note the debt-revenue difference and how it has evolved over time. A company's financial statements can show what affected those numbers and how they might be predicted to continue to shift.

Compare Stock Performance with Other Related Choices

The next suggestion is to examine if some inventories are performing close to what you choose to invest in. This gives you an understanding of how well a product is doing in the same industry and if it is really different from others.

Let's presume you have looked at Macy's stock (NYSE: M). On a map, you can find that Macy's stock is growing up or down in value without any clear long-term pattern. Look at other companies in the same shopping industry to see if Macy's is a successful company in which to buy. You may be searching for details regarding Kohl's (NYSE: KSS) and that the valuation of Kohl's stock has been slowly increasing. Owing to its success, maybe Kohl's would be a safer stock to invest in.

Check different inventories within the same area. If you would be operating with a retail stock, check out four or five market-oriented products and see which one is growing the most. Check those businesses' histories to see what renders these organizations successful or efficient.

What is Best for Short or Long-Term Needs?

Taking a peek at the patterns certain stocks make. How long have those patterns taken place? Perhaps a stock is decreasing rapidly like Sears, or as the Home Depot, it is unpredictable. An exceptionally unpredictable portfolio will be the best fit for day-trading purposes. The Home Store stock can be worthwhile for day trading since the stock fluctuates in value every day.

Meanwhile, it may be easier to hang on to a stock that has a long-term pattern. Is the stock you are involved in, without facing any opposition, steadily increasing in value? Isn't the stock at risk for some major losses in the future? If so, you may want to save and hang onto the stock for the near future. Realizing the right returns will take months or even years, so it'll certainly be worthwhile.

Signs a Stock is Better for Day-Trading

You don't have to swap any exchange that you do. You may take a few stocks over time that are guaranteed to grow in value and hang on to them for months. Here are a number of things to remember whether a stock might be safer for day trading or at least for keeping just a few days at a time:

A stock with a daily amount of or greater than 1 million.

The stock would be more prone to shift in value while the price is high. In only a few minutes, she might make major changes.

Profit holdings are larger.

When you sell a highly rated product, the chance for a big profit is greater. In a few hours, a stock worth $200 a share might shift its value from $10 to $20. Anything that is only $20 per share might be shifting for just a couple of bucks at a time.

Assets are highly unpredictable.

For day trading, a stock whose value varies from 1 to 5 percent every day is great. A stock with a higher volatility rate may shift its valuation so dramatically; you have to be ready to execute those trades.

You're not too preoccupied with the business history.

While it helps to learn how well a firm works and what it does, you may have just a few minutes or hours in stock at that business. At this stage, you do not really have to do any analysis (you can also do some study).

Signs a Stock Works for Long-Term Investing

Now let's speak at the other end of the spectrum in trade. This listing suggests signals that you can spend months in stock, rather than just a few hours:

Why a business earns profits is simple for you to clarify to others.

You might claim, for example, that you realize that Kohl's or Macy's earns its money by selling branded products and fashions to others. Every company that you appreciate is important and can quickly clarify.

For a corporation to remain operating, it doesn't require any control.

Look at the costs a corporation would have to keep operating. Perhaps a corporation will have to invest a lot of capital in equipment and personnel. In some instances, a business is only purchasing from vendors and exporting certain products. In the situation, figure out what it means for a company to run even why there isn't a lot of money to deal with. Any company which does not need a great deal of control may be easier to trust.

A firm has some type of good or service, providing a distinct advantage.

Macy's has several in-house and foreign distributors selling famous high-end products. Kohl's gives its consumers various incentive schemes. Sears provides garments as well as furniture, and also vehicle repair facilities. All three of these retail entities are distinct, but they all have similar stuff about them, which makes them interesting. These distinct characteristics, more specifically, help a company remain alive and successful.

The pattern of a stock is steady and doesn't seem like it will shift soon anywhere.

The most significant indicator of this is how effectively a commodity movement performs over the long run. Look through some moveable averages over the last couple of weeks to see how well a portfolio is doing. For, e.g., you can check a stock price over the past 10 to 15 Fridays. This shows how the valuation of the stock changed over time. Stock could be worth investing in if you think the moving average has been gradually increasing. Something that proceeds to go up is a safe investment.

There are still the right products out there that are easy to work out and grasp while getting completely understood patterns.

Chapter 3: Evaluating an SEC Report

One of the best ways to learn about what stocks to invest in is to look at the official SEC reports that are the issue of different companies. Any public company that has a stock must issue one of these reports annually.

How data of a stock is laid out in an SEC report is one of the best strategies you can use to find good stocks in which to invest. You have to identify a lot of specifics in the report as you look at these data.

Background of a Report

To see why incorporating an SEC report into your trading research efforts is so important, you need to see why such reports exist in the first place. Any SEC report is a document that must be sent to the United States Securities and Exchange Commission by a publicly-traded company. These reports were required since 1933, when the Securities Act was passed a few years earlier after the major stock market crash. The American government passed this to ensure transparency and specificity of all financial reports from publicly traded companies. This allows investors to make sensible choices about what to invest in. This would discourage them from making stock purchases that they do not fully understand, a problem that primarily caused the 1929 stock market crash.

By sharing all of its information with the public, a business ensures that fraudulent activities do not occur as likely as they do. Any business in which you may wish to invest should have a proper SEC report. The company report should be detailed, and many documents should be provided to prove the company's worth and operations. Any business which fails to provide sufficient SEC information could be suspicious.

10-K Report

The first part of looking at an SEC report is the 10-K report. This is a basic document that provides a complete summary of the performance of a firm. It is different from the report that a business gives its shareholders in that there are no electoral processes provided by the 10-K report.

This document is vital for understanding the workings of a business. It lets you see how the company operates and its different holdings and details. The information is valuable in its fullness. In fact, the 10-K report is the one thing you should analyze when looking at the SEC report above all others. It showcases the basics you need to know to make a worthwhile investment.

Summary of Operations

The first point to look at in the 10-K report relates to the operations summary. Including:

1. Background of the business

The background of the business provides information about what it is doing. For example, Apple's 10-k report (NASDAQ: AAPL) states that the technology firm focuses on making consumer products such as software, networking items, media players, and more.

2. Strategy for the business

The strategy includes how the enterprise moves forward. In the case of Apple, the strategy devises new products and services within the company's own tech platform. This includes, among other features, working with a wide array of third-party development programs.

3. Latest offerings information

The offers must include the physical as well as the non-physical items a company has. Apple's 10-k report has details of the different products it has to offer, such as the iPhone and iPad. It also reports on services and software programs such as the software for the iOS operating system and iCloud cloud storage. Offered general services. The 10-k report also gives details of what a company offers outside of its products. Apple's 10-k report says it offers an extensive customer service team located in the U.S. along with a couple of other call centers in various parts of the world.

4. Competition points

The 10-k report does not require specific names of any particular competitors. It should still include information on how other parties could be offering certain products or services in the same field. In the report, the information could also be found on what a company is doing to try and make itself competitive or distinct from others.

5. Data on research and development

The section on research and development should include what a company is doing to find new products and make them available. It can include information on how much money a company spends on R&D functions. Apple's 10-k report shows that, in 2013, it spent nearly twice as much on R&D operations as it did in 2011.

6. Licenses, patents, trademarks, and copyrights

Any new applications can be included for those legal markers. This shows how committed a company is to what it offers and how prepared it is for any legal issues that may arise. You could benefit from investing in a firm that takes care of its efforts. Don't expect to be overly detailed in this section. The company has only to list how it acquires legal protection to cover any applications that have been sent out, regardless of whether they have been accepted in full or not.

7. Foreign coverage

The foreign data refers to their operations outside of their base country. In its 10-k report, Apple lists outsourcing partners across Asia as well as a couple of other groups around North America and Europe. Apple lists this to let people know the company has a foreign presence for both where it sells items and where it makes its products.

8. Seasonal business

The report on seasonality has details of when a firm is doing much of its business. Apple says a significant portion of its sales occurs during the first quarter of the operation of that business. This is around the Christmas season when Apple is selling a large number of gift products.

In the 10-k report, you can use that point to strategize when you want to invest. In the first quarter of the organization, you would have better success investing in Apple because it is a moment when the firm is rising and flourishing.

Financial Outlook Information

The next part of the 10-k report relates to the financial approaches a company uses. A section that reads "Selected Financial Data" should list the financial data. The information may include the following:

- The net revenue from the operations of the business
- The Big Margin
- Costs for development and research
- Operating Revenue
- The effective tax rate an enterprise works with
- The total value of the assets an enterprise has

- The debt the company holds

How many employees a business has; this could explain part of why expenses may, in some cases, start to rise.

Financial information should also include historical points. Take the 10-k report, which was released to the public by Intel (NASDAQ: INTC). This includes information on the company's net revenue from 2007 through 2016. The report shows Intel's revenues in 2016 were nearly $60 billion. That total increased to $52 billion in 2013 from $35 billion in 2009. It is important to get historical information to understand how well a business is developing and how its finances have changed. The financial perspective has to be as thorough as possible to know whether or not something is an appropriate choice for your investment.

Balance Sheet

The balance sheet is the next section of the 10-k report. This should be listed near the report's section called "Financial Statements and Supplementary Data." The sheet is to contain the following information:

1. The company assets

These can include assets for both the short and long term. Such assets may involve currency, inventory, receivable accounts, and other investments. It should also include any equipment or properties that a business holds.

2. The liabilities of the company

Short-term liabilities are orders that could come to pass right now. Customer advances, payable accounts, and any taxes or interest that an enterprise owes should be included. Long-term bonds are debts. These include debts payable for bonds or any lengthy loans to be paid off. In this information listing, the short and long-term debts should be divided into their own sections.

3. Equity of Shareholders

This refers to the assets, minus the obligations. It's a baseline measure of how healthy a business is. The total focuses on what might be returned to shareholders in the event of liquidation of the company's assets and paying off its debts. A business whose total equity is increasing is always worth investing in, since that company stock has a better chance of adding value.

This section should contain information regarding both the preferred and current stock associated with a company. Preferred stock is for those who receive more dividends and may have more access to certain assets in the company. Common stock includes voting rights for major decisions a company makes. (Note: most of the stocks you'll find on the market are common stocks; preferred stocks are typically offered to business people).

The inclusion of these three points on the balance sheet is crucial. There are a couple of strategies that you can use to help you decide whether to make an investment in a company:

Focus on the assets underway. These are the assets that could be converted to cash.

Looking at the current assets helps you find out why the finances of a business may have changed in recent times and whether there has been a significant influx of sales or contracts.

Is it intangible to non-current assets?

Intangible assets include the overall reputation and goodwill a firm holds. A company such as Intel or Apple may have a considerable amount of goodwill because they have produced various products for many people, and each has a dedicated fan base.

Watch for depreciation, which could interfere with an investment.

Here the depreciation refers to the times when the value of the investment shrinks. In the course of time, physical equipment or goods may depreciate, causing the total value of the assets to fall.

Review how long the debts could last.

Some long-term debts might include loans that could last for ten years or more. Others may sunset after a year, thereby allowing a company more flexibility from an acquisition perspective on what it can do.

Calculate the ratio to debt.

The debt ratio can be used to help you figure out how worthwhile investment is. Take overall debt, divide it by total assets. A business with $15 million in debts, for instance, could have $25 million in assets. In this case, the debt ratio would be 0.6. In other words, assets clearly outweigh the debts.

What if it had reversed those numbers? A company with a debt of $25 million and assets of $15 million would have a debt ratio of 1,666.

An enterprise with a higher debt ratio will certainly be dangerous to consider investing in. This type of business would be in real trouble because it has insufficient assets. You should still look at why so many debts the business has attained just to find out what's going on in the business.

Income Statement

The income statement is a valuable guide to read before determining your financial plan. The statement of income refers to the statistics to represent what a company receives over time.

For at least the last three years of business, the statement should include facts. Anything else of history details helps provide you a better picture of where a company is heading and how any costs have been accumulated over the years.

The declaration of income should contain the following details:

1. Complete Wages

2. The proportion of profits

The distinction is the gross benefit or gross loss of the two points.

1. Operational expenses

These expenditures can include R&D, general operating costs, and other non-recurring expenditures.

To get the net taxable gain or loss, deduct the operational costs from the gross profit.

2. Income from running operations

This gain is what an organization receives between debt and taxation.

3. Tax and insurance payments

Depreciation expenses should be found in this portion or reported on a separate line, at least.

To calculate the net gain, deduct interest and tax from the profits.

Orient the plans on companies that gain adequate money when opposed to the costs they have. Taxes might be higher in value when a company is earning more profits, so that's only a normal evolution of how a company is progressing. Tax expenditures can differ depending on where the company is organized. This might affect the study since it might be a company in another area of the world where taxes are low or zero. In the beginning, the 10-k filing can inform you whether the company is organized outside of where it is headquartered, so you at least know that tax losses will not be important.

Cash Flow Report

The cash flow report is a cash flow study, a calculation of how much money is being exchanged inside and outside a company. It is a liquidity indicator since it tests how effectively a corporation can hold its activities alive. If a company makes the best decisions to pay off loans, control its inventory, or even its R&D operations, it lets you know.

The cash balance analysis contains more detail on what's going on in a company than an income statement. The concern with a declaration of income is that it just deals with issues relating to the currency. The cash flow report contains any asset and feature in the statement and gives you a clearer understanding of what the assets and role of a company are, in fact. That doesn't suggest you can disregard the income statement; all statements are crucial to know whether or not you can spend. Reporting cash flow may include:

1. The Group's total profits

2. The funds flow from activities

The cash flow relates to the income that has been invested over a period of time or received by the company. This may provide information concerning loan transactions, borrower settlement costs, and so on. A cash balance analysis may provide clear explanations that that is the location where the cash flow is. This may entail rises in payable accounts and reductions in receivable accounts.

Of course, you're going to want to choose an organization with a much greater cash balance. There are occasions where a corporation may have a negative cash balance as more capital flows out of the market.

1. The asset portfolios included

Cash used to sell or acquire valuable properties may be mentioned here. Which may provide descriptions of appliances, computers, chairs, stocks, insurance policies, or something else that is being utilized at a time. A company that invests more in its acquisitions will have lower cash flow, but it still continues to expand. Such new ventures may be used for potential gains and to render things more profitable or otherwise competent inside a company.

Such businesses may disburse more spending capital or at least save some of their assets for potential use. This is particularly true of software inventories. Tech businesses also budget large sums of capital for new developments or for whatever potential future demands they expect.

2. Cash earned or charged by support

It may mention the money earned by or charged to creditors and owners requires trading of securities or shares. Dividend companies can provide specifics of how they pay out dividends. If need be, certain businesses might buy back their stocks.

This 10-k report segment is critical in that it reflects extensively on how the company could develop. There are several factors that cause the cash flow of a stock to rise directly:

- Sales Extra;
- Taking out current long-term distribution arrangements for other firms or organizations;
- selling products;
- Sell off stocks or other commodities;
- Any investment that expanded until it was sold off; these involve some capital the firm has.

Cash flow decreases may arise due to a number of problems:

- Employee bonuses ought to be compensated out.

- Gain modern appliances or services.
- Bill for vehicle replacements and servicing.
- Having holders pay dividends.
- Lawsuits or other types of litigation; the damages may be factored into the valuation of legal problems.

This is only a short rundown of the cash flow decreases and increases you may find while looking for an investment.

A few helpful suggestions to consider while reading a cash flow chart are:

Although positive cash flow is often good, when the cash flow comes from activities, it is much better.

When the revenue arrives from sales, it means that the firm is producing adequate profits and that further products or new pieces of machinery are accessible to it. An organization with less than half its cash from sales may be too costly to invest in.

Is One Organization Increased Its Operations?

A company with negative cash flow may be halfway into an expansion project. This means the company is attempting to expand and has to invest money in coping with the growth. See what reduced the surge.

Look at the Loan Duration

Loans may be planned years in advance of being due. A loan can also be paid back earlier. Check if and over what time the debts are being charged.

To understand the meaning of cash flow, take a look at WorldCom's illustration. In the 2000s, the stock of the business dropped apart in a spectacular fashion. Many people saw WorldCom's revenue development was substantial, but they did not pay attention to the cash flow. What the investors didn't realize was that WorldCom's cash balance was very weak and substantially weaker than net profits. WorldCom could not spend and be losing money amid all its rise in sales. Any investor who saw weak cash flow from WorldCom may have made the right step and chose not to invest in the stock directly. Given how WorldCom broke apart, the safest bet must certainly have been to keep away.

Legal Proceedings

An overview of a report's court action is important. This applies to the litigation or other complex legal cases a company is going through. There are cases outside of regular proceedings.

Let's switch back to a 10-k filing from Apple. In their 2013 paper, Apple published details about a few court proceedings it had encountered.

Apple was losing about $370 million in a 2010 lawsuit against a corporation that argued that Apple had infringed those patents. It also covered a 2012 event in which Apple was awarded over $1 billion by another action.

The segment on legal action should provide information on the official identities of the court cases concerned and how much money they were worth irrespective of whether the judge favored. Every detail should be given about whether the action was launched.

You may want to look for more details on every company's court actions by investigating the cases on the organizations' pages that handled such cases. For example, a lawsuit considered by the Department of Justice in the United States may be investigated electronically at www.justice.gov. You will need to go and www.uscourts.gov to provide more details about lawsuits being conducted within those U.S. jurisdictions. These pages will provide you with comprehensive details on legal hearings and additional material specific to certain events.

In this section of a 10-k filing, a corporation can be clear and transparent on the legal proceedings. An organization that is able to provide as much detail as possible regarding these cases is much easier to trust, and the business is not reluctant to discuss any of its issues. You can still glance at such unofficial pages when a corporation may also want to withhold details regarding its legal problems.

Risk Factors

The 10-k study describes the risk factors a company faces. These considerations provide worries a company thinks would have a significant effect on its potential earnings. Think of it as SWOT analysis' W component.

The 10-k report by Intel mentions various risk factors that could harm the company. The study shows how the organization is having trouble forecasting demand for its goods. It also addresses how Intel experiences substantial rivalry and is therefore exposed to several factors in overseas markets that may potentially create a difference in how much the organization is capable of earning sales and maintaining itself operating.

The threats mentioned here can involve both the global sector and business-related concerns. Intel reports that it is a danger of product flaws or failures that may harm its goods. This risk could result in recalls or major costs, not to mention the possibility of undermining Intel's credibility.

Both of these points on the 10-k report are important for you to evaluate while determining which stocks to invest in. Review the whole report before conducting a transaction so you can appreciate where a company is heading and how it might actually affect its valuation.

10-Q Report

A 10-q filing parallels a 10-k filing that reports on a company's quarterly job.

Let's look at a 10-q filing, published in July 2017 by the Coca-Cola Corporation (NYSE: KO). This was from April until June 2017, with financial details across the year.

The 10-q study by Coca-Cola comprised a variety of important things:

1. Financial statements related to corporate income, operating expenditure, taxation, and varying expenditures

Many of the financial aspects outlined in the 10-q filing are similar to what is included in a 10-k study. This also offers a clearer understanding of what a business just did.

2. Information about any major changes that occurred during the previous quarter

In its 10-q filing, Coca-Cola reported that it had acquired a plant-based beverage firm and also franchised some of its operations in China.

3. Agreements signed with some parties

At a specified period, these arrangements can be transactions between particular individuals for services and goods from separate companies and offers.

4. Lawsuits and risk factors pending

In certain instances, you would refer back to an organization published in the last 10-k report. This is about situations where the consumer has not had something new happen.

You should also provide information to some court proceedings which are currently pending.

8-k Report

The Latest Filing is also regarded as the 8-k audit. Companies discuss this because they have significant activities they wish to let the public know about. The research is also on something that allows a business to rise in scale. In some situations, the research is on certain daunting topics that may be warning flags about the investing plan. An 8-k filing for consideration of any of the following may be filed:

- Issuing insolvency
- Entering or rejecting a binding content deal
- Completion of a big takeover bid
- Any incidents that trigger an adjustment to a financial commitment
- Cases where forecasts that a company is supposed to receive are drastically adjusted in value; this typically occurs when something's quality declines
- Changes to ethical business policy
- The presentation of core problems and inventions to be placed to the ballot of shareholders

The 8-k Coca-Cola Business study published in mid-February 2018 is one indication of that. The firm released an 8-k filing claiming that the organization had an excellent financial performance for the fourth quarter of the previous fiscal year. The study contained detail about many of the financial changes happening at the moment. In December 2017, Coca-Cola submitted an 8-k filing reporting a resignation of a key member of the business management. In October 2017, another research from the same firm claimed the business had a positive performance in the third quarter.

There are no restrictions on how many 8-k files a company may put out. You'd have to glance at how it mentions these. When writing these reports, an organization can be very comprehensive and straightforward, so customers can consider what leads a business to move in any manner.

Internal Functions

SEC reports may provide descriptions of all the internal operations that an organization requires. It provides a thorough overview of how the company is run and who is in charge, as well as any unusual acts that certain persons participate in. There are three basic records to analyze when examining an enterprise's organizational operations.

Proxy Statement

The proxy statement applies to details from management and the company's reports. It must be submitted before an annual meeting where shareholders are permitted to vote on operations taking place within the organization. The study gives you an overview of how the company administration functions and how the people concerned could get compensated. It also mentions potential questions about conflicts of interest that individuals might have with such auditors.

To grasp the workings of a proxy document, let's look at the document issued in April 2017 by Southwest Airlines (NYSE: LUV). The declaration contained the following points:

- Details about how citizens should become interested in voting
- How democratic procedures work
- The specifics of the persons concerned and any conflicts of interest they might have

The Southwest Airlines proxy statement stated that owing to numerous reasons linked to expertise and abilities, separate Board members could continue to retain their seats—the individuals were identified citing their experience in education, prior employment in the aviation sector, and so on.

Details Regarding How to Pay Employees

Southwest listed unique incentive details that executives will be entitled to receive depending on those success criteria. This provides the volume of revenue handled at a specified period. Performance rewards and promotions can be laid out in a proxy document. It indicated requirement of future payments, as well as other incentives such as private car use or unique travel facilities.

Functions Report

The classification of who is on the audit committee has been listed to describe how the auditing method will be structured inside the company.

You will locate corporation proxy documents by doing the following:

1. Go to the SEC website and check the report on EDGAR.

2. Join the individual company that you want details for.

3. Scan for a report that is titled DEF 14A. This gets its name as the final proxy statement, according to Section 14(a) of the Stock Exchange Act.

What is interesting about the proxy statement? The proxy statement is essential for a company to notify shareholders regarding the corporate executive functions. It helps us realize that a company has a reasonable strategy in motion to affect the path the company would take in the future as those decisions are to be taken.

You should suggest participating in firms that have open and clear proxy records. Sometimes those companies are easy to trust, and they want customers to grasp their operation's workings.

Schedule 13D

Schedule 13D is a part of SEC filings, covering details about who owns shares. A firm must file it within ten days of a person acquiring 5 percent or more of any security. This provides information on how much of the company's shares might be managed by one person. It could be a sign that one person could have a heavy influence on a business. The Report on Schedule 13D must include:

- Details on safety
- Information about the person who was securitized
- That should include the contact information and background of a person. Any such person's criminal records should be listed, as appropriate.
- The financing source for the transaction
- The money occasionally comes from leveraged or borrowed funds. A transaction that uses money is always better when the investor actually has complete control.
- The reason someone acquires these shares; it's also called the transaction purpose
- This could be because an investor is very much interested in a particular company and feels the stock is undervalued. It could also be a sign that someone is trying to acquire a significant portion of the company. Even those who try to get involved in a hostile takeover should be listed here.
- Any contracts or relationships within the business which the investor has with other people
- Letters and other documents telling how the transaction took place

The form in Schedule 13D is part of the SEC filing that should be reviewed for details and to determine whether someone wants to acquire a significant number of shares.

Form 144

Form 144 deals with how the stocks are made publicly available. Form 144 must be filed when the company plans to sell stock to someone associated with it. This includes an executive, a director, or another figure.

Form 144 is a simple two-page document. It has the following details to be filled out:

- Name of the Stock issuer;
- Title of the securities class which will be sold;
- The number of shares to go on sale;
- The market value of said shares;
- How much stock is outstanding;
- When it is expected to sell the shares;
- The names of the securities exchanges used at a given time;
- Information about any other securities that the person selling the shares has sold in the last three months.

Form 144 should be a factor in your investment strategy as you look at how the shares are made publicly available. Sometimes a report on Form 144 is a sign that someone in a company wants to retire and will sell off their shares. In other cases, it could be a sign that something big will happen in the business, like someone else buying out part of that entity.

Added Tips

Anything that goes into the SEC reports of a company will give you a good idea of how a business is run and what makes it exceptional or distinct. While the listed information is worthwhile, there are many intricate parts of an SEC report that you should also delve into. These features tell you more about the stock and can help you formulate your investment strategies.

Review the EPS

Seeking the EPS is a valuable strategy to use. This refers to one stock's earnings per share. Although a company does not have to declare that total in its SEC report, you can still easily figure this out:

1. Look up the net income shown in the report.

2. Divide that net revenue by the number of shares held by the investors.

3. That should give you an idea of how much money each share is involved in.

This is a good measure of how well an enterprise is doing. When the EPS is high, that means the business grows and evolves. This might be a good time to invest, but you should still look into why the total is moving up as much as it is. Sometimes the EPS may be increasing because some of its shares were bought back from others by the business. Also, the EPS could go down because more shares were issued by the business. Whatever the case may be, you must determine how the EPS is formed and why that total is where it is situated.

Don’t Forget Assumptions

An EPS could include a series of company assumptions that produce the document. These are based on past earnings, total forecasts, and general business plans as time progresses. Decide how realistic those hypotheses are. A business with a small growth rate of 1 to 2 percent could say it has expectations of 3 to 5 percent growth. This is sensible because it shows the company is growing and becoming more visible. However, as it seems unrealistic, a business that claims it will experience an extremely high increase, such as from 2 percent to 15 percent growth, should be avoided. Any business that doesn't make assumptions couldn't think about the future. It might take for granted that certain functions will remain sluggish or, in some way, lacking.

Consider Economic Conditions

Consider the overall economic conditions of the undertaking in question as you review the SEC report. Sometimes that could involve the economy as a whole. In other cases, it only involves a smaller economic segment. Consider how the economy evolves or not.

A company's net income or near earnings should be compared with the sales revenue it receives. More importantly, it should be analyzed in relation to what the business environment might be like at a given time. The business climate is sometimes healthy, or it might be that a business has difficulty growing and developing.

Conditions within a region in which a company operates could also be a factor. One part of the world could be a focus for an international organization. Yum! Brands, for example, are focused on the United States, Canada, the United Kingdom, and China. These four markets have their own single economic climate. Examining the international factors surrounding a stock gives you an idea of how some regions help or hinder a business. The gains a company has in China could, for example, offset the losses in the US.

Watch for One-Time Changes

Looking at the details of an SEC report, look carefully at some individual one-time changes that might occur as they could have a direct impact on your investment.

There are many reasons why an enormous one-time change could appear on a report:

• An enterprise could have invested in some new equipment or inventory. These include totally new things a company has never had any use for before. This could indicate a company attempting to expand.

- It may also recommend that there is a lawsuit or other legal action that an undertaking has just experienced, which could have resulted in a substantial amount of money paid out as a result of a court fight.

- The reason for the change could be an acquisition of another company.

Watch for Confusing or Vague Content

Another aspect to note when reviewing SEC reports is that there are many confusing SEC reports that could be. They could contain lots of terms you don't know about. Perhaps the reports include vague documents, or certain bits of information are not listed, even though the SEC states that they should be listed. This is often a sign that something a company is trying to hide.

What If a New Version of a Report Is Issued?

A business might sometimes issue a new version of an SEC report. The most common reason this happens is the inaccurate accounting practices a business has engaged in. Perhaps a company may have participated in false accounting by knowingly misleading about the revenues.

Any company which issues an SEC report revision may not be trustworthy. Look for details about why you updated the report before contemplating purchasing the product.

What About the Chairman's Letter?

The letter from the chairman is a text in a report from the SEC, which most people overlook. It is basically a report to customers as to what a company is doing and how it is doing.

The letter has a lot more to it than you would expect. Reviewing a letter from the Manager is one of the strongest techniques you might use to uncover the way an organization is going. It all comes from the chief of first-hand market experience. The Chairman should state when reading the letter:

- Inside the company, the financial strengths and problems are focused on leverage, cash flow, and other factors.

- The difficulties which the organization faces. These involve problems relevant to rivalry, industry concerns, or even the environment at large.

- Current steps are conducted to render the company financially more competitive, regardless of whether they require growth or cost-cutting acts.

- The continuity of the approach of the company, even how the method being employed, varies significantly from what it was a few years ago.

- Detailed and simple to understand the post. The Manager, after all, is the one whose career may be on the line based on how well a company does.

SEC files can be difficult to find because they can be complex and comprehensive. The more you study what's in an SEC report, the better it would be for you to determine the business you should take advantage of by investing.

Chapter 4: Understanding the True Value of Stock

You might have a strategy to find cheaper stocks while you are looking for stocks on the market. But thinking about various underlying factors in stock is even more important. Sometimes the value of a stock isn't as big as the official total says it is. That is, it overvalues stock.

At the same time, a firm is doing very well, but this is not reflected in the stock price. Would you like to buy a stock for $150 per share only to find out later that there was at the same time another stock with a better prospectus available at $30? If you knew what it had to offer at the time, you would have probably preferred to take the latter.

You will need to look at several points relating to how well a stock performs, so that you can make the most of an investment. This chapter deals with some strategies to use to determine if a stock is overvalued or undervalued.

P/E Ratio

A useful strategy to use when reviewing the value of stock really is to understand the P/E ratio. That is the ratio of price-earnings. This measurement demonstrates what investors will spend on stock. Investors will expect to get more earnings overtime when the total is higher. The stock is considered undervalued if the sum is poor. That means the stock is trading below what the perceived value could be. It could make buying an interesting product, thanks to how at this juncture it is considered a minor bargain. The P/E ratio measurement may be obtained like this:

1. Take in stock market price.

2. Split earnings by half. The EPS is the net income divided by the shares outstanding.

3. That gives you the ratio P/E.

The total value of the P/E ratio refers to the value that the stock market holds on that product. The investment market likes this better because the amount is larger. That is, the stock is something that consumers would like to purchase.

Here is an example of how the P/E ratio functions. Heading back to Macy's, you could see the stock priced at $26.26. The EPS is now at 2.28. This is focused on the $697 million net profits being split by the 304.57 million outstanding stock Macy's owns. By dividing the value of the stock and the EPS, we get a total of 11.52.

What does this example mean, then? It suggests an investor would be willing to pay $11.52 for each dollar of current Macy earnings. This is an inexpensive sum, since it means consumers would not pay that much on the stock to buy. The low P/E ratio indicates that if you are looking to buy anything a little cheaper on the market, Macy's stock may be worth investing in.

What If a Company Is Losing Money?

When you look at the P/E ratio, a company that is losing money will have an N/A mark on its stock report. Although you could technically calculate a negative ratio to show that a firm is losing money, it's easier to use the N/A listing as an indicator that people don't necessarily expect to gain much from the stock based on their earnings. That may be a sign of too risky a stock. It could also be a sign that a business may have undergone some expansion plan or legal issue, which could cause it to lose money temporarily.

In any situation, the only thing to do is figure out if a corporation is losing revenue. Look into the company's previous results to see what could have been the P/E ratio during better periods. Sometimes the P/E ratio could only dip briefly as a business grows and will rebound back to its original value once those efforts have been completed.

The Optimal P/E Ratio

Image of the Macy indicates the business is earning profits and not failing. Is an 11 percent P/E ratio good? There are no clear solutions as to whether a stock has the strongest P/E ratio. If you are trying to find decent value, you can look for stocks with low overall P/E. A stock that trades its earnings a few times can be cheaper than something that trades 12 times its value or more.

Consider several stock P/E ratios within the same sector. Stock in the technology sector with a P/E ratio of 25 may be interesting, but another stock in the same industry with a ratio of 14 maybe even more attractive.

Watch for Inflation

When looking at the P/E ratio, be aware of what the inflation rate is. Typically, this measurement is lower when the rate of inflation is high. This is because a firm's earnings may be skewed somewhat. As the dollar's power increases, it will seem as if a company is making more money. That rise is due to more dollars being factored into transactions. The cost of replacing assets is on the rise, just like the prices of other market staples.

Consider how the rate of inflation has changed over time as you look at a stock's historical data. Did you notice cases where the P/E ratio has dramatically shifted? That could be due to the rapidly changing inflation rate.

Inflation just takes a couple of months to make a difference. The inflation rate in the US was at 0 percent in May 2015. That total went to 1 percent in February 2016. In November 2016, it would become 2.1 percent. It takes a few months to make a sizable change to the inflation rate, but that shift will be noticeable when you look at investments.

Price/Earnings Growth Ratio

The next metric to remember while analyzing the real valuation of a stock is the price/earnings growth ratio. This is an indicator of whether a stock is underpriced or whether the valuation added to it is strong. It could mean the stock is an incredible bargain based on the findings you find.

It is a calculation that can be measured using the following equation:

1. Calculate stock ratio P/E.

2. Divide this by the increase in average earnings per share.

Say a corporation with a share price of $ 50. Last year's EPS for that business may have been $4. The amount may have been as big as $6 this year. Then you measure the P/E ratio by dividing 50 by 6 to hit 8.33. Now split the earnings by taking six separated by four separated by 1. That'd earn you a 0.5. This is calculated as a percentage point, which is 50%-earnings per share rise is 50%. Dividing 8.33 by 50 is tantamount to 0.166 PEG.

The PEG in this sample can sound marginal, but when combined with how the market is rising, the business market is selling at a drastic discount. Hence customers pay less for a company's stock that is beginning to expand. With time, the valuation may be higher attributed to the business proving to be more secure.

The PEG offers you an indication of what to expect from a stock you may have kept for a while. It demonstrates the upward trajectory that a stock may be in. I would recommend you stay a bit longer on a stock with a good Board. Even you should store the stock as a preference for day trading as you can check the stock many times a day to create multiple additional trades.

Use Historical Data

The easiest approach to operate with the PEG is to make the most of historical evidence. The illustration listed reflects on improvements in the valuation of a stock over the past year. While this read-out will be helpful, to have a better understanding of how it is changing, you may need to dig at more historical details regarding the PEG.

You may, for example, measure the PEG as it was in 2013. You can calculate earnings per share growth from 2012 to 2013 and see if, from the latest data, this correlates with stock. After that, you will use the same formula just to see how the PEG is adjusting with the development from 2015 to 2016 for the stock value from the latter year.

A stock of that PEG is one that is beginning to purchase more customers. With stock rising and industry growing, consumers are becoming more conscious of what's available. They are will start investing in the specific stock.

Price/Sales Ratio

The next technique to consider is to look at the ratio of price/sales, commonly known as the PSR. It reflects the valuation of the assets of a business as opposed to profits. A stock of a firm that has strong sales suggests that the business is profitable.

The Price/Sales ratio can be measured by doing the following:

1. Find the complete amount of securities outstanding.

2. For any of the last twelve months, add the cumulative revenue.

3. Divide the number of securities in those transaction figures.

4. Divide the current share value by phase 3 performance.

5. This shows you the Trading PSR based on the last twelve months.

You may also swap the cumulative revenue over the past twelve months with the revenues for the new fiscal year, if you wish. It would offer you a more direct response, even though the total may not be that great. Numbers may be used as a guide for the next fiscal year. The assessment over the last twelve months is more objective and reflects on what the market has improved.

If the PSR is low, this means a stock is inexpensive. Compared to the profits that the business receives, it has a minimal expense. Therefore, it is always advised to get in when the PSR is poor as a purchase.

The worst aspect of the PSR is that it's all sales-based. It is tougher for a company to update its revenue figures than changing the forecasts that an accounting committee could make.

Many revenue figures are steady and operate through periods that vary throughout the year. You may foresee how the PSR adjusts based on how an organization does in the sales department and whether the actual profits are projected to improve or not. This provides a simple element of consistency in determining whether to invest in a corporation or not.

Review Many Businesses in the Same Sector

The easiest approach to operate with the PSR is to audit as many companies as possible within a market. This might provide you a tentative insight into what could be a standard PSR in that area. This may entail, for example, calculating three or four inventories in the software industry. A low-ratio company may have an undervalued stock as opposed to the global industry. That is, the money is free. What is high in value can, therefore, be more costly than required. Major variations may also mean that different firms have their own objectives or intentions to expand or run.

Analyze the Book Value

Another technique to consider when evaluating the real worth of a stock is to take a deeper glance at the book value of the stock. This applies to the valuation of the properties kept in a portfolio less than the liabilities plus any intangible assets owned by the firm.

The book value corresponds to the inventory kept by an entity on a balance sheet. It determines what the company's owners will get in case the corporation was liquidated. That's a guess, but it's worth investigating. The most significant argument about the book valuation is that it determines how a company operates. An organization with a higher book value could be one that has ample reserves to hold it running.

The Main Concern

There are concerns about how every time the book value does not function. A fast-growing company may have a misleading book valuation as the business continues to acquire more money and attempts to make any practical improvements about how it runs. Businesses with fewer physical assets may pose a challenge. A bank portfolio may have a high book value, for instance, since that bank has many physical branches and ATMs. An online bank stock is distinctive in that the online banker has no other branches and does not have much to no advertised ATMs. As for every other metric, you need to know what the book prices are for different firms in the same market. Think of what makes a company invest too much in its inventory, only to maintain and work its general activities.

Even the intangible assets that an organization has could be a concern. Perhaps because of a legal dispute or a scandal involving a particular product or service, the credibility of a company has been destroyed. While it could restore credibility over time, it might put a dent in stock. It is not simple to get an exact estimate of the overall effect that such a problem might have on stock.

Evaluate how a company performs when analyzing its revenue, earnings growth, and book value, among other points, while looking at stock prices. There's a good possibility a stock might be a great offer than what you thought it would be.

Chapter 5: Working with Great Trading Platforms

I If you don't have a good trading network to deal with, any scheme that you devise for your savings would be useless. A trading site is a software you'll be performing the trades directly. Either of such sites should be accessible via a broker or a financial organization.

For a day trader, the trading platform is a must. The trading mechanism is a normal progression. It used to be that transactions between specific traders or other parties will have to be done in person. There has been the usage of interactive channels since at least the 1970s. The earliest interactive channels will enable users to find current market price statistics, thus encouraging them to submit signals saying they want to do business. The high-speed online environment has developed such that exchanges can accommodate trades at once. People get access to pricing in real-time. What you need is a link to the internet.

Analytics Points

A trading platform should offer you different metrics that can help you distinguish stock choices. Whilst with software, you can find quotations and maps in real-time, you need to be mindful of several other items.

News Feeds Are Vital

A Forum for Trading may have news feeds. This involves stories from various news agencies, including Associated Press and Reuters. The news feeds can send you details on everything that's going on in the business. A platform can also scan for unique stock details using a stream.

A quest for news feeds is one easy process:

1. Check out the stock in which you intend to buy.

2. Check on the stock market and the emblem that it uses.

3. Join the contents by mentioning them as Exchange abbreviations: Symbol. E.g., if you decided to find details about Cedar Fair Amusements, you might need to enter "NYSE: FUN" in the quest. This lets the software realize that you are searching for the stock of the Cedar Fair described under the symbol Pleasant in the NYSE.

4. Find out the outcome. The results may provide prediction information, SEC reports, and many more. It might also contain some pending incidents.

Try seeking news that's as recent as practicable. You will still use older stock records and get a sense of when a stock has shifted. Anything fresh is often instant and will have a significant influence on the valuation of your stock.

Proper Security Is Needed

The software you are utilizing must be safe, such that your financial information is not compromised or robbed. It needs a secure authentication scheme to enter a username and password to validate your identity.

Encryption is often a must to step through a network. This involves decoding transfers that you are doing so that outside powers cannot hack through a link and understand what you are doing.

Even a format can be used to document all completed transactions. The specification may provide details of where a transaction is made, how long it has been for, and so on. Such a requirement helps you to maintain notes so you can prove that, over time, you have made clear transactions.

Support for backups can often be offered on a website, which provides provision for backup servers in situations when the main one may be disabled. It could provide copies of all the details being exchanged, in specific knowledge on the records of both. All those reserves should be subject to the same protection as the primary material.

Financial Points

In a trading network, such additional financial costs may be listed. See and concentrate on what to invest in finishing deals, or even using a platform:

About how much each exchange would pay, each network has its own price. You should only pay a couple of dollars for each exchange. There may be a fixed rate on a specific deal or a charge, depending on how many securities you purchase or sell. Often because you have more stock, the payments are higher per unit since this is called a bulk sale.

Trades of options include a surcharge on contracts. The additional payment per contract may be nominal in value with an option. It may be inferior to a dollar.

One minimum account can be mentioned. Before you start trading, a lender may ask you to have a certain sum of money in your account. This means you're open to platform trading. Before you start trading, you may need to get $1,000 or more moved to an account with that site. In compliance with SEC requirements, you will require the $25,000 or more in your day-trading portfolio. Any sites may be running exclusive deals. An offer with a qualified deposit could be a guaranteed cash bonus. If you deposit $1,000 or more into an account, for example, you might get $100 in extra money for trading.

Each platform has special margin rates of its own. The margin rates offered for options could fall within a few percentage points of the current value of a stock. The standards which a platform uses may vary depending on how long the stock option will be open.

Can This Work In Lieu of a Stock Screener?

If you have a screener to work with, the details from a Trading Platform will be more effective. A dedicated stock-screener account would make it easier for you to find the specific stocks you like. A trading platform won't help you show inventories. Some platforms do offer extensive features for research. They could include their own trigger points and dimensions, allow warnings not to include. You'd have to look for information about how each platform works and what analysis they're offering, and how they can function with you. But a screener is much more detailed and offers you a more comprehensive insight into how you could spend your money and what you can anticipate while making a sale.

What Are the Best Trading Platforms?

Trading platforms have many choices. Investigate as many of these options as possible so that you know what might be suitable and worthwhile for you. Some of the trading platforms are backed by big brokerage houses.

Ally Invest

Ally Invest is a trading platform that lists complete charts of how well stocks move. The platform originates from the popular provider of online banking services. Using this costs $4.95 per trade and does not require any minimum account. Ally Invest also doesn't work with commission-free ETFs or mutual funds. Such investments could cost you extra to buy over the platform. You can also get discounts through Ally Invest. If you're making at least 30 trades in a quarter, you could spend $3.95 each. A day-trader shouldn't have difficulty reaching that threshold.

This solution reveals points that are worthwhile but also frustrating for online banking and financial services. Thanks to a lack of physical branches for its operations, Ally can charge its customers less for services. To some people who want direct contact with a broker, not having physical sites could be a problem.

TD Ameritrade

TD Ameritrade offers a more robust and comprehensive approach to providing inventory information. It features free research tools to help you identify stock patterns and signals. Also valuable is TD Ameritrade's extensive streaming news support, as it provides information from Zacks, Dow Jones, Credit Suisse, and many others. That does cost $6.95 per trade, a little extra to use. When you open an account here, you could get a few hundred dollars extra in a cash bonus, but the bonus will vary depending on the size of the account you have. Also, TD Ameritrade has different trading centers and locations throughout the United States. If you have a need for trading support, you could visit one of these places. You can also access the various branches of TD in Canada through its subsidiary of TD Canada Trust.

Trade Station

Trade Station is famous for providing a comprehensive and detailed trading platform. Recently, the group became popular as it lowered its original minimum total account from $5,000 to $500, allowing more people to enter the platform. (That doesn't mean you should only have $500 in your account because day traders need more money to fill their positions.) The cost of stock trading may vary depending on the investment. While a flat rate of $5 is available, you could also choose a price point per share based on the volume of trading on the stock. This would involve spending commercially up to $0.01 per share. To qualify for this deal, you'd have to spend at least $1 on the trade; it's clearly a deal designed for people looking to make bigger transactions on the platform.

Over a hundred indicators can be used to work on the platform. Using a stock screener, you can create your own individual indicators based on certain parameters you want to work with, though that might not be as many as what you would get.

Interactive Brokers

Interactive Brokers offers a trading platform that costs $0.005 per share to use and has a minimum account of $10,000. This is intended with a view of frequent trading. It provides a good assortment of investment options and lower margin rates. It does, however, charge inactivity fees for those who do not frequently speak trade. Interactive Brokers also don't offer many educational services for prospective traders. The system is clearly geared towards experienced traders.

Charles Schwab

Charles Schwab was one of the most trusted investment brokerage firms in the US. The organization, which has been in operation since 1971, has hundreds of branches in the United States. For people who need commission-free ETFs and index funds, the firm has its own electronic trading platform for day-trading. The group has Morningstar, Market Edge, and many other popular firms as research resources. The platform lays out stock specifics. Charles Schwab charges $4.95 per trade and demands a minimum of $1,000 from your account. It does not charge any fees for the inactivity.

EOption

EOption could benefit those who are looking for a base platform. There are not many fancy features to this. It only displays a base chart for each stock. It doesn't give you many research options, though that information will be provided by a stock screener. EOption fees $3 per trade, with a minimum account of $500. This platform is best suited for experienced traders with stock screeners that can work as opposed to the research features other platforms offer.

This trading platform information proves they're all varied but can be worthwhile. Make sure that you have the right materials ready to access one of those platforms to start trading.

Don't Forget Simulators

Trading platforms often include simulators to help you acknowledge how the market functions. These simulators focus on education: how to read a layout of a chart, how to execute a trade, and so on. Working with a simulator as close as possible to the actual platform is a necessity so that you know what to do before you actually do business. Check to see if a simulator is available on the platform you choose. Simulator training can make a world of difference. A program like this will help you identify a lot of factors related to how stocks change in value and how patterns can be identified.

Chapter 6: Identifying Patterns in a Stock

Some of the most popular stock market strategies are geared towards patterns. These are instances where, at a given time, something could change within a stock. Patterns show how the price of a stock moves while giving signals suggesting something will happen. There are many patterns, and when you look at how a stock is evolving, it's easy to figure them out. You can use these to plan your strategies on how you enter or exit trades or when you figure out what kinds of trades you should be doing.

Note: All patterns are identifiable by looking at a traditional stock price chart based on candlesticks. This would show you how something's value moves up and down consistently within a short timeframe.

Reversal or Continuation?

The most important thing about those patterns to notice is that they come in two ways:

1. Reversal - A reversal is where a trend had ended before a pattern started. The stock may have gone up before the pattern, but thereafter the stock will go down.

2. Continuation - A continuation shows that the change in stock prices will continue to move even after the pattern is complete. The pattern could be a brief occurrence, but thereafter the stock will continue unabated.

You can use these points to determine how you should trade in a stock. You may consider buying a stock for later sale, or you may be able to place a call or a put option depending on how the stock moves. Either way, you can always invest in a stock irrespective of whether its value is moving up or down. An interesting thing about continuations and reversals is that they can go on for a long time. It's hard to figure out how long one of those events will be, but you can be sure that something will more than likely happen after a while when a pattern occurs.

Pennant

The Pennant is the first pattern to be observed when a stock is found. It's a continuation pattern showing how the stock will continue to grow in value. At this point, the stock seems to struggle to move up or down in value, but after a while, the stock will break out of the pennant and continue to move towards the same position it was in at the beginning.

The Pennant indicates:

1. The value of a stock will start to grow or fall sharply. The change could be for the stock to gain or lose a few percentage points of its value. The change should be noticeable, however valuable it may be.

2. The value then should start going in the opposite direction. After a sizeable increase, it will slowly decrease, or it could go the other way around.

3. The values of the stock rises or drops will shrink in size after a time. With each candlestick, a stock could change by just a few pennies in value. Sometimes the total volume or range within which the value of the stock changes in a period of time may be minimal.

4. The stock will have little to no variation in its value after a while.

5. When the stock suddenly breaks out, the pennant will end and experience an increase or decrease in its value. This should be a complete continuation of what the stock had been experiencing before the pennant began.

The pennant's layout will let you know that the value of stock either stabilizes or is about to erupt. When the volume of trading and the value change shrinks to next to nothing, this is a sign that something is about to happen. Sometimes, depending on how the pennant started, you might find that the value could go up or down after a while.

Enter a pennant when you notice changes coming down to very low totals in each wave. Watch how the pennant is formed, and see how it breaks out of stock. At the opposite end of the trend, you can place a stop-loss order to protect you against the potential of the stock, not continuing in the same path or if the pennant lasts a bit longer than expected.

Bullish or Bearish?

A pennant can either be bullish or its value bearish. A bullish pennant is one that begins on a slight rally. In the beginning, the stock price will go up and then stabilize. The stock will probably shift back up in value once the pennant is formed.

A bearish pennant features a price that falls substantially before the pennant forms. The price may start to go up a bit, but after the pennant ends, the value will go down. You could probably say the same about any other pattern that you find. The pattern changes are all worth checking to anticipate that certain changes might grow and evolve.

The Flag – a Related Pattern

A pennant may occasionally occur in a more rectangular shape. That is, the value doesn't necessarily increase or decrease by much, but remains within a steady range. This establishes a flag pattern, which is in a flag-shaped pattern with the candlesticks on a chart moving. Whether the flag is bullish or bearish, you can still identify by looking at how it started. The first few price changes in the flag should give you an idea of how the flag moves in value up or down.

Think of the flag as if it were a series of oscillating waves throughout, with the same amplitude. The only difference is that the time periods on that wave will vary between the highs and lows. Ultimately, when you notice a sizable breakout from the flag, you would have to enter your trade.

Can the Pennant Go in the Other Direction?

Most pennants are made to go right to the left. That is, the biggest change in price will appear on the left while the smallest will go to the right. There are times when you can form an inverse pennant. This is where the volume of trading and changes in stock begin to gradually increase, eventually transforming into one big trade at the end of the pennant.

Not as easy to find reverse pennants as traditional ones. You will find a reverse pennant more likely after it's finished. Sometimes these reverse pennants might let you know how the price moves and how the stock is about bullish or bearish people. Just look at the ends of the reverse pennants, you'll get an idea of how a stock is developing.

Strategies for Using Pennants

You should use some strategies on the market to trade pennants:

Watch how the changes in the candlesticks vary as the pennant advances. Sometimes a majority of sticks move up in the pennant. They may, in other cases, go downwards. Either way, after the pennant is fully formed, it might be better for you to get into commerce. You might try to make small micro-transactions that last for a few minutes depending on where the pennant flows, but even then, it may be hard to determine how long the waves will move along and how many up or down candlesticks will form at a time. Seek out as many pennants as possible in stock. Reviewing multiple pennants gives you an insight into what a stock sentiment might be. You could see bullish pennants growing bigger. This suggests investors are more appreciative of stock and willing to make investments in it.

Trade, where possible, during stock upside parts. Trading at this point helps as you identify points where the value of a stock will likely rise in a shorter period of time. This would work only for a brief moment before something begins to shrink in value.

See if a pennant contains any significant outliers. These include cases in which one stick is larger in the middle than the other. An outlier is suggestive of stock uncertainty. It shows when the outliner moves downwards that a possible increase may not be as strong as it might be. Look at how long a pennant may be on the move. The pennant may sometimes last for a couple of days or even some weeks at a time. A pennant could last for a few hours, in most cases. This is because people will respond swiftly to stock changes. They might notice that a stock that trends upward and is stable in value might be worthwhile acquiring before the value might burst up again.

Wedge

The following pattern is a wedge. This is akin to the pennant, but it uses a different form. A wedge is a pattern where the wave of price reverses. After a while, the range in the price of a stock will begin to narrow. The stock will break out after the wedge ends and move up or down.

What distinguishes the coin from a pennant? A wedge is organized within a certain range based on the differences between stock prices. An example of how a wedge can be formed here is:

1. You may notice a trend where the price of a stock moves up and down and then down again. A stock could start at $100, for example, and then move up to $120 after a few days. After a few more days, the stock would then fall to $105.

2. The extremes are beginning the wedge between the first values. Just like with a pennant, the wedge will feature two lines. The first line begins at the $120 part, and the other begins at the $100 mark.

3. The wedge lines will move inward, based on stock range changes. You might notice the stock will go from $105 to $115 and then to $112

in a couple of days. As the gap between price extremes begins to shrink, the lines will become narrow.

4. The wedge will shrink to where the price may appear to break out after some time. By looking at how the wedge began, you can identify whether the wedge is bullish or bearish. If the wedge started with the price moving up, then there's a chance the price will break out after the wedge ends.

The Three Types of Wedges

The main strategy to use when trading wedges is to look at how the wedges are organized. There are three shapes of wedges that you might notice, with each being different based on how the value of a stock is going to change over time:

1. Rising wedge-This is where the highs and lows of the wedge keep moving up. You can tell when the wedge is rising that the stock is about to trend downward. You will have to sell your stock when the low on a rising wedge breaks beyond the lower bar. This is a sign that the stock is about to take a dramatic decline in value and possibly move further downward. This could occasionally lead to a falling wedge. This is the next wedge.

2. Wedge falling-The wedge falling is the opposite of the wedge rising. The ups and downs continue to decline. You should buy the stock from the top part of the wedge when it breaks out.

3. Symmetrical wedge- A symmetrical wedge has a relatively similar design to a pennant. But the gap's narrowing won't be as close as it would be to a pennant. You can see if the wedge will move up or down when you notice how the wedge started. This is just like a pennant as a wedge, which begins to increase in value and will surely continue to rise.

These three wedges are designed with different arrangements, but they are all vital to help you see where a stock could be going. Reviewing the wedge layout is vital to trying to get a trade option ready, which is the next item to look into here.

Take Profits on Options

The take profit should be analyzed if you have a wedge-based trade option. The profit from taking refers to the starting point of a wedge. When the rising wedge begins, it is high at the start of the falling wedge or the low. You can order an option that lasts for a certain period of time and is geared towards making a profit. At this point, the best strategy is to decide how long a wedge will develop. This might give you an idea of how long the option that you wish to place might be. You should keep the option long enough to give the stock the chance to return to the point of profit-taking.

This is irrespective of how long it might take to move the wedge.

Cup and Handle

The cup and handle have an intriguing shape, which you will notice quickly. This can indicate not only a continuation of the value of a stock, but also a reversal. More relevantly, this shows the value of a stock will rise after a brief dip. In the end, as the pattern ends, the value of the stock will move up in value. The cup and handle are arranged in three parts. They are focusing heavily on dramatic market changes:

1. The Cup-This is where stock value begins to bend in value. At the start, it will dip below a certain value and then move back to around the value it was when the cup began.

2. The Handle-The handle is a line that shows up around the cup end. This is a line that shows a slight downtrend. This is comparable to what you might see from a downward-moving pennant or wedge.

3. A breakout-After the handle is finished, the breakout appears. The breakout happens when the stock value begins to rise beyond what the handle is showing.

This is an intriguing organization, showing how the value of a stock could change. What is very interesting is that the pattern of the cup and handle might repeat itself several times over.

How Deep Can the Decline Be?

The cup and handle decline should not exceed 50 percent. Be aware of this may be a sign that a stock is in real danger when planning and developing as a decline of more than 50 percent. In case it goes too deep, it would be harder for a stock to recover. More importantly, it is an indication of general instability or insecurity among investors regarding how that stock could perform and evolve.

Reversal Pattern

In a reversal or continuation layout, you can find a cup and handle the trend in one stock. Let's look at those points first:

1. The stock price must be falling. -- The stock should have fallen in the last few weeks or months.

2. A sizeable decline is beginning to develop. The decline that begins the cup should be bigger and more consistent than the preceding declines.

3. In the middle of the cup should be a couple of small candlesticks that don't change much in value. That should be a sign that the stock is moving upward.

4. The stock then starts recovering and reaches the other end of the cup. The cup's two ends should be equal in value. The cup shape will vary, but the ends will have to be the same.

5. A handle will be formed for a short time with the stock going down in value.

The handlebars are subjective. The bars can be positioned in any way you think fit.

6. As with a pennant or wedge, the stock finally breaks out of the handle and moves upward in value. The stock should continue to an upward trend. Your method at this moment is to look at how well they handle formed to make a purchase while waiting for the stock to break out.

Continuation Pattern

The pattern of continuation is similar in a way to a reversal, in that the stock is will go down, up and down, and up again. The variation here is that while a reversal involves the stock going down before the cup and handle start, the continuation pattern occurs when the stock rises in value before the formation.

By looking at any significant decreases in the uptrend, you can identify when the cup starts. You might notice some small-sized candlesticks followed by a large red one that goes down. Here the cup should start.

An Option Target Point

You can use the cup and handle trade options to give you an idea of what the target should be. With a few steps, you can calculate the target for a trade of options:

1. Revise the cup's height. The height is the difference between the cup's start and endpoint and the lowest total value. Let's say the cup started and ended at $6, and the stock dropped to midway through $4.50. At this point, the cup should be at $1.50 in height.

2. Add the height of the cup on the handle to the breakout point. The stock may have a handle that falls down to $5.50 before the stock breaks out, after reaching $6 as the cup ends. Add the $1.50 to the $5.50 to get to $7.

3. At this point, the price target should be shaped. The price target of $7 can be used as a goal for options trades to reach your option. At some point in the future, you could contract to buy a stock at $7 and then sell

it with a sizeable profit if the stock is valuable much more than $7. You'd need to look at how long it can take to reach the target.

Of course, at this juncture, you have the option of just engaging in traditional trade. If you feel it will take a while for the trade to move on, you could do this.

Added Cup and Handle Trading Strategies

For your investment plans, there are a few extra strategies to use when getting a cup and handling trade:

Review how well-shaped the handle is. A shorter handle is a positive sign. The stock is moving up very soon. A handle could possess a minimum number of sticks. There's a better overall sentiment among traders about a stock when the handle is shorter. This suggests the stock is fast moving up. This could be perfect if you want to engage in a short-term trade. When you look at how the rally moves, you'd have to be cautious and if it could stop fast.

Use a target price that is up to at most two cup heights over the long term. For long-term trading, the best idea is to use two cup heights for how the stock will move up in value. The cup and handle should suggest the stock is moving up in value and becoming interesting to investors. Staying at just two cup heights is best as it reduces your risk and keeps your expectations under control. This also prevents you from losing too much in case the stock doesn't continue to move up in value.

Place a stop-loss command at the bottom of your handle. Although the risk of the stock going below the bottom of the handle is minimal, in the event that the stock continues to decline, you should still add a stop-loss order around that point.

When the handle starts, a short sale can work, but you'd have to watch out for its length. When the handle is formed, you can sell short of taking advantage of the drop in stock value. Note that a handle will last only for a few candlesticks at a time. Keep in your short sale about three to five sticks, so you can take advantage of the decline before any dramatic shifts occur.

Is This a Guarantee that a Stock Will Actually Go Up?

Although the pattern of cup and handle shows the value of a stock will go up, there is still a chance that stock will experience a significant decline. The best way to tell when the stock risks decreasing afterward is to notice how deep the cup is. This is a signal of how strong the movement could be and whether any gains on this investment could be difficult to maintain or support.

A cup with a very small dip has a greater chance of falling in value than a stock with a deeper dip. A handle that is also very narrow in size may also later decrease or at least take some time for it to recover and move up in value.

Can the Handle Move Upward?

There are times when the handle will actually move up in value on a cup and handle. This is a sign that a stock is favored by people, but you still have to be careful. A handle upward is only going to have very small increases. Some declines may appear after the handle, but at this point, the stock should still be moving upward. It may not move as fast and require you to stay with a longer trade, but it might be worth looking into.

An upward handle also may suggest that after the pattern is finished, a stock will not increase its value by as much as one might expect it. A lot of the trade will have already taken place during the formation of the cup and handle. At this juncture, the public may not be as bullish on the stock as they notice that its growth rate has stalled.

Head and Shoulders

One of the most common features you'll see in a stock is the pattern of the head and shoulders. It consists of six trends in a stock that goes in opposite directions of one another. The value of the stock may change, but it always returns to a pivot point. At the beginning of the head and shoulders trend, that point is formed and, at the very end, will be the same. It's around the point your strategy should come into play as you make a trade based on where the stock is about to move and how far it will go in that direction. The stock will break out when the head and shoulder pattern ends. It'll continue to move in a particular direction. There are two viewable positions in the pattern of the head and shoulders:

Top Position

The first position is the head and the top of the shoulders. This is a bearish pattern showing the stock may fall in value giving traders the belief that the stock will continue declining.

In the head and top of the shoulders, there are six points to see with each part of the definite pattern a distinct segment of the human body:

1. The left shoulder occurs when a rising value of the stock is about to fall or is stuck at the same total.

2. The first pullback happens when the value of the stock drops and is ready to go up.

3. When the stock moves up, the head is formed and is then about to decline. The head-on position should always be the highest point.

4. The stock will revert to the first pullback value. The second pullback forms this.

5. After the stock price moves up again, the right shoulder is formed and stays put for a little before falling. The right shoulder may be higher than the left shoulder or lower.

6. The breakout occurs when the stock price goes under the pullback mark and continues to decline.

Trading the Top

A useful strategy for this top position layout of the head and shoulders is to put a short-trade around the breakout level. At the breakout level, you can sell shares and then repurchase them shortly after when the stock starts to decay. Before the downward trend becomes more pronounced, the value will keep going back to or over the breakout point. You can also see how quickly the stock's value could begin to decline. You might see cases where the value of the stock is steady, but every once in a while it will experience slight declines. This can be used when planning trade-in options, so you know when to place a put order.

Using the Price Target

A good strategy for a place option on top of the head and shoulders is to place an order regarding the price target you set in this case. Here is what you can do to help you get this to work:

1. Take the right shoulder and extract it from the point of breakout.

2. At this point, you should have the head and shoulders high.

3. From breakout, subtract the height.

4. The result is the target that you have for the stock value decrease.

A stock with a $35 right shoulder and a $30 breakout, for instance, will have a $5 high. To get to the $25 price target for a put option, this should be subtracted from $30. This should be the mark you would like to get the stock down to when you invest in this option.

Also, you have the option to play percentages when you set a price target:

1. Review the right shoulder decline to the breakout point.

2. Calculate the decline-percentage. In the above example, as it goes from $35 to $30, the stock will have declined by about 15 percent.

3. Set a target under the breakout point based on the percentage total. The target would be 15 percent below $30 at this point. The target is set to be around $25.50.

You can use either of those options to set the price point. The total will be near the same, whatever you choose.

Bottom Position

The bottom position is the next thing for measuring calculation. The setup of the bottom head and shoulders is, in essence, the reverse of the top position:

1. At the start, the stock will go down in value.

2. The left shoulder is formed around the end of a pattern in which the value descends.

3. When the stock moves back up in value, the pullback positions occur.

4. The head is still to be lower than anything else in value.

5. The stock should move into the breakout point after moving back to the pullback position for the second time and then forming the right shoulder. The breakout point should be fully surpassed at this juncture, as the stock is starting to rise in value.

For the head and shoulders bottom, you can use the same target price measurement as what you use for the top. When calculating that price point, you can use either this same difference between the right shoulder and the breakout or the percentage difference between the two.

The setup at the bottom is perfect for a call option. See how the stock responds when it decides on the correct target price.

Trading Ideas for Head and Shoulders

Waiting for the pattern to complete itself before you enter a position is the most effective technique to use when trading the head and shoulders pattern. You should never assume the pattern continues all the way through. The earliest you might consider trading this pattern is to trade or launch the option around the top right shoulder part. This is around the time when the stock trend should go in the direction that you expect it to.

After the breakout point is reached, you can also wait for a few spots to see where the stock moves. Look at how fast it may take the stock to move to a certain point and that it does not struggle in any way. When you get the head and shoulders pattern to work for you, you have to be cautious.

Triangles

The next pattern to look at is the pattern with the triangle. It is a pattern of continuation, although it can sometimes be a pattern of reversal. When the price changes in stock start to narrow, a triangle develops. Here is a basic idea of how a triangle might be formed:

1. A triangle starts right as the stock heads down or up in worth over a few periods of trading.

2. Eventually, the stock returns in the opposite direction. This forms the line, which constitutes the other part of the triangle.

3. The stock is continuing to move back and forth. As the stock moves, the differences between the back and out points will be smaller.

4. The triangle is finally formed to perfection. There should be a breakout at this point where the stock is moving in the direction it was going at the triangle starts.

As the highs and lows of the stocks form, the triangle continues to alternate and become smaller in value. A triangle could show stock with $35, $30, and $25 highs with multiple points of $15, $20, and $22. That means the triangle shows a spread overtime of $20, $10, and $3. Such shrinking spreads will form the triangle and reveal the stock's potential to break out of the pattern. The breakout point is vital as it indicates when the earlier trend continues. It is here where it is possible to order an options trade or a straightforward stock purchase.

Triangles are popular among investors because the potential for reward and risk is about the same. People may use stop-loss commands near a triangle's opposite end to keep their losses from being too intense. In the meantime, examining how well the form of the triangle gives the investor an idea of how a stock could potentially increase its value.

The triangle shows no matter what happens, a trend is very resistant. That trend will continue to move in the same direction it had initially moved in. This shows a sense of consistency regarding how the stock is moving.

How the Triangle is Different from a Pennant

The triangle shape is clearly similar to what you'd see on a pennant. A pennant indicates the value of a stock moving briefly in the opposite direction of a continuing pattern. A triangle shows the stock moving inside the same value without much change of value experienced by the stock. It is essentially a pattern delay, except that there are no significant changes in the value of the triangle.

Can a Reversal Happen?

A triangle has the potential of showing a reversal in a stock's trend and appearing not as likely as a continuing trend. See how the triangle closes and how the stock continues to change in value. Sometimes a stock with multiple candlesticks in the triangle going the other way of the original trend could cause a reversal because the momentum is beginning to pick up where the stock is going in a different direction over time.

Three Kinds of Triangles

There are three specific kinds of triangles that you will see forming in a stock. These are separated according to how the stock's value may change at one or both ends. These show similar changes to what you'd find in other patterns.

1. Symmetric Triangle-The symmetric triangle is one in which the lines move toward one another. This forms the pennant-like shape that shows that inside the stock you hold, there might be some sort of even movement.

2. Ascending Triangle-When the lower line is rising, an ascending triangle occurs, but the upper line is at a consistent value. For example, the highs could be $30, $31, and $29.50, while the lows would be $22, $26, and $28. The stock's swings are getting smaller in value, but the stock doesn't necessarily move up. This type of triangle is a sign that the stock will probably decrease in value. You can set the breakthrough point a little earlier than if you prefer the triangle should end. You may notice when stock will peak.

3. Descending Triangle-The downward triangle is the opposite of the upward triangle. It shows the stock will more than likely continue to move in value. The lows are all at the same peaks, while the highs keep shrinking before the stock finally breaks out.

Determining the Target Price

When placing a trade from a triangle, the target price for an options call or a put should be carefully measured. There are a few steps to be employed:

1. First, set a stop-loss at the bottom or top part of the triangle. The positioning should be determined on the basis of trends in the stock. If the stock is moving up in value, place the stop-loss at the bottom. Do the opposite of ever weaker stock.

2. Measure the height from the bottom of the triangle end to the top of the start. For example, the top part could be at $40, while the bottom might be at $30; at this point, the total is $10.

3. Subtract or add that total from or to your breakout point.

In the example, the target price should be $50 for a call option. A put option should have a 20 dollar target. The overall goal is to look at how the bars move within the triangle and how the stock will change. This gives you a better chance of investing in quality whilst understanding how strong a stock could develop over time.

Double Top or Bottom

The top and bottom doubles are a popular pattern of reversal. This shows a stock will head high or low but will not go too far beyond the listed peaks. The stock will go in the opposite direction after reaching those peaks from where it had been moving.

How the Double Top Is Formed

The double top features a stock that at first trends upward:

1. It will eventually reach the first stop as the stock moves up in value. That's the highest value the stock will attain.

2. The stock then pulls back in value. There are no standards on how much of a difference between the pullback value and the first top should be found.

3. Then the stock rallies back up to reach the second top, which should be about as high as the first.

4. The stock then moves down to its original low pullback.

5. There may be a chance that the stock will begin to move up in value or stay the same, but the stock will eventually break below that total pull back, thus completing the double top.

The double top can give an idea of when a stock might be traded, as it is within the pattern. This pattern works particularly well if you want to put an option onto the stock. Look at how this is where the second top is formed. This is the point where a short sale or a put option can be entered.

How the Double Bottom is Formed

The double bottom is formed in the very same fashion as the double top but the other way round:

- The double bottom starts when there's a downward trend in the stock.
- Twice, the stock will appear to be reaching its lowest total.
- The stock will move far beyond pullback value after a while and begin to go up in value.
- The double bottom is perfect for calling options. When you review the trend, you will notice how the stock is about to rise in value.

Selecting a Price Target

Regardless of whether you buy and sell the double bottom or top, you can set a price target for anything that you want to invest in. Here's how to set a target price:

1. See where the top and bottom doubles are formed. You could see, for example, that the double tops on a stock are at $45 and $44.

2. Use the point between the two peaks at midway. You'll be using $44.50 as one border for this.

3. Consider where the opposite ends of the trend lie. Get the point at midway between those two. The bottom parts that appear after the

double tops, in the example, are around $35 and $33. So the midway would be $34.

4. Find the difference between the two totals which you've collected. Subtract $34 off $44.50 to reach a $10.50 difference.

5. Add or subtract the total to or from the point of breakout. Since the double tops show the stock will go down in value, you have to take $10.50 off the breakout. The second bottom part was $33, so let's use that as the mark for a breakout. The target price you should use then would be $22.50.

In short, you'd put an option on the price that goes under $22.50. You could also use this as a means of seeing if the stock is going to rally at the $22.50 mark if they get there. Either way, you have to work with a benchmark to identify how the value of the stock will change.

Where to Create a Stop-Loss

When you get a stop-loss planned on your double bottom or a top stock trade, you have two options to work with:

1. Create a stop-loss between the breakout point and tops or bottoms at the midway point. You would use a stop-loss total of roughly $38.50 for the double top example listed above. This is in between the top $44 and the breakout label of $33.

2. You can also opt for a stop-loss around the top or bottom double spot. A $44 stop-loss could be used to stop you from losing anything in case the stock exceeds that original peak.

You have the option to store the stop-loss at other stock values if you wish. These two options are recommended because they are less risky.

Space between Each Top or Bottom

To see how it is developing, look at the number of candlesticks in a double top or bottom pattern. A good trading pattern in between the bottom or top and the opposite end should have about four to seven sticks. This indicates how the stock tries to pass a certain total but struggles to do so. This also shows that traders have some sense of control due to consistent top and bottom swings. If you start noticing that the spacing between the top and bottom parts is consistent, you might feel more confident in a trade.

Can a Triple Top or Bottom Occur?

It is possible that a double top or bottom could have three peaks or valleys instead of two. This will not always be the case, but when you consider how the double top or bottom might clearly show a sense of uncertainty among investors, it is a possibility.

The third peak or valley will be slightly off the first two, in a triple top or bottom. The first two tops on a triple top could be $50 and $52, while the third top would be $46. This is a noticeable shift from the others and adds some confirmation that the stock will head in the opposite direction from where it first moved. There'll not always be triple tops or bottoms. If that happens, then the third instance will not be very intense.

Pocket Pivot

The pocket pivot is a distinct feature you might see in a stock. This happens when, after a consistent decrease or rise, the stock experiences a slight change in its value. You might notice, for example, five or more candlesticks where the stock either continues to go down or has an extremely minimal increase. Anyway, the stock would fall. You'll see a significant rise in the value of the stock on the sixth candlestick. That rise may be small, but still noteworthy. In a pocket pivot pattern, there are three things that need to be noticed:

1. The inventory needs to go in the opposite direction.

2. At this juncture, the change in stock value should be significant. It should be higher in value than the changes that had come before it on the candlesticks. For example, on one stick, a stock might have declined

by 40 cents, and then on the next by 50. The pocket point shows the stock is 60 cents up.

3. The volume of trade on the stock should be higher than in the last few trading periods. The best pocket pivots occur when the volume is nearly twice what it was before the pivot happened.

Compared to other investments, this is a rather small pattern and one that can repeat itself on a chart many times over. You may see a pocket pivot occurring every few days or even every few hours. This is because a cycle is set up in which people are willing to buy the stock and then quickly sell it off. A pocket pivot shows the stock in question is well-controlled, and the investors get an idea of what they want to do with it. Use this part of a trade to see how a stock moves, and you get an idea of where it will be heading.

A stop-loss order may be applied where necessary to the opposite end of the pivot point. This is enough to maintain control whilst attaining a decent value.

Each of these patterns shows that a stock can move in many directions on a stock market chart. Be aware of how these patterns get established, so you can have an idea of not only where a stock will head but also how the prices might change within a pattern.

Chapter 7: Buying Stocks on Margin

You might want to make a trade, but maybe you don't have the money to do it. This is fine, as many brokers will enable you to buy stocks marginally. Margin-buying is a simple concept. To pay for a trade you wish to complete, you borrow money from a broker. You're will use that money to buy more stock shares. You could also use the money to access a very expensive stock you couldn't normally afford. Margin trading is a risky strategy, and it's so risky that you might not be able to make a margin account with some investment brokers unless you have a history with that broker. To properly know how margin trading works, you must follow a couple of specific rules.

1. You will need to apply for a margin account to get started. A margin account differs from that of a cash account.

2. You must also sign a margin agreement and agree to the terms for margin trading, which a broker set. This should include information about how large a trade margin can be and what the trade rate is.

3. You can do a deal. You could have $20,000 in a margin account, for example. You might see a stock valued at $400 per share. You might ask to buy that stock from 100 shares. That would need $40,000, though.

4. The amount of money in your account will go toward the part of the cost after you make the trade, while the rest is a broker's loan.

5. At some point, you'll need to pay back the total value of that loan. That will include margin-rate interest. That makes it all the more important to look at that stock's performance. You can always sell the stock at the right time and cover the loan and interest costs. This only works when you step into a successful position.

6. You'll also need totals to your margin. Your margin account may have certain limits on what you are able to borrow at a time.

Margin Rates

The margin rate is the interest charged on a loan from a broker. Going back to the previous example, you might have been given a 7 percent rate on a margin of $20,000. That means you'll have to pay an interest of $1,400 on the margin trade. The rate is determined by the broker which you are using. For example, for people who deposit less than $25,000 into their margin accounts, Charles Schwab has a margin rate of 8.575 percent. That number is reduced to 7.075 percent for $100,000 accounts and then to 6.825 percent for $250,000 or more accounts. Merrill Edge charges 9,625 percent for $25,000 or less accounts and $100,000 for 7,125 per cent.

The good news about margin trading is that usually, you can borrow up to 50 percent of the total value of the position you want to enter. This is the maximum, which is typical. New margin traders should be able to borrow about 25 percent of their portfolio total. A new trader with a budget of $20,000 could buy about $5,000 in margin-processed trades. Often this limit is used because a person may not have enough margin trading experience. The broker who offers this deal just keeps the risk under control. It's becoming easier to do more with more buying power. You may be given a higher total margin to work with as you have more money in your account, and you continue to be profitable with margin trades. That can get you to the 50 percent value you're aiming for. You might try to buy $10,000 in stock, for example. You may have $5,000 you want to use in cash to pay for the investment. The other amount could be an offer on the margins.

A margin trading company could have limits on how much money you can spend on the trade. For example, you might need to have $15,000 or more in an account to trade in $10,000 on a margin trade. Such rules are applied by trading firms to ensure that people have the necessary funds to carry out trades and repay the loan and any margin-related charges if the trade goes south.

Examples

The following are examples for both again on a margin trade and a loss.

When a Gain Occurs

1. You have a $30,000 Margin Account.

2. You see a stock you would like to buy, but you need to use a margin. In particular, you want to get $150 worth of 100 shares of stock trading. You'd have to spend 15,000 dollars on commerce. For a margin trade, you can always use a part of your $30,000.

3. You will have to spend $7,500 on initial trade, and the other $7,500 on the margin. The margin would have a 7.5 percent interest rate. The interest rate again varies depending on the broker and how much you have put into your margin requirement.

4. When you decide to sell the trade, the stock increases to $190 in value. That $15,000 investment now has a value of $19,000.

5. Along with interest on the loan, you must repay the $7,500 margin. In this example, the interest would be $562.50.

6. From this trade, you'll have made a profit of $3,437.50. The profit is based on how the value of your original $7,500 grew to $9,500. The interest would be withdrawn from commerce. You should have made a substantial profit in the end.

This particularly illustrates how, when you work with a margin, you could get a greater profit from a successful trade. Just 50 shares of stock would have been a trade like this without margin. The $7,500 you are investing would turn into $9,500. You would have earned $2,000 from this trade, but that's far less than you'd made if you'd used a margin trade involving more shares. This is why so many people love to trade margins. It is considered a practice that gives them a greater chance of making a bigger profit than using their own money.

When a Loss Occurs

Obviously, you need a margin trade to be successful in making a profit, but losses could result from trade-in margins if the stock does not increase in value.

1. You paid $200 for 100 shares of a stock with $10,000 coming from your own account and $10,000 coming from a margin loan. This would also include an interest rate of 7.5 percent.

2. Before you sell the shares, the stock goes down to $150

3. You'll only make $15,000 if you sell the shares.

4. You must pay back the margin loan of $10,000 plus the interest charge of $750.

5. That results in a $4.250 loss.

Now let's say you went with a straight cash transaction in which you got 50 shares without using a margin for purchasing 100 shares. You'll invest $10,000 in the stock and then sell it to $7,500 for a $2,500 loss. If you spent more money on your margin trade, the potential for you to lose money could be even worse. What is more, if the stock falls further, the damage would be much worse yet.

For Which Stocks Can You Use Margins?

Please be advised that with each stock, you cannot use margin trades. You can't use margin trades on initial public offerings, penny stocks, or other stocks that could be considered highly risky.

The Board of the Federal Reserve determines which stocks may be marginally tradable. The Board will decide how those stocks are to be used based on various factors, such as how much money is involved, among other factors. The Board aim is to prevent investors from spending too much money on risky inventories.

Margin Calls

Margin calls are used when the value of stock spikes when you want more cash available. If a stock is making a dramatic decrease, you may need to pay more cash or stock to cover the losses involved. In the meantime, if the price has a huge positive spike, you might be asked to pay the broker back. This is to allow the broker to have the funds available on short notice for managing the trade.

The total value of a margin call should be about 10-20 percent of the total investment. That does not mean that there is absolutely going to be a margin call. The best strategy to use here is to look at how the stock has moved and looked at any case where the stock has experienced a dramatic fall in value.

Strategies for Margin Trading

Margin trading is a great way to make more money, but it is only experienced traders who should make margin trades. The potential for a profit could be enormous, but the margin involved can also aggravate any loss you encounter. You can use a few margin trading strategies to keep potential losses from becoming a burden. These focus more on keeping a sense of control.

Keep Your Margins Small at the Start

Just because you could at the beginning get twice the size of an investment when using a large margin trade doesn't mean that's the best idea. You must keep your margins in check whilst at the start using your own money. For example, in the beginning, you can stay with a 10 percent margin. This keeps the danger of a margin trade lower while providing you with a sensible introduction to how those trades work. A smaller trade margin is best when the stock that you want to trade is slightly more unstable. A stock that can change in value in less than a week by 10 percent or more should only be purchased with smaller margins.

Look for Stop Orders

For margin trades, stoppage orders are even more important. You can use a stop order to keep the failures down, but looking at how such orders work for-profits might be even more important. It is best to add a stop order a little over your stock's original value, as this ensures that any margin calls that might occur are minimized.

Avoid Speculation

It's also critical that when looking at what might actually occur with a stock, you avoid any kind of speculation. Speculation is problematic in that it makes an emotional decision easier for a person. This expects a stock to possibly move up in value without actually looking at various factors linked to the stock history.

High Rewards Mean Higher Risks

Although you can understand a profit from your marginal trades, as you would have been able to buy more stocks, this is still a very risky endeavor. As with any type of investment, when the reward is also great, the risk is greater. Because you trade on the margin, you work with more shares than you might otherwise have been able to buy. You are expanding your buying ability, but you also risk losing money.

In short, margin trades are exciting because they can give you a better chance of making a big profit. You also need to watch the value of a stock carefully and how it could change as the losses could be even worse.

Review with the broker you wish to use the terms of the margin trades.

Chapter 8: How to Identify Bad Stock News

We are living in a time when it's very easy to mislead people. We look at social media stories that claim to be real, and we assume they are accurate, but in reality, those stories are just rumors or falsehoods that random people spread about. Perhaps the worst false stories relate to certain stock investments. You may hear stuff about stocks worth investing in, but that information may not be correct. Those news stories may sometimes suggest that something could happen that will cause a stock to drop in value. Sometimes those who want to manipulate stocks are planted by the reports. Often many traders make deals based on a fake news story. Be careful to read any news story. There are several tips you can use to identify bad news stories so that it doesn't mislead your investment strategies.

Social Media Is Risky

The first sign that the news story stocks is when it is published on a social media website. The problem with finding these tips on social media sites is that those sites are often filled with fake accounts that people like running. Some people like to spread rumors. You can tell that a stock tip on social media that you find is bad if:

- The person posting that message is anonymous.
- The organization giving this “useful tip” is unknown. You can not verify the group responsible for posting this on a social media site. An unverified account is one that nobody, in particular, can confirm to hold.
- The tip listed could include misrepresentations, inaccuracies, or other errors. These fundamental errors, such as referring to Cedar Fair stock as having the symbol CF instead of its actual symbol

FUN, suggest somebody is rushing to post something online and has no accurate information.

Do your own due diligence to see if there's a stock worth it. Look online to see if the stock in question is legitimate and if the tip information can be confirmed through stock review.

Avoid Anonymous Sources

When reading stock tips, one thing you might hear involves anonymous sources stating certain items about a stock. You might hear stuff about a stock being a good deal, or perhaps something about a company that might impact the value of a stock. Do not believe anything from anonymous sources: It simply may not be legitimate. Many sources claiming anonymity may not have a direct understanding of the stock over which they are posting rumors. Sometimes a news source may take an anonymous tip without considering the impacts, or maybe they have further motives to post the rumor.

Who Else Is Reporting?

You might find at times that nobody else reports on a specific stock. You might see that no one wants to discuss stock-related things based on value changes, acquisitions with which a company could be working, and so on.

You may come across a stock tip listed on some site as an "exclusive" tip. That place could be claiming it's the only place you'll get that information. Did that entity has claimed other exclusives in the past? Have great stock-investment stories been released before? Be aware of any person reporting stories that nobody else is discussing and is certainly not a story you would like to trust. You never know where the story might have originated. After all, that "exclusive" label could be just a case of somebody trying to say something interesting and having no basis in truth.

Review the Fine Print

In any news story you read, you have to look at the fine print no matter in which stock you want to invest. A news story will sometimes say the stock tips come from a person who was paid to disseminate that information. A case where compensation is given to someone for offering tips needs to be disclosed in a report. It's often a sign of concern, as the news report could just be a promotional advertisement for a stock.

Additionally, there are times when a person who writes a story says he or she has some position to discuss with the stock. One person who holds that stock could write a story about Boeing stock. At the bottom of the story, that writer must state that he or she holds some stock in Boeing. This suggests the writer may be biased and maybe trying to hide information that could hurt the value of the stock. They need to take storylines like this with a grain of salt. The writer might, after all, just write a positive-sounding series of stories because that person wants to push the stock to a more advantageous position for him.

Where to Find News

Although it's easy to fall for fake stock-related news stories, you don't have to constantly struggle with those issues. For stock news, you can go to various useful places. Here are some of the best places to consider when retrieving stock news:

- **Investopedia** regularly offers information about various trading events and service providers. Simulators are also available to assist you in reviewing how stocks trade. The site does well to report margin trading, options trading, and many other investment firms.

- **Yahoo Finance** focuses on specifics when reporting on inventories. It includes information on how stocks are traded based on volume, P/E ratio, and many other technical considerations.

- For a long time, **The Wall Street Journal** has been a reliable option for financial information. The Journal can be found throughout the country on newsstands, and can be shipped to your home, but that does cost money to get regular access to what the WSJ offers.

- Thanks to its solid platform, **Bloomberg** is a popular name for business news. It also offers various reports, which are based on certain markets. Bloomberg's information is detailed and gives you all you need to know about a stock.

Do not forget to check what your stock screener or trading broker could offer. They must include detailed and regularly updated information from the sources noted above and from others. Look for your own additional information too.

There are plenty of legitimate sources that offer details of quality from which you can profit. False information is plentiful, but if you simply know where to find legitimate information, you do not have to struggle with it.

Chapter 9: Penny Stocks

The stocks you read about here are the ones that are expensive to invest in. You don't need to stay with those expensive inventories. You are given the option to select penny stocks. Penny stocks are stocks of firms trading at very low values. The SEC says a penny stock is worth less than $5 per share and will not be listed on one of the major exchanges. Penny stocks sound interesting on the surface because they are so cheap. At the same time, these investments are risky and difficult to work with, because when you trade them, it's impossible to figure out where they might go. There are some things that you can do to successfully trade them out.

What Is a Penny Stock?

A penny stock is a stock with a very tiny market cap. Besides having shares of less than $5 each, the company's market cap is worth about $50 million to $300 million and is not necessarily a globally recognized group. There are also some smaller markets where the stock trades. Penny stocks are traded over the counter in the US. That is, the trades are managed without exchange between the parties. Both the OTC Bulletin Board and Pink Sheets list information on how to organize these penny stocks. The most notable feature of penny stocks is that their values are very small. Some of those stocks may not even be worth one cent per stock.

The small real estate company Metro spaces, for example, trades as an OTC stock under the symbol MSPC. Metro spaces had been trading at $0,0001 per share at the beginning of 2018. Not all penny inventories are so cheap. Another OTC stock with the POTN symbol, Pot network Holdings, is a stock of a company dedicated to hemp products. The business has a stock that traded at around 50 cents per share for much of 2018.

The general thing about penny stocks is they're very inexpensive. As you will read next, however, these inventories are extremely risky.

Serious Risks

Hard to Prepare Trades

Many investment brokers aren't going to work with penny stocks, believing they're overly risky and hard to find. They may also be struggling with planning orders because the markets involved are slower than the larger ones. There's also the concern about what happens when a single trade shifts stock value.

No Real Standards

Although many stocks have strong standards of how they are to be traded, in penny stocks, you won't find those. Such a stock doesn't have to meet any significant standards to enter an exchange. An OTC penny stock has no information to file with SEC. The OTCBB does ask that the stocks it lists file with the SEC, but this is not particularly necessary. You can still check the SEC to see if there are proper filings for a stock you want to invest in, but that can be hard to find.

Hard to Find Information

The next issue surrounding OTC penny stocks is that you may not get sufficient details about what's available. You won't find much information about penny stocks, as news agencies won't report about them. These firms are too small to actually take some of these news agencies seriously.

You may want to read information about penny stock tips to check out, including stocks that might fascinate people to invest in. Those reports are often made by people who have positions in those stocks, with heavily biased information. They may also give you symbols and names, but not enough information about what you might expect from those stocks; that makes it more difficult for you to actually get the details you need. What is even worse is that it is not easy to access those stocks through a website. If you've tried to type "OTC stock quotes" into a search box, you might just come across a bunch of topics listing details on those quotes. This only helps make penny stocks more unreliable due to the lack of information available in the process.

Do You Know the Businesses Involved?

Check out the Pink Sheets to see some of the currently listed businesses. Recognize any one of these? Have you heard about Nutate Energy Holdings before? What about the holdings of Pazoo or Textmunication? Until now, the odds are you've never even heard of these groups.

Figuring out what makes these businesses tick could be a challenge. When you enter a Pazoo search, you will not see the company's website as the first listing on pazoo.com. Instead, you'll see a bunch of links to sites listing information about how the Pazoo stock works on the market and what trends might be noticed in this penny stock. It would take you a while to figure out that this is a wellness and health group which sells online nutritional products.

This is one of the biggest concerns you need to be aware of regarding investing in penny stocks. While penny stocks may seem intriguing, it's almost impossible to figure out what's popular with the stock or why its value might change.

Easy to Inflate or Adjust

Have you ever noticed cases where the value of a penny stock has undergone a dramatic change in a very short time? For example, Reach Messaging Holdings, an OTC stock underneath the RCMH ticker, experienced a significant, very short-lived bump in its value in February 2018. The value of the stock was $0.0003, but it soon moved to $0.0008. It then went down in just one day to $0.0003, and eventually to $0.0002.

What if, at this point, you had a million shares in RCMH? You might have bought them when the stock was $0.0008 believing the stock would continue to rise. You'd spent $800 on the stock. With that stock falling back to $0.0003, you'd have lost $500 on your capital expenditure. Simply put, you went with the conviction that the stock would continue to rise in value, but that stock actually sagged out.

That RCMH stock could have increased in value because there was a massive trade in that stock by one person. That person may have bought 10 million or more RCMH shares and then sold them off in a couple of hours or days after a sizeable increase in the stock. Even worse, that person could be somebody from within the company. This is a legitimate penny stock problem that many people don't even think about. It just takes one person to inflate or deflate the value of a stock. This, in fact, often happens with inventories that are not very liquid. A stock that does not have liquidity will not change much in value unless one individual manages to place a huge order and get a considerable number of shares sold or bought all at once.

Pumping and Dumping

A related issue is the pump and dump strategy with which penny stocks often struggle. Although it isn't illegal, it certainly feels like it should be because it manipulates the value of a penny stock directly and is often done by someone from within the business, such as:

1. A person buys a significant number of shares in a stock. Usually, this is for penny stocks, although theoretically, it could happen with any stock. Many penny stocks lacking volume makes them more likely to be targeted by pump and dump schemes. They manipulate much easier.

2. That person then tries to promote a stock by offering false or potentially misleading statements regarding the ability of the stock to grow. In the past, this was done by phone using cold calling techniques. People can now go to social media or create their own topic writing to promote those stocks.

3. Then people fall for those statements and buy the stock. Usually, the people who choose to buy those stocks are willing to invest in them

without thinking twice. They could be emotionally driven to invest in those stocks and not thoroughly investigate the company.

4. The person who started the scheme will sell off his shares after enough people buy the stocks in question because that person will have made enough money from the people buying the stock.

5. The people who fell from this trick for the pump and dump scheme could lose hundreds or even thousands of dollars. There are very significant problems with the pump and dump scheme.

What if You Do Want to Invest?

You can still invest, if you wish, in penny stocks. The risks of doing so are high, but it doesn't mean they need to be out of bounds. In fact, if you use a few basic strategies, you could earn money from penny stocks or at least reduce the risks involved. Alongside some more in-depth strategies, many of those are common-sense measures.

Do Not Pay Attention to Success Stories

Have you ever come across some site talking about penny stocks and hear someone report he or she has made tens of thousands of dollars in penny stocks trading? This sounds like a great suggestion and encourages you to invest in those stocks. The truth is, success stories like these, as exciting as they are, are often not legitimate. People who claim they made big bucks on penny stock trading are in the absolute minority. These are people who simply went through a few lucky streaks. Knowing what to find in a penny stock is, of course, critical if you are to succeed. There are so many risks and issues on the market, luck is sometimes more important than simply looking up information about what's available on the market. So you should never assume that these success stories will come true for you.

Don’t Hold Penny Stocks Too Long

Decide how long your penny stocks will last. You never know when something will change at any given time and can quickly shrink in value.

Look at how stock in Glance Technologies has changed over time. Around the beginning of 2018, GLNNF had a value of $1.40, but in about two months, that stock fell fast to 60 cents.

Many people buy massive quantities of shares in penny stocks, and it's no surprise that people might experience significant losses. After all, many could buy a large number of penny stocks because they're cheap, and more needs to be bought to make a decent profit. If someone holds a stock too long, that person is at risk of having massive drops in the value of the stock.

Buying and selling a penny-stock the same day is perfectly fine. No matter what you do, avoid holding that stock for more than a few days. There's always a chance you'll lose more than you could earn. The lowest stocks should always have a minimum holding time.

When to Sell?

A good strategy for selling penny stocks is to sell them when you have a 20 or 30 percent return. For example, buying 100,000 shares of a stock at $0.01 and then selling them at $0.012 is great, as you go from a total of $1,000 to $1,200. This is an ideal return of 20 percent. Some investors may hold the stocks assuming a stock could really move forward. Someone could assume the same stock will move up to $0.01 at $0.1. Investing in the stock would be extremely difficult to go from $1,000 to $10,000. Even if it did, this would take a very long time to happen. Of course, when they reach a 20 or 30 percent gain threshold, smart investors will have sold their shares anyway, making it nearly impossible for the stock to actually make that huge increase.

On a related note, you should try to add a stop command to your transaction to prevent potential losses from becoming a threat. Then again, some brokerage firms might not actually offer such orders on penny stocks due to the extended risk associated with them. The risk of a pump and dump event might make it so that the actual value goes well beyond what your stop order was for; at that time, you don't want to have a stop order at $0.1 only for the stock to drop to $0.06.

Watch Company Information

Some firms might claim their stocks are growing well. Company management may, however, skew its documents toward the more positive things about a stock. Some of the positive stories might also be inflated to make them sound more interesting and valuable than they really are. Companies are not necessarily required to tell you certain things about their stocks. They could be working very hard to make their stocks more intriguing for you without revealing any real substance. Always take whatever a company says about its stock and how it changes with a grain of salt, so you don't fall into any investment traps.

Choose Stocks with a High Volume

The next tip is to stay with stocks that have a good volume of trading. These are the inventories people actually buy. These could include stocks traded by a lot of people, thereby reducing the risk of a stock pump and dump scheme. Everything that has at least 100 million trading volumes is always worthwhile. That means that within the last 24 hours of trading, at least 100 million shares were traded.

That tip has one major caveat. You need to look at how the volume changes for a penny stock, based on what is shown in the read-out chart. A chart, for example, could show one or two massive spikes in a stock price. That means one person controlled a great deal of trading. It could, of course, be a sign of a pump and dump attack as well.

It is always easier to trust any stock with a graph or chart that is a little more variable and doesn't have lots of odd shifts in its value.

Avoid Trading More Than Needed

The specific number of penny stock shares that you can purchase could be limitless. While you might be motivated to purchase one million stock shares at a value of $0.0005, that could be a serious risk, in fact. You'd spend $500 on an investment that, if you're not careful, could be going south rather quickly.

On the contrary, try to keep your penny stock holdings from being worth more than a hundred dollars. A better idea is to stay with 100,000 shares at $0.0005. You would only spend $50 on your trade, but at least you won't lose a lot of money if the stock decreases rather than growing as you anticipated.

Never Sell Short

When you think about it, selling short films sounds like a great idea. You can borrow penny stock shares that appear to have been pumped up, sell them, and then buy back those stocks for a sizeable profit. The truth is that you could lose so much money from the trade than you could afford. For a penny stock, the time period for a short sale could be far too long.

Review Your Position

Consider how your position is organized based on the size of the volume of the stock. Never trade more than 10 percent of the volume of that stock. If you did that, you would end up inflating the stock price. Investing far too much at one time only adds to the overall transaction risk involved. When getting this part of the trade organized, you need to be careful.

When working with penny stocks, remember that you are fully aware of what you're going into in the process. If you are not careful, such stocks could prove to be dangerous and harmful to your investment plans.

Chapter 10: When to Sell a Stock?

Throughout this guide, you have experienced several times when you can reach a stock spot. If it is a strong upward trend or even a tendency indicating a major long-term market shift, the opportunities you have to get into a market are different and worth evaluating just how useful they are. And you'll have to sell your stocks for a bit. Never believe you should hang onto some stock for as much as you want. Instead, when you market something at the right moment, you can care about it. This chapter is about choosing the best opportunities to get the stock sold off.

Look at Dividend Changes

Look for every situation where the valuation of the profits on the stock is beginning to decline. Study stock and company to see what triggers the transition. There might be serious problems inside the company, such as a lack of sales or court proceedings that trigger the valuation of the dividend to shift. And the slightest dividend reduction can be a source of alarm. A single decline may be a huge issue for your savings, with dividends worth pennies apiece. Losing one cent of a stock's 10,000 shares will result in a $100 reduction of the dividends. That, of course, is only one indication of what might happen.

Review Your Price Target

A successful buying approach is to stick with a defined price point. This can be the extent to which you like the stock to be independent of the form of trade you join. Start by looking at the expected returns per unit. A quarterly outlook for the next year will help you gain an insight into what's going on with a warehouse. This involves a study of how an organization generates its profits. This can help you define an estimated pace at which the stock will expand over time. See the earnings per share (EPS) forecast with caution. This is only a prediction of what will happen inside the company, depending on several variables. Clearly, you will have to use a stop-loss plan at this stage in case an organization failed to meet its estimate.

When the Volume Slows

The amount for your stock would have a major effect on your stock's progress. What happens when the demand begins to taper, and the stock isn't as common as it once was? The lack of volume may be an indication that your stock would not be going the same way you'd wanted it to go. A stock that had risen in value could display resistance as its amount diminishes. This means that consumers are not as willing to purchase a product as they used to be. Soon some people will start selling the stock. But you can sell your shares as quickly as possible, but that you can make sure you move out of a position until it becomes less enticing.

When a Business Is About to Go Bankrupt

When a business falls bankrupt, it can be catastrophic. There is a possibility that a company will arise better than ever out of bankruptcy, such as what happened to numerous automotive firms in the U.S. A bankruptcy is more about making sure a corporation will reorganize itself to prevent a tough condition from getting worse.

The problems affecting a company may be too severe. A prime example of this is the discount store chain Toys R Us. The company moved through a period of closing stores in 2017 after it filed bankruptcy and then confirmed the second round of closures in 2018, leading the market presence of the brand to decline drastically. The major challenge is the bankruptcy will preclude a company from becoming sustainable and sustainable for investment. The valuation of the stock would more than certainly collapse as a consequence of what is going on.

Signs of a Possible Bankruptcy

If you find that a stock will collapse in value with clear indicators of recession, you can sell the stock. People will not experience damages because of an impending recession until it's too late, and the recession eventually occurs.

An organization is trying to slash its expenses but does not explain that it is doing so.

Many senior administrators or executives affiliated with a company might be quitting the company. If they realize the trouble is increasing and they want to get away before things get worse, they might quit early. They might also provide more comprehensive internal details on what's going on within the company, which allows it to fall apart.

Management may even be quiet and unable to share details on what is going on or whether such strategic decisions are being made.

Revenues fall dramatically and do not seem to display any indication of rebounding in their prices.

The cash balance statements may even disclose any important improvements. These involve improvements in how equipment maintenance plans can adjust and other routine efforts.

Tax Considerations for Losing Stocks

A large aspect of situations when the securities are losing value is they may provide you with a potential tax write-off. Any short-term losses you incur from stock purchases can outweigh short-term profits. When they drop value, you should sell your investments to better manage any taxes you'll have to pay. Particularly during the latter part of the year, you might do this if you have something that you've kept for a while, and you have to get rid of it. If you can lose revenue on the stock's disposal, you're at least going to hold your taxes off so high.

The short-term gains and losses would be registered separately from the long-term gains, the losses from a more mature portfolio that may be utilized by non-day traders before filing taxes. Check any of your holdings to decide if selling your shares is acceptable for your tax planning purposes at any particular period. For more guidance about what may be done to reduce your tax burden, please contact a local accountant or other tax planning specialist in your field.

Avoid Emotional Concerns

Moving a stock is often challenging, but moving anything you've had for a long period can be much tougher for you. You could feel that the stock that you had was something that you needed to hang on for as far as possible. You may have assumed that this will continue to increase in value. Perhaps it might also be the first stock you've ever traded-in.

You should still apply to your portfolio long-term stocks, but it doesn't suggest you can keep buying those stocks indefinitely. You have to disregard the emotional aspects of keeping a warehouse. You may be burdened with certain feelings when you try to hold your investments healthy.

How Much Money Should You Spend At One Time?

To get something out of day-trading is crucial to making enough funds for your stock trades. You should be conscious of how much you pay on a single transaction. It's real; you cannot pay more than you can manage on a single purchase. Is there some particular sum of money you can invest in each contract? There are no guidelines about how much expenditure an individual should be investing in. You ought to have a fair bit of common sense.

Here are a few suggestions:

Plan a Percentage Limit

Developing a percentage cap is the first method for handling capital through trades. That is the particular amount of the investments that you are planning to use in a deal. The optimal percentage cap for your investments is 1 percent. If you have a balance of $25,000 for day trading, you can just be paying $250 per sale. That keeps your risk of trading too high. When the fund expands or shrinks in size, the 1 percent sum can always be utilized. If your portfolio winds up heading towards $26,000 in valuation, you can still use a $260 cap on a sale. You do have to stick to the 1 percent cap so you don't run the risk of wasting more than you can handle. Do not deviate from the norm except through your portfolio shrinks.

Review the Cents Per Risk

The second technique to use includes calculating the cents by chance. This is a calculation of the difference in cents between your stock entry point and the stop command you apply to it. If a cents per risk ratio was too big, you would choose to spend less capital on a project. If the value is a little similar to the original price, you will have more.

How Big of a Position Should You Have?

Holding a target of 1 percent for your transactions is important, so you can think of how many securities you purchase at a time. This quick equation can be used to get an understanding of how large the place should be:

1. Take the entire sum of capital you'll be placing at risk.

2. Divide location by danger by cents. (In decimal terms this would be; 50 would be 0.5.)

3. You can know the total amount of securities you will be buying.

Let's presume you're plan to spend $250 in a portfolio despite getting 50 cents to stop order. You'd divide by 0.5 $250, which is equivalent to 500. That is, you can acquire up to 500 shares at once. Be mindful of potential transaction payments related to the portfolio contracts. Although this does not cost as much as the whole transaction itself, it also pays to recognize at least the charges while preparing the trading strategy.

On a note similar to this, there can be occasions that you need to round out the request. You do not have the opportunity to sell 250 or 270 stocks. Instead, you can be asked by a broker to exchange 200 or 300 securities. You'd have to round the amount up or down, but for an even sum, the dealer would have a simpler time to conduct the deal. You have the option, but if necessary, it is better to select the lower number. Use the 200 share option for this example.

This would obviously be less than 1 percent of your overall assets, so at this juncture, that's perfect. You also need to spend wisely on the stock, so you can finally step ahead and improve your position later on. The smaller order will be less at risk, but that's another matter.

A Sense of Balance

You need to keep the finances in check. Putting so much capital into a stock could result in you spending more money than you can manage. There's still a risk a project fails. The last option you might do is to drastically shrink your investments to where you can't afford a reasonable investment anymore.

You can't afford to actually make inexpensive trades all the time, though. You ought to invest a reasonable sum of money in your company if you wish to make anything substantial out of your company. Anyone who invests less would definitely not be reaping the rewards of becoming a good day trader.

How Are Preferred Shares Different from Common Shares?

On the surface, it seems that preferred stock securities are identical to common shares. It reflects one's ownership of a company. The stock price is often focused on the roles of earning and selling. Preferred stock shares can have the same value as common stockholders or are similar to the value at least. Preferred shares send you dividends that are settled upon at the point of a deal, whereas dividends that differ in value depending on profits and other things are paid out by common share. For a preferred share, you'll recognize the size of the dividend per year.

In particular, the dividend may be considerably higher than a common share dividend.

Nevertheless, a preferred share would not grant you are voting privileges in the relations of the business, such as the sale of common stock. That would not actually be a concern when you understand the value of the preferred stock.

What About Maturity?

A significant aspect of dealing with common stock securities is how long you get to hang onto the stock. When the preferred stock hits maturity, you get the initial investment back plus any dividends on it returned. This is a good idea, but it will take a while to hit maturity with the preferred stock. For it to happen, you'd have to wait around 30 to 40 years.

Obviously, with day-trading in mind, that's not something you can do. For anything, that will only be offering you a daily source of income that you can use to invest in the future. This is advantageous in that even though the preferred stock sinks to zero, you can always get the maximum valuation of the portfolio. At maturity, the entire amount would be paid out, thereby granting you maximum coverage for the existence of the product. It's a lot different from the common stock because if the stock really dropped to nothing, you will get none.

Why Would a Business Issue Preferred Shares?

A corporation will sell common stock certificates to investors as a way to collect funds for business activities. This occurs when a company has sold common stocks and bonds daily. However, usually, companies delay until they have sold common stocks and shares since they are not since difficult to sell as the preferred stock.

A business may terminate the dividends on preferred shares. This doesn't happen very much, so there's still an opening. In reality, it is feasible for a corporation to do this and not to fear being sued for default.

This is separate from loans where a corporation will default if the debt in such assets cannot be paid off.

A corporation will also benefit from preferred stock tax incentives. A business would not be expected to pay taxes on any of the funds it collects for the stock. Growing the overall sum of capital it won't have to pay back is better for a company because it doesn't take a long time to get preferred stock released on the market.

The firm would compensate investors' interest depending on how the stock does. Fortunately, this benefit would not be liable to taxation for the company. A large amount of the tax load is thus lifted entirely. However, the business selling the stock would not benefit from such tax advantages.

Important Concerns

You have to be careful, as tempting as is the chosen product. You could begin by looking at the interest rates correlated with preferred stock. Try to purchase the stock at a cheaper cost, as profits would have a greater opportunity to rise with time. Something that has a high cost is most likely to receive smaller overtime payouts. Moreover, rising interest rates trigger increases in returns on other stock-related assets. That cuts into the dividend gains you'd make.

You have to be very vigilant of how, with time, the common stock aligned with a preferred stock varies. The dilemma is that as stock values go up, the corporation that sold them will cash in common stock securities. You would also lose the valuation really going up on the preferred shares. You could earn compensation on any shares you lost, even though the compensation will not come similar to what you'd get if the shares matured.

Will These Strategies Work For Other Types of Investments?

All the points in this document you've read about are planned with stock trades or options in mind. For any other project, you may be involved in, you may suggest partnering with certain techniques. The amazing thing in the business environment today is that consumers have plenty of various opportunities to participate in.

People will transact stocks and options as well as securities, mutual funds, and more. Cryptocurrencies can also be used in any sector today. Don't believe the techniques you've read about here would fit with all investing forms. The concern for so many of today's equity assets is that they all have multiple factors that may directly affect their beliefs.

Commodities, for example, are also influenced by geographical factors and patterns on what customers would want or what companies might use. Mutual funds are also distinctive in terms of how they offer professionally designed solutions assembled by experts to their investors' benefit. There are cryptocurrencies every where. In reality, the products you invest in differ from one sector to another. For example, the energy industry is distinct from the retail or hospitality industries. Different variables can significantly affect how patterns grow and how market prices may differ.

Such assets outside the stocks are often expected to wind up dealing with the same patterns and metrics as stocks. The Doji can predominate on a foreign currency pair. A pennant, cup, and handle or some other pattern of exchange may appear on a merchandise transaction.

In order to obtain details about certain specific projects, you will also have to deal with several key principles. The issue with non-stock investments is that they are very drastic and complex in the variables which affect them.

Overall, if you plan to use the points you have gained regarding other forms of investments in this text, you should be exceedingly cautious. If you do, you can still use them, but that doesn't guarantee they would work.

Chapter 11: Links and Steps to Activate with a Broker

Investing profitably allows you to use the same brokerage firm that fits your financial priorities, training qualifications, and personal style. Choosing the right online financial manager that fits your requirements, particularly for new shareholders, may make a big difference with an interesting new investment portfolio and severe loss.

Although there are no entirely convinced-fire means of guaranteeing returns on investment, there is indeed a way of setting oneself help and protect by choosing the investment account that better fits your description.

In this tutorial, we'll examine anything that you can search for in your perfect broker, from the apparent to something not-so-accurate (as how simple it really is to get help from a real person when you really need it).

Key Points

• Exposure to the markets is cheap and easy due to a number of retail brokers operating online portals.

• Various online traders are tailored for a particular category of the customer— from lengthy-term buy-or-hold newcomers to professional, successful day trades.

• Picking the right broker online needs any proper research to have the best out of your investment. Obey the measures and recommendations to pick the right one in this post.

1: Remind Yourself About Your Desires

Take a minute to zero in on what is really essential to you that in a trading site, before they start pressing on broker advertising. Based on the financial goals and also where people are along the investing learning process, the solution may be subtly different.

When you're just heading out, features such as simple educational tools, detailed glossaries, fast access to help personnel, and the opportunity to learn trades until you actually play with actual money might be priorities.

If you already have certain investing expertise into your belt but are ready to get ambitious, you may like more strong-level information or interpretation-based tools published by active traders and experts and a broad range of simple and technical info.

A genuinely professional trader, maybe someone who has already carried out dozens of trades but also looking for a different broker, would offer preference to sophisticated charting tools, dependent order rights, and the right to trade futures, bonds, shares, and specified-income instruments, and stocks.

Be frank on what you see on the investing path right now, where you'd like to go. Would you try to create an IRA and 401(k) retirement plan and concentrate on passive assets that will produce tax-free money? Would you like to look down your nose in day-trading and don't know how to get started? Would you prefer the thought of designing your entire portfolio and tailoring it, or are you able to hire a specialist to make sure it's done right?

Relying on the direction you follow, there could be even more queries that you may need to address when you acquire knowledge and develop your objectives. Beginning with any of these four key criteria for now, though, will help you decide which one of the broker's features we will cover below would be most relevant. We also provided some test questions below each general subject to help keep the analytical impulses flowing:

1. Are you an aggressive or inactive investor in general? Want to be very hands-on to do day- and swing-trades? Can you finally see yourself abandoning the 9-to-5 routine and being a maximum-time entrepreneur? Or, then, are you searching for a few good assets with little to no day-to-day contact to carry for the longer term?

2. How much do you understand? Which sort of trades do you like to carry out? Will you be the sort of shareholder that understands what they like to do and only wants a forum that allows trading simple and fast? or would you like the broker with such a broader arsenal of tools to help you look for chances? Which kind of stocks are you targeting? Stocks, ETFs, mutual funds? Would you want to exchange stocks, derivatives, or fixed-income instruments even if you're more sophisticated? What are retailing margins? Want exposure to contingent orders, longer trading hours, and currency trading choices?

3. Want to help? What type? Would you go towards the DIY road, learn how to view charts or financial details in order to discover and carry out your own trading? or would you like to employ a pro? How are you in the learning process because you decided to go for it yourself? Which kind of tools are you supposed to use to draw on your understanding? Need quick access to help workers? or will you discover what you have to know via online learning resources? Would you want to conduct trades remotely? or do you like to dial in and get a broker and support you with a procedure?

4. What are the targets? What do you invest in? Why do you choose an investment? Seek to supplement your daily salary to boost your existing living standards? Was there some special case or cost you'd like to fund? Would you plan to potentially be your main source of revenue for this? Are you seeking to set up private pensions, and if so, do you still want a retirement plan, or would you like to start a new one through your fund of choice?

Such queries must not be replied incorrectly. Be honest about how many of your important movements, energy, and struggle you are willing to put in the investments. Over time, your answers will shift, and that is good. Do not try to predict any of your desires and priorities for the remainder of your career. Just start right now, with what you have right now.

2: Narrow Down Your Area

Now that you're having a clear understanding of what your investment objective is or what essential services you are going to start looking for in your perfect brokers, it is time to winnow down your choices a little bit. Although many brokerage elements might be more essential to some shareholders than others, there are also some things that should have any reliable brokerage online. Checking the simple needs for such a wide variety of choices is a perfect way to easily narrow the spectrum.

Stock Broker and Trust Regulation

Is the courier a Financial Investor Security Company (SIPC) member? Usually, there should be a form of description or warning at the end of the homepage. The company can be easily looked up on the SIPC platform.

Is the broker a part of the regulatory body for the financial sector (FINRA)? It should be noted very clearly in a location that is easy to find. You can view brokerages on the website of FINRA's Brokerage Check.

Is the company protected by the National Federal insurance Company (FDIC) as it sells checking or investment accounts, or all other investment items? Investment plans—such as securities or mutual funds invested in commodities, shares, futures, and insurance policies—are not covered by FDIC, since the security of the assets cannot be assured. Moreover, if the company sells CDs, Term deposit Arrangements

(MMDAs), banking accounts, or investment accounts, the FDIC will completely back them up.

What form of protection do they have to cover you in the event that the business fails? As a participant of a SIPC, the business will provide policies with a cap of at minimum $500,000 per client, with $250,000 reserved for cash complaints. If the corporation conforms to the consumer rights Rule, further coverage should also be provided over and above the SIPC's minimum standards.

Is there some sort of protection against fraud? Does the business compensate you for fraud-related losses? Be sure that you double test what the company expects of you will be reimbursed. Figure out whether you need to have some evidence or take clear measures for your own safety.

What is it the new consumers assume? Start looking for brokerage user feedback online, utilizing terms such as "insurance allegation," "fraud defense," and "customer care." Obviously, online comments can usually be viewed with a pinch of salt—certain people feel like moaning. Moreover, when there are many users from various places that are all voicing the same claim, then you might want to further examine.

Online Monitoring and Account Safety

It's crucial to know well how your data is secured by a brokerage.

Does it provide two-factor protection on the broker website? Can you get the choice in response to your key to triggering a protection feature? Responding to security requests, obtaining special, moment-sensitive keys through email or text, or utilizing data security keys that fit in your USB, may be popular.

Which kind of software is the broker employing to keep the data secure? Find out how the broker utilizes "cookies" or cryptography and how that explicitly describes how it utilizes them to secure the account details and how it functions.

Will be the company still marketing details regarding consumers to third parties, including advertising companies? The response, of course, should be no.

Brokers Trading Deals

Since the sorts of methods, you will rely on your objectives; the following elements should also be checked quickly to weed out investment banks that will simply not make your life easier.

Besides regular (taxable) mutual funds, what sorts of funds does a broker offer? If you already have investment income, for example, find out how you should open a health savings Arrangement (ESA) or a correctional account for the child or even other members.

Can you access a bank account? See if the broker has Roth or alternative savings plans and whether you should carry over an unused 401 K and IRA.

There are different companies for various targets for investment? For example, find out how the broker has handled accounts on offer. Often, find out which various forms of portfolios have investment requirements.

Can you use the brokerage to manage employee retirement funds? This can apply if you are a proprietor of a business. These Account forms include Basic or SEP IRAs.

Would the fund have alternatives for Self-Directed retirement funds or the Single 401 K? What happens if you are the only team member in your small company?

3: Calculate the Charges

Although there could be some items more relevant for you other than payments, you could begin with a fairly good picture of how many you could spend to use some specific brokers.

For others, whether the product provides functionality that it lacks affordable rivals, a low prime might be acceptable. In fact, though, at valuation costs and selling profits, you ought to risk as necessary of the interest earned as necessary.

Beginning from the end result, you can quickly decide that stock traders have become too costly to accept and are not really suited to the type of investing operation you're focusing on.

Brokers Account Income

Will the broker make a fee for the account opening?

Is there a Total Deposit? Please remember that investment funds have a minimum investment of $1,000 and sometimes more than that, but that isn't relevant as a financial institution that requires you to deposit the lowest possible amount of money only to open the account.

Are there really any maintenance charges per annum or yearly account? If so, were they forgiven for bigger accounts, or can they be skipped effectively even though your checking account is low? For instance, if the holders concur to collect documentation digitally, Vanguard renounces its yearly fee.

Was the dealer providing equal entry to a trade site as a result of their membership? The online platform will ideally match your needs if you are just beginning out.

Is there a Pay-to-Play trading site Pro and Advanced? When you're a very seasoned user, it's crucial to learn whether or maybe not you should have to pay to update your profile or get to the speed-up software and services. For buyers who choose to position a certain amount of trades each year or spend a certain sum, certain specialized systems are safe.

What are those margin prices? Margin investing is for really professional customers only, who recognize the dangers. If you're a value player, the statement is not going to relate to you.

What is the total amount of loan and balance of the account? For greater quantities, most investment banks will give lower rates, so don't let that be a reason for the client to borrow more than they should.

Commissions for Trading

Will exchange fees depend on whether you have spent or how much you move through brokerage? Vanguard commercial rates, for instance, vary according to the size of the account, whilst also E*TRADE provides a lowered council to clients who buy and sell greater than 30 times a quarter.

William Schwab's fees are smaller than rivals; however, to create an account, you will spend nearly $1,000. Think you should look at the rates that are most applicable to you, depending on your expected balance of account and trade activity.

Will common fee rates extend to information visualization? If you prepare more than stock trading, make sure that you know whatever the fees are for trading options, securities, futures, and perhaps other bonds.

If you think for investment funds or ETFs, will there be payment-free choices? What's really the least investment? Be sure that investments that allow you to purchase and sell for cheap do not charge certain forms of fees anyway. Investments often came with various types of expenses, all of which can pounce on you. Check the proposal of every investment you are contemplating to make sure you grasp all the risks involved.

Will the company make any free or discounted transactions? The number of 'bonus' trades you earn may vary based on your outstanding balance, so be sure you double-check what's being offered for the level of your account that would apply.

Often, make sure to test what sorts of transactions apply for the reduced price—whether it's just for shares and whether it includes ETFs, futures, or specific-income securities.

Is the contract timetable favorable to the sort of trading that you can do? Are you compensated with more successful trading, or are you penalized? For example, prices for Vanguard are increasing from the first twenty-five trades for Specification and Main competitor clients, or after 100 transactions for Flagship Enable clients, as you see in the above chart. This means consumers focused on active, purchase-and-hold investments get the most value.

Conversely, for the first 30 transactions of every given fifth, E*TRADE provides discounted fees, and committed participants are paid most frequently by utilizing the site.

When the dealer offers consulting services, how many do they charge? Is there a certain balance of account required to pay for such services? When, for whatsoever the reason, you are not trying to run your own investments, make sure to pay really great consideration to advisor costs.

4: Check the Broker Network

Although every brokerage will provide a reasonably clear overview of all sorts of applications and services a trading broker provides, often giving it a quick drive is the only way to determine the consistency of the product. With brokers who require you to set up an account for free, the initiative to go through the sign-up phase might also be worthwhile only to reach the payment system if this is what's required.

If the company provides a web-based portal that can be used by anybody or a free online application needing no-string sign-up, do your best to use the software you may really need free.

Unless you're a more experienced investor, and there's no easy way to mess around in front of "Pro" software, you could get a decent understanding of a standard of the products from a brokerage only by gazing through the simple collection. Unless there is little that appears appealing in the basic model, it's doubtful that the advanced form would be value the trouble either.

But from the other side of their free services, some firms offer a vast array of gadgets and information, so just don't start writing off brokerage firms with just one platform.

We've also invested a fair deal of time shortening the options based on quality and simple account deals. Now that we have finally got to the fun part, make sure to consume days reading also at features in various areas available.

Go into the steps for putting a transaction to see if the mechanism runs smoothly. Take several stock quotations and other stocks, then press on each tab to look at what sort of data the website offers. Additionally, you can search out any scanners or other resources available to help you identify funds that follow clear requirements.

Answer to the questions while checking platforms:

What kinds of assets on the system may you trade? You would have already ruled out any systems that do not enable you to exchange the bonds that interest you. Make sure this website helps you to transact preferred stock, IPOs, stocks, futures, and a fixed amount of income securities automatically. If you do not see clear protections on the website, but you realize it's sponsored by the company, seek to look at your settings or perform a fast check and see if you can trigger certain apps to read about authorization criteria.

Are those real-time quotes? Do they flow? There are many places you could get a price estimate for just a given location, although not every one of them can have the latest up-to-date detail. Be sure you know in which you can find streaming knowledge in real-time to ensure the trades are timely.

For instance, Vanguard's web-based system provides quick-time data on its countdown clock personal profiles but requires refreshing manuals. Easy results at the quote stage were postponed by 10 min more than that. Schwab's electronic quotes often entail downloading guides, but all provide real-time viewing data across the free Street-smart Edge app and its cloud-enabled equivalent.

Can you create your own custom watch lists or alerts? If you are trying to be more of an affiliate marketer, in relation to email, you will probably like being able to get alerts via text and make different watch lists various criteria.

Do the framework supply inspectors, which you can personalize to discover inventories, ETFs, index funds, or any other bonds that fulfill your special requirements? Even if you're new and don't know what all of the choices literally mean, play with the different variables to have a concept of how easy to use the tools. A strong interface should be designed conceptually and simple to use.

What sorts of commissions can you put? Go into the movements for placing the trade, as well as look at what kinds of requests are being offered. A basic system should normally offer market limits, restrict, hold back, and stop boundaries. A better framework will also enable you to put chasing keep orders or consumer-on-close instructions.

If you're searching to do comparatively several transactions, and you're not concerned in a day- and swing-trading, there should be a basic choice of order types. However, if you're trying to look to get out of trading stocks gritty-gritty, you must look for just a wider choice. If you are more experienced, you will look for just the option to position contractual instructions that enable you can set up several transactions with different triggers, which will immediately execute when the requirements you define are met.

Do you really have access to the timing of orders and the implementation of trades? At least one simple platform will allow you to position good-for-day trades (meaning they could be performed at any time during working hours) or nice-until-canceled trades.

A more sophisticated platform allows you to position boundary orders with more variation, like put-or-kill (which cancels its order immediately if it is not filled out immediately) and Instantaneous or terminate (which cancels its order immediately if it is not filled in at least in part immediately).

Will you deal in Long Hrs.? Stock or ETF transactions arise during regular business hours—9:30 a.m.–4 p.m. Some may be traded, via Aps, at times of pre-market and post-hours. Each brokerage will have its own description of the different time periods covered by such extra hour sessions. E.g., Schwab has post-shipment trade starting at 8:00 a.m., while E*TRADE's pre-market sessions begin around 7 a.m.

Not all systems begin trading over extra periods, and some allow only after-hours trading, not during premarket hours. You can be paid a premium for longer trading hours; just be sure that you check the conditions of certain transactions and ensure that you are not caught by surprise.

Again, that feature might not be all that good for modern investors. However, checking the extra hours trading strategy of a brokerage is important for more experienced traders or others who are trying to be very involved.

Charting Characteristics

Now that you've been messing with the application a little more, take a closer look at a charting feature to test the options available for you.

Listen to what sorts of data it can map, how simple it is to move among charting studies and analyzing common or industry results, and how you should modify and save to later use.

What chart patterns are on a chart? Generally, the stronger, the more. So, at the least, higher times such as quantity, RSI, exponential moving avg, swing trading, MACD, as well as stochastics should be plottable. If one of those key guidelines is missing, it's time to move forward. Basically, a few business events, such as quarterly results, stock divides, and dividends, must also be plottable.

The following are instances of two distinct technological menus. These are less than the optimal alternative. Note that volume is not plottable.

It also has an impressive technological choice, which involves several choices for each form of indicator. It also lets you map the basic data and also has a search feature.

Could you use the same map to compare various stocks or indices?

Can you draw trends, free-form graphs, Prime numbers circles, or arcs, or any other markings on the chart?

Does the website have a trade publication or any other way to save your work? If you're going to speak charts or you're a seasoned investor making notes to keep track of yourself, finding a way to design and archive your graphs is a very useful resource. Things linked include:

• Aside from building historical trends, should you easily draw on the map to illustrate key things, so you can recall when to check later?

• Can you store the maps once you have adjusted them to your needs?

• May you make information for use later?

• Would you place certain comments on the table and make sure you recognize what they refer to when you glance at them later?

Some Other Options

Please note that many of these choices can be accessed only on a professional or advanced level. If you're a successful, experienced investor, you'll definitely want to have a brokerage that provides all those options. Whether you're a more casual investor or simply don't want to spend a fee for bells or whistles that you're not ready to, keeping to a standard free platform is perfect.

- Can you simplify trades with custom rules or with manufactured methodologies?

- Can the network be tailored to acknowledge specific price, indicator, and modulation diagram patterns?

- Can you set alerts to inform you when a contrasting pattern is found on the device?

Is the site or forum allowed to export paper? For shareholders, paper trade is a place to practice putting or performing transactions without even utilizing capital. It is a perfect place to train potential successful investors and investors with all levels of expertise to try out innovative ideas and refine their abilities without causing losses.

Is back testing enabled on the model? Back testing helps you to replicate a transaction based on the past results of your preferred defense, another method to check techniques to get familiar with the method before placing cash on a line. It's a way to put a retroactive, hypothetical transaction and then see what might have changed if you actually carried that out in actual life.

5: How Well Does the Stockbroker Teach its Customers?

While a reliable and efficient payment system is important, you should take a moment to discover educational deals from the brokerage and check out another search feature.

You ought to be capable of locating for words you don't recognize or to get guidance about how to view data because you are a value player. If there is a topic you have been beginning to wonder about and a measurement you do not fully comprehend, do a test run using the search feature and see what you can efficiently find the info you really want.

Know that, for one developer, what is elegant or eco-friendly can be a terrifying maze with meaningless web searches for the next, so it's essential to choose a tool that you can operate with.

If you've been navigating a site for about 20 minutes, you will be able to ask the following issues fairly quickly. If you can't, and a fast check for clear answers from the web doesn't deliver the details you need, it's usually an indication that the trading system isn't for you.

Quality and Accessibility of Stockbrokers

All of the world's educational services are worthless because you can't conveniently reach them. A strong forum or website will also give a wide variety of learning resources in different formats to ensure that consumers access the content they need efficiently and conveniently in a way that fits with their preferred style. Once we delve into the different categories of educational institutions that you can anticipate from a successful brokerage, make sure that such tools were user-friendly first.

What kinds of education programs do the financial adviser offer? The layout needs to start working for you, whether it provides video clips, podcasts, podcasts, or written books.

Where does the information originate from? If the trader syndicates from other pages, guarantee all certain pages are trustworthy. If the platform features a forum or other material by readers, then please ensure that the posting writers have expertise and knowledge, which you can believe.

How easy or intuitive is navigation to the site and platform? Make sure that going to the selling screen from a study page is a quick operation. You do not want to look like walking around in loops. Make sure the various topics on the site are easy to find.

Does broker sell resources for beginners? This might involve pronunciation guides or how-to papers, basic analyzes, diversification of investments, how to view scientific studies, and other topics for beginners.

How successful is the search feature on the platform? By typing into a common investment term or looking for subjects you have queries about, you can find this out. How quickly has the search feature been able to get the details that you needed? Is this knowledge available automatically, or do you need to scroll on a few sites to get through?

Here's an instance of a non-user-friendly search function:

Although Vanguard lets you use its tracking tool to map the relative power index (RSI), its search feature does not seem to know the expression.

Resources Monitoring

Is there enough review with respect to the security? This will provide multi-source analyst scores, real-time stories, on the market, as well as relevant sector details.

Is there any of the essential data accessible? For starters, stock portfolios will contain the issuance company's historical records, such as annual releases, financial results (like working capital, operating statement and statement of cash), dividend distributions, trading volume and repurchases, and SEC disclosures. Any insider-trading operation must also be warned.

Are business details open for U.S. and global markets? How about regarding information from manufacturing and from the sector? How thoroughly can you immerse yourself in the big picture circumstances affecting business performance?

6: Ease of Depositing and Withdrawing Funds

Is there enough review with respect to will security? Which will provide multi-source analyst scores, real-time stories, and the market as well as sector details relevant.

Is there any of the essential data accessible? For starters, stock portfolios will contain the issuance company's historical records, such as annual releases, financial results (like working capital, operating statement and statement of cash), dividend distributions, trading volume and repurchases, and SEC disclosures. Any insider-trading operation must also be warned.

Are business details open for U.S. and global markets? How regarding information from manufacturing and from the sector? How thoroughly can you immerse yourself in the big picture circumstances affecting business performance?

Removing Funds

How long would it take to recover the funds from selling the investments? Making sure you test the unified group with the numerous forms of shares that you are trying to sell.

What are income payments or tax payments? How quickly are those assets available to invest? For retiring?

How convenient is using the investment account to remove funds? Figure out how you can transfer through ACH wire, wire, or email and also how far it would take to get into your banking account for all those funds. Also, find out if there are any withdrawal fees.

Will the broker offer the option of adding a debit and ATM card to your credit card? It is often given for a mutual fund, as well as other times to use this service; you have to open a connected checking and saving account. Find out what other ATMs you can use if you have a card option, so there are some costs involved with using the card.

7: Support to Customers

By now, you've already limited your choices to one of two brokerage firms that actually blow you up in terms of money, functionality, and functionality. If you've reached the dream forum, or are already on the board, just take a couple more minutes to search a brokerage aid section you're contemplating.

When you're a potential user and feel stressed, make absolutely sure you can rapidly and effectively get in contact with the military members. When you're technologically inept, try to ensure your tech support department is easy to get in contact with and accessible 24/7.

Although these things won't make and break a brokerage choice, it's always important to know you recognize when and where to get support.

• Is there a designated amount where you should call a person asking for trade aid?

• Ensure you are informed of any potential phone-assisted trading costs.

• Can you call an automatic number for simple queries?

• Ultimate support what? And what were the Assistance ask-in hours?

• What are the operating hours for telephone lines? Will you dial 24/7, or do the phones only work outside office hours?

• There is an email for those that are opposed to contacting that you use to get timely support?

• Does the company use a safe network for internal transmission of relevant documentation and client questions?

• Maybe you are having a normal issue but don't want to annoy the member? Is there a viewable FAQ segment that responds to a large range of perspectives?

• How for tech backing? Are there specific phone lines, telephone numbers, or chat networks to access professional support?

8: Go and Take Next Moves

Whatever broker has by far the most active campaign, we realize it can be enticing to sign up for. However, good investing takes dedication to details far before you position your first order.

If you're planning to take trading a lengthy-term hobby, a long-term career, or even a way to boost your pension fund, then it's important to use the resources and tools that will help you deal for an enjoyable and successful experience.

Hopefully, by adopting an in-depth tutorial you've found the forum that would better fit your requirements, which they may be. On our stockbroker rating page, you will find support via filtering the various brokers.

Chapter 12: Common Strategies to Follow

We're going to speak about some of the more popular tactics that certain people may have learned about, even though they're not particularly familiar with how the stock market works.

Buying On Down Days

In general, that is not a terrible thing. The broker calls you up and advises you that there appears to be a down day on the street, and it may be a smart opportunity to pick up any stocks at the low.

As you'll have come to know, when it comes to capital market activity there are still two sides of a coin.

If you're someone with a strong market analysis system that focused your investment decisions on sound facts and numbers, then a down day might potentially be a moment when you might want to pick up any stocks you've purchased at a lower price. Also, a down day doesn't imply you're wasting any of your money on those better cost products. The astute investor will drive the positions in sections more frequently than not, with the expectation that a down day might quite well turn out to be a down week. That will indicate decent rates for products picking up.

However, if you are merely betting on the tips and calls of the broker, a splurge into the market on a down-day could become a cause for depression if the market doldrums continue over the week or even a month. You just purchased it, you figured it was a decent deal, and now it's gone down much more.

Buying on down days cannot be seen as a tactic alone but as part of a well-planned framework as a whole. There is, nevertheless, a claim that purchasing on down days may be a tactic too, and here is how it goes.

You buy on a day off. If the price drops more down the next day, you pay exactly what you paid. Then if the price drops more on the following day, you repeat the one from the previous days. You'd only made seven multiples of the original first-day purchase at this point.

You then pursue this buy if the downward go on before there is a rebound so that the market price does not fall below the day before, and so you sell it all off.

Since you've acquired product in higher numbers at cheaper rates, you've basically downgraded the expenses, and thus, when there's a market spike, selling off anything can be a benefit net.

The difficulty with this is the requirement to provide large quantities of money to continue the endless purchasing. Imagine something occurring for 15 days, how many multiples will it have been? Not something I'd suggest, so it's not worth the risk-benefit ratio to me.

Dollar-Cost Averaging

This is because many investment analysts and citizens are moving the shares and exchange-traded securities (ETFs)

Are you really trying? The basic principle is that you designate a date, claim the first day of the month to dive into the financial instruments in your currency, regardless of the market fluctuations that day. You're here.

Then do this regularly over the following months, with the period chosen over putting the capital into investing per the first day of the month.

You basically take out of scenario the timing of the market or actually randomize the timing of the market. By adding funds per month on a particular day in the period, you neglect the market dynamics at that moment of time in merely concentrate on reaching your roles.

Financial analysts prefer this concept because it makes the assets of the clientele easy to handle. Of note, the dollar cost measure, under such circumstances, still has its merits. It is our job to know what these requirements are and how the overall cost of the dollar can be exploited for our gain.

Generally speaking, when the economy is a rising trend, getting a set sum to spend on a given date would mean that you are only buying fewer units at a better price.

The same would be valid when the demand is downward heading, where the set volume will then cause a greater buying quantity at a lower price.

The average cost to most folk would be the commercial appeal of the dollar, the fact that it looks like an idiot-proof way to invest. Think about it; you're setting aside a comfortable sum per month or annum, or whatever period you choose. Then you literally plunge it into the stock or stocks that you have picked. More frequently than not, though, you will drive that into mutual funds or exchange-traded funds since they are, in reality, investments that are investing in various securities and properties, and so you believe that might be best for liquidity and stability.

For me, whether you intend to participate in the equity market and its relevant capital services, time should never be removed from the table entirely.

Why?

People, who happily have dollars in an average of one year or even two to three years, can lose half or a ton of their financial value just because they choose to participate in a bear market because their predominant plan was to go long or buy stock.

If one truly decided to sell or invest like an ostrich, so at least seven to fourteen years would need to be the minimum horizon. This is such that you can view yourself in two simultaneous economic cycles and thereby have a subsequent effect on the capital markets.

To me, the average cost of the dollar has its benefits, but you need to understand how to do it and, most specifically, to determine if it is really acceptable for your specific goals. This sort of investing plan will be perfect for people who have limitless stamina, have a decent career or extra cash flow every month rolling in, and don't even get concerned by the sums they're plugging into the markets. The crux of the matter is that they can spend a sum they feel really happy with, and that they would rarely not have to change the level of money even in the direst emergencies.

These people would profit from this approach because it suits them fairly well, ever since they actually don't have a crippling curiosity even weekly in researching the financial markets. While their earnings are good, they would find it exceedingly challenging to overtake timers in the sector. I tell this honestly and based on what I heard and learned. It does not knock on the cost balancing technique of the dollar at all.

Like I said earlier, numerous roads are leading to Rome, and everyone has their favorite route.

Indeed, the overall expense of the dollar may be perceived as a stand-alone tactic, albeit a very simplified one. However, those who wish to reap full profits from it will need to monitor and timing the sector, and others who only want to make their capital function better for them without suffering through problems would also need to consider a longer keeping duration or horizon.

Bear Market Strategy

This is basically a purchase on bad days' situation derivation. Generally, bear markets are known as such after the economy has experienced a drop of twenty percent in stock prices or where the stocks have been exposed to sustain downward pressure for several months or even years.

For me, bear markets can have numerous and varying mathematical metrics to decide by, so a rather easy approach is to head out into the streets and start talking to people you're accustomed to seeing on a regular basis. Taxi drivers, restaurant waiters, and maybe also primary school teacher! If neither of them would like to chat with you about the equity market, you're potentially in the money if you put your bet that the economy is definitely in the doldrums and the sector is somewhat bearish.

Everyone becomes a financial market whiz when the shares are optimistic, and that is where the word irrational exuberance introduces itself. By comparison, when no one tries to give their well-meaning suggestions about which stocks to buy or sell, and when even the stock market whisper will bring people into jitters, or advise them to keep away, then you definitely realize that the bear market is on its way.

The solution for the bear market is also fairly basic. Simply define the bear market era accurately, and what you do need now, though, is trust. And when other people are huddled at home with their cash fund collections, you'll head out into the street to purchase products.

Creating your confidence would require a clear and strong study of the firms that are piquing your attention, but still ensuring that you do not overestimate yourself in the department of capital.

Sell markets may be reasonably brief, although others can be reasonably deep, which is why the confidence of remaining engaged is necessary to understand the opportunity for benefit.

These sorts of scenarios do not exist on a regular or weekly basis, but it would be fair to assume that those concerned with day trading or short-term swing trading wouldn't have anything to do here. The bear market plan is really about people who normally have cash on hand, because they've done their homework in such a way that when the moment arrives they're beyond doubt and can behave in trust when they're backed up by anyone else.

One quirk is that others would also mix the method of cost averaging the currency with this tactic for the bear market. This involves foresight and confidence that the bear market is still on us, and then a clear scheme can be formulated to trigger regular stock and fund sales while the markets begin to fall. Some prefer this as opposed to trying to plunge in larger amounts in one go, while some tend to hold to their calculations and focus their investments on price ranges that they have determined to be of worth.

Again I would claim that, in both situations, there is no right or wrong. Most notably, a reasonable match for the customer needs to be the approach. As I would like to suggest, if you earn a hundred thousand dollars but are continuously shivering with anxiety and sweat-drenched, I would rather take advantage of ten thousand to sleep comfortably and without any worries.

The bear market strategy has its position and period for usage, but due to the very existence of being a bear market, it is not ideal for those searching for fast trades. It's a really nice way for me to spend the surplus funds for which you have no need and to sit invested in securities or instruments that can't earn profits for a few years down the line.

Day Trading

This used to be a fad because I was already battling the market. At this point in time, I believe it to always be. Many day-trading advocates will claim it's one of the easiest ways to sell and get wealthy. In the afternoon you reach and leave both of your places. You scout your stocks and plan them throughout the day. Within the trading time period, you make all your choices, and so after the market ends, you are a happier individual, and you will go to bed with no fears, unlike others that have current securities.

All this is well and dandy, but as I have already said, there will always be two sides to everything with respect to the stock market.

If you lock yourself up and only be willing to exchange within the time span of a day, what happens if you don't have any decent trades to pick from? Do you believe you'd have the opportunity to indulge in a transaction, or you would not really gain money for the day? What occurs if the condition of this sort of exchange is less than one day, two days, or even three days in a row? Could you guess how much tension and anxiety the day trader has to endure at this juncture? The day trader may therefore be compelled to participate in a deal that may not be the most desirable to get out of this. That represents an enhanced loss risk.

The typical counter-argument to this will be that the world of stocks, as well as financial instruments, is so large that at least one decent trade would certainly be set up every day. The world may be large, but your resources will restrict the degree to which you would comfortably evaluate the stocks you choose to sell. There is just so much that artificial intelligence and computerized aids will achieve, with the human brain also required for deeper research.

The other part of day trading where you have to remember will be on the benefit side. Suppose you sold a portfolio for the day; twenty points in the day went up, and you've happily banked with the income. It holes out the following day, when the market exchange only opens at a far higher price than the closing price of the previous day. This kind of scenario occurs when there are good reports from overnight or when the purchasing desire is too strong.

As a day trader, anytime some kind of upward sprint occurs, you are pushed into the periphery. You may be able to fall into the act and just leap through the structures and laws, and that will be the first move to foolishness.

Day trading is almost an opportunistic practice to me. If there is an optimal time to do so, we can do it. It's really much about how they used to do hunting and fishing—in seasons. When the season is perfect for day trading, we can do so because it really does increase your sharpness and contribute to your benefit capacity. We should have our other structures and strategies to focus on when the season isn't there. Trading on the day doesn't work all the time, so it is another useful weapon in the arsenal when it can be put to use.

One note of advice, however, to get the hang of day trading, you will have to learn more. This is attributed to the demands for pace and rapid decision-making, as well as the requirement for strong analytical skills. Often you could hear folks claim they're dealing from the gut, or they just felt like they had to get out of storage. Take them with a grain of salt, and dig into it further. Possibly these guys have had plenty of experience coping with the market or the specific product, which is why they are willing to operate on their whims and fancies, obviously. In reality, their brains have absorbed the knowledge they need, and then they can make the choices very easily.

Shorting

This side of the market carries a certain fascination and allure to certain folks, since about 50 percent of consumers are now mostly acquainted with the fact that stocks can only be acquired. They don't understand the idea that, according to trading terms and conditions, you can potentially sell short stocks that you don't buy.

Usually, short selling will enable you to sell quickly from a selection of stocks made accessible by the brokerage. This is because these are stocks that are held by the company or have received authorization from stock owners to accept borrowing. Short sellers will also be allowed to sell their non-owned securities, but would have to pay interest for the day their short positions remain operating. This same paying attention goes as we are even concerned for conditional contracts. (MFF)

Shorting as a tactic is once again part of the game that you may apply to your arsenal. Imagine the stock market situation where the bear market is just beginning. You realize that the price will drop by 20 percent or more, and if you have the opportunity to shorten those picked products, why not make a profit on the way down until you make the reversal and start buying the products on the cheap one?

Is it always important that you have to learn shortcut? I'd agree it's nice to know, and it's a safe choice to have available, but to be competitive in capital markets, it's not a must-have.

Taking the situation on the bear market that we spoke about earlier. If you didn't have the opportunity or simply didn't like shorting, you'd simply keep out of the market before the bear market sales kicked in and you began your long positions in your preference stocks. In the meantime, what will you do as the economy went down, you ask? You might be quietly sitting on cash doing nothing, or you could be trading in other sectors. Not all stocks work in unison, and as one is in the early stages of a bearish period, another may flow into the start of a bull run.

One thing I feel obliged to claim will be that short-term benefit appears to be higher. Exactly what do I mean?

If you were a stock too low at a certain point and you had the right call, the downward trend would typically be even smoother than if you were on the same call with the very same stock for a long time. This is why shorting income typically comes far sooner than longing income.

This stems from two primary impulses, covetousness and anxiety. In the case of shorting, the prevailing emotion that can be found on the stock exchange is anxiety. When a stock takes a dive, most committed people will not be willing to bear the impact and will want to get out fast. Their ultimate philosophy will not be to waste their capital in the stock anymore.

When we get a product that goes up in price, speculation is the biggest reason people come and drive the profit up in order that they will offer it at a better profit later on. Greed has a driving power marginally lower than terror because the human mind still needs to preserve what it has first. It cannot withstand everything it holds from separation. Therefore the fear of losing still trumps the reward greed.

That's just something you should take care of, but it's not a clarion call for you to leap on the shorting bandwagon anyway. I repeat that it is nice to recognize, but it is by no way sufficient for the financial markets to perform well.

Penny Stocks

When this technique really came into dominant action, I'm not aware, but to be frank, I never really used it actively. It doesn't mean I didn't take penny stock positions, but it does mean I didn't launch those positions only because they were penny stocks.

This approach relies primarily on small stocks, which are comparatively inexpensive in contrast with the more mainline stocks in play. When you take a stake in a penny stock, you will get thousands or even tens of thousands of them. The entire theory will be to wait in the market action for a tick up and then by dint of value, you are simply selling out the penny stock shares to cash in some gains.

A change of the penny stock approach will be to reach a few markets that you perceive to be positive and then buy positions of penny stocks that belong to certain businesses. This time around, the investment of penny stock wouldn't be huge, so you'd be looking for a bigger price change to understand the opportunity for benefit.

My positions in penny stocks mostly came into existence after I evaluated the stock, and I certainly didn't have the requirements that the stock could be a penny stock first.

For a cause, penny stocks adhere to the group and may vary from something like the poorly managed business to bigger structural stuff such as being in a sunset market. Performance and worth are also not to be used as the market plunge to what is called the bottom of the penny.

For instance, the sector may be terribly incorrect on times, or the penny stock business is doing a great rebound.

Much of my penny deals are around the fact that businesses are always known to have any appeal and development prospects, and it is only because of seasonal causes that hammered down the market price that it counts as a penny commodity. But if I say temporary, it could be either a quick or a long wait. We never do.

As such, in my view, the penny stock investing approach isn't really one that can hold up if the scheme was solely focused on getting the stock requirements to be penny stocks.

For me, that looks so much of a risk and smacks too much expectation. Hoping that every day the stock would go up, or hoping that the market would only fall so that the whole portfolio could be sold for a benefit. If you are in stock market optimism and there is little more to support your continued interest, it should be about time to put the exit order.

Know Yourself

I realize it has been stated before, but in the light of these widely heard investing methods, I would like to hear it once again.

Many of the tactics have their applications, as we have shown. What is more relevant now is to have a clear idea of how the personality for trading is, and then pick certain tactics that you think will be a good match for you.

An individual who dislikes glancing at the monitors and continually being bound to the computer will be a bad match for day-trading. An individual who likes relentless action and lives for instant gratification will be a bad match for strategy in the bear market.

There are no perfect size suits all tactics out there, as it is. What would be more realistic would be to gain awareness of the various methods that you find acceptable for yourself and then turn it into a cohesive framework that can be conveniently utilized by you.

Having said that, I would like to define those traditional techniques described above as being what I might consider the tip of the iceberg. We will explore the investment analytics schools a bit more in detail later, and it will actually open up deeper into the investment management environment.

Strategies from Schools of Thought

This section can cause an explosive debate. I'm all set for it because I was selling myself through all fields of learning. This is the controversy over conceptual analyses and scientific research that is ever-present.

Before I move much further, I want to illustrate the importance of research in the field of stock picking. The findings of a well-worked and thorough study are also a building pillar that will help reinforce the judgment in moments where everybody and all is telling the contrary of what you are doing. Research offers you confidence, and you have the steady strength and capacity to ride out the turbulent waters and stop market turbulence with certainty. More specifically, you build your own understanding of stock and marketplace. That is still priceless. And if you might be mistaken, but the mere fact that you've developed a perspective based on a comprehensive and well-worked framework allows you the freedom to fine-tune and change your business views as the path continues.

Dream of someone who doesn't have a vision of his shoes for a while. Instead, he depends on press stories, stock magazines, and traders to fill him with suggestions of what his next major move might be. Compare it to someone qualified to have business understanding and angle. True, he can also collect news and investment notes, and who can claim he can't draw encouragement from these resources to find a decent invitation to stock? The main distinction is that the individual getting taught would do his own screening and a thorough examination to shape his point of view. Then he should equate his interpretation to those portrayed in the material. If divergence is clear, so he will quickly let it go.

This is in comparison to the individual who has little experience. If he's letting go of the order, he'd be concerned if the stock eventually soars to the sky, feeling regretful. And he is still traumatized by each fluctuation in rates even though he is in stock, so he loses confidence.

Proponents of basic and theoretical analyses have been at loggerheads for as long as anybody can recall. Side strongly insists that their way of thinking is better and therefore inspires people in any path to take up studies.

I may try, for myself, to suggest that my comprehensive schooling was in the context of fundamental research. That means I was qualified in business balance sheet arithmetic and cash flow statements. We also learned to look at the business and assess its valuation so that we can foresee the course of the stock price.

It was enjoyable at school since the figures stagnate equally, and you didn't have to deal with feelings or the financial markets' hustle and bustle. Hypotheses created on paper stayed unchanged and did not alter. Company factors have not been entirely factored in yet. You didn't have cases of corruption or immoral conduct that might have a detrimental effect on market values. It was pretty tidy and sterile, with all.

Folks who believe strongly in quantitative research trust in the idea that the revenue, cash flow accounts, and the balance sheet displayed in the financial results are the key component of the puzzle they will use to break business code. They also belong to the prevailing mindset where they regard stocks as strict firms, and thus their cognitive process will revolve around evaluating the market environment and the like. Industry opportunities and entry hurdles will be at the top of their priorities if there is a decision to purchase or sell a stock.

Fundamentalists perform really well for me because they work in the context of long-lasting problems. The empirical bent of looking at a company's economics can take you to a filtration method. You should pick out the very powerful from the obvious ones, whilst at the same time, you can rank others that are apparently not as bad as what the market tends to decide.

As fundamentalists, we should pick out the strong firms because, in the case of some unexpected situations such as corporate abuse or exploitation, the only way is to wait for the stock to comply with the company standards.

That is also the issue.

Often it takes a couple more times until the business catches on, then you'd be willing to enjoy the profits only for making the right choice. On some occasions, it could take you years or eons. You gladly went in with the money and, in a certain amount of time, anticipated certain benefits, and yet those hopes fall flat. The world also doesn't want to know too well what you should do! At that time, the expenditure is static, and the monies are bottled away, unable to be used elsewhere for a better future return.

In a future where there was somebody with infinite wealth, I think he'd be a really content fundamentalist because he'd be willing to deposit funds in certain businesses he'd find worth the risk and then wait for the moment to develop. Since he has nearly infinite money, he will have no concerns about the potential cost of assets. Naturally, that is the perfect setting. We exist in the modern world, and so we would have little means to name ourselves.

At this juncture, it is here where technical observers step in to point out the obvious shortcomings in the conceptual school of thinking and then rejoice in the apparent advantages of the strictly tactical trading system.

At one point in my life, technological trading represented the Holy Grail for me; I was so stuck on it because I always felt that if I just discovered the right technological framework, my life would be set, and my business career would be free.

There are still several sellers of technological systems seeking to react to certain assumptions that getting "the" technical system will reflect prosperity, and passive income for all the rest of eternity.

Take it from me. In trade, there is no such thing as a holy grail. In some cases, only technological processes will perform better and recover all the gains and have the losses double in other cycles. Trading algorithms can see returns in certain frames, but in others, they do offer nothing but losses.

This is not meant to break the ego, just to say the facts and what it is. For all those people who clearly claim, they trust in the strength of their shifting averages, candlestick trends, and retracements of Fibonacci, you should be fairly confident that there may be more than you can see.

I felt like an energizer bunny when I first began practicing Strategic Trading. The name of the game during those days was Back Training. I'd concocted a combination of technical signals and then compare those signals back with a bunch of stocks to see the risk of loss of gain. I did it once non-stop for thirty days, and you know what, the outcome I received was a flat loss rate for a victory.

That, of course, did not dissuade me in the least, since I strongly assumed that the issue resides in the concoction of technological signals, not elsewhere. As soon as I managed to create the right balance of technological signals, everything will be fine. So I thought.

It was a few years of humbling and exhausting, and at the end of my rope, as I was almost on the brink of giving up, I chanced across the idea of market action or product volume action analysis as some may term it.

The idea is that all that is to be learned regarding the stock or investment tool has already been recorded in both the price and its movement. In the case of inventories, we even have the secondary regular inventory metric is helpful proof.

This was like a letter given by a deity to one who was approaching the end of his path. It made any sense to me, at last. I didn't have to think too much about stochastics, shifting averages, and Bollinger pairs. (If all these sound like a foreign language to you, just know it doesn't matter) Price and volume will be everything I cared for.

The theory was straightforward and enticing, but in the beginning, it was very difficult when attempting to adapt to the modern world. Regulation on rates was besotted of market increases. Such market ranges were considered to be bands of assistance and opposition, and you were supposed to devise strategies to compensate for occasions when rates plummeted across certain bands or when rates rebounded away from those bands.

I've been tottering down this road for about three years, and frankly, at that point in time, it didn't appear to me I was going anywhere. If you shot a stumbling sailor in a bar struggling to rush away and catch the shuttle, it will be a detailed description of my trading experience on the equity market at the moment. It wasn't until I learned, truly learned, and held copious notes of my trade newspapers that I actually made any headway for decent benefit.

My own interpretation and usage of the basic and scientific schools of thinking will ultimately be central to targeting and filtration. I focus on the simple side of things to open up my reach and narrow down can stock I should be involved in. The technical analysis will play its role in deciding where and when the lever to join could be pulled, as well as exiting stock positions. This was a collaboration between the two great homes, and it was a lucrative arrangement that catered my tastes.

I can understand if you feel rather deflated at this stage, or maybe a little interested. Deflated because I have confirmed without a question that there is no holy grail and intrigued about what I have achieved to build the revolution for myself.

I want to repeat the section of not getting a holy grail. I say it's just not my concern if you chose not to accept that and go on splurging thousands of dollars of your hard-earned cash on folk services that try to sell you. I would just point out that if such devices perform too well, the people who market them probably won't allow you to have your hands on them.

That is because the technological structures are struggling from what we term the impact of widespread use. If a certain critical mass of citizens decides to operate on the same technological signs, the exchange is essentially annulled. Even though these devices have not suffered from the consequences of widespread use, why would these people choose to sell them to you for a small amount per day? Clearly, they would actually make so much more each day using those devices.

There's just no free lunch in the world at the end of the day, and if anything seems almost too nice to be true, then it generally is.

Now for the section about my success, short of sending you a personal one on a single coaching session to lead you on what works for me from a professional point of view, it's going to be really challenging to write it down because it works for you too. There are some tips I kept during the climb up, though.

- Analysis of the trade journal and creation of links with market transactions

- Reaching at the initial stage of the wider time span. You'd want to venture through the lower time frames just once you have a defined collection of guidelines and structures.

- You don't need to rush; there's nothing in the universe who can push you to sell, so just take your time and start the exchange on your terms.

- Please make sure to include a list of rules to obey. Even if it's only a one-liner at the outset, create the practice of making guidelines so you'll have limits within which to work.

Some Other Useful Things

I'm going to speak about certain topics in this segment that I think will be very useful to someone who wants to make more money out of trading in the stock market.

Momentum Trading

Trading and trading policy of this type depend strongly on, as the name implies, momentum. In other terms, how we build and conduct this plan will be equally contingent on purchasing or selling interest at present and planned.

Strategies may be as easy as I can commit to joining the stock the next day at the starting price if the stock has had a distance up day. This is attributed to the assumption that the trader hopes to maintain the upward trend, and therefore making such a pass. Related situations may be rendered where there has been a break in the stock down day.

Here the crux of the matter is to recognize the energy that will hopefully continue for at least a few days. A longer time will, of course, be most welcome. Sometimes, people who are only doing momentum-based trading might not have such decent win-loss percentages with their transactions, but will cover up for that with their bigger profit margins. We should not depend entirely on momentum, but rather aim to integrate it into our trading processes.

I use a motivation for the additional boost to pull in the extra money for myself. But in cases when I might have missed my goal benefit for a specific product, if I see traction in the market counter, I can only let the place continue to run.

Recognizing that certain sources of energy waves originate from the press will be the way to distinguish permanent traction from others that may fizzle out easily. Therefore it is our duty to easily and cleverly discern, which bits of news have a real effect on the bottom line, and others are all everyday hogwash. Continuing to get the news that has a significant effect on the profit prospects and profitability of the business is very unusual, but we are still looking at and piece of news immediately in relation to our specific stock information. This also assumes the more acquainted you are with stock and business, the easier you'd be separating out actual news from the noise of the economy.

Trend Following

This can be considered a tactic and, at the same time, a common concept that the bulk of traders choose to obey. Trade the trend, pursue the trend, the trend is that your buddy will list among the many terms that make life better for yourself as you exchange and spend in the course of the pattern.

Only imagine it. If you have a product that has a price chart that essentially moves non-linear upward for a very long period of time, it would be fair to say that if your goal was to lengthen the product, you would have a greater chance of winning a deal.

I've been in those circumstances before, and I'll tell you it's essentially quick to only put your orders at the correct technical stage, wait for the stock price to fall back and go up to certain technical prices, and then watch your orders get filled out. After the retracement, when the market continues its upward rise, you stand by to gain a benefit or to control your portfolio positions.

Benefit taking may also be an agonizing choice since you tend to lock in gains but at the same time not having to leave so much capital on the table as the stock starts to meteor upwards. Often I do it with a part of the assets gaining benefit and moving my emotional stop losses to break even with my other current section. This basically generates a concept for me that I can see the actual stock portfolios as "free" for the already earned gains charged for purchasing these new stocks. Getting free stocks doesn't imply you should handle them differently, only then there's that little extra room you're allowing yourself to gain a little less or to generate a lot of money. In certain situations, it would typically turn out to be breakeven for this free part, or I am collecting almost twice as much income as if I were trying to cut off all as a whole.

My decision to undertake this step relies solely on my stock and business evaluation, as well as the existing technological condition. I would have to confess, of course, that the niggling sensation of taking a chance would typically be the main instigator for me to suggest making this leap, but the determination about whether to do so would always be focused on facts and statistics.

Trading in the movement certainly has its advantages, which is why so many people expound it and even make it their slogan. But it is often challenging to understand and refine into a functioning investment plan.

One of the biggest factors being that you have to be conscious of what span of time you are on as you look at the graph. There are numerous timescales, varying from minute charts to monthly maps. None would disagree with you that the longer the duration, the weightier such price charts will get. This is since an indicator on the month map is a reflection of the market movement for the individual stock over the entire month. The battle of the month between the bulls and the bears, as well as the cumulative total of the money they contributed to the war, are all encapsulated in the table of that month.

On the other side, a candle on the one-minute map will certainly have far less money invested into it relative to the month list, thereby reducing its confidence amount. Similarly, a pattern on a minute chart might be upward, but you may easily disregard the minute chart while the day chart or month chart is telling a downward tale.

Looking at higher cycle maps, such as day, week, and month levels, are best as you're starting off first. Compared to the longer time spans, the patterns depicted on these maps will have a smaller chance of turning out not to be permanent.

Another issue about pattern investing will be to have reasonable entry and exit locations. Let's say that you've finished your research and found the stock you'd like to pull the lever to enter in its upward trajectory. Currently, it is at $50 per share price. Any people could just pull the trigger and hop in at $50. Others should do what I normally do and park orders at fixed price levels that make us say $30. If the market retraces, which the market normally does, and there are barely any instances of the straight line shooting up or down, so, at a reasonable price, I'll get into stock. This also means I have nothing to risk than a person who goes in at $50 only because my price is, so to say, lower to the "park."

In general, when the stock entry price is higher to the bottom, where the bottom implies $0, then you have a more secure location, just like a lower center of gravity in physics rules.

An individual purchasing at $50 or an individual purchasing at $30 will seem different only because of the various entrance rates. The $30 guy will have more leeway to transfer the product. Think about it, if the stock price changes to $40, that's a $10 benefit for the $30 guy but a $10 loss for the $50 consumer. Naturally, a decent dose of strategic research will have to base this company with a sensible entry and exit stage. It is important to chart and decide the entrance and exit points from the technological level, and therefore the next thing to do is to have the mindset of being willing to leave the exchange.

What? Had I understood it, right?

Actually, you have finished. Have the emotional readiness to leave the company. Why do you think so? This is for the occasions where the retracement exists, but it does not reach the stage, which is logically calculated. But instead of falling to $30, it rises to $33, then stages a recovery afterward. This is also valid during occasions where there is no retraction, and the market tends to rumble from $50 onwards.

You do have cases like that. Therefore, you must still be prepared emotionally to let go of the exchange and step on to the next. That is also why the investing and trading framework should never be too limiting to provide either one or two triggers every year. Imagine if you skipped the last trading chance, you might have to wait until next year to have another one.

I would also like to point out that the $50 guy might not actually be incorrect in our case, but it's just my nature to err on the cautionary side. I will tell kudos to him if the $50 guy had the gumption and the money required to handle the possible bumpier trip than the $30 guy might. What I term a "jumper" will be the $50 man. Typically these guys leap into a market out of fear of losing out. Jumpers rule the roost in moments where the movement is roaring, and the press is on the spot, which also has significant structural effects. There's absolutely no place for people who want retracements entry because there's just zero.

You either hop in that kind of circumstance, or you pass on to the next possible stock. Mentality and temperament play a major part in whether you'd be an effective jumper. And we also recognize that the nature of investing is primarily influenced by the volume of cash at stake for any particular moment in time. If you want to train yourself as a jumper and yet find yourself missing the requisite mental criteria, beginning small will be the solution. When leaping, fear tiny quantities before you get used to the sensation of it. You will also be forced to scale up to a reasonable level progressively.

I'm not much of a jumper myself, but I leap when the chance occurs. Jumping is like every other talent in the field of trade and finance, always useful to add to your arsenal so you can rely on it anytime you find you need it.

How can you decide the pattern will be another problem for some people. While others would adhere to the concept of utilizing moving averages to evaluate the pattern, some might find Bollinger band use to be the only valid way to determine the trend.

After potentially thousands of hours staring at the maps, I've come to know that when the pattern is apparent, it's so clear that you don't require any metrics or new-catched technologies to tell you to claim this is a pattern. The Map visual analysis is what you need. I would prefer to stay on the higher time frame for me and then do a visual analysis to assess what seems like the imminent theme that is actually affecting the sector.

Going from top left to bottom right will mean a downward step pattern. Moving from the bottom left to the top right would indicate that the bulls will have power. If you try and search, because you can't find something that's clear, that's what we say by a trendless condition or a side sector. If a market moves sideways, that typically means the fight between the bulls and the bears is going on, and the outcomes are not yet clear.

Sideways markets are perfect circumstances for day trading, by the way. So, you have what you imagine is a sort of map in a pretty rectangular type. This ensures that the top and bottom borders are equally established for you to deal with day to day. We won't dive too much into the trading part of this day right now, maybe more in a future novel.

But there's no reason to over-complicate stuff; visual examination typically fits well since it's the easiest because when items are clear, they're generally in the truest shape.

The Need For Stop Losses

This idea was discussed at multiple sections in this book, but I felt it's worth a segment of its own, only because of its significance in the field of trade and investment.

A stop-loss or a decreased loss is simply a fixed price point that is the escape signal for everybody to get out of a poor deal. The idea of getting a quantity that will be acceptable for the person to sacrifice falls into play here.

Tell Adam that he has decided he's willing to bet $1000 on a certain offer to sell, and that he now has a hundred shares that are selling at a price of $40. Then it will mean that his stop-loss price will be $30 if the trade call is long one, so his $1000 risk capital would be divided by his one hundred shares to produce a $10 price gap. His exchange will then have space for a gyrate of up to $30, and if the price point drops below that, then he would close the deal, dust himself off, and then go ahead to the next.

This point is also the section where I would like to highlight the significance of closing the candle, or bar on which you are tracking the time period ever. If you're a day trader, you might be gazing at the end of the hourly light. That implies if the market price still falls below $30 on every hourly closing light, you'd be conducting the closure of the exchange. If you were a swing or long-term trader, though, you might look at the closing of the day candle or even the closing of the week candle. It would suggest you'd just conduct the exit plan when the market moves and ends on the day or week candle around $30 based on the time period you're monitoring. Keep in mind that regardless of the vast volume of money required to create and fight for the results of that specific candle, the longer the time span, the more confidence it would hold.

This argument would also contribute to another controversial field that has long been subject to discussion. Few people would say that if you chose to adopt this method, the cumulative number of damages that would be sustained would be more than the safe sum that one would spend. This is because as we are waiting for the day or week candle to end, after crashing through the predetermined point, the price may fell even further. Considering the scenario above, you could see rates at $25 or even $20 while your price range was expected to be $30. It will end in a double loss of the money you were able to fork out.

For me, I understand the drawbacks of using the stop loss in this manner, but I prefer to only do things this way because of the benefits things confers. The one big benefit you get by performing the stop loss upon closure will be that you'd be avoided circumstances when the price jumps dramatically up or down, and sometimes it doesn't close at all.

Take Adam and his stock as our example once again. The approved price for stop loss was $30. If his stock swings significantly within the hour, say $20, and yet he still tries to keep his composure and convince himself to wait until the closing hour, he may notice that at the closing hour, the stock price maybe has rebounded back to $35. And also produces what we term a pin bar or a hammer or what people might deem the candle handle.

What Adam has done by keeping his composure to get out of a condition that might have flushed his lack of stoppage. He's still in the game amid the intra-hour downward shift that turned out to be nothing but a terror.

These conditions may appear in all time frames, but keep in mind that the wider the time span, the more money to devote.

So what to do with the question of getting to pay about exactly what you were able to sacrifice initially? The solution is to transact in limited quantities. Imagine this period for Adam, instead of a hundred shares, he's only exposed to fifty shares because he knows the vulnerability of closing utilizing the stop loss, he's easily circumvented the problem, yet he's still held his safe losing number.

So when I say this, I generally get confronted with some hoots and derision, as some people would then suggest, won't the benefit opportunity be diminished similarly? The response is a yes, of course, and now I would like to inform everybody that it is all first about what you can and are able to sacrifice before we move on worrying about benefits. If we can maintain a solid basis on our expenses, so of course, gains can result. This is because the temperament for trading would be more secure and less subject to the whims and swings of the market wind.

Not all, of course, subscribes to this philosophy. Others swear by the touch and go stop losing, where it simply implies that if the price ever reaches $30, as in our previous case, then the trade will end. For any span of time, there is no discussion of waiting for a close.

Under this scenario, the trader will have better control of his loss number, so his trade would be out every time $30 is reached. That also implies, however, that his odds of getting flushed out of his stop would still be much better than a trader who used the strategy of closing-stop failure.

For me, the way things are handled is not right or wrong. Often it comes down to character and psychology in dealing. I see the folks who love lots of activity are more likely to use the touch-stop method of managing stop losses, while the folks who are a bit more reserved and smoother prefer to wait for further clarification and use the close-stop loss approach as a result.

I used to subscribe to the contact pause since it was the most common and showed the most. But I didn't like the idea that I was still on the right side of the exchange only to lose it when I was pushed out of place. It's almost like a double smack on the cheek. You make a mistake because, in the trading call, you wind up being correct. That's when the near stop for me came into action, and it performed great in my view so far.

These two methods of managing stop losses are, of course, much preferable to another form of dealing stop-loss, which has no stop losses. Honestly, I can't tell it, but here's my reiteration again, there's still a stop loss, even if it's only a mental price amount. Bear the degree in mind, and you'll need to conduct the escape until it's broken. It is a fight, a war in which any exchange. If a stop-loss is broken, you realize the fight has been lost, but the fighting is always going on as long as you have the capital. Still fail to a halt.

This will be one more thing to remember. Determining the price range for a stop loss needs to make sense from the viewpoint of business research. By what do I mean? In the case of Adam, the $30 price point was calculated simply by the sum Adam was able to sacrifice and by the value of his part. This is not the way it can be, and the scenario was just kept up to demonstrate how the stop-loss could perform.

You should really keep two points in mind with a trade call first. The purchase price, or the amount you are able to pay to share in the stock's prosperity, as well as the stop loss amount calculated by the techniques of market research. In certain situations, citizens turn to scientific analyses to get a stop-loss price. They can extract price ranges from their lines of assistance and opposition and have ears identified as possible stop losses. That is also why I also point out that the task of technical analysis is more of a precision method, whereas that of fundamental analysis will be more of a filtration device to get your fine, worthwhile stocks.

This also ensures you shouldn't have too close a stop while selecting your stop-loss rate. E.g., in the case of Adam, if his entry price was $40, and there appeared to be a slight amount of help at $38, and Adam was currently preparing his trade for the longer haul, it would be very hard to position his stop at $38. As a rule of thumb, a longer trading time will normally entail a greater loss of the pause. Similarly, if you play longer and miss a bigger rest, the benefits goals would typically be higher too. This is for each exchange to ensure a fair risk-reward ratio.

One thing I've been guilty of in the past was selecting and selecting tighter stop losses. That helped me to have greater share visibility and thereby gain more money, at least in my opinion! I'd pick a close stop and then genuinely hope the economy doesn't hit that amount. Any of my trades have been so unbelievably organized that I will be in a deal and then out of business within a few minutes, with a few hundred losses to match. This was especially so while I was still doing the lack of contact pause. It doesn't make sense to look fine on paper and assume the economy doesn't affect the lack of the end. Also, beginning to calculate the gain right before beginning the exchange is no good. Engaging in mental gymnastics like that will just waste your focus and leave you empty when you need it.

That is why virtually all trades that end up as winners start with the first issue of how much we might lose. All that's on offer is truth and statistics and less optimism and wishful thinking. It's crucial that we perceive things as what they are and not what we expect them to be.

Stock Screeners

These items are so popular these days, with most of them being accessible through web browsers and online. The primary usage of stock screeners will be to have some sort of automatic support while we deal with the boring task of searching out filtering firms.

With only a few mouse clicks, screeners will support a lot in this world with hundreds of thousands of stocks, and we'll have a more accessible shortlist of a handful of hundreds. Okay, it was almost a half-joke, but to be frank, occasionally, you still had to dig around a couple of hundred businesses to get to some deserving of being sold.

Insiders and Institutional Investors

As well as being the hard weights, these guys are also the ones who know most about their businesses. Knowing their records will give us a big leg up for institutional investors when it comes to our investment decisions.

Looking at individual pages documenting those trends and also reading the annual reports to get a sense of who is who and who is doing what would be nice, but it could create too much of a cognitive challenge. Imagine tracking the shortlist of fifty individual securities and maintaining track of insider and retail activity. That pushed the wall toward me.

An easier approach I find for myself would be to use the professional analysts' concept and trust it. The stock price has all caught that which needs to be understood. I keep on board the notion when it comes to tracking products that have already been shortlisted. Yet when it comes to getting the shortlist together, there's simply no moving away from the hard legwork that comes with the foundational research.

For me, fundamental analysis with its regular hard work would guide the way in the development of my monitoring shortlist of stocks; then, technical analysis would offer me the degree of pricing to implement my investing ideas.

Chapter 13: Common Mistakes to Avoid and Suggestions

If stocks move up, down, and sideways it is possible to benefit by selling options. With a fairly tiny cash outlay, you might use option methods to sell stocks, preserve gains and control huge parts of the stock.

Sounds nice, doesn't it? Here we have the pick.

You may also risk more by buying options than the overall sum you've spent over a fairly short span of time. That is why continuing with caution is so necessary. Also, self-confident investors will misjudge a chance and lose capital.

This section addresses the top errors that novice options traders usually make, with professional advice, as an expert in the business, about how you might trade wiser. Take time now to study them, so you can prevent an expensive wrong move.

Misaligned Leverage

Many rookies abuse contracts providing leveraging factor alternatives without knowing how much chance they are taking. They're also attracted to making quick-term calls. So, this is so often the case; it's important to ask: Is it a "speculative" or "conservative" strategy to buy outright calls?

A general rule to start option investors: if you're usually trading 100 stock lots, then stay with one start option. When you usually exchange 300 lots of securities—maybe three agreements— that is a decent volume of training to start with. When you don't have luck on small scales, the bigger scale trades would more definitely not be successful.

Not Being Responsive to New Initiatives

Most option traders claim they'd never purchase out-of-the-money stocks or offer the options in-the-money. Such absolutes sound stupid—till after you find oneself in a market that is working against you.

There have also been experienced options for investors. Confronted by this situation, you are sometimes inclined to violate all kinds of ethical rules.

You have also learned, as a bond investor, a common excuse for scaling up to keep up. E.g., if you loved the stock when you purchased it at 80, at 50, you have to love it. It may be enticing to purchase more on the exchange to reduce the total cost level. However, be vigilant: In the field of options, what provides a sense for shares does not float. Typically, boosting up as a potential tactic just doesn't make any sense.

Be accessible to exploring different approaches to invest in futures. Note, options are securities, implying that their values don't shift the same or have almost the same characteristics as the stock market. A decline in time, whether positive or poor, for the role, must also be taken into account in the strategies.

When things will change in your business, and you contemplate what was previously inconceivable, just honestly ask yourself: was this a move I took when I first started opening this status?

If the reaction is no, so do not.

Close a trade, cut down on your damages, or start a different chance that makes perfect sense today. Options give decent leverage opportunities on comparatively low assets, but when you dig deeper, they can explode just as rapidly as every position. Take a minor risk because it presents you with an opportunity to eventually escape a disaster.

Wait Much Long to Order Limited Options

This failure can be distilled down with one word of wisdom: Always be eager and able to buy out shorter options soon.

Too many traders may take too long to purchase back their sold options. There are many million explanations for doing this. For instance:

- You don't want the tribunal to the bill.

- You're hoping that the deal ends void.

- You're only looking to get a bit more from the exchange.

Just when to give the short options back. If OTM gets lost with your short alternative and you can purchase it back to profitably, take the danger off the table, do it. Don't be greedy about that.

For example, what if you offered a choice for $1.00, and now it's worth 20 percent? To start with, you wouldn't offer a 20-cent option, as it would just not be worth it. Equally, you must not believe scraping out the remaining few cents from this deal is worth it.

Here's a simple thumb rule: if you may keep 80 percent or more of the original income from the choice deal, you can definitely buy it back a few weeks later by a short choice because you took too long. This is a virtual guarantee, otherwise.

Putting in Spreads

Many traders with starting options seek to "pull-in" a gap by first purchasing the options and then selling a second options. They seek to cut losses by a handful of pennies. That's just not worth the chance.

Comfortable sound? That example has also fried most seasoned options traders and taught the valuable lesson.

When you decide to swap a set, don't "jump in" deal one set as a one-time deal. Don't needlessly take on excessive business pressure.

You could purchase a call, for instance, and then seek to schedule the selling of some other call, trying to get out of the second leg a little bit better. If the economy experiences a fall, this is a risky tactic, because they won't be capable of carrying off the profit. You may be faced with a call option with little plan to move on.

If you're trying the whole strategic plan, don't buy the spread but also wait approximately, hoping the economy will be moving in the favor. You may imagine you might market it at a better price later. This is a rather unlikely performance.

Also, view a split as one deal. Don't want to solve the pacing minutia. Before the economy keeps going down, you should get into a trade.

Ignoring the Stocks for Fair Markets Table

Person inventories may be very unpredictable. For instance, if a company has a large unpredicted news event, this could rock a stock for a couple of days. On the other side, even extreme chaos in a large company that is a member of an S&P 500 will certainly not make the index fluctuate significantly.

What Are the Story's Morals?

Options trading focused on benchmarks will protect your part from the tremendous changes that individual news reports may produce for selected securities. Take into account neutral transactions on big indicators, and reduce the unsure impact of news from the market.

Find investment tactics that may be lucrative if the sector already sits on indices, including a short break (also named margin requirements). Index moves appear to be much less intense than some other methods and far less likely to be impacted by media.

Traditionally, the short spread is built for income, even though the fundamental value stays the same. Short position spreads are thus deemed "fair to bearish," and short puts spread are "good to bullish." This is one of the main distinctions between longer spreads or short spreads.

Note, spreads include trading in greater than one alternative and thus incur and over one fee. Hold that in factors when choosing the options on trade.

Not Realizing What to Do at the Task

If you offer options, just periodically inform yourself that you may be allocated early, until the expiry date. Most new retail investors never dream about assigning as a prospect before such time that it occurs. When you haven't factored into the assignment, it can be confusing, particularly if you are operating a multi-leg approach like short or long spreads.

For instance, what if you run a call option spread and are given the short higher-strike option? Starting traders may panic or exercise the long option to utilize the stock for the lower hit. This is definitely not the right choice, though. Selling the long choice on the stock market, taking the residual time premium together with the intrinsic interest of the contract, and utilizing the profits to purchase the order, is typically cheaper. Then, at a higher price, you will buy the company to the individual investor.

An early appointment is one of the often-unpredictable market activities which are genuinely emotional. When it occurs, there is always no rhyme or explanation behind it. It is all true. And as the economy shows, it's a trick less than genius.

If delegated well in advance, go about what you will do. The greatest defense towards the early task is to let it play into your early thought.

Otherwise, it will lead you to make less than rational, in-the-moment, protective decisions.

Taking consumer dynamics into account will aid—is it more prudent to work out early, for example? A call or a put? Trying to exercise a put or stock sale right ensures the dealer sells the stock or gets cash.

Always question yourself: Do you like your money now or when it expires? Citizens often prefer cash now or cash later on. This implies the puts appear to be more prone to earlier activity than calls.

A calling implies that the dealer must be able to invest cash to buy the product relative to the game later. Waiting for and investing the cash later is typically human nature. When an inventory is rising, though, less qualified traders can squeeze the pin early, lacking to know that they are leaving a certain time premium mostly on the table. How will an early task be random?

Failure of Reality for Next Event

Not all market developments are predetermined. However, there are two important things to keep on top of while selling options- profits and dates of dividends on the stock market.

For starters, if you've sold puts and a payout is coming, it improves the chances that you may be allocated early because the choice is already in cash. This is particularly true if we consider the dividend to be increasing. That's the proprietors of options that have no dividend protection. Options traders will exercise the right to receive, and by the common assets.

Make sure things weigh pending. You'll need to learn the former-dividend date, for starters. Stay well clear of offering put options with unpaid distributions, unless you are able to consider higher assignment costs.

Trading with the company's securities during the price action normally ensures that you may face greater uncertainty— and therefore pay an elevated cost for that opportunity. If you intend to buy options during the profit-taking, then one choice is to buy another option and offer another, producing a spread.

Illiquid Options Trading

Cash flow is about how fast a trader could even buy this without causing major movement in price. A smart investor is one that often contains available, committed sellers and buyers.

Here's a way to talk about everything: Liquidity relates to the possibility the next transaction can be carried over at a rate equivalent to the previous.

Options markets are, for one basic explanation, more competitive for traders. Investment bankers swap only one stock, while rational investors can select from hundreds of strike prices.

For instance, investment bankers would rush to one type of, let's just assume, IBM stock; however, brokerage firms may have six separate expirations to choose from a host of strike rates. By nature, further choices imply that the price action would generally not be as competitive as the equity market.

A good reason like IBM is not normally a liquidity issue for stock traders and options traders. Narrower inventories creep into the issue. Take extreme Green Technologies, an environmentally sustainable (imaginary) energy business of some hope, can have only one stock that sells once per week by request.

The stocks on extreme Green Technologies are likely to be much more negative if the portfolio was illiquid. Typically, this will allow the gap between the offer and leading to a "to have the options excessively high."

E.g., whether the bid-ask difference is $0.20, then if you purchase the contract $2.00, that's a maximum of 10 percent of a price charged to determine the place.

It's never a smart decision to place your role right away at a 10 percent loss, even by picking a highly leveraged alternative with a broad bid-ask range.

Trading overleveraged options pushes up the expense of doing so, and on a yearly basis, price action prices are now greater than stocks. Don't place yourselves on a load.

If selling stocks, please ensure that the available position is at least 40 times the size of the connections that you choose to sell.

E.g., to exchange a 10-lot, the appropriate leverage must be 10 x 40, or perhaps a minimum of 400 open interest. Open value reflects the number of option contracts left with a market price and expiry date that were bought or exchanged to put it up. Any closing payments raise the open value, although it reduces the closure of payments. Also, at the end of each financial day the free interest is measured. Invest liquidity options to avoid extra expenses and pressures on yourself. There are tons of possibilities somewhere for liquids.

Search for resources that can assist you in discovering possibilities, obtain perspective, or respond when the urge attacks. Find out several Trade platform on smart devices.

Doesn't Have an Escape Route

You have always seen it before, a thousand times. It's important to manage the emotions when purchasing in bulk, much like stocks. That does not involve swallowing all the worries in a human-level way. It's far better than all that: Get a job schedule and adhere to it.

You have to have an escape schedule, time frame. Even though things fall at your side, use an upside-out stage, a downward escape stage, and well-advanced timescales for each departure.

What if you head out though early and drop it upside hand on the ground?

That is the preoccupation of a traditional dealer. Here's the perfect counterpoint: what about if you reliably made a profit, then check the probabilities of risks, and sleep well at night?

Establish a strategy for the exit. Whether you purchase or sell shares, an escape strategy is an utter necessity. This lets you develop more efficient trading patterns. This, therefore, maintains some power over the fears.

Evaluate an upside-down escape strategy, but the worst-case situation you're able to accept. If you accomplish your objectives on the upside, examine your place, and take all your money. Don't feel gloat. If you hit your stop-loss downside, you can clear your place once again. Don't subject yourself to unnecessary danger by betting that the high prices can return.

Perhaps from start to end, the urge to break this guidance will be high. Do not do it. You have to build a decision, but instead commit to it. All too many merchants draw out a schedule and then throw the strategy to suit their impulses as long as the exchange is done.

Call Options for (OTM)

Buying OTM strikes openly is some of the most challenging ways to reliably earn money in options trading. Margin requirement sell options cater to traders of fresh options since they are inexpensive.

That would seem like a reasonable place to begin: Purchase the best escorts alternative and see whether you can select a winner. Calls to purchase should sound comfortable as it fits the trend you're used to pursuing as a stock trader: trade away and seek and sell big. Yet if you restrict yourself to that technique alone, you will continually lose capital.

Try offering an OTM long position on an already held portfolio as the first approach. This method is regarded as a strategic concealed call.

What's good with protected calls as a tactic is that if the call is secured by a cash position, the danger will not arise from buying the right. This even has the ability to give you market profits while you're optimistic, but also able to sell the shares if the price goes up. This tactic will give you the "look" of how contract rates for the OTM option shift when the approaches to expiry and the changes in market demand.

Nonetheless, the danger resides in controlling a stock—as well as the danger may be big. Although offering the covered call does not create capital danger, it does reduce the upside, thereby increasing the possibility of opportunity. If the price increases and your request is executed, you face needing to buy the shares after the assignment.

Chapter 14: Facts and Numbers to Help You

This field is where we dive further into the fascinating environment of quantitative stock market research. It will be to look through the business figures and sort them out and see if they're making the grade for us to track. Often the main issue is how we can manage this?

The Value Question

This is probably one of the first items you'll experience when you run across someone who looks at the financial market from a fundamentalist's eyes. Does this business show worth, and is the worth that the investment market already realizes?

Some people live and breathe the notion that for trading in the stock market, you should depend entirely on fundamentals. They're not perfect. I've seen and been in contact with individuals who have never seen a stock chart in their life and who have gone on to create millions in capital market transactions. The following are among the more popular denominators among these people:

- Compared to the regular street Joe, they begin with more than usual amounts of capital.

- As a result, they seem to have an overall stronger grasp on their trading psychology.

- On days where the stocks have dramatic swings, they prefer to make their profits, which implies they are certainly not day traders or short-term buyers. Occasions that come to mind are like the collapse of the 2000 software bubble, as well as the turmoil of the 2008 mortgage notes, or the Lehman case.

- They don't need to depend on the profits for their everyday life and expenditures from their savings.

Fundamentals may be all you need to move ahead in the stock market investment sector. You use basics to pick up a decent product and then steadfastly wait for either the stock price to be down so that you can purchase the stock or sell it as the general demand becomes excessively buoyant to cash in on the greed of others.

It would require lots of patience, and then you will have to wait for the unspecified incident that will push the market price below the valuation you realize it has. Typically no brainers will be global incidents, impacting the entire financial price and getting the blow from both counters. This is how it influences all counters because the anxiety is too prevalent, without even waiting for any reasoning or thinking. This also suggests that the rates being depressed are more likely to only be influenced by expectations than to have some specific systemic problems inside the business. If the incident is only based on the particular business, perhaps further brain work will be required to sift through the evidence and noise and decide if the importance you've seen of the organization before still remains.

Investing in fundamentals is just a waiting process, where you are waiting to get in, and then you are waiting to get out again. It's not cut out for all people, to be frank. I mean, if we look at a typical scenario in a regular middle-class household when both parents are going off work, and you realize they get some extra cash every month that they put into their bank account. For some people who might have built up a modest nest egg of say $50,000, it will be simple to tell on paper, but tougher to do without some sort of work, as market prices are still poor.

Perhaps these people will be best off getting regular exposure and studying as well as knowing more about their mindset in investment and selling, which would then bring them in a far healthier spot through major openings provided in periods of financial turbulence.

Think also about the individual who wants to exchange today, since he might have a large amount to start with, but because of his choice to depend on that amount to produce his monthly profits, this fundamental investment approach will not be fast enough to maintain a healthy lifestyle.

But my opinion is that basic expenditure is all fine and can function well on its own two feet. It is about carrying a blade to a fight. It is a dignified tool to use. And I am posing this issue to you now. Why carry one blade if you can handle two?

My personal understanding of this is what I stated in the other segments earlier. For filtration purposes, I use fundamental research since it is the inherent power when looking at the fundamentals. You will see the power and competencies of an organization when it comes to figures and annual accounts. This means I'm just going to limit my trading and investment shortlist to businesses with a strong and proper role. I mean, if we're interested in Starbucks, we should actually summarize their company as selling coffee, and that's how we'd mold our thought and look at their business model's other aspects.

Getting the sword of fundamental analysis with you allows you the opportunity to select and choose from the vast pool of stock candidates out there, and that will improve your winning chances. And yeah, I'm going to remove the gun comparisons right here and now, in case it could annoy any people.

For instance, the other tool I would use besides reading the basics would be to use scientific research or map reading, as others might term it. If fundamentals provided the barrier, you would store and pick your businesses with, so the strategic analysis will provide you the timing and signals to take them out of the water and communicate with them.

One gives you a filtration device; the other gives you an interaction method.

Let's look at what we normally search for in a business and decide whether it is worthy of reflecting worth.

Increasing Profits

Profits reflect growth, and growth typically brings value to people like us investing in the stock market, which translates into a winning investment. What's better than winnings? Well, yields are growing year after year. That would actually be great news for any vested individual whose firm is seeing such development.

Usually, benefit numbers under the portion of the income statement can be conveniently accessed from the company's annual reports. Most reports these days offer at least a one-year comparison with the most recent collection of figures released, but that would not be enough. For the people who decide not to use the power of the internet, they will then hopefully have to collate and click through all the company's actual annual reports for ten years. It would be much better if you could get fifteen. Note, with their deep learning algorithms, when we have more data, our brain behaves like those of artificial intelligence, we consume and can process more.

I used to enjoy doing this, and I just like flipping through papers. There was something about the paper and its scent that just attracted me to it. But I have to admit, it's been hard work. Honest. You'd probably start looking at stars after you walked through three businesses. That is why I would urge everyone to make use of the technology that we all have at our disposal. You can easily look at a firm's ten-year results these days and focus on its profit metric.

A good measure will be a situation in which you see a steady development year after year. Usually, this informs you that the business has stable profits and is still expanding to meet the demand opportunity at the same time. For the gross profit, we will keep an eye out while paying more attention to the net profit figure. We want to see what the revenue and product costs are even for the business. That way, you will work out the profitability of the business, and that can be a helpful thing to have in your mind.

I have my sensors put out when I see steady growth that is then punctuated by a sudden spurt of growth. To be honest, I just don't like those circumstances and would most certainly need to take a closer look at them. This is the time that you really first got to get through the annual reports, potentially using at least three annual reports. I still take the previous annual report, the yearly growth spurt report, and the yearly report afterward. You'd like to explore what caused the growth spurt, and if it were sustainable, the main question would be. Many businesses have such spurts on paper, and it shows up extremely well, just to make it revealed later that a one-off sale of some commodity actually made money. It is our responsibility to find out what is happening, and to make informed, accurate decisions for ourselves, as it will build up our confidence as we move to the process of decision making.

Increasing Sales

The income or sales figures may also forecast the profits, and certain businesses report their sales statistics but do not book the profits until after the distribution of the programs or products. Revenue figures will be a decent benchmark for measuring any business, and, of course, we would like to see a year-on-year rise in sales as evidence of having a growing business in our sights.

For certain businesses, there might be little to no improvement in their revenue and profit figures, maybe one or two percent a year. Counters like Macdonald's would come to mind, and General Electric would. There are more secure, steady counters who have engaged their potential in the market and are likely to just cruise along. What they mean to the investor will be cash in dividend forms, as well as value development by company stock purchase backs. If well managed, these behemoths will typically sit on cash stockpiles, which are generally distributed to shareholders as dividends or used in acquisitions of corporate stocks.

Corporate stock acquisitions tend to raise the stock price per share as sales decrease the total number of stocks on the market.

Then others would wonder, what's the point of looking at such slow-growing firms? Remember, our job is to identify and filter those companies that are well run and meet our target pool criteria. Although these bigger businesses do not have the revenue and profit growth rates, they do show value when they have stock price depressions due to either external or internal shocks. That's why it's also a good idea to have a grasp on what would be a reasonable price for these stocks because you'd know whether it's under- or overvalued.

Granted, if we were able to choose, it would be fantastic to go every day of the year for growth firms, particularly when we are on the path to building more financial capital. For those that have a better slice of the pie or maybe a slice of silver or gold in the spoons that have been used to feed you, then the bigger firms with larger and more stable dividend payouts might make sense to park some money there.

For me, you will see steady growth year after year when it comes to measuring the revenue and benefit figures. It can be, but not super popular. Then what do you do with figures getting their ups and downs? A simple rule of thumb is to determine how many down years in the ten-year cycle are present. If it's more than three, I won't look too much into it, unless all those three years were packed closer to the front together, and the more recent figures are all showing steady progress.

The main point that I want to impress on everyone here is that with these numbers and details, we're trying to construct a narrative. No airy-fairy castles, just good old strong facts, and figures in the dream sort of thing. A business with some downturns and some unexpectedly punctuated development in ten to fifteen years will send me a message that either there is something wrong with the management of the company, or it's in a cyclical industry. If, after learning all of these, we are still interested in the business, then we will have the means to further investigate.

I want to go down the least road of resistance when it comes to me, though. What this means is that I would prefer to trade or invest in a business with steady growth, as seen in their 10-year study, rather than in a business with splotchy growth estimates. Some could argue. Yes, I may miss out on the unpolished gem, and yes, sometimes these splotchy numbers of growth actually mean something better. I still think, though, that with the universe of stocks as it is, there will always be a great chance for me to rope in the gains just as well as riding on the growth firms. You could call me lazy, but just me. In searching for the no-brainer growth stocks, I prefer to dump more effort than to spend effort investigating if a splotchy one is worth the hit.

Low Liabilities

We looked at revenue and benefit figures, but now we will look at the company's obligations and assets we may be involved in. It is important to take care of two main items for this chapter. The liability or obligations in the long run and the present liability.

We would prefer to see the capital flow of the business is sufficient to pay down the entire outstanding obligations with the existing liability, which is generally defined by the liability where the creditors will become callable within a year. The higher the cash-to-current debt ratio is, the lower we will score the business.

We typically use this formula debt-to-equity for the long-term loans to see the future health situation for the company we are investing in. Equity is the company's equity belonging to the owners, who are people like you and me. In this situation, we like the amount to be as little as practicable, so it will mean that the liability owed to creditors is even smaller than the worth we shareholders assign.

It's also a positive situation to have less leverage in the business since it means that the company does not need to draw into leverage yet to boost its expansion. This usually occurs when the business is in a fast-growing market with lots of demand or where the business has high barriers to entry into the goods or services and is willing to dictate competitive rates.

But ultimately, both firms seem to hit a point where they will find it easier to take on debt to finance their growth plans. The key here is that we don't want a possible goal organization to get pulled into a leverage pit where they take on too much leverage for their own gain. A debt-to-equity level of about 0.5 or less will be a fair gauge of what we strive to accomplish.

We really don't want to see a scenario in which the business simply requires loans to cover its operational expenses. This is typically a negative indication since it simply shows that regular net revenues or cashflow alone cannot cover the operational costs. This does not mean, though, that the business is beyond repair, as I saw companies who managed to achieve turnarounds after being saddled with debts. Speaking of shorting or short selling these businesses is indeed foolhardy, as I have seen too many people talking. If I can't purchase those businesses, why shouldn't I sell them short instead? Not many of these debt-saddled companies run the risk of falling under their own weight. For years or even decades, they will even be able to maintain this illusion of reputable activity, but it will be foolhardy to shorten these businesses only on the grounds of just one debt measure.

Increasing Return On Equity

The return on equity is the firm's operating earnings essentially measured by the owners' cumulative capital credited. This number reflects how much the capital will have played in the shareholder pot in the previous year. Higher net earnings would mean a greater yield, which would also imply a happier opportunity for the owners. I say, more value for one buck, right?

That this statistic is important is also attributed to the company's probability of offering stock. As stock redemption arises, the cumulative amount of trading securities is raised, which therefore means that the firm's gross asset valuation will rise as well. If the income of the business were to rise at a constant pace, yet would be faced with only a raise in equity that would be very bad news that more hands must share the gains.

A growing return on equity ratio will therefore be a very welcoming sight since it basically implies that the business is allowing greater use of its investments to produce further gains for its stockholders.

Perhaps, some people may wonder, does this same problem of making more people exchanging earnings arise during a market split? The direct response is no, and this is why. A stock split is effectively a scenario when a $100 per share is divided into usually two pieces, producing a scenario where after the break, it becomes $50 apiece. No extra capital appreciation is injected to expand the investor base.

Barriers to Entry

Another consideration to weigh for determining a stock's profitability will be the qualitative element of the entry barriers. How difficult will it be for rivals to join the same room with that business to offer a free for all?

Take Starbucks, for example, what it's offering goes beyond a cup of high-quality coffee. It's offering the atmosphere of Starbucks that occurs anytime all of its consumers walk into the shop. I say coffee is simple to make, correct? You might do that on your own, but why would you actually want to skip down to a Starbucks store to have them produce the particular coffee and then charge you a premium for it? That in itself is one of Starbucks' effective entrance barriers as good protection against it will be competitors.

Barriers to entry cannot often be caused by the business. They could very well be Government policy outcomes. For this case, let's go a bit afield here. They have a federal law in the South East Asian nation of Singapore, which requires all vehicles that are three years of age or older to go to an authorized agent for annual vehicle inspection. Only say what? In the nation, there are just a few such approved agents around, and that essentially renders it an oligopoly. To add to the appeal of this sector, it is a well-known reality that it is almost difficult to get the government to approve another new worker.

If you were an investor looking at this sort of situation, only concentrating on the entry factor barriers will send you very optimistic vibes on that. In a market with only two participants, you have a government regulation that practically guarantees demand for the services that are rendered. Some may be inclined to draw comparisons with Boeing and Airbus, but in reality, the business these two behemoths work in is very different. Purchases of aircraft appear to be cyclical in nature, with airlines preferring to put their fleet orders in the estimation of how their potential demand will be. As such, aircraft manufactures are therefore exposed to this cyclical stream of demand, which is ebbing and flowing. The market there is a relative constant for the automotive inspection industry. When the next customers come, you don't have to think.

Another form of hurdle will be the high expense of change, whether the consumer wants to move from one brand to another. This is true; just think about converting your desktop to mac. I think if you're a good member of the dual method, then kudos to you. And those born and raised on the computer, converting to the mac is sort of like giving birth, rough and unpleasant. Perhaps it will feel like a change for those who have been weaned on the mac to move into the computer.

We aim to have enterprises with as low entry obstacles as possible or just a few really high obstacles to get businesses. This means that due to potential competitors, the market that the prospective target firms are in will not be overcrowded out too fast. However, one point to remember is my belief that there would be no obstacle forever to end. Stuff often comes about, shifts in political policy, disrupts the infrastructure.

Any of these variables will induce transition and generate a ripple impact that breaks down a barrier's once strong fortress.

So the key here is to move into businesses that have strong barriers in effect and then see how the management is building paths to developing new barriers in readiness for the day that their existing barriers become redundant. I will call this a positive thing to have, but not specifically important in the initial stages of stock filtration.

Why? For what?

Just because you begin to weigh too many driving forces and mechanisms, there will actually be information overload. Attempting to see what one company's management is doing may be feasible, but it would seem utterly arduous because you have to do it regularly for five to six hundred years. When it falls into effect, there will be a real danger of getting complacent. In an allotted period of time, you have so many businesses to dig at that the brain would be tempted to stop the phase shortly. In doing so, it will sacrifice the normal robustness and close evaluation as well as the study of expression.

This is why I would advise people to work on looking for the obstacles to entry first, without knowing whether any proposals for potential barriers are being drawn up by management.

Another item to consider would be a simple heading. You certainly don't want to start considering entrance hurdles simply because you're too besotted with some single business. In general terms, the simpler the definition of the entry obstacle, the easier and better it can be. Anybody should attempt to describe it. Even better if the individual has an utter zero business or stock awareness. If they can see what you're attempting to convey in the shortest practicable period, in terms of the power and simplicity of the entrance barrier, you might have a champion here.

Management

The company's executive staff will be directly linked to access obstacles in dispute. It can also be classified as one of the barriers to entry if this element is considered to be high.

Much as the captain who is navigating the ship on the seas, the organization's manager or decision-maker will be equally responsible for bringing the corporation into the choppy market waters. A good, competent captain would ensure the safety and stability of the company, as would successful management.

The main problem here is to understand how to properly define effective and powerful governance. I say, for the most part, we're individual buyers, not hedge fund traders like Peter Lynch who can jet around the world and show in for a peek at the business headquarters. The good part here is, there aren't many items in this day and age of social networking that can't be ferreted out if you're of a mind.

We Take a Look at Their Track Record

Simply key their names into Google, and you should at least be able to take a whiff if they have some managerial expertise of some sort. Taking a glance at the present status of their former businesses and often take into consideration what their exit date was and traceback performance records of four to five years before transferring.

Another factor is looking at their specific interests about where they are living and what they are doing. Personally, with those people who are a bit more down-to-earth and a little less glamorous, I am more of a fan. That's not to suggest I haven't seen home runs with glamorous, noisy people operating businesses; it's just my own choice.

Generally speaking, I prefer to think that those who are a little less vocal will usually allow their acts to come out. They don't need huge mansions and flash cars but just let their performance speak for themselves. To take the famous Warren Buffett as an illustration, we won't have to search for it. Yeah, you might say he's an intense mite because the universe really doesn't allow them that way anymore. Ok, many other people are models with the less glamorous lifestyle, and I'm sure you can recognize them.

Another thing I would like to find out is the boy with the hand of the Midas. There's still somebody like that, obviously. An individual who suddenly turns around a worn-out corporation starts up new enterprises and immediately becomes a success. I'd like to concentrate more on the figures and hard data while the organization has such a dynamic boss. The reason I'm concerned about the company's value is some factor in the star leader's "light," because if that light is no longer available, the stock might take a dive. Often, when we meet such a dynamic man, there may be all-around encouraging reviews that can cause us to get quickly swept away at the moment we feel good. I'm still suspicious of this, but I will try to use statistics and evidence to anchor myself. If there are not enough figures, so I'll prefer to miss the business and follow the next better one.

Valuation

This may be a multi-billion dollar issue when it comes to simple research. Both funnies will like a figure that they can use to equate with the actual price of the trade. That's how people come up with words like under-or-above-value. The index to which the selling price is measured will be the amount deriving from the valuation.

So then, how do we extract the valuation number? If you were to conduct a quick google search, it turns out that you would be able to pull up at least three or four common forms of valuation approaches that Wall Street analysts are expected to use. Let's speak a little about them here, about the processes, not the specialists on Wall Street.

Next up will be the patriarch of both of them, the discounted study of cash flow. It's a process that requires several digits, as the name implies, and if you had to punch the digits on a calculator manually, it could take you a little while to hit your final destination. Believe me; I've done it before.

Luckily, we have outstanding spreadsheets and a plethora of other technical miracles that will simplify this phase for us to reduce the main numbers we are concerned about.

We would like to see what the company's actual net cash flow is. From the new annual accounts, that can be conveniently downloaded, so no issues here. The next number in question will be the expected pace of growth that you would like to add to the mentioned business.

How we will measure this will usually be to provide data worth about ten years in terms of sales and benefit. Then we review the growth rates periodically and take an average of nine years. If we have reasonable growth rates both in sales and benefit, the sensible course of action will be to choose the lower of the two ratios. I say, in most situations, to be careful is often safer. However, some people appear to be a little more a purist when it comes to that stuff, but they carry yet another combination of the two figures. However, as the case might be, the end goal will be to obtain a forecast pace of growth for the business that can fairly be counted upon.

I claim fairly since no one on earth can guess what the company's real growth pace would be. So many variables on hand may confuse the count, and we will have to make do with the strongest estimates we may obtain.

After the company's growth pace, we'll also have to determine the correct discount rate, which is typically the capital expense required to finance to run the business. For that, there's a sophisticated word named WACC. Simply it implies weighted average capital expenditure. There are equity and debt both in business. The loan expense will be the interest rate paid to the business by the lending sector. Think about the mortgage, which helps you to raise funds to acquire your house or vehicle. You have to pay tax on certain accounts. The same goes for the corporation, and the cost of debt will be the average interest. Equity expenses will be just the total yield on equity. WACC is then determined by taking correct debt and equity ratios over the company's net asset valuation and calculating the related costs.

While it's not particularly relevant about what we do, the purist in me just had to bring that out for the record. And WACC as well will be determined.

Equity Valuation Divided By Net Asset Value Multiplied by Expense Of Equity + Debt Value Divided By Net Asset Value Multiplied by Debt Expense Multiplied by One Half of the prevailing tax rate.

There you have it. Only knock out with WACC.

But since we have these three significant figures in discounted cash flow analysis, it will be sort of simple to produce the absolute golden number, which is basically the final amount of all operational cash flows carried out into the future using the expected growth rate, and discounted back into the present using the WACC.

Another way to arrive at the value figure will be by calculating price-earnings or multiples. In short, the PE ratio is assumed to be the product of dividing the market price by earnings per share of the stock.

Once again, some people will use around ten years of statistics to figure out the cumulative PE amount and add it to the actual earnings per share and get an idea of what the company's future worth could be.

If you are not still floating in a lot of ifs, buts, and expectations, it would be high time to realize that when doing DCF and even PE valuation, you would be doing a lot of that. And if the financial model may be complex at the end of the day, the fundamental reality is that it will still be based upon assumptions. Hypotheses that could be changeable or volatile because of the mere reality that we tend to look so much into the future.

Let's face it, in the seventies, people would actually have had a fair idea of what lifestyle might be like in the eighties. Now people would actually have a difficult time predicting how things might work out to be like in the next ten years. Technology is both the maker and the killer with the introduction of self-driving vehicles, artificial intelligence, and deep learning. Who is to claim you can't ruin or rebuild a company's expectations and dreams?

I mean, to be talking like this right now may sound like a super wet blanket. I say, maybe you should go, but what's the point of performing all those fundie analyzes? Everything goes down the pipe, and we can't foresee the future. Don't worry.

A preliminary reference for us would also be DCF or PE, or other kinds of financial models that pump out valuation figures. It is by no way the entirety of the decision-making phase to be the finish. If we get a DCF valuation figure, we have a very vague understanding of whether this business is above or underpriced at the moment. Our key foundation is to always process and shape a pool of prospective target firms utilizing all the fundamental facets of the research listed above. Going at progress from the viewpoint of sales and benefit, taking in qualitative factors as well as rounding things off with the value figures, it will be customized to the variety of businesses. We are not going to make judgments on purchasing or selling based on valuation amounts

Chapter 15: Constant Profits

This section would explain how to stay ahead in terms of profiting from the stock market. We still say stuff like, a number of times:

Many investors struggle to make profits off the equity market, even more so for retail companies, but at the end of the day, the house still wins.

It is safer to put your trust in mutual funds and highly paid professionals.

In most marketing materials for expensive stock trading and investing classes, this will be the moment where the content will say categorically that they had the unique response that would allow you to be the lucky one or ten percent who would reliably beat the market, harvest passive gains, all on a simple one-hour investing a day.

Sounds amazing, right?

The reality is that many supermarket companies are losing money, but many are still earning profits, and the only ones who would actually know for sure will be the tax department officials. As I said, the path from the stock market to gain and prosper lies primarily with yourself.

In order to study to appreciate how the competition operates, you have to invest in the time and commitment to have a fair chance to win it regularly. Here we will look through certain tips that will enable you to move into profitability.

Do Not Follow the Herd

This theory is also a basic yet misunderstood concept when it comes to capital market valuation issues. When it comes to precious trading insights and so-called insider reports, it's always quick to fall victim to the general flow of emotions. You want to move into the depths of it, and you will certainly be scared to lose out on what you see as the perfect opportunity to make money fast and effortless.

Banish Those Thoughts

We are simply coming at things from two slightly different angles, while not joining the group. In one, we don't encourage the simple seduction of stock tips by so-called experts to drag us and manipulate us. On the other side, we are not basing our own investment choices solely on what the general crowd is doing at the moment. At its heart, we will still depend on our intuition, derived from the comprehensive fundamental and scientific modes of research, to process and make the requisite judgments about sales and transactions.

That's not to suggest we're not open to suggestions that might be coming from others. That surely is not true. Holding an open mind is important, the more from which to understand. My analysis of this will be to interpret new ideas gleaned from others as just that—possible ideas. The filtration and analytical method that forms the foundation of the investment profession also need to be exposed to them. The ability to be caught away by the raw force of envy or terror in moments of intense emotion will be wonderful, so please try your utmost to stave it off. You're getting better off with it.

I've always found it simpler for me to avoid market calls during times of a bull run, as nearly any second person you encounter on the streets will be willing to talk on investments and give a bit of well-meaning sage guidance. I suppose a latent skeptic resides inside me, hoping for the smallest chance to pounce. Beyond the particular slant will be the foundation I have in the theoretical framework that I've come to depend on to make all of my investment decisions.

I realize that even though this proposed invitation to stock was to perform superbly well and my research did not lead me to take any decision for any reason or other, there will be some more concrete opportunities awaiting me. This eliminates the risk of losing out to basically none.

For circumstances when the stock market occurs, it is typically uncertainty that is more prevalent. On many occasions, people will offer advice to keep out of the stock market or get out of stock until it gets too late. I find it more challenging to tackle fear than envy, which is natural. That's also part of why bear markets are always faster to set up than their bull equivalents. People get inspired by fear more quickly than by envy.

Also, the way to overcome this is to remain concentrated and firm in the critical process. I realize, for me, that every choice I make would be the product of philosophical and logical study, and that gives me the confidence to carry the choice through. This moves to the system's next step.

Trust Your System

You should feel at home because you value the mechanism, whether it's a down market or a bull market. This is because you have the trust and understanding that the method can produce a steady share of chances for you to step towards profitability.

However, one thing you can remember here is that you don't just pinch some old collection of technical indicators and then mark the framework. I tended to do so early on, and it was a common sight, so I bailed out of my investment choices, mostly at crucial junctures that might have had me earn gains rather than constant losses.

When I talk about the method, it's something I've built for myself. For me, I use a two-step method that requires the stock filtration to be done by the fundamental analysis, then the technical analysis to determine optimum entry and exit points. Some people are concerned with designing their structures solely based on technological research, whilst some are only sticking to the basics. No solution is correct or wrong. I guess the most practical way of looking at things will be which method will be deemed the best framework for you to achieve stable income over a fair period of time.

I notice that marrying the two major analytics schools fits pretty well for me because it offers me a sense of confidence that much of the angles should be guarded. When you're designing your ideal method, you have to determine what will best for you.

The theoretical part of business, including the statistical study of commodities, has its positives. Even they have their share of issues. No method will ever assert outright dominance over the other, which is presumably why the one I use now always pulls elements from both.

You may notice that in designing your own ideal method, you have the same thoughts and perceptions as mine, and therefore build an amalgamation of the fundamental and the scientific. In other instances, you might be oriented more toward the scientific side of things, and the design might seem more like a graphical model. Whatever the case, the phase after the device is installed will be to thoroughly test it.

This is the position where you develop your faith.

Back checking is perhaps the most popular form people hire to verify a system's functionality and viability. For strictly technological tools, this approach is simple to apply since the test results can be collected within a matter of minutes these days. For the fundamentalists, back research is still feasible, but more manual of nature would have to be undertaken.

In reference to the quarterly or annual accounts, they will have to review the change in market values. Back testing is useful for establishing a device base, but a separate type of testing is required to show it stressfully.

The use of the device in either simulated or live trading will be forward checking or experimenting in real-time. Such research will catch both the thoughts of the uncertain and the resulting reactions as the request is eventually proved to be right or incorrect. I carried on research with my method with approximately a year before raising the stakes on-investment decision.

The downside to forwarding testing is that it requires time, basically. This is not a workaround. The nice thing about that is that if you see it functions regularly, you can develop a strong trust in the method. And if the device doesn't actually work, you will have learned useful experience of tinkering with it and coming up with more insights about how to make things better for you.

I will say, you should actually get away with doing forward tests for only six months at this stage. I will suggest, when it comes to this subject, that the longer the time, the better. Of course, this has got to be matched with the question of what happens if the device simply doesn't function. This leads to the crucial issue of how you are formulating your method.

Take an individual who believes he would like to invest based on leverage, for example. He provides an easy mechanism where, if his price reaches the 52-week high price watermark, he will go long or buy a warehouse. Since this is such an easy technique for him, he would be able to do back checking on this approach to verify its effectiveness. If he is pleased with the outcome of the back examination, he will then pass it on to the process of forwarding checking, where he will analyze the findings first hand. He would need to start worrying about the realistic implications of this technique, and during the live trading phase, he would have ample practice using it. He might care about choosing which stock to invest in when there could be several stocks in the same moment breaching their 52-week high watermark. He would also look at this methodology's total feasibility and make observations as to if it is worth following this course.

The method doesn't have to be very complex in general. It only needs to be important to you and, of course, potentially successful as utilized in the markets.

Market Timing

If you want to produce supernormal stock market returns, then I don't care what other people suggest, the timing of the market would be a talent you have to learn.

There will still be time to purchase inventories and time to market. A successful stock market company will require someone to take advantage of such two optimum timings and have the spirit to see beyond them.

Would you foresee returns to be reached if you only want to buy into a stock and keep it for posterity? Responding is true. You might, yes, but there will be better chances of having supernormal returns. There are also legends on investing about individuals who have spent $5,000 and, after 30 years, have earned back a million dollars. All those reports will not be that these acquisitions were in the next major wave of businesses. It is almost about moving into Apple in early 2000 or some of the software giants.

It is not a daily thing that certain chances exist, and if skipped, it could very well be a wait that lasts for a lifetime to come. I put forward the notion of market timing to overcome this problem.

If you're willing to absorb the market's ups and downs when it comes to business range, you don't need to really strike the jackpot.

Often, setting away the notion that you are going to purchase at the very lowest and offer at the very peak is fine too. Not a lot of people will do it. In reality, I haven't seen anybody at this stage of writing who can lay claim to regularly and conscientiously do it. We can consider reaching the seventy-fifth percentile level more frequently than not as a positive accomplishment. Selling the stock when it's a quarter away from the high point, and buying the stock when it's a quarter away from the bottom, to me, are commendable feats that will actually require several years of practice.

The other explanation that market timing is very important to producing the supernormal returns that one people expect in the equity market is the reality that the churning impact needs to be taken into account.

If, within three years, a stock were to increase by 100-point, it would be considered a fairly strong investment in most regions. Will it be possible if I were to suggest having five separate instances of 20 point increase within a year? First off, a 20 point increase will have a greater chance of occurring than a 100 point rise. Second, I'd only like to identify five separate places where there's a better chance of making a 20 point shift. It will also actually be better to notice five 20 point shifts in a year than to notice one 100 point step in one or two years. The argument I am suggesting is that with the timing of the business, you are able to generate a higher amount of profits over a greater range of transactions relative to getting all the earnings based on one or two firms.

Metaphorically, market timing will cause you to receive a dollar from any citizen on the globe, as opposed to earning ten dollars from everyone in your region. Will it be better to ask somebody to give you a dollar while you're worried about it, instead of asking them to part with ten dollars? The same goes for one warehouse. It would be a trifle tougher to bag a ten-bagger, as some Wall Street people would say it, due to having regular one bagger on yourself. One bag is equal to a fold increase of the purchase price for clarity purposes. This is one of the key reasons why I would suggest timing on demand to be one of the abilities that you will pick up while you advance in your investment career.

Here, nothing is completely crafted in stone or wood, as in many aspects in existence and in the markets too. Typically there are at least two sides of everything, and often even more than two. For this matter of market timing, amid my ongoing appeals for one to pick up this valuable talent, I do agree that for others, acquiring this ability may actually be pointless to them.

For certain people who are already guardians or husbanders with vast sums with assets and money, so I might sense that market timing skills would not be as important to them as they might be to the average retail investor. For these individuals born with incredibly significant quantities of wealth, they will genuinely carry out a buy and keep the same policy that will continue for centuries. This is because their immediate needs are now well covered for the resources they have at their hands, and the immense surplus can be guided into savings that will practically bear fruit in a lifetime.

Not everybody is a scion of certain family riches or has the chance to accumulate a massive sum of money within a very short period. Quite a lot of people are already trying to keep the cash flowing in, and it's fairly much at the forefront of our heads as to how best to produce further gains on the money surplus.

Ultimately, utilizing market timing correctly and with proper implementation will then encourage one to speed up the compounding rate for one's capital.

Conclusion

The market is only a market, no feeling and no connection attached to it. There's nothing exciting about this, nor is it particularly thrilling. For others, the major problem is that they choose to mess up the investment market with capital, or, more accurately, assets that they expect to buy.

Please step away from the pedestal, and turn aside from your feelings.

The more dispassionate and comparatively calm you are willing to keep with respect to capital market activities and machinations, or any asset sector, the easier that will be with your overall investment effort.

To me, the best approach of this book will still be to go back to the fundamentals, whether an experienced trader or novice. Have a clear idea of what type of business you're working with. For starters, if you plan to restrict your search to just the S&P 500 index stocks, then research such stocks and come to understand the behavior of the index like you might change your own body.

This, of course, may not happen immediately, and to strive for it will take regular, diligent action.

The next move will be to devise the hunting plan or hunting method with the clearness of the goals. This is where hundreds of people will be gunning for the simple way out, seduced by this or that ready-made machine offered by glib salespeople who pledge for a commitment of only one hour a day to roll in riches.

Little is really good for free. Only think of the duck swimming serenely on the lake's shore, when in reality, it is actively paddling to stay afloat under the waters. This can also be a harbinger about how the particular structure builds.

You can run into dead ends, and in anger, you can start pulling the hair out of its roots. That is completely natural. What counts most here will be the tenacious endeavor to build your own workable method. I can just advise you- don't give up. Eventually, you would be able to locate the framework because when you believe it and start seeing the steady benefits from it, even the struggles they followed, it would make their effort worth it.

It's my sincere wish that you might produce steady gains from the investment market, and who knows, maybe one day you'd be able to leave your day job and live to live entirely off the stock market income.

Never give up.

Day Trading Forex:

The Forex Basics Explained With All Trading Strategies. A Proven Method To Become A Profitable Forex Trader. You Will Find Inside The A-Z Glossary To All Technical Terms Used

Written by:

Nathan Real

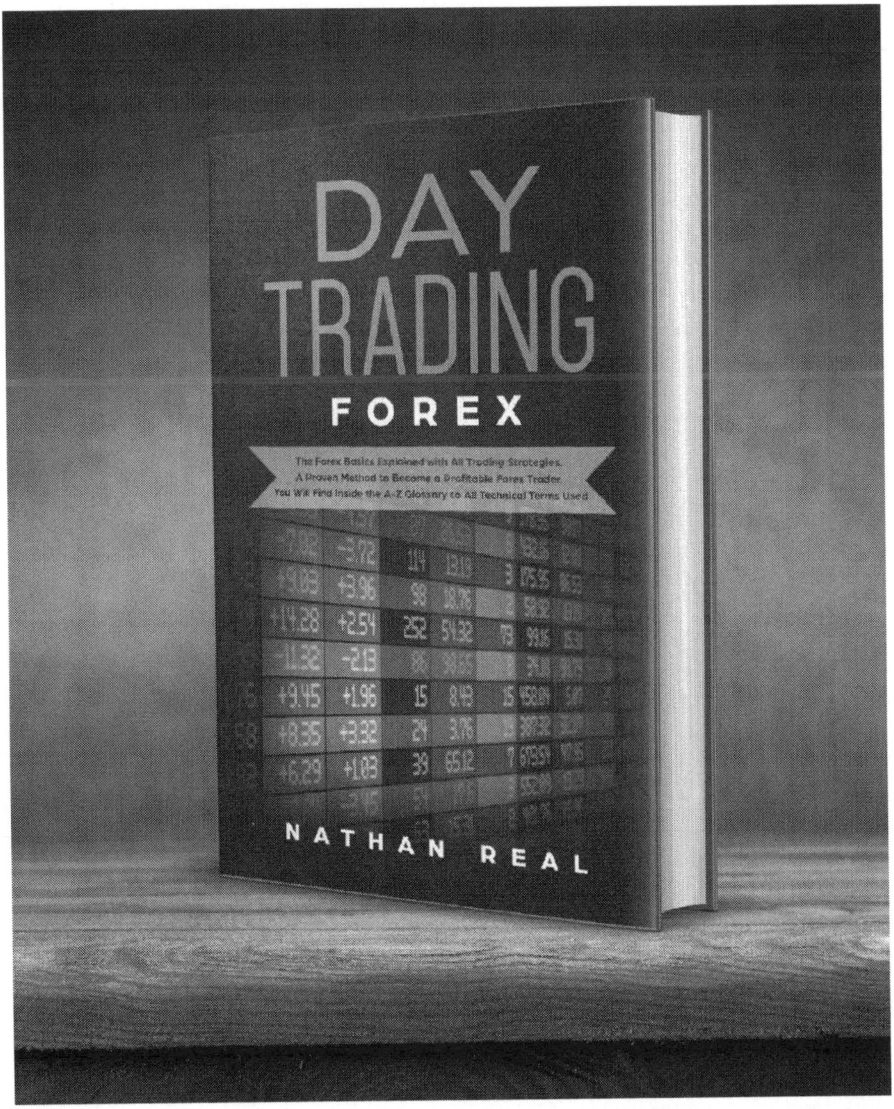
DAY
TRADING
FOREX
NATHAN REAL

Introduction

Congratulations on purchasing *Day Trading Forex* and thank you for doing so.

There are plenty of books on this subject on the market, thanks again for choosing this one! Every effort was made to ensure it is full of as much useful information as possible, please enjoy!

Who Is Involved In Foreign Exchange Trading And How It Is Carried Out?

Since large financial companies, corporations and funds have their own banks and carry out transactions through them, we, mere mortals, conclude agreements with banks or brokerage companies to service our operations in the Forex market.

In the foreign exchange market, as you understand, it is customary to make transactions in certain volumes. The minimum lot participating in the auction is $ 100,000. However, not everyone has such a sum. And in order for you to be able to complete a transaction, a brokerage house or a bank provides you with an interest-free loan for the duration of the transaction. Such a loan has a name - "leverage. As an example: if the leverage is 1:10, and the lot is, say, 100,000, then you need to have $ 10,000 on your account. The higher the allowable leverage, the higher the volume of transactions that can be made with the same amount of capital placed with a broker. The higher the volume, the higher the profit or loss. The larger the leverage provided, the more money management opportunities.

I see skepticism in the eyes of the reader. So, someone thinks, bankers "out of love for the neighbor" do nothing. There must be some kind of hook and not just a hook, but a real ship anchor. You are of course right. Naturally, there is such a hook. Bankers really know how to count their money. What is their interest? Remember the currency exchange office: there is a column "purchase" and a column "sale", and there is a difference between buying and selling - this difference is called the spread.

So *spread* - this is the difference between the purchase price (ask) and the sale price (bid). Spread is the profit of the exchange office. And Forex is the international currency exchange market for currencies. And who is one of the participants in Forex currency trading? That's right - large banks. Draw an analogy. As soon as you enter into a trade, the spread is calculated from your account immediately. Spread is the profit of the bank. Therefore, it is financially beneficial for a bank to have transactions completed as often as possible. And we, traders, benefit from leverage and the opportunity to work in this market. We are interesting to the bank, and the bank is interesting to us. This is a mutual interest. Therefore, we choose the most attractive and reliable terms of trade. The choice of a bank or a brokerage house is very important.

So, finances are placed.

The meaning of Forex trading is to buy some currency, wait for a favorable exchange rate change and then sell more expensive than you bought it. Uncle's operation clearly shows us an example of speculative trading. The result of such an operation is to obtain, by changing the exchange rate, a difference that will make your profit. And by the way, if you think that any currency will become cheaper, then you can sell it in the expectation that the rate of this currency will decrease and you can earn on its fall. However, many argue this way: in order to sell something, you must first buy something. No, this is not necessary, since there is such a rule on Forex: we carry out all operations with the currency that is the first in the currency pair. Selling, say, a couple of euros/dollars, we sell euros for dollars. That is, selling euros, we buy dollars.

On the price chart, the appreciation of the first currency is displayed by moving the chart up, and the cheaper - by moving the chart down accordingly.

- If you think that the chart of any currency pair will move up, then your action is to buy, after a certain price up - closing the transaction and taking profit.
- If you think that the chart of any currency pair will move down, then your action is to sell, after a certain price down - closing the transaction and taking profit.

Chapter 1 - How Does A Buy-Sell Operation Happen?

1. Opening an account (brokerage company or bank).

2. The program (for example Metatrader, find it from Google).

3. Decision (buy-sell). Request.

4. The transaction (it takes a few seconds).

5. Receive a report on the transaction in the form of an open position on the terminal. Consider the concepts that are often found when discussing operations on the Forex market and which you and I will need to keep up to date and speak the same language.

- *Quotation,* or *exchange rate.*

A value showing how much of one currency you are willing to pay for another currency at a given time.

• *Currency pair.*

A currency pair is, for example, the designation EUR / USD. Here EUR is the base currency, USD is the counter currency.

• *Forward and reverse quotes.*

A direct quote shows how much of any currency (for example, rubles) is contained in one US dollar. Examples:

▪ USD / RUR (American dollar / ruble);

▪ USD / JPY (American dollar / Japanese yen);

▪ USD / CAD (American dollar / Canadian dollar).

The reverse quote shows how many US dollars are contained in a unit of national currency. Examples:

▪ GBP / USD (pound sterling / US dollar);

■ EUR / USD (Euro / American dollar);

■ AUD / USD (Australian dollar / American dollar)

• *Cross rate.*

This is a quote without the participation of the American dollar. Examples:

■ GBP / JPI (pound sterling / Japanese yen);

■ EUR / CAD (Euro / Canadian dollar);

■ GBP / CHF (pound sterling / Swiss franc).

• *Paragraph.*

If (recalling the exchange office) we say that 1 euro can be sold for 1.3910 US dollars, and bought for 1.3915 US dollars, then the minimum change in the value of the currency EUR / USD is one unit in the fourth decimal place, which is called paragraph. In this case, we see the euro/dollar quote, in which the spread is 5 points.

• *Open foreign exchange position.*

This is the amount of currency bought or sold, the value of which changes over time according to a change in the rate of a given currency. I will explain this with an example. Suppose you are planning to buy/sell a currency pair. To do this, do the following:

1) Install a special online trading program such as Metatrader;

2) Send a request to buy (or sell) a currency pair;

3) Receive a currency quote from a broker;

4) If the price suits you, make a purchase (or sale) of a certain amount of currency.

From the moment of the transaction, you will be listed as an open currency position.

Every business has its own specifics of communication and some special terms. When you fall into the midst of professionals, sometimes it seems that you are talking like compatriots but in some completely incomprehensible language. The most amazing thing is that they understand each other. You have just begun to discover this amazing and fascinating country called Forex, and in order to better understand everything, you just need to learn a few terms that will be often used in the future. For example:

- stop loss - limit losses;
- take profit - take profits;
- sell - sell;
- buy - buy.

As soon as you meet a new term, write it down (with decoding) and memorize! I remember how difficult the terminology was for me. Brains simply refused to perceive unusual information for them. How I envied those who freely juggled with all sorts of intricate phrases and, which was completely strange for me, even seemed to understand what he was talking about. Then I came up with a way out of this situation. I simply wrote on the leaflets all those specific expressions (with explanations) that were, at that time, gibberish for me and scattered these leaflets in all accessible and inaccessible places. No matter where I was, as soon as I reached into my bag, pocket or desk, I stumbled across these "strange" phrases (for example, buy - buy, sell - sell). My household members openly laughed at my venture, but when you see the goal in front of you, you perceive everything else as some kind of cost. This did not bother me.

Every night before going to bed, remembering how once poems were memorized at school, I took a notebook with lectures and read them aloud. Someone reads newspapers, some detectives, some historical literature, and I gave lectures on Forex with little understanding. After a couple of weeks, I suddenly discovered that I began to understand what was being said about in my notes. That is, at first the language gets used to pronounce these seemingly unusual terms, and then the brains begin to turn in the right direction. And away we go ...

The basic principle of working on Forex is quite simple. There are buyers on the market, they are often called "bulls" (the bull is trying to raise the price with its horns), and sellers are called "bears" (the bear is trying to lower the price with a paw). So there are buyers and sellers. It is profitable for buyers to buy cheaper, and sellers - to sell more expensive.

Consider this as an example. Let's say you come to the market. To the regular market. Saw something that you liked. And, like any buyer, you want to buy this wonderful little thing, but not at the price that the seller offers you, but at a lower price ... And the seller, in turn, is ready to sell you this wonderful little thing, but not at that price which you offered him, but for the most part. Both your task and the seller's task is to find the parity price that will suit you and the seller will be profitable. And you begin to bargain, trying to find the price when "and the wolves will be full, and the sheep are safe". And having found mutual understanding, you disagree, very pleased with yourself, each with his own interest.

In the foreign exchange market, there is also a bargain price for buying and selling. Only here you can act as a buyer and as a seller. It is not necessary to go one way. What makes the Forex market wonderful. You yourself determine what is more profitable for you at the moment - to buy or sell.

BUT, in order to correctly assess the situation on the market and determine the nature of the transaction (purchase or sale), it is necessary to understand on the basis of what laws the price movement is taking place. To do this, consider the Dow theory because it is this theory that is the foundation of our success building called Forex. Dow theory is the foundation of the basics. Each postulate of this theory is a kind of brick in the base of the house. If one of the principles is violated, the building will lose its stability. Therefore, the study of the Dow postulates is one of the most important rules for working in the market.

By the way, do you know who Charles Dow is? After all, it is he who is called the man who discovered Stock America. The Dow Jones index fell ... Or rose by such a number of points ... Have you heard? Why is it that Dow and his friend Jones are remembered not once a day, but every time they cover and analyze world financial markets?

Charles Dow was born into a family of farmers. And after reaching sixteen, he got a job as a typewriter apprentice in a weekly newspaper, and then as a reporter. As he gained experience, he developed an interest in economic topics. And Dow was able to realize this interest by moving from a provincial newspaper to the daily The Providence Star, where he began working as a reporter, effectively becoming the progenitor of the genre of financial journalism. And it was Dow who came up with the idea of issuing a newsletter with a summary table of stock price changes every day. It was an innovation! At first, this information looked like an insider, companies at that time preferred not to advertise so openly and regularly about changes in the value of shares for the general public. However, fortunately, Charles Dow changed the situation by proving the profitability of such information for the great manipulators of the exchange - after all, by public statements about price changes, they could stimulate the movement of shares in the direction they needed. Thus, it was Charles Dow who changed the basic principles of the stock exchange. Moreover, he, together with his friend Eddie Jones, derived a single stock market index, assigning equal weight to each stock and calculating percentage changes in prices, thereby leading the rates to an average value. It is the Dow Jones index that is designed to determine some general direction of the market. And who knows, dear reader, maybe it is for you to supplement the basic postulates of the Dow, to derive a new index, which will be called your name. After all, the foreign exchange market provides a lot of food for the mind ... and opportunities.

From the school curriculum, you remember that theorems are what need proof, and axioms are what is taken for granted. I did not set myself the goal of proving to you the very obvious truths, just try to take the Dow theory as an axiom.

Technical price analysis. Dow Theory. Everything else – Fog...

Any business has its own laws, requirements, and a set of rules that are mandatory. The foreign exchange market is no exception.

As I already noted, Forex has certain patterns, considering and applying which you can earn. And the basis of these laws is the Dow Theory, the basic principles of which we will consider. First of all, find out what technical analysis is.

Technical analysis is the analysis of exchange rate charts using special methods to obtain a forecast of further price movement. That is, with its help, we can predict where the price may turn out, to understand that at this stage it is more profitable for us to buy or sell.

So, the Dow theory is based on the following postulates:

- price takes everything into account;
- history always repeats itself;
- trend is your friend;
- different indices must confirm each other;
- trade volumes should confirm the nature of the trend;
- the trend is valid until there are clear signals of its change. Let's look at these postulates in more detail.

Price Includes Everything

It means that all factors - predictable and not predictable: economic, natural, political, anthropogenic, etc. - are taken into account by the market and are reflected in price dynamics. One of the politicians announced his resignation, an economic crisis broke out, there was a terrorist attack, an earthquake ... All of this will affect the price chart. Wow, perspective! Are you puzzled? And although such disasters rarely occur, it doesn't make it easier for you ...

What to do now? Do not enter into a deal? In fact, everything is very simple. Trend is movement, movement is life. Each of us has his own way in life, his own principles and habits. Nevertheless, there is something that unites us ("We are so different, but still we are together" - remember?). And we all obey certain laws - moral, legal, the law of God, and the goal of all these laws is not to plunge the world into chaos. We obey the trend of life, and price obeys the financial trend. Do not forget that it is people who move the price, so they project their behavior and principles onto it. Imagine this situation: you are setting up an interesting experiment, watching a performance in a theater, or simply getting into an elevator to your floor (looking forward to an evening break), and at that moment the light is cut down. Suddenly! Maybe the accident at the substation, maybe the electrician messed up something, or maybe the lights were turned off for non-payment - like an energy crisis ... What will you do? You can fall into hysteria, bang your head against the wall, stand in a proud pose, saying that you won't go to the theater with your legs anymore, and you probably won't go home ... Or you can just sit around this situation. All the same, everything will return to normal, the switch will be turned on, and life (like the trend) will take its course. And in order for this situation to not take you by surprise, you need to take care of emergency lighting!

On Forex, this emergency lighting system is called stop loss (limit losses). We will talk about this later

History Always Repeats Itself

The movement of prices is historically repeated, which is manifested in the repetition of identical figures on price charts. The fact that history always repeats, we found out at school. We were told what happens to those who have not learned her lessons. And the signs of a revolutionary situation when "the tops cannot and the lower classes do not want to live in the old way" are inevitable precursors of the coming revolution. On Forex, everything is like in life. Before a big move, the price chart first draws certain configurations that signal an upcoming event and invites attentive traders to participate in such a significant event. The more detailed you look at and analyze the history of the currency, the more obvious the signals it sends to you will be.

Trend Is Your Friend

Each of us has friends. And we love our friends and accept them as they are, with all their advantages and disadvantages.

You can have several of those friends. Include in this list another faithful comrade with whom you must go hand in hand. His name is Trend, Just Trend. This, as they say, is not just love, but love with interest. God forbid you to stand in his way and try to at least change something in him. Let me give you a good example.

Imagine a mighty river flow, and you are walking along the bank of this river. On foot, you have to go to your destination for about three hours, and if you board a boat, and here, by the way, it is also a boat station, then you will sail, say, in an hour. The river, in this case, will help you get much faster to your goal than if you were walking. She is your friend and helper.

And suddenly a crazy thought comes into your head - to reverse the river flow ... And in the place where the water flow is the strongest! Here and now, urgently! .. You imagine yourself in the role of a lone hero ... "Let me be alone with this element - whatever happens ..." - you tell yourself ... and begin your struggle with the course of the river. What nonsense, you say, dear reader, this is Sisyphean labor ... And you will be right. Why turn around if you can board a boat and adrift with comfort and speed to your destination. And as for the reversal of the current, one might think already in a more comfortable environment, having weighed all the pros and cons without emotions, taking into account all the features and bends of the river ...

Therefore, do not reinvent the wheel, do not seek adventures on your own head, and do not complicate your path on the Forex. A trend is a celebration for a trader. And going with him is much more profitable in one direction. Both morally and financially. "Trend - is your friend."

Let's now understand what a trend is. *Trend is* a directional price movement. The movement is in accordance with the trend. We have already noted that price follows the trend. There are upward, downward and neutral trends (side corridor).

• When *ascending (bullish)* tendency, each subsequent peak and each subsequent decline is higher than the previous one.

• When *descending (bearish)* trends, each subsequent peak and each subsequent decline is lower than the previous one.

• In the *side corridor* or *flat, the* price is in a certain range – practically at the horizontal corridor. Usually flat is a harbinger of big changes - the price, as it were, accumulates strength for further movement.

Dow identified three categories of trend:

• primary (in the literature there are other names, for example, the main, or long-term);

• secondary (it is also corrective, or medium-term);

• small (it is short-term).

Dow gave the greatest importance to the primary trend, which lasts more than a year, and sometimes several years.

The secondary (intermediate) trend is corrective (that is, having the opposite direction) with respect to the main one and usually lasts from 3 weeks to 3 months. Such intermediate corrections range from 1/3 to 2/3 (very often half, or 50%) of the distance traveled by prices during a previous trend.

Small trends last no more than 3 weeks and represent short-term fluctuations within the intermediate trend. In the development of the main trend, we distinguish 3 phases:

• 1st phase (accumulation): the most far-sighted and informed investors begin to buy since all adverse economic information has already been taken into account by the market;

• The 2nd phase begins when those who use technical methods to follow trends join in the game. Prices have already risen, and economic information is becoming optimistic;

• 3rd phase (final): the general public enters into action, the hype begins on the market.

Guess which of those who decided to participate in the movement is likely to be at risk? Most likely, it is the one who succumbed to the hype and got into the "catch-up" deal. Now move on to the next postulate of the Dow.

Different Indices Must Confirm Each Other

Dow believed that any important signal to increase or decrease in the market rate should go in the values of several indices (that is, it is advisable to make a decision by receiving the same signal according to the largest number of applied criteria).

When you make a decision, you rely on different factors. It can be rumors, facts, someone's subjective opinion, advice, intuition, life experience, etc. in a word, you try to make the most complete and real picture of what is happening, relying on many objective arguments.

When you make a decision, you weigh the pros and cons. The more pluses are in the "for" column, the more rational your decision is and the more comfortable you feel when making it. That is, if several factors at once, independently from each other, tell you that your vision of this situation is correct, then it is easier for you to make a decision. In the foreign exchange market, you also have someone to rely on and consult with. We will talk about this later.

It is important to remember that when entering a transaction it is necessary to receive several confirmations, independent of each other, but signaling the same thing.

Trade Volumes Should Confirm The Nature Of The Trend

The Dow considered trading volume to be an extremely important factor in confirming the signals received on price charts, that is, the volume should increase in the direction of the main trend.

Directional Movement Must Correspond To Large Volumes

Volumes are often not taken seriously in the Forex market, more importance is attached to this parameter in the stock market. Meanwhile, in the foreign exchange market, they can provide very useful information. Judge for yourself.

Suppose the indicator shows significant volumes on the market, but the price chart is closed by a small doji candle. This means that there were a lot of purchases and a lot of sales, but the price remained bargained in a narrow range. No one succeeded in shifting the price, which means that the situation on the market is still uncertain and it is better to refrain from entering the market. Or another example. Let us see the level breaking through, and the daily volumes are small. This is most likely a false penetration since the market sentiment does not imply any strong movement, it is only a speculative penetration that will turn into a fall.

The trend is valid until there are clear signals of its change

It's very important to understand that the trend, started his movement will strive it move on! The price will go up until it goes down. Similarly, the price will go down until it goes up. This means that the *price prefers to continue its movement, rather than turn in the opposite direction.*

This, of course, is great, you say. But how to understand that the price will continue its movement and will not turn in the other direction? We will discuss this moment with you in the near future. In the meantime, just remember these simple principles that you will be guided by when working in the financial market. And I want to end this chapter with a story about the wonderful athlete Florence Chadwick.

In 1952, she tried to sail 21 miles (30 kilometers) from Catalina Island to the coast of California. She sailed for 15 hours, but then was exhausted, she was dragged from the water and taken ashore. She did not reach the target half a mile (750 meters). The next day, at a press conference, Florence said: "Fog is all that I could see, if I saw the coast, I would swim."

Now you understand the laws that govern market prices. And if suddenly fog falls on your boat, remember that Forex obeys clear laws. And don't let the fog obscure your goals!

Chapter 2 - Graphic Method Of Technical Analysis

Any tendency (trend) can be divided into shorter tendencies making it up. The computer itself builds price charts for you. Charts cover different time periods. A chart is often called a chart. A chart is a chart of the exchange rate.

We introduce the following notation:

- monthly chart - Monthly (M);
- weekly schedule - Weekly (W);
- daily chart - Daily (D);
- 4-hour chart - 4 Hours (4H);
- hourly chart - Hourly (N);
- half-hour chart (ZOM);
- 15-minute schedule (15M);
- 5-minute schedule (5M).

Charts are linear (line chart), column (bar chart) and candlestick (candlestick chart). On a *line chart,* prices are connected by a curve. In this case, you can connect either the selling price, or the purchase price, or the average between the selling and buying prices. The program indicates on the basis of what prices the schedule is built. Typically, lines are built through selling prices. The line graph is most often used in print media but for analysis, it is not suitable.

On the *bar graph,* each vertical bar indicates a price change for the time period you select: if the chart is 5 minutes, then in 5 minutes, if 60 minutes, then in 60 minutes. I will also mention some of the notifications used by me in this book:

- Min - the minimum price for the selected period of time;
- Max - the maximum price for the selected time period;

- Open - the first price, or the opening price, the price movement begins with it;
- Close - closing price, the bar ends on it.

If the opening price is lower than the closing price, then the body of the candle is white. This means that over a given period of time, the price has made an upward movement.

If the opening price is higher than the closing price, then the body of the candle is black. This means that over a given period of time, the price has made a downward movement.

If during the selected period of time the opening price is equal to the closing price, it is said that the market is in equilibrium. Such a candle is called a *doge* and is indicated by a "+" sign.

Graphic Analysis Lines

Wonderful lines that allow you to understand what is happening on the market are called *trendy:*

• a line that price cannot break up and which, as it were, restrains the chart from above, called resistance line ;

• a line that the price cannot break down and which, as it were, supports the chart from below, called the support line.

These lines are drawn at the ends of the candles. They provide an opportunity to make purchases, warn events, allow you to recognize the situation on the market. The meaning of constructing such trend lines is to specify for themselves the direction of the trend and outline its boundaries for ease of perception. If the price violates the boundaries of the line drawn by you, then there are changes in the structure of the price movement. The following options are possible here:

• change of direction;

• a decrease in the speed of movement and, as a consequence of this, a change in the trajectory of the curve of the price chart;

• the price fell in place and will stand for some time.

That's all, there are no other options! The main task is to correctly draw these lines. If it was possible to draw in parallel both the support line and the resistance line, then the two lines are called a *channel,* or a corridor.

If the lines and the channel go at an angle, then we are dealing with a trend (rise or fall), and if the lines and the corridor are horizontal, then the price is in this range. Often this price range, as already noted, is called a *flat.* Usually flat happens before a strong price movement. At this moment, the price seems to accumulate strength before the jerk for its further movement.

Remember that lines are needed to determine the direction of trends, as well as determining clear price boundaries for the movement of the exchange rate in the framework of this direction.

In addition, we are currency speculators ... So, we take into account the principle of the market: buy cheaper - sell more expensive. And we determine when it is more profitable to buy or sell. We have already said that profitable purchases are made from the support line, and profitable sales must be made from the resistance line.

Pending Orders

However, the situation is not always so straightforward. Suppose you turn on the monitor and do a market analysis:

1. Determine the direction of the trend (looking for signs of a downward or upward movement).

2. Based on the trend, determine the nature of the transaction (if the trend is up, then you are the buyer today if the downtrend is the seller).

3. Define a line of support: this is a line of purchases - it is from her that you need to buy.

4. Define the line of resistance: this is the line of sales - it is from it that you need to sell. And you find that the price is somewhere in the middle of the market. That is, she did not go either to the line of resistance or to the line of support.

What to do in this case? Not to get into the market when the situation is incomprehensible? We have a way out - place *pending orders.* The principle of their installation is as follows:

• if the trend is *up,* then today you *buy;*

• if the trend is *down,* then today you are *selling.*

If you buy, the question arises: where is the best place to buy? If you are a buyer today, then you are buying, but not from the current price, but from the line support (i.e. cheaper than the current price). In this case, you place an order to bounce off support lines (buy limit). But it could happen that the price does not reach the support line, but immediately the current price will rush towards the trend - up. Then the following rule applies:

If, during an upward movement, the price breaks through the resistance line, it accelerates upward. In this case, an order break is placed on the resistance line (buy stop). It is placed above the resistance line because if the price breaks through this line, the uptrend seems to give it an additional impetus, and the price practically flies up, as if rejoicing in its victory over the resistance. In fact, it breaks the stop loss lines set above the resistance, closing the aggressive positions of those who opened for sale against the trend and opens pending orders of the same traders like you who placed breakout orders. This is what gives her an additional impetus. It's like a kick towards the trend. Why they say that the trend is your friend! From any situation, he will pull out and help to earn. Place two orders at once: both for a rebound from the support line and for breaking through the resistance line. Which one works, that will give you a profit.

If suddenly the price does not reach your lower order (which, of course, is preferable, since buying cheaper is the goal of any buyer), but the impatience of traders can be so great that their desire to push the price up can overpower common sense and adjust the price before a big move, then an order to break through the resistance line will work and you will be yours on this holiday of life called a trend.

Now we'll explore the second option when the trend is downtrend, which means that today you are selling. In this case, the opposite question arises: where is the best place to sell?

If you are a seller today, then you are selling, but not from the current price, but from the line resistance (i.e. more expensive than the current price). In this case, you need to place an order on rebound from the resistance line (sell limit). But it could happen that the price does not reach lines of resistance, and will rush along a downtrend to break through the support line. Then we use the following rule:

If during a downward movement the price breaks the support line, it accelerates downward.

In this case, an order to break through the support line is placed below the support line (sell stop). It is often advantageous to place two orders at once: both for a rebound from the resistance line and for breaking through the support line. If the price rises to your upper order first - great, you can cancel the lower order that you set to break through the support line. And you can, if the deposit allows, set another position for adding. If the price does not reach your top order, an order to break through the support line will turn on. And in any case, you will not stay on the sidelines, but go in the direction of the trend.

So, let's summarize the principle by which pending orders are placed.

1. The direction of the trend is determined:

- if the trend is upward, buy orders are(for a rebound from the support line and/or for breaking the buy stop resistance line);

- if the trend is downtrend, sell orders are placed (for a rebound from the resistance line and/or) for breaking through the sell stop support line).

2. Stop losses are set (we will consider the principle of placing these orders later).

3. Take profits are set (we will consider the principle of placing these parameters later).

I highly recommend you to master the principle of placing pending orders. Very often, especially for beginners (and not only for them!), this is one of the most important aspects of working in the Forex market.

Trend Work

When something is not clear to you, do not hesitate to ask again if the opinion of this person is really significant for you. The simplest, safest, fastest and most profitable that can be in the foreign exchange market is to work in a trend. A trend is truly a celebration for the trader. As a rule, very good amounts are earned in a short period.

How To Work On The Trend?

You need to choose a schedule that we will consider the main (days, weeks or months), and determine the direction of price movement for the selected period. For example, you can take the daily chart as the main one and find out where the price goes during this period: up or down. This will be the direction of the trend. After that, you need to take a schedule with shorter periods: 4 hours or 1 hour. This chart is of interest when the price movement is not in the direction of the daily trend but in the opposite direction. Next, you need to wait until the price curve on the 4-hour chart starts to turn towards the daily trend. With an uptrend, we buy, but not from any point, but at a temporary drop in price, which we are looking for in a shorter time interval.

In a downtrend, we sell, but not from any point, but at a temporary increase in price, which we are looking for in a shorter time interval.

If the price crosses your trend line for the first time in the presence of a long rise or fall, always remember that then, most likely, a short-term price rollback will follow, which will be replaced by a continuation of the trend.

Before the upward trend changes to the downward trend, a time must pass when the price stands practically in one place, but constantly makes splashes in the direction opposite to the trend, painting the price reversal. Similarly, before a downtrend changes its direction to an uptrend, time will pass. And at this moment, the price will paint us a turn-up. What these reversals look like, we will consider in a later chapter.

What Are The Signs Of A Trend Change?

• Price crosses the support line.

• If such an intersection occurred during an upward movement, then there will be a fall in the prices.

• If such an intersection occurred in a downtrend, then there will be a fall in the prices.

• Price crosses the resistance line.

• If such an intersection occurred during an upward movement, then there will be an accelerated price increase.

• If such an intersection occurred in a downtrend, then there will be a price increase.

• The price in the presence of a corridor does not reach the resistance line.

On the price chart, this is the very *first sign of future changes.* This will be either a change of direction or a decrease in the pace of the trend, that is, the price will begin to change more smoothly.

Channel Work

The horizontal channel is usually determined on the daily chart. To build a channel, it is necessary to identify the largest and smallest peaks where the price is able to "go", and draw support and resistance lines at these peaks.

How To Work In The Channel?

Visually divide the channel into three approximately equal parts.

• If the channel is horizontal, then:

• when the price comes to the upper price range, we sell;

• when the price comes to the lower price range, we buy;

• when the price is in the middle range, we do not enter the market, but we are waiting for the situation to be clarified.

• If the channel is upward, then we give preference to purchases from the lower price range, and in the upper range, we close the deal with profit.

• If the channel is downward, then we give preference to sales from the upper price range, and in the lower range, we close the deal with profit.

The Obvious Is Unbelievable

It is no secret that many people treat Forex not as a serious business, but as a casino. Lucky - or no luck ... Who knows how the cards will fall ... Thinking about these things, I remembered a trip to Monaco. The main attraction and income item of this country is, of course, the casino in Monte Carlo. Being in Monte Carlo and not visiting such a "landmark" place?

No sooner said than done. Previously, I outlined the budget, which I defined as risk capital. Of course, I understood that this was not Forex with its principles and rules, but only a random combination of circumstances, but nevertheless my heart was worried by the idea that conditions were being lost here (but someone won !!!) and there were the most famous people in the world. Although what am I flirting with? Anyway, somewhere in the depths of my soul there lived a little hope and demanded to chant: "Miracles! Miracles! "But what if I find myself among the handful who wins? .. They show me on TV - like, a tourist from Russia won - ... twenty million dollars! ... Here I accept congratulations from friends and acquaintances ... Here is my own red Ferrari ... Illusions were shattered. No miracle happened. I had to leave the casino with a motivational song: not lucky for me on cards, lucky in love !!! Although I really wanted to continue the game and a provocative thought did not give me rest - what if? .. But Forex taught me discipline. I told myself: stop loss worked, stop. At least I visited the most famous casino, I didn't look with Dmitry Krylov's eyes, but with my own eyes, I saw rich grandmothers lazily pressing buttons of "one-armed bandits", shocking gentlemen bored with a glass of wine, brutal men driving up on the most expensive Lamborghini cars "," Bentley "," Porsche " and, like in a movie kissing when meeting each other, their beautiful companions of a beautiful life ... And I got one more convincing proof that in the casino you can count on luck, but Mr. Forex - very demanding. He is the gentleman who appreciates a competent approach and sober calculation in transactions. As Jesse Livermore said: "At all times, people have acted in the market in the same way, driven by greed, fear, ignorance, and hope. That is why numerical characteristics and models are constantly repeated".

The name of this section is not accidental. We will analyze with you those market entry points that are so obvious and work in 90% of cases out of 100%, that sometimes it seems incredible.

Remember the school curriculum in geometry: you can draw one straight line through two points. On the currency chart, we also draw one straight line through two points, that is, we take two peaks from the bottom, for example, with an upward movement, and draw a support line along these peaks. So, in almost 90% of cases (mind you, not in 50%, you're lucky - no luck, but in the vast majority of cases!), When the price comes to this line for the third time, there should be a rebound from the support line in the direction of directional movement. This is the first pattern that we will take into account when analyzing the market. For convenience, we will call the point one the point of purchase from the uptrend line at the third touch.

It should be noted that the higher the timeframe on which you placed an order to bounce off the support line, the greater the distance the price will go. So, if the rebound from the daily support line is, say, 300 points, then the rebound from the 4-hour support line can be 150 points. This applies not only to this particular point but also to other points that we will consider. However, this is just an example for ease of perception. In each case, you need to be guided by the situation. The market appreciates creativity!

The main sign of a downtrend is that each subsequent peak and each subsequent decline is lower than the previous one. That is, we draw a downtrend line at two points, and when the price approaches this resistance line for the third time, we place a sell order. Point 2 - sale from the trend line at the third touch.

From the Dow theory, you have already learned that the trend that started the movement will tend to continue. And the price, of course, can rest against the trend line and push off from it more than three times. However, the more often it will "approach" to the trend line, the more vulnerable this line becomes to break through. But in any case, it is necessary to "absorb with mother's milk ", which is necessary to buy from support, and from resistance to sell. Because the trend is going up until it goes down. And likewise, the trend goes down until it goes up. I present your surprised faces: “Fun. You will not say anything. But how to understand when he will go on a U-turn? ”

The fact of the matter is that the trend does not unfold instantly. That is, while it is going up, we are trying to buy from the trend line. But as soon as the price breaks this trend line and, what is important, “fixes” below it, remaining for some time below it, we joyfully rub our hands in anticipation of a good prospect and begin to search for the moment of entering the market in the opposite direction - for sale. It must be remembered that before an uptrend is replaced by a downtrend, time must pass, and during this period the price stands almost in one place. This standing in a narrow price range is often called a “flat."

It is in this range that the price draws a reversal for us. How does this reversal look on the chart? So, the price, breaking the line of the uptrend, most often returns to this line. Some people call such a reversal the back loop, others call the approach from the back, and others call the “zigzag”. But no matter what you call it, it is important that this point is a wonderful signal of a market reversal.

Sale From The Counter-Trend

In a downward movement, the resistance line “crushes” the price from above. When the price breaks through it and closes above it for several periods, and then returns to its former resistance line already as a support line, painting a trend reversal upward, this is for us a signal to enter a buy transaction from a counter-trend.

Purchase From The Counter-Trend

In addition to inclined trend lines, there are also horizontal levels. The price is always between two fires: either the resistance line is pressing on top of it, or the support line is holding it below.

Each of us has a purpose in life. And, as a rule, there is something, say resistance, which is an obstacle to our progress towards this goal. And when a person overcomes this obstacle, he begins to believe in his own strength, asserts himself, strives for further growth and sets his life standard for himself already higher. The market price is driven by people and their emotions. Therefore, the price is affected by the same psychological factors.

For example, there is an upward movement, but it meets an obstacle in the form of a horizontal line of resistance. Overcoming this resistance, the price asserts itself, closing several periods above it and returning to this resistance defeated by it already as support, is gaining strength there to storm further targets, takes everyone with it and strives for new triumphs.

Purchase From The Resistance Level After Breaking Through An Upward Movement

Our life consists not only of ups, but also of falls. And each of us must have noticed how difficult it is to climb up, but how quickly you can fall, literally fly down. But even falling, we rely on the support of loved ones who are trying to stop the fall and help us start climbing again. And if we are not ready to accept this support, we push off from it, resisting, and continue our decline until we find the bottom from which we can actually push off.

So, in a downward movement, if the price breaks through the support level and closes several periods below it, this indicates the seriousness of its intentions to continue to fall. Then most often the price returns to the line that it broke, and bounces off it already as if from resistance.

Often we ourselves create difficulties for ourselves, which we then successfully overcome. And since it is the human factor that influences the financial market, it is we (people) who move the price and project the features of our behavior on it. And point 7 demonstrates this clearly. Let's consider it in more detail.

There are the following two rules:

1) in a downward movement, if the price breaks through the support line, it rapidly falls down;

2) with an upward movement, if the price breaks through the resistance line, it flies upward acceleratedly.

It should be noted that the longer the time period for which the price has overcome support, the more serious the processing of the order will be. That is, if the price overcame such support in the weekly period, then it is possible to fix 300-400 points of profit, if in the daytime - then 200-250 points, and with a 4-hour period - 80-120 points.

By analogy: when a resistance line is broken, a trend gives an acceleration to the price, and the price starts flying upward, collecting stop loss along the way and receiving an additional impetus for growth from this. In this case, they place an order to break the resistance line (buy stop). Of course, the rest of the market participants are connected to this, their warrants to break the resistance line are triggered, and the price rushes up more rapidly. And again, do not forget about time periods at which a breakthrough occurred, and based on this we set a profit. These seven points are a kind of stencil.

“Press the button - you will get the result, and your dream will come true!” - the “Technology” band once sang. Maybe this is about Forex? These points work in almost 90% of cases at all periods, but the most reliable, of course, is periods up to 4 hours. And of course, it was not for nothing that you and I said that it is necessary to study the history of currency pairs. We are reacting to the same event with no different characters and temperaments! And who moves the price and projects their life perception on it, including their complexes? That's right, we are with you. And we are different ... And the nature of the movement of all currencies is also different. Therefore, it is worth tracking which of the points most often is realized by one or another currency pair. After all, each of them has its own passions and small weaknesses.

I remembered a trip to Nice when on Saturday early morning we went to the local exit market. An analogue of our Moscow "Weekend Fair." The spectacle is very colorful. It is interesting to look at both buyers and sellers. Since the French prefer to eat in cafes and restaurants, they buy at the markets what is useful to them on a picnic, including greens, vegetables, fruits, meat, fish. Therefore, the main assortment of the market is approximately the same. But in what quantities! And how bright, neat and festive on the shelves! And with what dignity and how friendly you are smiling sellers, local farmers, whom the city dwellers greatly respect! “Bonjour, Madame!” The pessimist may object: “Yeah, we know the price of this beauty!” Probably all genomodified! ... I was faced with just such a reaction. And not only on the story of the Nice market but also on his article “Obvious - Unbelievable.”

One comrade wrote that it can't be as cool as I write, that it looks like a genome-defective product - “type” everything is beautifully written, but in reality? .. I have only one answer for such people: study the market, gentlemen, and then you will begin to trust him. Why should I trust? You don’t know me at all ... I’m just telling you my observations about the market, and you should draw conclusions and only you. I will not even argue on this subject. Just tell you one parable. There are optimists and pessimists. And the optimist says: “Look, what a wonderful weather! The sky is blue, the sun is shining brightly, the birds are singing, it smells like ozone, I want to live! ”The pessimist listened to an enthusiastic speech, looked around for a long time, and finally remarked:“ Did you see that little cloud? “It will ruin the weather.” I am not an unrestrained optimist, but the principle “There are no problems - there are situations, and they are resolved,” seems to be the most acceptable. All problems must be addressed as they become available. In the end, if you are afraid that it will rain in the cloud, grab an umbrella. In this case, I'm talking about stop-loss (see section 5). And "Ostap suffered ..." Well, I was somewhat distracted.

Observe currency pairs, test them, choose those that are close to you in spirit and perception for work. Learn the patterns and earn! Who's stopping you?

Just Moose

Spring, grass turns green, the buds on the trees swell, the sun warms. An elk grazes in a forest clearing. Suddenly a young elk pops up into the clearing. Seeing her, the elk loses its head and, hoping for an acquaintance, runs to the elk. But the moose cow, flirting, jumps out and starts to run away. Elk is after her. Here she jumps through a stream - and an elk through a stream, a moose cow through a bush - and an elk through a bush, a moose cow through a knoll - and an elk through a knoll ... So they ran for half a day. A moose cow jumped over a log, while a leg of a tired elk turned up, and, jumping over a log, he caught on to it and fell to the ground with all its might. The moose cow stopped, looked around and, seeing that the moose did not get up and did not continue the game, began to approach him. Then, playfully flashing her eyes, she decided to introduce herself: “Elk, female! And you? ”Elk sadly: “ Elk ”, then, dropping his eyes down: “ Now - just an elk. ”

Forex is not the only gymnastics for the mind, it broadens our economic horizons, disciplines us and gives a very worthy financial equivalent to our brain costs. Therefore, risks are a topic that needs to be considered first. After all, forewarned means armed! Think about the emergency lighting which was about the Dow postulates.

How To Set A Stop Loss?

In a downtrend, the stop loss is placed above the last peak before the price crosses the support line on the price chart. I put the loss limiter 5 points higher from the peak plus the spread. Stop-loss during an upward movement is placed below the last peak before the price crosses the resistance line on the price chart. I also put it below the last peak by 5 points plus a spread.

Stop loss is set immediately after opening a position. During a profitably open position, try to position your stop loss as close as possible, to break-even level. The point is that when you already have a profit, you can reset your stop order to the level of the price of opening a position. If the rate goes back again, then when executing the order you will not incur losses.

Stop loss must be used in calculating the profitability of the transaction.

In the latter case, first of all, you need to calculate the ratio of estimated losses in case the price goes against you (stop loss) and projected profit (take profit). We have already examined how to set a stop loss, and take profit is determined when a signal is received that is directly opposite to that which was received when opening a deal. That is, if we made a purchase from the support line, then we determine the nearest resistance from which sales can begin, and it is in this area that we set take profit. And only the ratio of stop loss/take profit should be decisive for you when deciding whether to enter the transaction. If the risks are 100 points, and the closest resistance line is 70 points away, think about whether to stand in a deal and risk losing $ 1000, expecting to earn only 700. The risk/profit ratio should be 3: 1, maybe 2: 1. All the rest is risky operations. And you need to be aware of this. And also, in my opinion, a very important point. You must not allow yourself risks exceeding 10% from your deposit. Otherwise, you risk your deposit. Consider a simple example.

Let your deposit be $ 5,000. This means that your risk capital is not more than 50 points (10% of 5,000 - 50 points), and you calculated that your risks in a particular transaction will be 100 points. According to all the rules for setting stop loss, it doesn't work out less. However, you can afford no more than 50 points, otherwise, the transaction will be considered risky and may lead to greater losses than you can afford. There is only one conclusion: do not get into this deal, but consider other options on other currency pairs where your stop loss does not exceed 50 points. My students often ask me: "What currency is it better to set?" And I always answer - on the one where the entry point will be prettier (according to the classics - with all correct reversals), and always with a minimum stop loss acceptable for your deposit. Indeed, conjugated currency pairs, as a rule, "go on the road" almost simultaneously, but at different speeds. And often when in one currency the price has already reached her goal, on others, she is just approaching her. But they will leave at the same time! Although at different speeds. Here, where the price beautifully invites you, there and expose a position. And certainly with a stop loss. Resist the temptation to open a risky deal. This is troublesome. And just financially unprofitable.

Examples

So, we decided to sell a pair of Eurodollars.

1. We determine the nearest resistance level from which we will put up a sale.

2. We determine at what level the nearest previous peak was in a downward movement, and we plan to set a stop loss above this peak.

3. We determine the closest support level from which purchases can begin and set take profit a little higher from this level.

4. We calculate the profitability of the transaction. Our estimated profit is 250 points, and the risks are 100 points. A 2: 1 ratio is satisfied.

5. We put up a deal. For this:

1) place a sell order at a price of 1.2810 from the resistance line;

2) put a protective stop order at a price of 1.2900 (and up 5 points plus a spread). Since the movement is downward, then any subsequent peak and subsequent decline is lower than the previous one.

3) place an order to take profit at a price of 1.2553.

We consider this situation further. Let the price break through the resistance line and the trend change, becoming upward. As a result, we embark on the purchase of a pair of euro-dollar and reason in the same way.

1. We determine the closest support level from which we will place a purchase.

2. We determine at what level the previous decline was during the upward movement, and we plan to set a stop loss below this decline.

3. We determine the nearest resistance level from which sales can go, and just below this level, we place an order to fix profit.

4. We calculate the profitability of the transaction. Our estimated profit is 250 points, and the risks - 70 points. That is, a 3: 1 ratio is satisfied.

5. We put up a deal. For this:

1) We place an order for a rebound from the support line at the price of 1.2553;

2) We place a protective order at a price of 1.2482 (and down another 5 points plus a spread). Since the trend is upward, then any subsequent peak and subsequent decline is higher than the previous one.

3) place an order to take profit at a price of 1.2811. As you can see, there is nothing complicated.

A person walking towards his goal has a certain store of knowledge and life experience - it is this experience that gives a person confidence that he will achieve his goal. And so the price strives to take profit so confidently when it is protected by its stop loss.

Good luck, traders! More profits and less moose!

Open Window For A Trader

The old fly selflessly beat its head against the glass. Probably an hour and a half. It flew back, turned around and, fiercely buzzing, fearlessly went to the ram. The young fly ran up and timidly asked: "Excuse me, if not a secret, why bang your head on the glass when it's open next ?!" The old fly answered, barely moving its jaws: "You are silly! Because you are young! Any fool can fly out of an open window! But what about joys? Flew, flew, flew, flew! Do we live for this ?! And here you work with your head until it swells until the floor merges with the ceiling! And when there is nothing to buzz anymore - here you are crawling to where it is open! If you knew how good I am now!". The young fly tried not to look at the old head's swollen head, and she continued: "My dad has been banging his head on the glass all his life. Mom deceased was beating. And they bequeathed to me: only overcoming difficulties will you feel like a man!"

- *From the monologue Semyon Altov*

Sometimes a trader resembles the very old fly made up by life experience, which beats through a closed window, although a window is open nearby. That is, it complicates the analysis of the current situation so much that it forgets about the simplest signals that the market gives us.

First of all, we define the *basic principles of* work:

• saving deposit;

• increase in deposit.

This is not my know-how. This is more of Warren Buffett's (namely, this person topped the list of the richest people in the world according to Forbes magazine in 2008 - he has something to learn). He defined some rules as follows:

Rule number one - do not lose money.

Rule number two - do not forget rule number one.

It should be noted that, only by learning how to keep your deposit, you will begin to increase it. Namely, principle 1 - saving the deposit - dictates to us the necessary rules for entering the market. So where to start?

Of course, with the choice of the currency pair with which you plan to work. The principle of selection is very simple. It consists in choosing the most secure and cheapest currency in terms of deposit.

First of all, we pay attention to the following characteristics:

- collateral amount;
- spread
- item value;
- volatility
- technicality.

Security Deposit

Deposits are different for everyone, and it makes no sense to stare at the same GBR / CHF pair if you have a deposit of, say, $ 3,000, and this currency pair has a security deposit of $ 3,000. You can determine the security amount yourself by opening a transaction on a demo account and looking in the column “Security amount” or “Terms of trade” on the company’s website where you opened your account.

Spread

We pay a spread for entering the transaction (the difference between buying and selling). The spread can be found in the "Market Watch" column, or you can look in the "Trading Conditions" section of the "MetaTrader" program. On the same GBP / CHF pair, the spread is 10 points.

Item Cost

On the GBP / CHF currency pair, 1 point costs $ 12. Now let's count.

You will be charged 10 points x 12 dollars = 120 dollars for entering into a transaction on the GBP / CHF currency pair, with a security deposit of 3000. This means that 3120 dollars will be deducted from the balance when entering the transaction. What is your deposit? 3 times more? Then everything is all right. If less, think: do you need it? The risks are high. As a familiar trader says: “I’m not greedy, but home-like.”

Volatility

In order to assess whether a currency pair you like can afford, take a look at what kind of movement it has. Choose a couple based on your psychotype. One would like to say - choose in the same way as you choose your wife (husband) - as in life. Remember the words of Zhenya Lukashin from the movie "The Irony of Fate, or Enjoy Your Bath" about the upcoming marriage: "I just imagined how it would flicker before my eyes: back and forth, back and forth - and so all my life! Brrrr! "? Of course, a currency pair can be changed, but I do not want to waste time. Therefore, to begin with, determine your priorities.

I would like to mention someone's motto of life: "I see the goal. I believe in myself. I don't notice the obstacles!". That is, if you are a dynamic person, accustomed to make decisions quickly, welcome to a couple of pound yen. With it, you fly 300 points this hour, and the next 200 points in the other direction! And it inspires you, you enjoy life - adrenaline, in a word. And someone argues differently: "Slow down, go further!", "Measure seven times - cut one!" That is, your character requires a calm, balanced approach. It's not a question, there are pairs for you, and the dollar-franc is one of them. This couple will give time to think and decide on entering a deal.

For example, if we consider such conjugate currency pairs as USD / JPY, EUR / JPI, and GBP / JPI, it is noteworthy that when the price moves for the same period of time, USD / JPI may pass 50 points, EUR / JPI - 75 points, while GBP / JPI - all 150-200 points. This is called volatility. From the point of view of greed, of course, I would like to choose GBP / JPI (still, such a scope!), but bearing in mind that security is above all, it is advisable to choose USD / JPI. "Less is better" is not me, but the classic of world communism has spoken. And hit the nail on the head. In general, each currency has its own rhythm of movement, like cities. What a comparison! The first time I felt that every city has its own rhythm when I got to Nice. The rhythm of life really surprised me. I will describe it to you a little, maybe in a strange way ... But it was precisely such associations that he called for me.

A vigorous, frying dog runs, following her, holding on to a leash stretched like a string, a panting, panting granny. The dog barks awkwardly, the grandmother swears viciously at her. At the same time, both are happy. This is a scene from our Moscow life. The rhythm of the city leaves its mark on everyone who lives in it, including animals.

The city is an ancient grandfather, barely moving his legs. Behind him on a sagging (!!!) leash, a lazy well-fed dog walks slowly, calmly looking around ... grandfather paused, and the dog imposingly sat down on the pavement. Grandfather exchanged a couple of phrases with the dog - he answered him lazily, waving his tail. And they continue their journey. At the same time, both are happy. This is nice. This is her rhythm.

What rhythm is more comfortable for you - only you know. It's up to you to choose: calm or adrenaline is more attractive when working in the market for you personally.

Technicality

This term means how much a particular currency (judging by its history) is predicted in terms of its movement. History always repeats itself. This is an axiom. Of course, adjusted for the time. It is important to examine from history what particular patterns the currency pair of your choice responds to. After all, each of us reacts differently to the same situation, although rarely anyone violates the laws of life. And it is the human factor that plays an important role in the movement of prices, that is, all those complexes and habits that are inherent in a person apply to the movement of currencies.

So, the currency is selected.

The next step is *graphical analysis.* The principle of its implementation is as follows:

1. We always analyze from a larger period to a shorter one (that is, M → W → D → 4H).

2. Remember, in cards where the ace is older than the king, and the king is older than the lady, that the levels and trend lines drawn on the monthly chart *(Monthly, M),* more significant, they are "more important" of the lines drawn on the weekly chart *(Weekly, W),* and weekly "more important" than the daily *(Daily, D).* This means that if, for example, the daily trend is upward and at the same time the price rests, say, at the weekly level, then most likely a

rebound will follow from this level. Another example, let the weekly trend go up and the daily trend down. In this case, the daily trend (it acts as a correction) when approaching the weekly trend is likely to rebound.

So, on a monthly chart we determine:

- support and resistance levels.
- trend direction.
- turning points.

We determine the same parameters on the weekly and daily charts. We define support and resistance levels in order to find out the range at which is trading a currency pair. This gives us the opportunity to "trade in the channel". It is very important that after breaking through the support or resistance level, we have the opportunity to put the deal from the broken level in the opposite direction. It should be noted that the "older" the level that the price overcomes (that is, the timeframe where this level is determined), the more significant movement the currency pair expects.

We determine the direction of the trend based on signs of the direction of movement. Remember the signs of upward and downward movement.

What Are Turning Points?

The price, breaking through the support line, in most cases returns to it as a resistance line. Someone calls this moment the "back loop", some call it the "approach from the back", some call it the "zigzag of luck", and some call it the correct breaking of the support line. It doesn't matter what they call it, it's important that this moment is a turning point in the trend and gives us a signal to enter the trade from the counter trend.

You should not start every day with a monthly chart - it is enough to view it once a month (after all, we are not the owners of banks to place our orders, focusing on the distant future). Similarly, we view the weekly schedule once a week, and the daily - daily. So, we take the daily trend as the main one. It is in the direction of the daily trend that we determine the nature of the transaction.

If the daily trend is upward, then today we buy, but buy not from any price that we see at the moment, but at a temporary drop in the price that we are looking for in a 4-hour period. That is, if the daily trend is directed upwards, then we are looking for a correction on the 4-hour period (when it is directed downwards) and when it turns around, we stand in the direction of the daily buy direction. I bring to your attention the real deal of December 5, 2008.

1. Received daily signal of a price reversal.

2. We switch to a 4-hour period and look forward to a reversal for the purchase already in this period.

3. When the price breaks the resistance line and closes several 4-hour candles above this resistance line, this indicates the seriousness of its intention to go up. We joyfully rub our hands in anticipation of a wonderful movement and place a buy order, and in case the price does not fall exactly to our order, we place another order to break up. We place a stop order after the last peak since the trend is upward and every subsequent peak and subsequent decline is higher than the previous one. And we rightly believe that the price will not fall below it. And finally, where do we take profits?

It is this reversal for sale that is a signal to take profits - 1650 points. And - drove down with the market until the next turning point up. Remember the important feature of any trend: the trend never reverses and does not go in the opposite direction at once. Before the up trend changes to the down trend, time will pass. During this period of time, the price actually stands still, making "outliers" in the direction opposite to the trend. This may be misleading. If the price crosses your trend line for the first time in the presence of a long rise or fall, then always remember that next, most likely, a short-term price rollback will follow, which will be replaced by a continuation of the trend. If the price begins to cross the line of support or resistance, then a change in direction occurs. Simply? Let it be simple, the main thing is that without a headache you are taking profits and there is no need to constantly sit in front of the monitor, reacting to the slightest price movements.

Let's summarize and work out the necessary algorithm of actions. This will be our business plan.

1. The choice of a currency pair.

2. The choice of the schedule, which we will consider the main (we decide on the interval - days, weeks, months). The trend in this chart will be taken as the main trend. That is, we look at where the price is going on this chart: up or down (we recall signs of an upward and downward trend). This will be the direction of the trend.

3. Opening shorter charts. If the main chart is daily, then open the 4-hour and hourly charts. These charts are of interest when the price movement is not in the direction of the daily trend but in the opposite. It is necessary to wait until the price curve on the 4-hour chart begins to wrap towards the daily. That is, if the daily chart shows an upward movement, and the 4-hour chart shows a downward movement, we are preparing for the upcoming deal. That is, we are waiting for a 4-hour chart reversal towards the main daily trend and stand in its direction.

4. We determine and set a stop loss.

5. We determine and set take profit (warrant for profit-taking). The main argument for closing positions will be a signal opposite to that which served as a motivation for opening a currency position.

6. We determine the ratio of stop loss and take profit. This indicates the profitability of the transaction. The ratio of potential profit and loss should be no less than 3: 1.

Trading should bring a sense of joy in life! And if you are in front of the computer all the time, you can lose this feeling! Therefore daytime signals - reliable assistants to traders. Why beat on the glass every day, because the window is open, dear traders!

“To be or not to be? That’s the question ... ”, or “Castle Tactics”

Castle tactics are also called locking. What is she like?

Let's say you got into a deal and bought from a trending daily line with an upward movement. The price goes in your direction, gives you a profit. And you observe that it is approaching, say, a weekly resistance line. Keeping in mind that weekly levels are older than daily, you rightly believe that a rebound is possible from this level. At least the resistance line needs to be sold. You have learned this. But you are sure that the trend has not finished its upward movement. At least he hasn't painted a U-turn yet. In this case, without closing the purchase transaction, you can place a sell order. At the same time, it is important to note that the collateral amount that was collected from your deposit by the bank during your purchase transaction, remains unchanged when you open a sale transaction. For example, if you bought a pair of Euro-dollars, the security deposit for this pair for this period is $ 1,423, which is reflected in your terminal. Now you place a sell order for the same currency pair. The transaction is opened, and the security deposit shown on your terminal remains the same - 1423. That is, it is not burdensome for your deposit. I emphasize once again that the collateral amount remains unchanged if two opposite (for purchase and sale) transactions are opened for one currency pair.

Your further actions are that you, not paying attention to the castle, act as if you are planning a new deal.

• If the price bounces from the weekly level, you are waiting for a reversal towards the upward movement and close your sales, leaving only purchases - and your profit continues to grow.

• If the price breaks through the weekly resistance level (nothing lasts forever under the moon - sooner or later all levels break through), you calmly wait for it to return to this level already as to the support level, and close your sales at zero, and the purchase continues to grow. Personally, I really respect and love positive locks. They give us the opportunity to enter transactions without pain (if it is against the trend, then on rebounds) and replenish our deposit.

There is also the so-called negative lock. What is he like?

Let's say you get up to buy from an uptrend line, as taught. And the price suddenly, instead of a rebound from this trend line up, was predicted to break through this line down. In this case, where, according to all laws, you should have set a stop loss, you instead place a sell order. In this case, this order to break through the support line replaces the stop loss. Then, instead of closing a trade at a loss, you open the opposite order. That is, you have two orders: to buy and to sell. In this case, the collateral amount remains the same, as in the previous case. That is, it does not affect your deposit in any way.

Your further actions are that you seem to forget that you have a castle, otherwise you will begin to “pull facts by the ears” and come up with something that is not there, opening your castle before a signal is received.

So, you determine the nearest level (in this case, the level of support), rightly believing that purchases will follow from the support. And in this case, close the sale and release the purchase. Theoretically, it’s enough for you that the price rebounds by the size of your castle. If, for example, the difference between buying and selling was 70 points, the price is enough to go through 70 points and your deposit will be saved. You can also add support to the purchase. This tactic is called averaging.

When you get into the castle, you cancel the stop loss and take profit, since the castle already implies the preservation of a certain delta. It gives you the opportunity to calmly navigate, because you kind of fix your profit or loss, depending on what type of lock you use. If the castle is positive, then your delta with a plus sign, if negative, then your delta with a minus sign (although it is strange to call it that ...).

I do not recommend setting a negative lock instead of stop loss, although this, of course, is tempting. Some experience is needed here in order not to fall under the hypnosis of the market and to open this castle on time. But back to the tactics. The meaning of averaging tactics is to put another deal to buy from support. In this case, you will have two purchases open, one from below and one from the support above. As a result, when the price is somewhere in the middle of the way up, you will have a plus for the lower purchase, and the same figure for the upper purchase, but with a minus sign, and zero will be reflected in the terminal. That is, the deposit is saved, you can close the transaction and start analyzing ...

Let's analyze another tactic, which is called the addition. What is this tactic?

Let's say you put up a deal. Bought from a trend line (or maybe sold from it, if the trend is downtrend). The price goes in your direction. Profit is growing. The mood is improving. But most often, after a certain movement, the price goes for a correction. We have already discussed this. You can stand in a positive castle. Or don't get up. This is your own business. But when the price comes to the support line, what would you do if you hadn't already opened a buy deal? That's right, you would have bought (of course, not thoughtlessly, but having assessed the situation in the market and having checked your business plan). And in this case, if the purchases do not contradict your plans, you can add another purchase order. As a result, you will have two purchase orders open: one from the bottom, the other from the middle. In this case, your profit will begin to grow at a double pace.

What's Better?

I don't know! And, it's true. Having caught the moose, having burnt up and analyzed the situation, you are ready to work again. And when you stand in a negative castle, you are in constant tension, choosing when to open it, and the slightest movement not in your direction is perceived as a disaster. It is very difficult. In addition, you are forced to reject the real deals that the market offers you. You are fixated on one currency pair. But you could make money on other deals.

Apparently, depression is contagious. I can not explain to anyone else why at the same time five people from the dealing got into pound-yen deals. And this currency pair in certain trading circles is known as an antidepressant. After all, having opened a deal on it, you can forget about everything that tormented you before that ... The meaning of life, unrequited love, the reappraisal of values, etc., etc. - everything fades into the background. Because you are always in the market. Day, night, morning, evening. She can fly 400 points in one direction, and you relax, waiting for further movement. But it was at this moment that this currency pair suddenly sharply adjusted in the other direction, and with even greater agility. And you have to decide whether to urgently become in a positive lock, or to close a deal with what you have, or to put a stop loss at the opening price, and then look for an opportunity to open the deal again in the same direction, because the stop loss, likely to close the deal. "And the eternal battle, we can only dream of peace" - this is her motto ... Pound-yen - the girl is certainly interesting, but also capricious. And jealous ... Demands that you constantly keep your ears on top of your head. The cure for depression, in a word. And it was for this pair that five traders got into deals.

And this was not a herd feeling, because three out of five were at home at the time of the transaction, did not consult with anyone, and did not discuss it with anyone until they entered the transaction. That is, the market signaled its readiness to hike down and offered to participate at him. His signals were noticed, and away we go ... First, the market gave to earn and then began to turn up. But after the sale, it's somehow difficult to readjust to the purchase. The stereotype of thinking works. Five traders amicably opposed the rise of this currency pair, stubbornly selling it and getting into negative castles. The trend was upward, but these brave guys carefully did not notice this.

And as you know, winners get everything. Perseverance - it, of course, causes respect. But when it borders on obstinacy and unwillingness to see the real state of things, it begins to resemble a struggle with windmills. I hope you remember what they called Don Quixote? When any of them approached me with their arguments in favor of the sale, I always asked only one question: "The direction of the trend?" Ascending! .. There are no more questions! .. However, it seemed that these five were bold, arguing, tried not only to convince each other of the correctness of their conclusion but also to get as many supporters as possible. Probably, at that moment it seemed to them that the more people start selling this pair, the faster it will unfold. A club of pound-yen lovers was organized. The guys shared the duty at night. Someone was sleeping, someone was awake, in order to signal the whole five if necessary. Like in the book "Timur and his team." The arguments in favor of sales began to border on some insanity. I remember how Sergey approached me, by the way, a very sensible person, and in all seriousness began to explain that the yen is very responsive to ... Moon phases. He shoveled the story for several years and deduced the pattern. Like, when the moon decreases, the yen begins to grow, and when the moon grows, the yen weakens. Or vice versa, I don't remember exactly. "Serezha," I tell him, "why only the yen reacts like that, and other currencies?" "And the Japanese are more sensitive," he answered without blinking or doubting. Trying to appeal to common sense, I go up to another one of these five and with a laugh, I retell him a conversation with Sergey. What Oleg (his name is) tells me: "Yes, I know. I met one guy here. I talked to him on Skype. When I told him Sergey's theory, he was surprised that we just found out about this - they always trade like that ... on the lunar calendar. "And I still laughed at the stories of Mikhail Zadornov.

One morning I come to dealing and I see that the palm tree, which was in the corner by the table, is missing. “Where did you deliver the flower?” I ask the guys. After hesitating, they finally give me an answer. Say, he is unhappy. “In what sense is unhappy?” I wonder. “Directly,” Anton answers. “When he was gone, the pound-yen went down, and when he was transferred to us, everything changed.”

In short, Feng Shui went on the move ... I'm trying to joke: “Maybe it makes sense to take hostages and not let them go until large-scale sales begin? And if they don’t listen to your requirements, threaten to be shot? ”The guys didn’t take jokes. I understand that the nerves are on the limit. It was a very long marathon. As a result, not everyone reached the finish line. Not every deposit can withstand such trips ... Moreover, swaps on sale are negative (swaps are charged for transferring a position from one day to another). If they saw their goal, but they saw only fog.

This story is intended once again to remind you: do not be stubborn. The market is none. Not evil, not good. He will not spare you. And he does not need to be loved, he must be studied. And try to watch from a distance. Impartiality. And focus not on the phases of the moon, but on trends.

Chapter 3 - What Should We Build A House On? Thoughts Or The Foundation?

"If it seemed to you that you understood what I said, then you misunderstood me" – Alan Greenspan

First, some little classics. Economic data and their impact on exchange rates:

"Buy rumors - sell facts" ... How many of you have not heard this expression? Probably heard many ... What does it mean? Imagine that the market is awaiting the Fed's decision on the interest rate and believes that it is likely to raise the rate, as the economic situation in the country predisposes precisely to this. An increase in the interest rate, as you know, is in favor of the national currency, and this currency begins to grow. And here comes the day the decision is made - the interest rate is really raised by the expected number of points, and it is after this that the rate of this currency goes down sharply. It seems that everything is clear: the market bought the currency in advance on rumors of interest rate increases and sold it when these rumors became a fait accompli, that is, it was confirmed because the market won back the advance in advance. Simply? Of course! If not for one "but". This is theoretically clear to us and clear in hindsight ... And when you turn on the monitor and to take advantage of the situation, you begin to study the opinions of leading bank analysts as to whether the rate will be raised or not ... As a rule, the opinions of specialists, in the end, are 50/50. Usually, it looks like this: "Most likely, the bet will be increased if ... (here there are a number of reasons for raising ...) But you need to consider that ... (here there are a number of reasons for leaving the bet on that same level ...) and even (oh my God!) a decrease is possible, because ... (there are a number of arguments in favor of this scenario)". That is why I took the words of A. Greenspan as an epigraph to this chapter. There is always a chance that events can go according to different scenarios. And how do we behave in this situation?

First of all, let's understand what fundamental analysis is.

Fundamental analysis is not predicting any indexes, speeches of politicians and economists. Fundamental analysis is a comparative analysis of economies and their pace of development in the two countries whose currencies we are considering. For example, if you are considering a pair of EUR / USD, then you need to compare the economies of the European Union and America. In principle, it is not so difficult to put together all the economic indicators, compare them, understand who is currently in a winning situation, and place a bet on him. But ... tell me, do you seriously think that we are getting absolutely reliable data? Take off your pink glasses and become realistic! Politics manipulate the economy and society, and this is usually justified by state interests. There is secret economic information that is not accessible to the masses since it is a state secret. There is an outright falsification of data, again, based on the interests of a particular country. There are, of course, financial companies with a large staff of employees engaged in analytical research to correctly predict the development of the economic situation in the country. Can you single-handedly conduct a detailed comparative analysis of the economies of different countries? To filter and analyze a huge number of indicators, and not always publicly available? Most likely, no ... Unless you yourself own this information first hand ... And the point is not that you and I are deliberately misled. Have you ever heard the expression: "Always tell the truth! But not all! .. "? "Chef! Everything is lost! - I want to scream and hide in hysteria".

Imagine meeting your lender. You have two options.

1. You are perplexed and start telling that now you are insolvent, that everything is falling apart and you are unlikely to pay back the loan soon. Your wife (husband) has left you because he considers you an insolvent loser, a bore; all friends shy away from you like a plague, rightly believing that it is contagious. Nobody believes in you, and life is rolling downhill ...The finish!

2. You meet with the lender, radiating joy and confidence in the future. You have prospects and plans for the near future. And to achieve financial heights you only need time and a little extra cash infusion. With those, it will turn into a wonderful project that you have already calculated and a business plan has been drawn up for it. Basically, your project is already planned. The lender becomes interested and is ready to lend funds for it ... But you, as a decent

person, considered it necessary to inform your creditor, since the project is very profitable, it would be very pleasant for you to work with him to thank him in the future for patiently waiting for a return debt, with a higher percentage.

Of course, option 2 will work. And note: you were honest, because you talked about prospects and your plans. The principle "Pontov do not spare! Don't give money! " is inherent not only to people but also to states (because it is believed that the state is the guarantor of the interests of its fellow citizens). And do not be indignant that the GDP for the last quarter was revised and turned out to be much lower than the previously submitted one. You just need to understand how to make money on it and what you should pay attention to first of all.

I remember how I tried to calculate how the market reacts to the release of a particular news, hoping to find a pattern. And it turned out that the same news in one month could cause sales in the market, and in another - purchases. At these moments, my indignation knew no bounds. I showed my acquaintances to traders the notes made a month ago when the market reacted to the same news in the exact opposite of how it does it today. And the questions: "How to live further?" Who should I believe? "- were at that time the most relevant.

Another point that worried me was how quickly I needed to respond to the release of certain data and put up a deal. I did not have time to finish reading "What and how?" in the running line, and the market already "whistled" by 100 points. And what do you want to do in this situation? Jump into an outgoing train?

In fact, "the chest opens simply". Let's just assume that the heads of state are going to gather (say, the G-7, now the G-8, or the G-20 ...), and the American president says that the country's economy is experiencing some difficulties, and therefore to revive economic indicators required to "reduce the cost of the dollar". The estimated period necessary to improve the economic situation in the country (according to experts' forecasts) is 2-3 years. It will not be possible to sharply reduce the price of the dollar overnight: firstly, it will lead to a sharp rise in the price of other currencies (which, of course, will not please other countries), and secondly, for America itself, the process of "reviving" the economy cannot happen in one night. There are thirdly, and fifthly, and tenths.

But we will not go into the jungle of the economic jungle, we need to understand the process of the trend. As you know, the main trend lasts for several years. So, the president testified, so to speak, of his intentions, and the process began. The trend begins to unfold in the direction of the dollar. How? Very simple - there is news that starts to provoke the sale of the dollar, politicians, economists speak out, expressing concern over the current state of things in America, which also affects the exchange rate. But since the trend is designed for several years, the dollar cannot be at the target point ahead of schedule. And if the price begins to fall at a faster rate than expected (which threatens to accelerate the movement), then at that moment some news comes out, some politicians come out who suddenly say that everything is not so bad! Very well. And the price goes for a correction. In order to wait for the next push to continue the trend.

It turns out that news is only a catalyst for price movements. And in principle, it is not so important for us, traders, what kind of data is released (meaning, with an increase or decrease). Another thing is important - the time of their release. Because it is at this moment that the news can trigger a price movement. Consider the price movement on the example of the release of data "Nonfarm payrolls". So, classically, the market reaction after the release of these data takes place in three stages.

1. Usually, the first impulse sets the direction of price movement. Price makes a sharp leap. The nearest support or resistance line is usually 50-70 points. Large investors take profits. Price rolls back a bit. But the direction of motion is given.

2. The bulk of professionals are connected. The movement is the longest. About 100-150 points. Then again, profit-taking.

3. After the departure of London, the Americans turn on. As a rule, this is another 50-70 points.

This is a classic. All traders are always looking forward to this day. They call it that - the day of the trader. In one day you can earn a year in advance (this, of course, depending on which deposit you should go with). But a month in advance - that's for sure. I know traders who worked only once a month. It is the output of the Nonfarm payrolls data. And the rest of the time they rested. But the market "in the classics" goes less and less.

Now, most often I work on data output as follows. I spend the analysis thirty minutes before the release of the data. First, I select the currency pair on which I will put up the transaction.

1. I determine the nearest support and resistance lines.

2. From support, I place a pending buy order.

3. From resistance, I place a pending sell order.

Most often, the price at the data output now makes a false fall, but not in the direction of real movement, but in the opposite direction. Thus, a pending order is opened, and I cancel the second order.

What events are worth paying attention to? I recommend this list:

- G8 meetings;
- presidential elections;
- major meetings of the Central Bank;
- potential changes in modes;
- possible defaults on debts of large countries;
- possible wars as a result of growing geopolitical tensions;
- six-month speech by the Fed chairman in the US Congress.

It is events of this magnitude that are designed to send a trend for correction or give a new impetus to the movement. But once again, I note that these events can only be an occasion to a reversal or acceleration of the movement, which the price, as a rule, draws in advance. And your task is to analyze the price movement schedule regardless of what the media suggests and put the deal in accordance with your own conclusions.

I want to dwell once more on one important aspect that can be used. Have you heard the expression “trading on the difference in rates”? What does it mean?

Japan has the lowest interest rates. Therefore, the most profitable and safe way is to take the yen from a bank in Japan, buy a higher-yielding currency for it in countries where the interest rate is higher than in a bank in Japan, for example, a dollar, euro or pound, and receive a higher percentage from banks in the European Union, America or England . Who likes what? A win-win! Imagine, in one place we take the currency at one percent, invest it in another currency, where the interest rate is higher (say, 2%), and we simply put the difference from interest rates (1%) in our pocket. Remember how in the commercial: “You and I are sitting here, but the money is coming. Yes, dad? Yes”. This is exactly the case. But not for us, mere mortals. Most likely, we will not be able to get a loan from a bank in Japan. But we can make money in the Forex market using this knowledge. Indeed, at this moment, the yen begins to become cheaper, since it is being sold. And there is one more nuance. When the fiscal year closes in Japan, the yen needs to be returned to its homeland. This process is called repatriation. Therefore, those who took the yen from the Bank of Japan and bought other currencies for it are forced to do reverse operations. That is, they sell the dollar, pound, euro and buy the yen. At this point, the yen begins to rise in price ... It is known that in Japan the fiscal year closes in March, and yen usually starts to buy from the end of February. At the end of August, the results are summed up and the fiscal year in the USA and Canada closes, which also plays in favor of the yen. At this moment, she, too, usually rises in price. And traders usually use this in their trades.

But such events do not occur every day. They must be taken into account and used in your trading strategy. But how to plan your work for every day?

So, you are working, for example, on the EUR / USD pair. Printed out a weekly data release calendar for these zones. We paid attention to the time of the release of that news that could provoke a price movement and put up the positions for technical analysis before (notice - before!) the release of this news. As a rule, the price draws market entries before the start of the movement. If these inputs are not very beautiful, we do not rely on the case but wait for a more understandable situation. You must be able to wait too! This is my view on fundamental analysis! Maybe categorically, maybe it will seem primitive to someone, but practice shows that ease of perception is a reliable ally of the trader. This is my point of view, possibly incorrect, but it is mine, tested in practice, and therefore I trust her.

Chapter 4 - Indicators: Friends Or Traitors?

"... If a friend did not whine, did not ache, but walked, let him be gloomy and angry, and when you fell from the rocks, he groaned, but held! If he was following you, as if in battle, At the top he was drunk, So, how you rely on him yourself..."

- V. Vysotsky

In every man, lives the dream. And everyone wants to achieve it with the least cost: moral, physical and material. Everyone, without exception, at the beginning of his journey in the Forex market believes that you just need to find the right indicator - and here it is, your dream, in your pocket! And if there is no such assistant, he must be invented or written yourself!

I remember my puppy joy when, testing another new indicator and getting profit from its signals, I rejoiced internally: "Here it is happiness!" Get only the signal "buy", "sell", "wait" - and take profit. But at the most unexpected moment, the indicator suddenly began to behave inappropriately in relation to the price, that is, it gave false, as I thought, signals, contrary to its forecasts. At such moments, I called him a traitor and began to search for another, more perfect, in my opinion, instrument.

And only when certain statistics on the performance of indicators were collected, an understanding of what, in fact, they are. After all, as you know, "if the stars are lit, then someone needs this."

So, the indicators. What are they doing on our monitor? They calculate what happened to the price over a certain period of time. That is, an indicator is a mathematical embodiment of price movement. This means that it is not the indicator that controls the price, but the price that controls the indicator! It is not the indicator that unfolds and "drags" the price, but the price unfolds and "drags" the indicator behind itself!

Conclusion 1. The price is primary, and the indicator value is secondary!

That is, first we conduct a graphical analysis, and then look for confirmation of our views on the indicators. The law of life dictates the following pattern to us: there is some new idea that leads to an upswing, then a certain period of stagnation (stabilization) follows, and if there are no new ideas, there is a decline. Forex obeys the same laws of life: rise → flat → rise (decline). That is, the uptrend is replaced by a flat, and if there is no news that can act as a catalyst for the price movement further up, the trend changes its direction in the opposite direction, turning into a downtrend. And at each of these periods, certain groups of indicators work. Trend indicators that work with directional movement are called *trendy*. Indicators that capture market turning points and give signals in a flat are called *oscillators*.

Conclusion 2. Indicators are divided into trend and oscillators.

First, we find out whether directional movement or flat reigns in the market and then select the necessary type of indicators.

Trend indicators are a good tool for market analysis, with strong movements they can give synchronous signals, but with market turns, they often lag behind its movements. There are a lot of indicators. It is important to choose the indicator, the signals of which will be clear to you and will give confidence when entering the market. Let's analyze some of them:

• Moving Average (MA) is a common indicator name, although it is correctly called a moving average;

• Convergence-Divergence of Moving Averages (Moving Averagers Convergence Divergence, MACD);

• Parabolic (parabolic) system;

• Bollinger Bands (BB).

Oscillators, as we have already noted, capture reversal changes as well as market turning moments. They can give synchronous and leading signals. True, with the establishment of a strong trend, these signals are unreliable, and often false. These include:

• stochastic oscillator;

• Relative Strength Index (RSI)

• Commodity Channel Index (CCI) indicator

• tempo indicator (momentum).

We will not now find out how the values of all these indicators are calculated (this can be done by reading the special literature), but we will analyze the principle of their work and the rules of use in market analysis.

Moving Averages

There are three types of moving averages:

• Simple, or arithmetic mean, moving averages (Simple Moving Averages, SMA);

• Linearly weighted moving averages (Linearly weighted Moving Averages, LMA); rarely used;

• Exponentially smoothed Moving Averages (EMA), are applied most often.

The moving average is a graph of the average price, it is a line imposed on the graph of this price. How does moving average work?

• If the indicator chart crosses the price chart from the bottom up - this is a buy signal.

• If the indicator chart crosses the price chart from top to bottom - this is a sell signal. Advantages of moving averages:

• easy to determine the direction of the trend;

• can be used as a support or resistance line.

If the graphic support line coincides with the mathematical one (that is, with the line of the moving average), then this is the strongest support area, from which purchases are most likely to start. And by analogy - if the graphic resistance line coincides with the mathematical one, then this zone is attractive for sales.

The period of moving averages is determined empirically from the history of the movement of the currency. For each time period and each currency pair, you need to select your period of moving averages. The disadvantages of moving averages include the systematic delay of signals.

Moving Average Convergence-Divergence

Moving Averages Convergence Divergence (MACD) is a simple oscillator from two exponentially smoothed moving averages. It is depicted as a line.

To clearly indicate favorable moments with periods of 12 and 26 for buying or selling, a signal line is plotted on the MACD chart - a 9-period moving average of the indicator. How does it work? The intersection of the MACD lines and the signal line is a signal to buy or sell. Where the lines crossed, the price moves there. This is where the MACD property manifests itself as a trend indicator. In my opinion, this indicator shows divergence very well and clearly. Divergence is the difference between the price value and the indicator value.

That is, we take conclusion 1 as an axiom that the indicator repeats the price movement, and, based on this, we have the right to assume that if the price goes up on the chart and shows a peak, the indicator follows it and draws the same peak. If the indicator does not reach the maximum, it means that it catches that the bulls are already not strong enough to move the price higher, and correction is possible. This is called divergence. Similarly with the downward movement. Moreover, divergence on the indicator often coincides with strong levels of support or resistance on the price chart, which is a definite signal for us to work on the rebound. That is, it is necessary to consider the totality of signals, and not having seen the divergence showing the direction down (up), rush to the market urgently ...

Often, divergence is used as a signal to enter the market by trend or to add positions. Let's say the dollar-yen trend is going up, both current and long-term. A MACD also draws a bullish divergence up ... If you see that the hour has closed below the past, and MACD is above the past minimum, buy immediately! Do it in the first seconds of the next hour, maybe even at the end of that hour; although it is not yet closed, but everything is already visible and everything is clear. The difference between trend and counter trend divergences is huge. According to the trend, this is an occasion to buy from strong support (or sell from resistance) or an excuse to add, which is risky against the trend. Expand a trend due to some kind of divergence on the indicator? So take it and roll over? It's difficult! The disadvantage of MACD is signal lag.

Parabolic System

This system was developed as a mechanical stop loss system. Suppose you have a profitable position of 100 points. In this case, you expect further price movement in your direction, that is, an increase in profits, and do not rush to close the position. You have a completely legitimate question: where to put a stop loss to protect your profit from a possible price reversal against you and what will be a signal for you to take profit? This indicator very clearly demonstrates the levels of setting stop losses.

The parabolic system is generally shown by points located below the price chart if the price goes up, and above the chart if the price goes down. Since this system shows stop order levels, a point is the price at which it is necessary to place a stop loss, but not exactly on it, but departing from it by at least the spread.

The signal for a transaction based on the line of the parabolic system is the intersection of the price chart with it. This moment signals either a trend reversal or its temporary stabilization. Another signal of the line of the parabolic system is its direction, which characterizes the current trend: in the case of a positive slope of the line of the parabolic system, this is a bullish trend, otherwise - a bearish one.

The advantages of the parabolic system include the fact that it responds to changes in prices over time, allowing you to determine the direction of the trend and the time of the transaction. There are two periods of life of the parabolic system line - maturity and old age. With their consideration, it is necessary to perceive signals.

In a mature period, the price chart, as a rule, runs parallel to the line of the parabolic system, and in "old age" these charts begin to converge right up to the intersection. Accordingly, the received signals can be divided into the correct ones, given in the mature period, and the false ones, related to old age.

By the way, I have a student who works exclusively along the lines of the parabolic system. When he came to me and we began to learn to draw lines of support and resistance, it turned out that these magic lines were given to him with great difficulty. He could not understand their purpose and functions performed by them. And since the desire to work and earn money was huge, and the deposit allowed certain risks, the parabolic system came to the rescue. He took a 4-hour period from the eurodollar and, as soon as he noticed the beginning of the movement, he immediately stood in the direction of this movement. My arguments about how unprofitable it is that the price often makes a correction after determining the movement and he has to stay out of this correction, although he could have entered into a deal at a better price, etc., they did not perceive. But those qualities that have developed over the years in it (and my student - a hereditary military man, now a pensioner), namely discipline and strict adherence to the developed action plan, brought a good result. His deposit is increasing monthly by an average of 20%. "Not a bad increase in my pension," he says.

How does this work?

1. The daily price direction is determined by a parabolic system. Positions open only in this direction!

2. Work is carried out only in the daytime - that is why the euro-dollar currency pair was chosen.

3. The closure of each 4-hour candle is monitored (from 10.00 to 22.00), so there is no need to constantly sit at the monitor!

4. When a signal is received on a parabolic system, a position is opened in the direction of the direction of movement.

5. A stop loss is set (for a point that appears on the line of the parabolic system plus 5 points plus the spread value).

6. As soon as the profit allows, the stop loss is reset to the opening price.

7. Stop-loss should then be dragged along like a suitcase until a signal is received that is directly opposite to that which served as a signal to open a position. After that, the position is closed.

But I repeat once again: the deposit should allow quite serious risks, otherwise "the game is not worth the candle". By the way, you can experiment with moving averages.

Bollinger Bands

Bollinger Bands is a trend indicator based on the moving average line. His work is based on the fact that 5% of prices should be outside the indicator lines, and 95% should be inside, that is, between the BB + and BB- lines.

Moreover, in a bullish trend, the price throughout the trend, with the exception of corrections, is between the upper Bollinger line (BB +) and the moving average line. In the case of a bearish trend, the price lies between the lower Bollinger Boundary (BB-) and the moving average line.

If the price rises above the upper Bollinger line, and then falls, crossing it from top to bottom, it is recommended to make a decision on the sale, since the bulls growth potential has been exhausted.

If the price crossed the lower Bollinger line from the top down, and then crossed it again, but from the bottom up, it is recommended to make a purchasing decision, since the price pushed off its support line in the form of the lower Bollinger line. There are also auxiliary signals confirming the main ones.

• The convergence of the Bollinger lines is observed in a calming market and at the absence of strong price fluctuations. If the convergence of the Bollinger lines occurs with a slight bullish or bearish slope, then a weak signal is sent to continue the previously existing bullish or bearish trend. If the convergence occurs "horizontally", this is a weak signal for a reversal and the beginning of a new trend.

• The divergence of the Bollinger lines may occur with the strengthening of the current trend. or the beginning of a new one. If the discrepancy corresponds to an increase in transaction volumes, the signal from the indicator is of great strength.

Of course, there are much more indicators than I described here. Which one you will use is up to you. The main thing is to clearly know which signals it can and should respond to. To do this, first test the indicator on the demo account and, only after receiving a stable result, add it to your friends list. But, as they say, "one friend is good, and two is better". Therefore, it is better to focus on the signals of not one, but several instruments. And if they say “buy” or “sell” to you in chorus, this will add to your confidence when entering a deal. And if suddenly the indicators begin to conduct each conversation, evaluate it as a signal “wait”. You must be able to wait too! And remember that the price dictates the necessary actions to the indicator, and not vice versa.

Oscillators

Now let's talk about the oscillators. As you know, price fluctuations occur in the financial market. The price goes up, then down, again up and down again. Outwardly, these fluctuations look rather chaotic. But this is at first glance. In order to systematize the oscillations, oscillators were developed. The oscillator is like a pendulum that swings from its extreme values to normal averages.

Stochastic Oscillator

The most popular indicator used in the Forex market is the *stochastic oscillator*. I remember as, testing stochastic (as traders call this oscillator) and having a very vague idea of its work, I was guided solely by the fact that the price was in the overbought (oversold) zone. This is a traditional stochastic signal that forms when the fast and slow lines cross. I joyfully rubbed my hands, getting a signal, got into a deal and took profits. “Here it is!”, I sang in the shower, “My lifesaver,” I affectionately called him. And suddenly ... thunder broke out in the clear sky. The trend began, and my favorite indicator, which I began to trust as much as myself, suddenly began to “stick” to the upper borders and send me false signals. But then I did not perceive them as false, but took them at face value and honestly got into transactions, practically without looking at the price chart, but only focusing on him, my beloved. As a result, I got up against the market, violating the first commandment of the trader “Trend is your friend”. Others made remarkable profits because for a trader a trend is a holiday: for a short period you earn serious amounts. And I ... I got one “stop” after another, and Ostap Bender’s phrase “We are strangers at this celebration of life” revolved in my head.

Then came the understanding that those laws that apply when driving a car do not apply to pedestrians. A pedestrian walks on his own paths, and more precisely, on sidewalks ... So it is on Forex ... What works in the side corridor (in the flat) does not work with strong price movements, that is, with a trend. And those indicators that do an excellent job with the trend, in the lateral movement of prices can afford some liberties. The laws of wartime undoubtedly differ from the laws of peace.

Since it works very well in the side corridor, and Forex is a 70% flat market, stochastics can be called a real assistant to the trader! Therefore, we will analyze first of all the advantages of this oscillator:

• catches changes well at the turning points of the market;

• often gives synchronous and/or leading signals at the side corridor.

Disadvantages:

• the presence of “flat” Asian sessions, when the clock oscillators are discharged and distort their performance;

• with strong market movements (with a trend), the stochastic “sticks” and “lies” on the overbought, oversold lines, starting to give false signals.

How does it work?

With a general increase in prices, closing price indicators tend to the upper limit of the price range, and vice versa, with a downward trend, closing prices tend to the lower limit of the range. Two curves are used in stochastic analysis: % K and % D.

The second curve is more significant as according to its dynamics one can judge the most important changes in the market. Stochastic oscillators show the ability of bulls or bears to close the market near the upper or lower edge of the range. With the rise, the market tends to close near the upper edge of the trend. If the bulls can raise prices during the period, but cannot close them near the maximum, stochastic lines begin to decline. This gives a sell signal. The same is true with the purchase.

Traditional stochastic signals are formed at the intersection of fast and slow lines. Sell signals are generated when the fast line crosses the slow line at the overbought zone (the curve is in the zone from 10 to 15). It should be borne in mind that ascending fast and slow lines can intersect, so be sure to wait for the stochastic slow line to turn around. A buy signal is formed when the fast and slow lines cross in the oversold zone (when the curve is in the range of values from 85 to 90).

In this case, if the weekly trend is bullish, and the daily stochastic lines have fallen below their lower line, a purchase order should be given. If the situation is just the opposite, then you should sell. Despite the fact that the stochastic is a good helper in lateral movement, it has a wonderful trend signal. This signal is called the daily trend jump.

How does it work?

Suppose there is a directional trend, the stochastic, of course, enters the area of limit values and has been in this area for a long time. And when the price goes for the first deep correction (the fast line of the oscillator crosses the 50 mark), this serves as a signal to enter the position along the trend.

The most serious buy and sell signals appear when there is divergence or a discrepancy. A bearish divergence occurs when curve D is above 70 and forms two dropping peaks, and prices continue to rise. With a bullish divergence, on the contrary, curve D is below 30 and forms a double rising base, and prices begin to fall.

Relative Strength Index

The Relative Strength Index (RSI) is a leading or coinciding oscillator that determines the strength of bullish or bearish sentiment, tracking changes in closing prices over a certain time interval.

How does RSI work?

RSI fluctuates between 0 and 100. Horizontal support lines, indicating the boundaries of overbought and oversold, should cross the highest highs and deep lows. Usually, they are carried out at levels 30 and 70. When a strong trend movement is observed, then you can perform some shift of the lines. In strong bull markets, they can be at levels 40 and 80, and in strong bear markets - at levels 20 and 60.

So, when the RSI rises above the upper support line, this indicates the strength of the bullish trend, as well as the fact that the market is in the overbought zone and is ready for corrective sales. And when the RSI falls below the lower support line, this indicates the strength of the bearish mood in the market and at the same time that it is worth preparing for correction, that is, for shopping.

The disadvantage of the relative strength index is the fact that any strong trend, regardless of direction (up or down) usually quickly makes the oscillators take critical values. In such cases, by mistakenly assuming that the market is overbought or oversold, you can close profitable positions prematurely.

The first appearance of an RSI value in an overbought or oversold area is usually just a warning! A stronger signal for motivation to act is the appearance of a curve in the critical region a second time. Overbought or oversold is a situation that arises when quotes, due to excessive demand or supply, reach unreasonably high or low values, respectively. It is one of the few indicators that gives signals, not after the price has already begun its movement, but before the beginning of this movement. This can be noted as the advantage of the relative strength index. That is, the dynamics of the RSI chart over several time periods is ahead of the dynamics of prices on the chart, which allows us to predict further price behavior.

To use this wonderful signal, draw trend lines on the RSI chart. Suppose there is an uptrend both on the price chart and on the RSI. Suppose that on the chart the price rests against the trend line, but on the RSI it has already broken it down. This suggests that you should not put up for purchase at the moment according to the trend: most likely, the price will begin to correct downward. That is, when the RSI chart breaks the uptrend line from top to bottom, a sell order should be placed.

Conversely, if the RSI chart breaks down from the bottom upward trend line, you should place a buy order. It is important to consider long-term signals, daily and/or 4-hour. It is imperative to wait until the closing of the 4-hour period and/or day. Otherwise, it may turn out that you will break the trend line, and at the end of the 4-hour period this will turn out to be a "fall" (false break) and the RSI chart will close above the trend line. Using this signal for a longer period, you will realize how wonderful he is. How many times he helped out and helped to earn!

I will tell you one case from practice. November 2007, a pair of euro-dollar. The price is in the side corridor for about three months. Side corridor 600 points wide. Traders buy from below support, close profit at resistance and open deals for sale. Long-standing in the side corridor somewhat dulls vigilance. Although every time we wait for a breakthrough of the corridor, remember that the resistance line is the best selling price. I place a warrant from her for a rebound from the resistance line. On the morning of February 26, 2008, I turn on the monitor and, as always, start viewing from the daily charts ... And I see that the RSI tail, which broke the trend line up yesterday, has remained above the broken line today. This is a daily signal to break up! I urgently cancel the bounce order from the resistance line and place an order to break it. And away we go! 900 points up without correction. The new high of the Euro-dollar, and, of course, thanks to my friend RSI for the help and signal that came to me!

Divergence on the RSI occurs when prices rise to a new high. Bullish divergences give a buy signal. This occurs when prices reach an even lower value than before, while the RSI reaches a minimum higher than the one during the previous decline. The buy signal will be especially strong if the penultimate minimum of the RSI is below the lower support line, and the last is above it. In the case of a bearish divergence, the picture is exactly the opposite. A sell signal is especially strong if the penultimate peak of the RSI lies above the upper support line, and the last is lower.

To summarize.

Overbought - This is the state of the market in which there are no bulls among the bulls or their buying opportunities are running out and they cannot raise prices to a new height.

This time, there is some lull in the market, prices do not have a strongly pronounced bullish direction, and the oscillator turns down and breaks over the border of the overbought zone after some time. This bulk of the oscillators indicates the damping strength of the bulls and the imminent reversal of the trend. Similarly, the oversold state occurs when the oscillator reaches a lower value than the previous ones. In this case, the oscillator is ready to begin growth.

On the charts, overbought and oversold levels are marked with horizontal auxiliary lines. At the same time, for the daily chart, lines should cross only the highest peaks and oscillator troughs in the last 6 months. Their position should be adjusted every 3 months. Oscillators can be in the overbought or oversold zone for many weeks when a new trend begins, giving a premature signal to counter-trade. In such cases, we should proceed to the analysis of trend indicators.

What else is worth paying attention to is the so-called commodity currencies. These include AUD, CAD, NZD, CHF (gold, copper, nickel, oil) and USD. Why commodity currencies? Because the American dollar (like the Canadian one) reacts to the movement of gold. If the price of gold goes up, then the dollar will go down. What is not an indicator? If oil goes up, then the dollar and the Canadian currency will go down. It is necessary to track the movement of oil prices.

Conclusions Regarding Indicators And Oscillators

So, we examined indicators and oscillators. Each of them, as well as you and I, has its drawbacks and unconditional advantages. It is important to remember that it is necessary to use the indicators and oscillators that most traders work with. Swim against the tide of the market - this, of course, increases adrenaline but does not guarantee the fact that you will get out of the water dry. Do you need it? And the signals, obvious to the majority, will move the market in the direction in which this majority will place orders. How much I work, I hear so much from traders about some new mechanical systems that can calculate everything and give a signal about entering the market. More than once, cherishing the hope of a miracle, I dreamed of an indicator that would calculate everything instead and give me a signal: “Buy it!” Or: “Sell it!”, And then: “Take profit”. But each time, such an indicator turned out to be an illusion. Think for yourself: if you could come up with such a system, who would start to offer it (this system) for widespread use? The developer himself in a short period would have earned a state equal to that of Soros. The question is, why does he need us? Therefore, "God rely on God, but don’t lie!"

We conduct a graphical analysis, determine the direction of the trend and based on this information we establish with whom we are better off contacting - we have friends for all occasions! They are always ready to help. There is a trend (directional movement) - we turn to indicators. There is a lateral movement (the price fluctuates in one range) - we turn to the oscillators. At the same time, we take into account their shortcomings and focus on their advantages! And of course, we earn! Good luck, traders! And she, as you know, loves the winners.

Chapter 5 - Candles: Eastern Tales or Western Rationalism?

"Why are we all called Eurasia? Eurasia is when there is more of Europe than Asia. And we have more Asia than Europe. Therefore, we are not Eurasia, we are Asiope ..."

- M. Zadornov

It is no coincidence that I quoted these words from the monologue of M. Zadornov as an epigraph to the chapter on candle analysis. Because the confrontation between Europe (it is the West for us) and Asia affects not only the culture, religion, upbringing, etc. but also the analysis of price charts on the Forex market. Combining the Western approach with the eastern analysis, you can get much more confidence when entering a deal than relying on only one of these systems. Indeed, Western rationalism, enriched by subtle oriental maneuvering, will always be in a better position. By the way, in comparison with other countries, Russia has much more opportunities for a flexible approach. The geographical position of our country itself suggests that our thinking is tuned to two waves at once, and as you know, our thoughts determine our actions.

Honestly, the topic of candlestick analysis appeared unexpectedly. Once, while discussing strategies for conducting transactions, I talked with the traders of our dealing and asked who exactly uses Oriental analysis in their analytics. Opinions, oddly enough, were divided. Some categorically denied the candlestick analysis, pointing to its shortcomings, while others sang odes praising its virtues.

First of all, let's look at what candle analysis is, what are its advantages and disadvantages (and are they?) In comparison with a graphical analysis of price movement (that is, Western analysis). To do this, we define the terminology of Western and Eastern technical analysis. What is western analysis? This is an analysis of price movement charts.

Western analysis implies the definition of:

- trend direction;
- the turning points of this trend;
- support and resistance levels;
- breaking through these levels; and, based on the foregoing, determination of entry and exit points from transactions.

As a matter of fact, it was we who analyzed the Western analysis in the chapters "Obvious - Incredible" and "Open Window for the Trader". Adherents of the Western school say: "Why should I look at the candles if I see a general price movement? It (the price) already gives me information about the direction of the trend, about the reversal of movement, about the formation of shapes ... Candles distract me ... ". In fairness, I want to note that I myself thought for a long time that way, using exclusively Western technical tools.

Then came the fascination with candle analysis, which is also called oriental. Why is it called oriental? Partly because the Japanese invented it. And they are very influential participants in most world markets. I admire how elegantly and accurately oriental philosophers notice the details of being.

The transparency and plasticity of the language, the depth, and flexibility of thought are amazingly captivating. The Japanese are famous philosophers. And it is not surprising that they, on their distant islands, invented a new analytical method with a very romantic name - *Japanese candles.* And they did it long before the appearance of exchanges in the West and their attendant financial instruments. Candlestick charts are much older than their Western counterparts, which, of course, cannot but inspire confidence.

How do you imagine a Christmas party? Soft white snow, a warm comfortable house, which smells of Christmas tree and oranges, a pleasant twilight in the room. And of course, lighted candles ... It is they who give the familiar atmosphere an atmosphere of tranquility and mystery.

A person can watch for hours without stopping at the rain, water, and a burning fire. And he can look at how others work. By the way, the last statement, perhaps, is not valid in trading. Because real professionals from trading prefer to work on their own. Just consider other people's money - not accustomed. Accustomed to count their own. So, the eastern analysis is the analysis of the candles.

Candle (candlestick) is a term for the oldest and most common type of Japanese technical analysis.

The thick part of the candle is called the body. The body is the distance between the opening price and the closing price. If the closing price is higher than the opening price, the candle body remains empty. In this case, they say that the price is going up. If the closing price is lower than the opening price, the body of the candle turns black. In this case, they talk about the price moving down. There are candles without bodies. For such candles, the opening price is equal to the closing price (or almost equal). They are called *doji.*

The thin lines above and below the body of the candle are called shadows. The top of the upper shadow is the maximum of the candle, and the bottom of the lower shadow is the minimum of the candle. Let us dwell in more detail on some signals that candles give us.

Doji

Doji (or "Candle of equilibrium") often signals what the market is in equilibrium. The appearance of such a candle in a trending market can often mean that the market has lost its momentum and is ready for a correction. Of course, only the appearance of a “doji” does not mean that the price will abruptly change direction. The chances of a reversal increase if the market is near the level of resistance or support and if the market is overbought or oversold.

So, if the price approached the support level or resistance level and closed with a doji candlestick near it, then most likely the price is preparing for a rebound from this level. If at the same time, indicators enter the overbought or oversold zone, then this is another additional signal to enter the market for a rebound from the level. Thus, the eastern analysis complements the western, which gives us more confidence when entering the transaction.

If the "doji" appeared after a long rising candle, then we can say that the shadows of this candle and the "balance candle" form a resistance level. From him in the future may begin sales, albeit temporary. If the “doji” appeared after a long downward candle, then we can say that the shadows of this candle and the “balance candle” form a support level, from which purchases can subsequently begin.

The body of the candle is a kind of indicator. It demonstrates to traders a confident direction of movement and characterizes the strength of the trend. Shadows of candles also carry very useful information. Consider this with a specific example. If the white candlestick does not have shadows, then this can be considered as a positive indicator characterizing the strength of the upward trend. But, looking at such a candle after the close of the day, pay attention to the shadow that it left on top. This shadow indicates that the upward movement could not consolidate and the price quickly pushed down from the resistance level. Attention deserves the fact that the price was near the resistance level, from which sales began. This tells us that the bulls do not have enough strength to continue the upward movement. The same is true for a downward movement. The price begins to move down, but, faced with the level of support and even "punctures" this level, can not gain a foothold below it. Only shadows in the form of false falls remain below. This state of the market is a turning point in the downward movement: the bears could not gain a foothold below support and thereby confirm their superiority over the bulls in an effort to move the price further down, and purchases started from support.

Looking at graphical analysis in a Western context, you and I have already analyzed the trend reversal patterns. Candlestick analysis is much older than your western counterpart, so it would be logical to assume that similar reversal patterns exist in candlestick analysis. What is a reversal signal in candlestick analysis? First of all, these are absorption models, which are a combination of two candles. There are two types of absorption models.

• Bullish model - appears in a downtrend, when the white body of the candle “Absorbs” the black body. This model signals the strength of buyers - there are much more of them on the market than sellers, demand exceeds supply.

• Bear model - appears during the upward movement, when the black body of the candle “Absorbs” the white body. This model signals that supply exceeds demand.

You ask: and then what? There was an upward movement, a black candle engulfed a white one. Or vice versa, there was a downward movement, a white candle engulfed a black one. Such an absorption is a reversal signal. And when to get into a deal? The technique is very simple: in the bullish model, the lower of the two lows is used as the support level, while in the bearish model, the largest of the two peaks is selected as the resistance line.

How to use the signal of a single candle and formulate trading rules based on these signals? First of all, we should focus on candlestick models that provide a vision of the whole market picture.

The most complete information on the current market situation is provided by candles formed over long periods (month, week, day, 4-hour timeframe). The shorter the period under consideration, the greater the percentage of error is laid at the entrance to the transaction. Please note: it is necessary to consider the formed candles that already have an opening price, closing price, maximum and minimum, and not those that are in the process of moving! This is one of the basic rules used in the market.

Now let's move on to the signals that need to be analyzed using single candles. Let us dwell on candles that have a long upper (lower) shadow with a small body located at the upper (lower) border of the price range of the session.

Summary

Candle "Hammer" - a long lower shadow and the closing price near or strictly at the maximum. Candle "Shooting Star" - a long upper shadow and a small body located near the lower border of the price range of the session.

The Hanged Candle - a very long shadow below small body (black or white) near the upper border of the price range of the session and a short (or absent) upper shadow. This candle is similar to the "Hammer", but the "Hammer" appears during the downward movement of the market, and the "Hanged Man" appears during the upward movement of the market.

We will consider candlestick patterns in the overall market picture. As the saying goes, words cannot be erased from a song.

"Hammer"

Candle "Hammer" - an indicator of a turn-up, but only if available downward trend. A necessary condition for the formation of such a candle - signal on a purchase is a serious recession or an oversold market. It should be borne in mind that after the formation of the "Hammer", the market often rolls back to the support area that the shadow of this candlestick forms. Some of the traders immediately after the formation of the "Hammer" rises to buy, someone more conservative waits until the price tests the level of support formed by it again, and only then a buy order is issued from this level. The choice depends on your determination and temperament. The price shows us the classic Hammer. The long lower shadow reflects the determination of the bulls, who managed to raise prices so high from the session lows. The subsequent rollback rested in support of the "Hammer", leaned on it and "springed" up, giving everyone the opportunity to join the upward movement and earn about $ 3,500.

Consider the same situation from the point of view of the Western analysis of price movements - we will build a trend line of support. The line is built on two points, and when the price comes to this line for the third time, there should be a rebound from it - after all, the most "chocolate" purchases from support.

Western and eastern analysis complement each other. Agree, when you are invited to buy two signals at once, then the entrance to the transaction becomes obvious.

"Shooting Star"

The "Shooting Star" candle is an indicator of a turn to the bottom, its long shadow from above signals that the bears managed to reverse the upward trend and pushed the price off the highs. The necessary conditions for using such a candle as a sell signal are the overbought market and the upward movement preceding its formation.

Consider the price movement chart of the EUR / USD pair. With directed upward movement, the market closed the day with the "Shooting Star" model, signaling that the bulls could not keep the closing price near the reached maximum. At the same time, the market was in the overbought zone, which also signals that the price is ready to decline. It is possible to put up a sale deal after the formation of the "Shooting Star" or after repeated testing of the level formed at the price of 1,5900. Impatient traders place their trades immediately after the formation of this model, while more conservative traders wait for a return to the resistance level and put a sell order from it.

Consider the same situation from the point of view of Western analysis. The price breaks the trend line of support and closes several periods under it, and then makes a return to this line already as resistance. It is this area of resistance that is most attractive for sales. Attentive traders, considering only such simple daily signals, earned about $ 3000 in three days.

"Hanged"

The Hanged Candle is a signal of a turn at the top, which should appear in rising time. The long lower shadow of a candle can be misleading, which it would seem that speaks about the activity of buyers, but such a strong drop during the session demonstrates market instability. The "Hanged Man" small body indicates that the upward trend at the top of which this model appeared may be at a turning point. An important signal for the market to turn down is the appearance of the next bearish candle, especially if this bearish candle closed below the Hanged Man's body, confirming its intention to go down. If such a signal did not follow and the market closed the next session above the body of the “Hanged Man”, then we cannot consider this model as a sell signal.

In order to use the Hanged model as a sell signal, the following conditions must be met:

• the appearance of this model in an upward movement;

• a small body (black or white) located at the upper price range of the session;

• the length of the lower shadow usually exceeds the length of the body by three or more times;

• upper shadow missing or very small;

• Mandatory bear confirmation in the next session, so that the body of the "Hanged Man" is blocked by the next bear candle.

With these signals, the market often informs us of upcoming movements and our task - do not miss these signals and make decisions on entering deals on time.

But always remember and do not forget the basic rule of market analysis: do not overdo it with a decrease time interval. The shorter period you take for trading, the higher the probability that the signals used will deceive you, because the shorter the period, the more noise. This approach combines eastern and western analysis. As in cards where the ace is older than the king, and the king is older than the lady, so in the analysis: weekly levels formed using the candlestick absorption model are more significant than those formed on the daily charts.

There are a large number of different models of candles - with romantic and not very romantic names - but this is a completely different story ... In order to tell about each of them, one chapter, of course, is not enough. On the other hand, this is an occasion to meet with you again, dear readers.

In my opinion, what we have sorted out is enough to clarify a simple truth: it is more advantageous to use eastern analysis in a single complex with western. Often they complement each other. It is the candlestick analysis that gives us a more accurate entry into the transaction - develop the habit of using candlestick signals for a longer period, and then your positive results will be able to exceed your expectations.

This is not a Christmas tale, believe me!

“It’s better to be rich and healthy ...”, or Rake, which should not be stepped on!

At first glance, for an inexperienced person, the Forex market is a kind of Brownian (chaotic) movement in which it is quite difficult for a beginner to navigate. Since over time you learn to trust the market, the confusion and sense of fear with which you first entered the market fade into the background. I unexpectedly experienced this forgotten feeling, inherent in all newcomers, when traveling to Vietnam, when I watched the traffic on the city streets. Nevertheless, it is amazing how thin the line separates our daily life and work in the market.

Traffic in the cities of Vietnam is a separate song. Since the Vietnamese are no longer using bicycles (only schoolchildren in rural areas move on them), the bulk of people prefer riding scooters. You froze by the road, watching the movement of, say, a hundred bikers? This feeling is nothing compared to when an avalanche of scooters is approaching you. It seems that there are thousands of them. Moreover, they all honk, I suspect, not unsystematically, but it is difficult to understand what they want. No, they, of course, understand. I find it difficult. When I first saw how from the far right lane, literally perpendicular to the road along which this live mass of mopeds was moving along the river, someone turned (probably he just urgently needed to the left), I was literally dumbfounded: " Daredevil! Poor thing ... ”- flashed through my head. But ... None of this happened! Calmly, without slowing down, this “kamikaze" safely turned into an alley. Such scenes are not uncommon, but quite a common thing. Moreover, those who are on the machines are quite loyal to the tricks of their fellow citizens. Maybe they themselves just recently moved from mopeds and they have a “genetic memory" in them? But their restraint and patience can be envied!

Conclusion

Thank you for making it through to the end of *Day Trading Forex*, let's hope it was informative and able to provide you with all of the tools you need to achieve your goals whatever they may be.

Finally, in order not to be excruciatingly painful for the days spent aimlessly, you need to make certain rules for yourself that you will use as a guide to action. Before deciding to enter a deal, you need to reasonably answer questions that will help you understand the market and correctly place an order. As an example, I will cite the rules that I follow when analyzing the market, and when deciding to enter a transaction.

1. Before the start of the working day, you need to have a clear work plan.

2. The need for a trade operation must be confirmed by a signal.

3. The signal should be formed according to the criteria of the work plan.

4. Calculate the level and set a stop loss by calculating the profitability of the transaction.

5. If you have doubts about the correctness of the trading decision, then explain to yourself the objective validity of these doubts in accordance with your plan.

6. If doubts are justified, it is better not to make a decision on the purchase and sale, but to wait. Sometimes clarity in understanding the market situation does not come immediately.

7. If you are very nervous, then you should not make a deal. It's better to go home and do something far from financial transactions.

8. If you get the idea that you are one hundred percent confident in the direction of the price movement, wait and carefully think it over again. Often there is a situation where everyone says: "No brainer, where the price will go," but it is at such moments that the price presents unexpected surprises.

9. Try your best to maintain a sober mind and a rational view of the direction of the price.

Finally, if you found this book useful in any way, a review on Amazon is always appreciated!

Swing Trading

the Beginner's Guide on How to Trade for Profits with the Best Strategies

and Technical Analysis. You will Find Inside the A-Z Glossary to All Technical Terms Used

Written by:

Nathan Real

SWING
TRADING
NATHAN REAL

Introduction

These days, the only thing you need to become a trader is a computer and good internet access. As a result, the number of people trading in the stock market has grown significantly in the past few years. The average Joe can take advantage of the opportunities available on the stock market to make a profit from the movement in stock prices.

There is also a much wider array of resources available to the prospective stock trader. Within a matter of minutes, I could access several websites and videos offering me stock strategies from experienced traders. It has never been easier to educate yourself and enter the market as a trader. I can keep informed in real-time about the stock market from the grocery store or the beach using only my cell phone. As a trader its important to have information readily available so that you can respond to changes in the market and make a profit.

But what is trading? We often hear about people trading on the stock market, but what does this mean? How do people make a profit simply by buying and selling shares and stocks, and what are their strategies? How do they know which stocks to choose and which trends to watch? A trader makes money by taking advantage of the upward and downward movements of stock prices. The simplest breakdown of trading is 'buy low and sell high'. This is how traders make a profit in the stock market. But you will learn that there is much more to it than that. There are other tools and methods that traders use. Understanding these tools requires an understanding of different types of markets.

Usually, when we refer to the market in this book, we are talking about the stock market. If you aren't very experienced in trading, then this is probably the market you are most familiar with. There are many other kinds of markets where traders buy and sell to make a profit. When we refer to the stock market, we are talking about the market where shares in companies are sold. These are often referred to as securities. When you buy a stock, you are buying a certain percentage of ownership of that company. When the value of the company increases; the value of your share of ownership will increase. If the value of the company decreases, then your percentage of ownership will hold less value.

The value of the company is mainly determined by the company's success and profitability. But there are other factors which affect the value of a company's stock. The overall performance of the economy can affect the performance of an individual company. A company might be extremely profitable, but suddenly they are involved in a scandal or a major lawsuit which causes the price of shares to go down. A good trader will keep track of these factors in order to monitor the health of their stocks.

As a trader, you should think of owning a share as if you are the owner of a business. Famed investor and hedge fund manager have said that when you are considering purchasing a stock, you should treat it as if you are considering purchasing the entire business. If you were going to buy a business, think about what types of questions you would ask beforehand. What would you want to know about the person managing the business? Do they have the experience and skills necessary, and would you trust them with your hard-earned capital? What kind of product or service does the company provide? Think about the long-term prospects of that company and whether the company is doing a good job of staying relevant in the ever-changing world. Of course, you also want to know if the company is making a profit. When you buy a business, after all, you buy it with the expectation that it will make you a profit. You should buy shares of a company with the same mindset.

In addition to trading shares in companies, people can also trade raw materials. The materials we use to build houses or consumer products also have a value that is determined by a market and influencing economic factors. Raw material like steel doesn't always trade for the same price. A shortage of machinery or a rise in the cost of steel production will affect the price of steel. Companies who produce consumer goods are constantly dealing with the rise and fall of the cost of raw materials and these changes will affect how much they are able to produce at a given time. If the price of steel goes up, then construction costs will also increase. Traders can make money by anticipating these changes in the price of raw materials. This is known as the commodities market. Traders on the commodities market buy some amount of raw materials, usually on paper through a brokerage firm, anticipating that at some point that raw material will be valued higher and they can capitalize on the price discrepancy. A brief glimpse at a chart of the price of steel over the last year won't look much different from a chart showing the price of a stock or a security index; it will be made up of peaks and values where the price of that raw material has risen and fallen over time depending on external factors.

While the technical aspects of commodities trading are similar, a trader in commodities must pay attention to different indicators than someone who trades in stocks and securities. Where a stock trader might watch for news about a certain company and the development of their products, a commodities trader might keep a close eye on steel manufacturing firms and their levels of production, or how import and export taxes are affecting oil companies in the Persian Gulf.

When we buy stocks in a company then we are also buying the risks associated with owning that business. I could open a business today, and five years from now the business could be worth significantly more money. The business could also go bankrupt after six months, which means I would lose all the capital I invested in the business. Traders should never forget this when they are considering buying a share in a company. Remember to treat it like you are buying the whole business. The business could be profitable, but it could also lose money which means that you will lose money.

Most traders will mitigate the risk by not pouring all their capital in one stock. By investing all your money in one company then theoretically you would make more money if that stock did very well. But, if you put all your money in one company and the company goes bankrupt, then you'll lose the entirety of your investment. Instead, traders diversify. If I had $1000 dollars to invest, rather than taking $1000 dollars and placing my faith in one company I would be better off breaking that $1000 dollar up, putting $100 into ten different stocks.

Companies sell stocks as a method of generating capital for growing their business. Businesses need liquid cash to operate, meaning they need the money that isn't tied up or committed to other expenses. A company that wants to expand will issue stocks in the hopes that people will buy them, resulting in cash flow that the company can reinvest into developing new products.

People choose to invest in the stock market as an alternative to saving money in the bank. By putting your money in the stock market and leaving it long term, you are letting your money 'work' over time so that you make more money. Banks try to encourage saving by paying members interest rates. A bank makes a profit by lending money from the pool of its member's money. In return for putting your money in the bank and allowing it to do lend your money to other people, they pay you an interest rate. Interest rates used to be a good incentive for people to save their money in banks. If they put money in the bank, then the value of their money would grow over time with interest rates. Nowadays, interest rates that banks provide are typically too low to even beat the inflation rate which means that if you're keeping your money in the bank long term then your money is losing a small amount of value.

To understand this, you must understand how inflation works. Over time the price of products and services slowly increases. People's wages ideally increase to keep up with the rate of inflation, so that they can still afford a consistent level of goods and services. The downside of keeping your money in a bank account long-term is that the interest rate you receive from the bank won't keep up with the inflation rate. If the price of goods and services rises on average by 2% over the next year, but the bank only pays you .25% interest, then the actual value of your money has gone down. This means that you'll be able to buy fewer goods and services with the same amount of money in the future.

The advantage of investing is that even if you are a long-term, low-risk investor, your money will grow at a rate that keeps up with the rate of inflation. If the inflation rate over the next ten years averages at 2%, and you have a well-diversified portfolio of stocks that returns about 8% per year, then you're beating the inflation rate and making profit. You're not only increasing the dollar amount of your money; the actual value of your money is increasing.

Diversifying your portfolio profit can play a huge role in reducing your risk, especially if you are a long-term investor. While the stock market may have periods of time where it drops in value, the historical trend for the entire stock market is a gradual increase year after year. If you diversify your investments, you might have one or two investments that don't do as well or even perform poorly. However, you can expect the cumulative trend of your stocks to be an increase if you've diversified properly and chosen stocks in reliable companies.

While many people have a perception of the stock market as a place where you can get rich overnight, this requires a mindset that is somewhat akin to gambling. To be a successful investor or trader, you must put in a good amount of work evaluating companies and choosing the right time to buy a stock or enter a market. The one thing this book will not do is teach you how to get rich quick, or how to make money quickly. This book will, however, give you tools to begin trading with well thought out strategies. You will also learn how to minimize risk so that you can profit from your good trades while minimizing losses when you make a bad trade.

This book will cover one of the specific trading mindsets among a wide variety of approaches. This type of trading is known as swing trading. It's a trading that is differentiated by the time frame and the strategies used when a trader is approaching the market. There are three main categories that traders and investors typically fall in to; there is the day trader, the swing trader, and the long-term position trader. While each of these different types of traders will compete in the same markets, the strategies and approaches that they use will differ. They might buy and sell the same securities and commodities even; but the indicators that they will watch for will be different, the signs for when to 'buy' and when to 'sell' will vary.

An average Joe like you and I would be called a retail trader. When we trade on the stock market, we aren't doing it for a firm or a financial agency. Our investing efforts aren't part of a corporate finance plan and we don't run a hedge fund. These people would be referred to as institutional traders. Warren Buffet would be considered an institutional trader because private investors entrust him with their money, and he invests it for them. In order to be an institutional trader, you must meet certain criteria and have the right qualifications. Most of the stock market is comprised of the institutional traders who manage hedge funds and mutual funds. Compared to institutional traders, you or I would be considered small fish. Our volumes are considerably lower. We own less stock and our profits are smaller. We, as individuals, don't have the same impact on a market that an institutional trader might have.

For instance, if a major financial institution suddenly offloads a high volume of stock then this will likely have a noticeable effect on the price of that stock. In this case, investors would see this as a warning sign and the value of the stock would go down. On the other hand, if a major financial institution suddenly acquires a huge amount of stock in a certain company, it may be a sign to investors and traders that they should buy this stock as well.

Financial institutions often have entire teams devoted to the research and analysis of certain stocks, which means retail traders often look to them as a source of information. If a large financial institution makes a move, then traders will assume that there is some meaning behind it.

Just because a financial institution can make these types of waves in the stock market does not mean that they are immune to the risks associated with trading and investing. As a matter of fact, in some cases the opposite is true. Because they have such an enormous number of stocks, it's more difficult for a financial institution to abandon a position when it starts to go south. The high volume also means that there is a higher risk; there is more money on the line. Think of the difference between a massive ship and a small fishing boat. The massive ship can carry more tuna, that's an indisputable fact. But if a storm is coming, the fishing boat can turn around in a hurry; whereas the ship needs more time to change its course.

Even though, as a retail trader, you'll be competing with these major financial institutions, you can take advantage of opportunities that they wouldn't be able to. You will be more flexible and more agile when the stock market changes its course. You'll be able to enter a position quickly when you see an opportunity or exit a position equally fast when things are moving against you. Institutional traders don't have that luxury.

Chapter 1: What Kind of Trader Are You?

When people refer to retail, 'stay-at-home' traders they often call these people day traders. Retail traders can fall into many different categories depending on the type of strategy they employ. But what is the difference between a swing trader and a day trader? Is there a difference?

If you are a retail trader, then there are three categories that you could fall in to. Traders can either be classified as day traders, swing traders, or long-term position traders. You might even fall into more than one of these categories. You could use a mix of all three. The key difference is in the time frame of the position that these three types of traders will use. The three types of trades also require traders with different mindsets and strategies. They require a different degree of focus on the market, and some types of trades require a more active trader.

We talked earlier about the different types of trends, and how long they last. The trader who works with the shortest time frame is the day trader. The day trader looks to ride small, short term fluctuations that last less than a day. A day trader will be less focused on the overall trend in the market, and more focused on the small adjustments that happen throughout the market during a single given trading day. When the market opens, the day trader will have no positions from the day before. Instead, they will choose all new positions. By the time the trading day ends, the day trader will have exited all the positions they chose at the beginning of that day. Day traders can utilize short selling, options, and bullish techniques to make a profit. Day trading tends to lean heavily on technical analysis. A day trader might be less concerned with the actual company than with the patterns in the company's stock on a given day.

The downside of being a day trader is a time commitment. Most day traders use day trading as their main source of income; spending the entire day from market open until close watching movements in the stock market. You can't really be a passive day trader. In order to day trade successfully, you need to have enough time on your hands that you can monitor your positions minute by minute and make decisions as things unfold in the market.

Because the movements in day trading are typically small, the profits are also small. This means that a day trader relies on a high number of smaller successful trades. Hopefully, when you add up all your trades, you will have enough money to pay the bills. This means that a day trader must have a larger amount of starting capital in order to make the profits of day trading worth it. If you don't have a good amount of capital and a willingness to quit your day job, day trading isn't the most practical option. In fact, I recommend that people shouldn't even consider day trading unless they have a healthy amount of experience in the stock market. Most people who attempt to become day traders will fail.

Sure, it is possible to make a lot of money very fast as a day trader. But that means its also possible to lose as much money, just as quickly. Day trading isn't a safe way to get rich, and its not a trading strategy for novice traders. It requires an in-depth understanding of the intricacies of the stock market, and the discipline to study and make high-stress decisions.

If you imagine day trading to be a laid back, work from home type of job, then you'd be mistaken. Day trading is a high-risk pursuit. Day traders must make decisions in a matter of minutes, or even seconds, about high volumes of their hard-earned money. The job does have its benefits; you can work from home and make your money independently of a boss. You don't have to commute to an office every day and you can take a day or two off without getting approval from HR first. These benefits are attached to a job that can be high risk, with a high degree of day traders burning out not long after their first trade.

But there is an alternative option. The risks and the rewards are slightly lower, as is the required investment of time and money. If you picked up this book, then you probably already know that day trading may not be the most feasible option for you as a trader. As a swing trader, you can still maintain a day job if you have access to a smartphone or a computer intermittently throughout the day. For a trader who is still learning the ropes, swing trading gives you more time to consider your positions which mean that the stress factor is slightly lower for a swing trader. Rather than being forced to make a guess on a position in a matter of a few minutes, swing traders can consider their next move over the course of a few hours or an entire day before they decide.

If you picked up this book, then you're interested in the second type of trading. Swing trading is like day trading; you're watching for short- and medium-term positions dependent on smaller adjustments in the overall trend. Swing traders have more time. The medium-term trends tend to move more which means that a swing trader will have the opportunity to profit more from one trade, but they will make fewer trades than the day trader. Slightly larger margins mean that a swing trader doesn't need quite as much capital when they initially invest.

If you want to trade actively, but you don't have the experience or the capital to trade full time, then swing trading is a good option. If you can monitor your portfolio from your phone or work computer, then you should be able to operate as a swing trader. The biggest factor in choosing what type of trader you want to come down to the lifestyle you want and skill level you possess.

The third type of trading that people employ is long term and position investing. While this type of trading doesn't really fit within the scope of this book, many swing traders and day traders will choose to hold these types of positions in order to diversify their strategies. A position investor will plan to hold on to a stock for a significant period; choosing a stock that they think is undervalued or has the potential for growth in the future. Fundamental analysis is the most important thing to a position investor. If you are interested in a company over a long period of time, then you will analyze the fundamentals of stock before deciding to invest. A position investor will probably expect to hold their position for years, using their investment as more of a savings tool than an active trading tool.

Position investing is considered the lowest risk form of investing. If you have a well-diversified investment portfolio then the average of all your stocks should go up over time. If you hold onto those investments through all the dips and peaks, then your initial investment will hopefully have grown.

The most important consideration for choosing which type of time frame strategy you want to use will be dependent on your personality. What is your temperament and ability to handle stress, and how much time do you have to commit to trading? There is nothing wrong with choosing the lower risk route of position investing with the occasional swing trade. In fact, most retail investors and traders fall within this category. For many people, this is the right place to be. If you are more risk-averse, then the stock market may serve better as a savings tool than as an active source of income.

There is a whole spectrum of trading that you can take part in, from position investing to day trading. The trick is to find the strategies and the level of participation that suits your life and your willingness to take risks. If you figure out what type of strategies suit you then you will be more likely to stick with trading and less likely to suffer from the burnout that is common among new traders who bite off more than they can chew. It's not a bad idea to start trading with simpler strategies and slowly move towards more active types of trading. Most experienced traders will have a portfolio that contains a mix of different types of investments with different time-oriented strategies. You can be a swing trader and a day trader and a position investor all at once. Just make sure you know what you're doing so that you don't overwhelm yourself.

There is also a difference in the amount of capital required to begin trading with any of these strategies. Day traders require the most amount of capital to begin. Most day trading accounts require a minimum investment of $25,000. This is not a small amount of money, and more than most beginner investors are willing to use. They require more money because their margins are smaller.

Swing traders require less. You can start a swing trading account with as little as $5000. It would be difficult to swing trade with any amount of capital much lower than that. Some people manage to swing trade with accounts that are as small as $1000, but this makes it difficult to diversify. If you're a long-term position investor, then there is really no minimum threshold. However, the same problems exist for long term investors; with less money, it will be more difficult to diversify, especially if you are managing your portfolio independently.

Chapter 2: How to Buy and Sell Stocks

In order to buy and sell stocks, we must go through someone called a broker. A broker's job is to connect buyers and sellers on the stock market. If you've ever seen videos or pictures of the New York Stock Exchange, you've likely seen brokers moving around between the screens talking on the phone and brokering deals between traders.

You and I can't go to the New York Stock Exchange and start buying and selling shares independently. We must go through a licensed brokerage. With the advent of the internet, the cost of finding a brokerage has gone down and there are more options available that are more attractive to smaller retail traders. This has opened the door to new strategies and has made retail trading more accessible to anyone with a computer and internet access.

It doesn't take a large amount of money or an expensive broker to make some money on the stock market nowadays. The only requirements are the willingness to take on some degree of risk and the ability to read a few different types of charts. A good predilection to market research and financial analysis will also help. All the information you need to be an effective trader is available through your phone or home computer.

There are many different types of brokerages available through the internet, where you can manage your portfolio and make trades in one place. The type of brokerage you choose will depend on the amount of money you're investing as well. We'll talk about this later on in the book, but choosing a brokerage is the first step in trading or investing and it requires some thought and research once you've learned a little more about the different types of trading strategies and what sort of features you consider to be the most important.

When you are looking to buy a stock, you will see two different prices. The first price is called the asking price. It's a little like the 'buy it now price'. As an alternative, you can also buy a stock at the bid price. The bid price will be lower than the asking price which means you can get a better deal on the stock if the broker is willing to part with the stock at that price. Just like any time you make a deal, whether on the stock market or at a garage sale, offering a lower price means that there is a chance you may not get the stock you're bidding for. This means that if you're trying to quickly enter the market in order to capitalize on a trend, you might miss out if you bid and don't get the stock.

Whether a not a broker will sell you the stock for the bid price is dependent on many factors. The stock market is an experiment in the laws of supply in demand which means that a broker will make his or her decision based on these laws. If the stock is in low demand, you may be able to buy it for a price much lower than the asking price. If not, many people are buying the stock then the broker will be much more willing to part with it for a low price.

On the other hand, if the market indicators show that a stock is quickly on the rise and traders are seeing an opportunity forming, then the demand for that stock is probably going to increase. If you offer the broker a bid that's too low, then he'll probably turn it down because he can find someone to pay more for the stock.

Keep this in mind when you are going to purchase a stock. You might be able to save some money by buying a stock below the asking price. But if you have a feeling that the stock is in high demand, don't try and low-ball the broker because they will probably find a more willing buyer and you will lose the stock altogether and miss out on whatever trend you're following.

As traders, we can trade with two different kinds of accounts. When you sign up with a broker you will have the option of choosing one or the other. Most brokerages will give you a choice between the two. For many new traders, they open their account and are asked whether they want to open a cash account, or a margin account and they don't know the difference.

The main difference between a cash account and a margin account is the way they allow you to use your available funds. If you went to a bank and asked to get a card, you'd be given the choice between a debit card and a credit card. If you choose to get a debit card, then the card acts much like a regular wallet. You can only spend the money that you have in your wallet, you can't spend money you don't have on hand. If you choose to get a credit card then you have the option to purchase things, pay the bank back later. When the brokerage gives you the choice between a cash account and a margin account, your options are similar.

If you open a cash account and deposit $10,000 dollars, it means that you can buy $10,000 dollars' worth of stock. It's like a debit card. You can buy as much stock as you want, splitting your account however you want, by purchasing the stock with the cash available in your account.

This is the most straightforward way of managing your money whether you are getting a bank card or opening a brokerage account. However, there is a reason that people decide to get credit cards. With a credit card, you have more flexibility. If you have a bill to pay now, but your paycheck comes next week then you're able to pay the bill and cover it later.

By opening a margin account, you receive flexibility from the broker, who is extending credit to you so that you can buy stocks and pay later. If you open a margin account with $10,000 dollars, you can use the broker's credit to purchase stocks while the $10,000 acts as leverage for the credit.

Let's say that your $10,000 is tied up in stocks that you can't sell at the moment, but an opportunity has popped up that you want to take a position on. You don't have the cash on hand immediately, but you know that in a few days you'll have the cash so you can pay the broker back at that time. The added flexibility of a margin account means you can take advantage of opportunities even when you don't have cash on hand.

The flipside of the margin account, just like with a credit card, is the added risk of borrowing money with the intention of paying it back later. If you leverage your $10,000 to purchase more stocks on credit, then those stocks go down in prices then your losses are more than if you had just purchased the stock in cash. You'll lose on the stock dropping in price, but you'll still need to pay the broker back for the full price. Your broker might also get nervous that you won't pay them back. The broker might make you sell those stocks you have as leverage, and if you are selling them at a bad time then your losses will be even worse. You'll lose not only the money from the bad trade, but you'll lose the stock and the potential earnings from the shares you purchased in cash.

If you want to minimize risk as much as possible, then the best choice is to choose a cash account. This is often a good idea for newer investors. But if you avoid the risk by choosing a cash account then you will also lose out on the added benefits of using a margin account. Some swing trading strategies require a margin account, so you'll be unable to apply these strategies. There are ways to maintain a credit card in a safe and conservative manner, while still enjoying the benefits of having credit. Margin accounts can also be used safely if you minimize the amount of leverage you use and limiting your use of credit to certain scenarios.

Before choosing between a margin and a cash account, make sure you read the terms that apply to your brokerage. Many brokerages have rules for how much you can leverage and minimum amounts for opening a margin account. Once you've finished reading the rest of this book you will have a better idea of what types of strategies you want to use, and which account will be the most suitable. If you want to keep your trading simple and minimize risk when you are first starting out, then consider opening a cash account. But keep in mind the added flexibility and the ability to capitalize on opportunities when you don't have the cash immediately available. A higher potential for profits always comes with added risk, and vice versa.

Once you've opened your account, you'll start to watch the market, maybe even picking a few specific stocks to watch. You're watching in order to choose a good position. When traders refer to a position, they are talking about the stocks that they decide to buy or short in anticipation of the stock moving up or down. The most basic example of a position is buying a stock anticipating that the price will go up in the future so that you can sell it at a higher price.

While it may seem obvious that people make money on the stock market when the prices go up, there also traders whose strategies depend on the stock market going down by using a method called shorting. It's a higher risk strategy that is quite common among day traders and swing traders.

Short selling works like this; a trader has a gut feeling that the price of a stock will drop soon. They've seen the indicators and they think the stock is overvalued for whatever reason, and they anticipate a decline in the price followed by a high volume of traders offloading the stock at the same. But how can a trader profit off this scenario?In this instance, the trader doesn't own any of this stock. So, in order to short sell, he or she borrows shares of that company from the broker and then sells them. Remember that this trader anticipated a drop in the price of this stock. Now that they've sold it, they wait. Eventually they will have to pay back the broker for the borrowed stock. If they were right about the stock price plummeting, then by the time they pay their broker back for the shorted stock they will only have to pay back a fraction of what they bought the stock for. They make their profit in the beginning by selling high and buying low, rather than the ordinary trade which happens in the reverse.

The risk with short selling, of course, is that the price of the stock might go up instead of down. It might turn out that the gut feeling you had about a stock being undervalued was wrong; instead of the price plummeting as you expected, it just keeps going up.No matter how high it goes, you will have to buy the stock back for your broker. If I short $200 worth of shares hoping that tomorrow they will go down, but instead they are suddenly worth $300 this means that I'll have lost $100. You might consider waiting, maybe you mistimed the drop, but the shares might still go down. You wait a few days and now the stocks you shorted are valued at $400. So, you received $200 from short selling, but you owe your broker $400. The dangerous thing about short selling is that you have no idea how high a stock price can go up. If the stock is overvalued and the price has been rising, then there is a chance that it could continue doing that and it may not stop in foreseeable future. With short selling, it's a lot trickier to turn the boat around and minimize your losses.

The advantage of short selling is that when you rely on the stock price going up to make money, you usually must wait much longer to see the price rise. When the price of a stock rises, it usually increases slowly over time which means that someone anticipating a stock price increase must wait longer to see the same profits as a short seller. When the price of a stock drops, it drops quickly due to market psychology. You can make a quick profit with short selling.

Some people question short selling, saying that it poses a moral hazard. Profiting off a market that is going down, or a business that is doing poorly.

The questionable ethics of short selling have led to regulation of short selling which means restrictions on the times that traders can short stocks. For example, you can short sell in a market that's already in recession. The market has been moving upward for a trader to engage in short selling.

In the early days of the stock market, people who try to make money by instigating a price drop. A large group would short sell a stock at the same time. A high volume of short-sellers at once would cause the market to panic and people would start to sell their own shares creating an artificial drop in price.

Proponents of short selling argue that they are doing the stock market a favor. They are helping to predict downturns and warn the public about overvalued stocks. In 2008, short-sellers made billions of dollars by anticipating the collapse of the housing market, short selling a large volume of stocks right before the Great Recession.

Short selling is an important tool because it gives us a method of profiting in all kinds of situations. You don't need to wait for a stock to go up in price in order to make money. You can make money off a stock whose price is going up; known as a bullish stock. You can also make money short selling on a bearish stock. The bull and the bear are classic wall street symbols for the different types of market trends. A bull market is named after the way a bull attack by thrusting its horns up, so a bull market is moving up. The bear market gets its name from the downwards swipe of a bear's claws when it attacks. Financial analysts often refer to stocks being bullish and bearish, while the market might be a bull market or a bear market.

For a market or a stock to qualify as being bearish, then we need to see a downward trend over a given a trend over a period. Not every downward movement in the price of a stock makes the stock bearish. If analysts start referring to a bear market, the stock market would have to have experienced a loss of 20% or more of its overall value. A bear market must occur over an extended period. In 2008, when the stock market experienced a great recession, stocks were bearish for over 17 months.

A bear market is often, but not always, correlated with an economy that is not doing well. When growth starts to slow down in the market, investors begin to feel less confident about the economy. After all, what goes up must always down? Investors see the slowing growth and anticipate a drop. They'll either start investing less or selling off investments to protect themselves from the drop that they anticipate.

When a significant number of investors begin to act this way then the demand for stocks will go down, which means the price of the stocks will go down and the drop will be exacerbated by the collective panic. Many investors begin to fear a bear market when the prices for stocks are peaking but the outlook for the companies, they are investing in begins to drop. The market will remain bearish until investors anticipate it to turn around again.

A bull market happens when the value of the market is increasing over time. Not every increase in the market is bullish, but like bear markets, the market value needs to be increasing for a good amount of time for it to qualify as a true bull market. When the market is bullish, investors will see this as an opportunity. They expect the prices will continue to rise, so they buy stock in order to make some money from the increase.

So, with swing traders buying and selling a stock, they have an opportunity to make money off of the market in a variety of conditions. The simplest approach is buying low and selling high. Making money on a bullish market is less risky, and the most straightforward. It's also the way an investor will make their money if they are waiting for a profit from a long-term investment. If you want to make money on a bullish market, then the best time to buy a stock is often during a bearish market. If you use this approach, you will have to be willing to wait for however long it's necessary for the market to turn around and move upwards again.

The short-selling stock has the potential for quick profits, but they come with higher risk. Short selling is one of the most common methods of swing trading. Unlike buying stock and hoping for a bullish market, short selling requires less patience because the time frame is shorter. You must be aware though, that this means you can lose a lot more in a shorter amount of time. Short selling is a more active swing trading strategy that requires an astute trader who is willing to keep up with market trends as they unfold.

Keep in mind that some brokerage companies, especially for small-time traders, don't offer short selling. For example, Robinhood is a popular app for many beginning investors because it has no trading fees which mean that you can trade with even a small amount of money without your profits being eaten away by fees.

This brings us to our next section where we will discuss the different types of swing trading. Knowing a little bit about these strategies will help you choose a broker. You can identify which brokers have these tools available. An important factor to consider is the fees that the broker will charge. Depending on the amount of money you are trading with, these fees will quickly add up if you're making multiple trades. If you're only using a small amount of money, then you'll spend more money on fees than you'll be profiting. Therefore, it's important to think about the strategy you want to use when you're swing trading before you choose a broker. Different brokers will come with different features and will enable different strategies. The amount of money you start with will also be an important consideration.

Once you've chosen your broker, you will have to decide which type of account is best for you. Whether that's a margin account or a cash account, you will have different advantages depending on the one you choose. Of course, your skill level and your level of experience should be an important factor when you're considering a broker. A margin account might give you more flexibility and might make it possible to achieve higher profits, but the risk will be higher. How much do you want to risk when you are first starting out? There are a lot of things to watch for when you're trading stock; sometimes the best solution is keeping your trades simple when you're first starting out.

We mentioned Robinhood as a popular choice for beginning investors. You can trade with a smaller amount of money because there are no commissions for trades. The biggest downside to using Robinhood is the fact that they don't allow you to short. If you are a beginning investor only interested in trading bullishly, then this won't be a problem. If you're a more experienced investor and you want to tap into the profits from short selling and use strategies that only work on a bearish market, then opening an account with Robinhood will be limiting. There's nothing wrong in starting with simple strategies and smaller amounts of capital. For this, there is nothing wrong with choosing a service like Robinhood while you learn the ropes and do your first trades. You'll save money on commission fees and you will have a relatively simple setup to begin trading. You might read this book and think you've got a pretty good grasp on swing trading and jump right into using multiple strategies on a complex platform. The truth is, once the ticker starts moving and you must make decisions, a lot of the information you retained will be lost in the heat of the moment. Remember, there is nothing wrong with starting out using simple strategies.

You'll also want to think about what the brokerage platforms will provide in terms of technical assistance. Most decent trading apps will give you the ability to monitor your portfolio in real-time, but there are added features that can be helpful when you start using more comprehensive strategies. In order to streamline the process, buying and selling stocks should be as easy as possible through your brokerage account.

In addition to that actual trading of stocks through your broker, many apps offer a comprehensive analysis in real-time. Many apps also offer the added benefit of access to market research and in-depth coverage of certain stocks. This by itself shouldn't be the only selling point. Most of the research provided can be found on your own. If you want to have the research available in one place, then using an app that provides this will be useful but not totally necessary.

What is more useful is finding brokerage fees that can send you text and email alerts about a stock movement. If you're a swing trader then you probably aren't monitoring the market during every minute that it's open, but you should be able to keep close tabs on it especially if you are anticipating a movement. If you are waiting to decide on a position, your brokerage can send you text alerts when the price of a stock goes up or below a certain alert price. This enables you to keep track of your stocks or potential opportunities even while you busy at work or running errands. You never know when an opportunity may present itself.

Stock Options

Another way to add flexibility to your trading strategy is by using stock options. Stock options are especially popular in recent years because they can be an effective way of lowering risk while also giving you the ability to hedge several positions at once without tying up your capital until you know you want to make a move.

Options consist of puts and calls. When you buy a stock option, you are paying a broker to hold a stock a certain price for you. Let's say a new kid moves into the neighborhood, he has a trading card that you think is worth a lot of money. You want to wait to buy it, but you think that other kids in the neighborhood will want it as well. You tell the new kid that you think that trading card is worth $7, and you offer him $2 to hold the price at $7. The next day, the rest of the kids in the neighborhood see the trading card and offer him $10 for it. But you've already made a deal, paying him $2 to hold on to the card for you at a fixed price. You buy the card for the fixed price you've agreed upon, and then turn around and sell it to the kids offering $10. This is essentially how an option works.

When you buy a stock option, you are purchasing the option to buy it and sell it at a higher price later down the road. Let's say instead that you give your neighbor $2 to hold the price at $7 for you. Tomorrow the kids in the neighborhood show up, but they don't think the card is as valuable as you do. They only offer him $5. You decide in that case, not to buy the card from him at $7, because it's not worth as much as you thought. Instead of being out $7, you are only out $2 because you didn't purchase the card outright. You just paid the cardholder to hold it for you at a certain price.

With stock options, you're paying the broker to hold it at a fixed price. If you see a stock that you think might go up, you can buy an option from the broker to hold it at the current price. If the stock goes up, then you will make a profit because the broker will still sell it to you at the discounted price. If it goes down, then you'll only lose the option fee rather than the entire price of purchasing the stock. Stock options allow you to set a price for yourself without committing the amount of capital it would take to buy the stock outright.

The fee that you pay the broker to hold the stock at a price is known as a strike price. In options trading, if the stock doesn't do as well as you'd hoped then ideally you will only lose the strike price rather than the entire price of the stock. If your broker is sitting on a stock valued at $15, you can pay them $3 in order to hold the stock at that price. If the value of that stock goes up to $22 next week, then you pay your broker $15 and then sell the stock. Your call on this option will have made you a $4 profit. What if, however, you pay your broker $3 to hold the stock at $15. Next week the price of the stock drops to $10. If you had bought the stock outright then you would have lost $5. By buying an option on this stock, you instead will only lose the $3 you paid for the strike price.

Typically, options have expiration dates. You can't buy an option and hold onto it indefinitely; the broker will set a day and you must choose to exercise the option by that day. Brokers will usually sell options in sets, with 100 shares per set. It allows you to gain an advantage in several opportunities, without committing to the risk of tying up too much capital. Trading options are a way to keep your portfolio flexible and react to the market, rather than being fixed to a position. It's a way to make your portfolio more diverse even when you are working with a smaller amount of money.

There are major advantages to shifting your strategy towards trading options. On the flip side, they are also more complicated than normal trades. It requires a good amount of organization to manage your options, which is usually done the best when you have some experience as a trader. When you own a stock, then you know what price you bought it for and what you stand to gain or lose at any given time. When you own stocks, there isn't any confusion when you look over your portfolio. If you trade options you will have to pay closer attention to your buy and sell price, as well as your strike price. You must not only sell for a profit but sell for a profit that is large enough to cover the cost of your strike price. Choosing to use an option and selling a stock too early can result in a negative result, even when the trade was positive. It's an easy mistake to make when you are first learning how to trade options.

Another advantage of option trading is the number of opportunities at any given time. Options traders can be flexible where regular bull and bear traders become fixed in a position once they've entered it. For beginner traders, I recommend spending some time using simpler strategies before you start to try options trading. While options trading has an added degree of flexibility, it is much more complicated. There are entire books devoted to different options trading strategies, with strategies much more involved than swing trading strategies. Its good to understand what's out there in terms of potential strategies, so you can plan and choose a broker that will enable you to use these strategies in the future. Like any type of trading, options traders need to be diligent and focused in order to be successful. Passive beginner traders should probably shy away from options trading when they first start.

Exchange Traded Funds

Another way for small-time retail traders to diversify their portfolio is by using exchange traded funds. If you are a beginner and you don't have a lot of initial capital, then exchange traded funds are a good way to stretch your money to create a more diverse array of investments. They are easy to buy and sell and they don't require a large degree of capital to invest in, so they are simple to use and a good way to learn the stock market.

The diversity of exchange traded funds is their main advantage. The spread between the bid and ask price is typically lower so buying and selling are straightforward. Exchange traded funds are a combined list of stocks within a given sector. If you were smart, then you'd choose a sector where you already have a good amount of knowledge. That way you'll know what pieces of information to watch for. Having some technical knowledge about the companies you own share in gives you an advantage because when you are doing market research or research on specific companies, you might notice things that someone else would overlook. Just like if you were to buy a business, you would have more success if you bought a business where you understood the product and the relevant market. You'd know what companies to watch for and what new technologies might cause a change in the market. I recommend that as a beginning investor you pick ETFs in a sector that already interests you, where you won't mind doing research.

Diversification is one of the most important ways to minimize risk. The value of some stocks may drop, but overall the value of a well-diversified portfolio is more likely to go up. If you want to diversify your portfolio as a new swing trader, then this is the cheapest way to do it. ETFs can also be traded using the strategies we've already mentioned, such as short selling and options trading. It's worth reading up on exchange traded funds if you are a new investor and you want to add a little more horsepower to your trading strategies.

Chapter 3: How to Read the Market

By now we have talked about a few different types of trades that a swing trader can use. All these types of trades, whether you are using short selling or options or buying bullish stocks, require you to examine market factors to determine where you are most likely to make a profit. But there are thousands of stocks available on the market which you could take a position with for swing trading, so how do you know which stocks are worth watching? What types of indicators do successful traders look for?

In this chapter, we focus on the tools used by traders and investors to study the value of a stock and to make predictions about our expectations. As traders, we use two different types of analysis to make predictions or guesses about the projected value of a stock. The first type of analysis is called fundamental analysis and when we do fundamental analysis, we are looking at the actual business indicators relevant to stock, like the way we would evaluate the health of a business we were going to buy.

The second type of analysis is called technical analysis. When you look at a financial website like Finviz, you will see dozens of different numbers and indicators as well as numerous charts, all tracking different parts of the stock market. We call these technical indicators. Traders look for patterns and trends in technical indicators to make predictions.

Fundamental Analysis

Fundamental analysis is a way for traders to get insight into the performance of a business over time. Recall that we compared buying stock to buying an actual business. If I wanted to purchase a brick and mortar store, I'd be interested in looking at the numbers of how the business is performing. Fundamental analysis is very similar to the type of analysis you would do if you wanted to buy a business. You'd probably want to know things like how much profit the business is making, or how much debt the business has.

These indicators would give you a good picture of how the business is performing so that you could make a prediction about its long-term prospects.

Is common sense that buying an unprofitable business would be a higher risk than buying a business that was doing very well? But it follows that the profitable business would be much more expensive to buy. We use fundamental indicators to determine whether the price of the stock matches what we think the stock is worth based on our fundamental analysis.

If we wanted to know the profits that a business is making, then we want to know the profit that a stock will get us. The first fundamental analysis measurement is called **earnings per share.** When we buy a stock or a share in a business, we are only buying a small percentage of that business. With earnings per share, we are calculating how much of the profit we will get for our own in the company. You can find the earnings per share of a company by taking the profit of a company and dividing it by the number of shares that a company has issued. The better the earnings per share are, the higher the value it is given by the market. A stock with high earnings per share is seen as valuable because people expect the company to continue to make profits.

The next thing you would want to know about a business you are buying would be the prospects for earning in the future. A company that is profitable today still needs to innovate and compete in the market so that it can continue to be profitable tomorrow.

If you wanted to see how business was growing, you would look at its growth over time. Has growth been stagnant? Has there been a decline in growth over the past few years? By looking at growth over time, you might have an idea of what the prospects look like for the company. Traders and investors use what's called projected earnings growth to determine the prospects for growth of a company so that they can find the value of the company. To find the projected earnings growth you would divide the price of the stock by its earnings per share, and then divide that value by the growth of earnings per share.

Not every analyst will use the exact same formula for calculating projected earnings growth. While this information is typically free to access companies' earnings reports, different companies may use slightly different methods of calculating projected earnings growth. Keep this in mind when you are looking at projected earnings growth so that your comparisons are made using consistent data.

Projected earnings growth is a useful tool when combined with earnings per share. Of course, if you see high earnings per share but a low price for the stock, you might think you are getting a good deal. If you take a closer look and see that the projected earnings growth is low or declining, then that might explain the reason why the stock is discounted.

While you might think you are getting a good deal based on earnings per share, the project earnings growth is a good tool to double-check and evaluate whether the prospects are good for the company and whether that high earnings per share will continue.

The same applies to stock with the opposite fundamentals. Maybe you see a stock that has low earnings per share, or the price for the stock seems too high relative to the earnings that you'll receive. Based on these fundamentals you might conclude that the stock is overvalued. However, a high projected earnings growth might give you enough reason to suspect that the prospects for the company look very good, even if their actual earnings per share are low now. After all, if you are long term investment then you will be looking for companies that will grow over time. You could argue the projected growth earnings are equally important as earnings per share for a long-term investor.

A company can evaluate the value of its own stock, which might be different from what the market will pay. This is known as the price equity ratio. A company uses its own fundamentals to determine the value of its stock and then compares it to the value given by the market. Using this ratio can help you determine if a company is undervalued or overvalued. A company with a high price equity ratio may be overvalued, while a company with a low-price equity ratio might be undervalued.

Another way to earn money through owning stocks is in dividends. Dividends are returns paid by the company for the shares of that company which you own. It's like the company giving you a small piece of their profits in return for owning some stock. Some people choose to reinvest their dividends in order to extend their ownership of a company. Not all the company's income is paid out in dividends though. A good percentage of the money earned by a company goes back into the company to pay expenses and grow. Another fundamental that traders can look for in a company is the dividend payout ratio.

This amount of income that goes back to the shareholders, relative to the total income with the dividend payout ratio you are basically finding out; how big of a cut am I getting, relative to the entire pie?

Some companies will have higher dividend payout ratios, so this is another type of fundamental. Obviously the higher the price, the higher you would hope to get in return for the dividend payout. If you want to know how much you are making in dividends relative to the price you are paying for the stock, you would look at the **dividend yield**. You can use the dividend to compare the amount you will get in dividends relative to the price, and then compare this across companies. If the dividend yield is low compared to stocks at similar prices, then this is a negative indicator.

Companies need to own assets in order to function. Assets can be anything from machinery to materials, to intellectual property. Assets cost money, which means that the return on these assets is important to shareholders. You want to know that the assets are not only being paid for but that they are paying for themselves. If a company has a lot of assets, but their income is low relative to these assets, then this might be a red flag as a potential investor. The company is spending a lot of money on these assets, but the returns aren't that impressive relative to what the company has invested. The fundamental used to determine this is known as return on equity. To find equity, take the cost of the assets less the debt incurred to buy those assets. Then divide the company's income by that number. This will provide you with a return on equity.

Keep in mind that what is considered 'good' return on equity will depend on the industry. Different industries will require different assets, so the cost of operating the business and the margins will be slightly different. The overhead costs in one industry will be completely different from one type of company to the next.

An airline may have very expensive assets with smaller margins than an insurance company. Don't confuse yourself by comparing the return on equity of two companies in totally different sectors, because the comparison won't mean much. Instead, compare the return on equity for similar companies. If you are looking at buying stocks in Northwest Airlines, compare their return on equity to that of Lufthansa. Then you can compare the efficiency of two companies that provide the same service which requires similar assets.

On the other side of equity, a company also will manage some level of debt. While debt may seem like a dirty word to the individual, it is a tool that corporate managers can use to leverage their capital in order to grow and expand. Companies will take on debt in order to buy equipment or hire specialists to design a new product line. It's not unusual for companies to have some amount of debt for a variety of reasons. If a company manages its debt effectively, then they can drive expansion.

If you were going to buy a business, you would want to know if that business was in debt and why. You'd also probably ask if the company had an effective plan to pay off the debt. How much debt does the business have, relative to its assets and earnings? If we are planning to trade, we would ask the same question about a company whose stock we considered taking a position on. In order to make an assessment on a company's debt management, we would look at the fundamental known as the debt to equity ratio.

How much does the company owner in assets, and how much are those assets worth? What is the ratio of this equity to the level of debt the company has taken on? The debt to equity ratio will help us answer these types of questions. For the most part, it's a good sign if a company has less debt than equity.

The next fundamental and the one that brings us back to our first point will help us determine whether the company is profitable or not. If I want to buy a bike shop, the obvious questions would be; how many bikes do you sell per month or per year? How much money do you make on repairs? Now apply those questions to a stock purchase. How much product has the company sold, be it goods or services? Multiply this by the value of all these goods or service, and you will end up with total revenue.In short, you're looking at how much money the company is taking in. Ideally, you'll be looking for a company whose total revenue is steadily increasing if you're interested in a long-term investment. Conversely, if a company has shown a steady decline then the stock price will also decline.

Why is Fundamental Analysis Important

To summarize; if you're a swing trader then you should take an interest in fundamental analysis. Knowing the health of a company that you want to buy a share of is the first step to investing and trading intelligently. Just like buying a business, you would want to know how that business is doing, and how it will do in the future.

With the accessibility of the internet, these fundamental indicators should be easy to find. Publicly traded companies should have earnings reports, investor reports, or financial reports which are tailored towards prospective investors doing research on the health of their company. While at first, it might seem daunting to look through these extensive reports, it is invaluable to you as a trader. Now that you understand which fundamentals to look for, you narrow the scope of your research and study important indicators more efficiently.

Fundamental analysis is also helpful because you will be able to compare the health of companies within the same sector. When you limit your research to a sector then the fundamentals will have appropriate context. With fundamental analysis, you are acknowledging that the price of the stock does not tell the entire story on its own. Look at the health indicators of a company, as well as the macroeconomic influences. The see how other companies are performing in the same circumstances. Try and give yourself a complete picture of the business before you decide to buy stock in the company. At the end of the day, treat it as if you are buying the entire business. What sort of questions would you ask the previous owners before risking your hard-earned capital?

Technical Analysis

We mentioned earlier that there are two different types of analysis that swing traders apply when they are trying to evaluate potential positions. Now, you have learned how to research the performance of a company, and how its internal indicators can influence your decisions on trading. That is the basis for fundamental analysis.

The second type of analysis is called technical analysis, and it involves the study of patterns in order to make decisions about trading positions. Technical analysists use historical data and statistics to examine patterns in the stock market. While these patterns may have variations, there are some patterns which are consistent and knowing how to recognize characteristics of these patterns will enable you to anticipate movements and make judgments about the psychology of the market.

While you are anticipating movements in the market and trying to determine your own positions, there are millions of other traders trying to do the same thing. Around the world, many of these traders are watching the candlestick charts and trying to make the same predictions that you are trying to make. All these traders are competing with the same thought in mind; making a profit.

Market psychology is important because sometimes the stock market anticipating a movement can become a self-fulfilling prophecy. If thousands of shareholders think that a stock price will plummet and they decide to sell off their stocks in a mass exodus, then the price of that stock will plummet. As a swing trader, you are trying to profit off short-term movements in the market. These short-term movements are often caused or exacerbated by the collective hive mind of traders anticipating the same thing. So, it is important for a swing trader to be able to use technical indicators to give them a clear picture of how other people are trading.

Technical analysis is dependent on economic theories and theories about the stock market that analysts have developed over time after studying the historic movements of the market. While fundamental analysis gives you a snapshot of a company and some indicators of long-term health, technical analysis is a more direct approach to try and predict stock prices using statistics.

Much of the market depends on the laws of supply and demand. Supply and demand will ultimately be the determinants of the market price of a stock. The more people want a stock, the higher the demand is. The demand for a stock will decrease when the price that stock increases. The more people are willing to pay for something, the higher the supply will go. Supply and demand interact with each other in markets until they reach a level of equilibrium. The price of the stock will sit at this equilibrium point.

On the stock market, the price of a stock is determined by the market factors affecting supply and demand. Many trade theorists believe that the price of stock accounts for all the factors in the market, which means that the price of a stock always reflects the true value of that stock determined by supply and demand. Trade theorists who follow this school of thought believe that the price is the only real indicator of all these elements combined. This is a belief held by many technical analysts.

The belief that the price of a stock is the best indicator of the market is a key component Dow Theory. If you follow the stock market, then the name Dow should be very familiar to you. The Dow Jones Industrial Average is a major index in the modern stock market.

It was named after Charles Dow, the founder of the Wall Street Journal and the architect for many modern theories of the stock market that are now important tenets for technical analysis. The Wall Street Journal started as a two-page pamphlet for investors in the 1870s but was eventually transformed into a full-fledged newspaper.

Charles Dow was an early component of the idea that the price of a stock reflected all the supply and demand factors in the market, and the market was always at the efficient equilibrium based on current market characteristics. In economics, this is referred to as the efficient-market hypothesis.

In the stock market, a stock has three directions in which it can move. A stock price can either move up, down or sideways. In science people say 'every action has a reaction. Dow believed the same thing about the stock market. Everything that happens in the economy, or to a business and their market, will influence the movement of stock prices within that market.

Technical analysts look for trends or movements. There are three different types of trends or movements, as defined by the Dow Theory. Number one is the main movement. This is the overall trend in the market, the long-term trend. This trend can be a few months long or even a few years long. This trend could either be downward, or bearish. The trend can also be upward, or bullish.

Within the main movement, there are other smaller movements. A graph that showed the movement of an index over the last six months might show an overall trend moving in the same direction. If we look closer, 'zooming in' on the chart, then we will see that within the bigger primary trend there will be smaller upward and downward movements that last a shorter amount of time.

The next category of movements is called the medium swings. These medium swings may last from a few weeks to a few months. They generally move about 30-60% of the main movement. As a swing trader, you will be looking for trends within this time frame.

If you were to zoom in on the chart even closer, you would see that within even the medium swings, there are upward and downward movements that may only run from a few hours to a few weeks. According to Dow Theory, these are called short swings. While the main movement may be heading in one direction, short swings and medium swings may move up and down. These medium and short swings are the types of movements that swing traders and day traders look for because they are shorter term.

Each of these movements can also be broken down into terms explained by the dynamics of market psychology. The breakdown splits each movement into distinct 'phases', each phase representing an action or reaction from traders as economics events unfold within the market. During the first phase, traders who first see the writing on the wall begin to take a position on a stock, usually going against the grain of what the rest of the market is doing. This phase is called the accumulation phase. During the accumulation phase, not much happens to the price of the stock because most investors are still trading with the current, and those traders who anticipate the change make up only a small percentage of them. After some time, the market begins to catch on that a change is either starting to take place or is about to take place. This phase is when the largest amount of movement happens to the price of a stock. People start to catch on to the coming movement, and mass amounts of investors begin to take a position. This phase is called the public participation phase. Ideally, as a trader, we'd like to get our position before this phase so that we can enjoy the benefits of it. After these first two phases, the trend will play out but eventually it the trend will begin to slow. The third phase starts when the first investors begin to sell off their stocks and leave the position in order to make money elsewhere.

The next important tenet of Dow Theory is the one that we have already discussed, on which the other rules are based. That is the belief in the efficient market hypothesis, which means that all relevant information is already reflected in the price of the stock. According to the Dow theory, every new piece of news or information about a company will be quickly interpreted and reflected in the price of a stock. If new information about a company came out during the trading day, then this information will quickly affect the price of that stock.

When Down was creating his first pamphlets to interpret trends in the stock market, indexes worked a little differently. Companies were far apart and on opposite sides of the country. When people first began using indexes to measure the overall trend in the economy, they primarily made the index from a combination of railroad companies and manufacturing companies. These different types of complementary companies typically moved in the same direction; if factories were making more money and increasing their output, then railroads would be moving a lot of raw materials and finished product across the country. The Dow Jones Industrial Average was created with this idea in mind. The performance of these companies should be moving in the same direction, on average. When these companies start to move in opposite directions of one another, it is a sign that a change will take place in the market soon. This methodology is still in use and it makes up another part of the Dow Theory. The average of the indexes must be moving in the same direction in order to indicate a trend.

In addition to the indexes moving in the same direction, there is another way to reaffirm the existence of a trend. One of the most basic indicators that swing traders use is volume. Volume is the number of trades made during a given period for a certain stock. There are a number of reasons why people might trade a stock, so if the stock price changes but the volume are low then that doesn't necessarily mean a trend exists. But if the price of stock changes, and there is a high volume meaning that a lot of traders are buying and selling that stock as the price changes, then this is a good indication that you are seeing the beginning of a trend.

The last tenet of Dow Theory has to do with the end of a trend. If you are watching a trend and wondering when it will reverse, trying to anticipate that best time to leave your position, then this tenet is important. If you watch a trend, you will see that the trend often doesn't remain consecutive. There might be small reversals within the larger movement itself. If you react to every one of these small reversals, then you might leave your position at the wrong time.

These small dips within the overall trend are referred to as noise; they don't always mean much. Eventually, one of those small reversals will stick and the trend will change. It's very difficult to tell the difference, as the market is making small upwards and downwards movements all the time.

Therefore, according to the Dow Theory, we should assume that the trend is continuing until we have very clear indicators that the trend is ending.

While it is impossible to accurately determine whether a movement is a real reversal or not, technical analysts use different sell signals to make an educated guess on whether they should sell or keep holding. These signals can be helpful in determining the reversal of trends, but more importantly, this will tell you what other traders are watching for when they are anticipating a trend reversal. We'll outline some of the more common sell signals that technical analysts use. Again, it's important to note that these signals don't always tell us the correct answer, and we'll have to consider other indicators and market factors before we make a decision on what position we want to take.

Below, we have an example of a very common sell signal at what could be the reversal of a bear market.

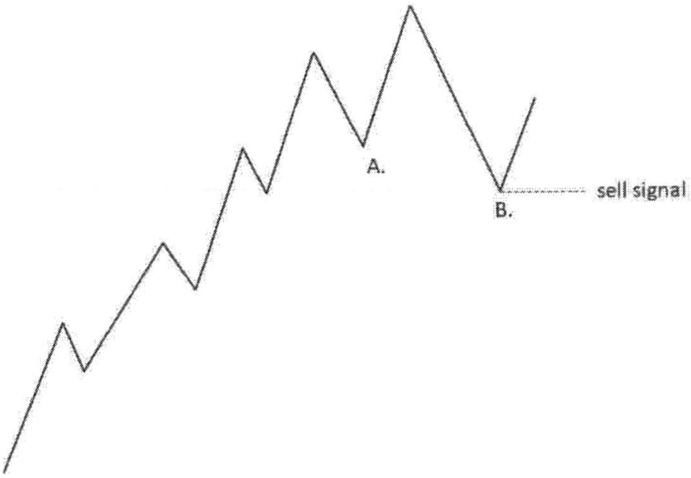

You can see that the market has been bearish for some time, although there is noise in the upward trend. So far you have ridden out the noise and the price of the stock continues to grow, which means if you held on to the stock through these small reversals then you stand to ride with the growth. But how would you know when the reversal is an actual reversal and not just noise? While there is no way to know for sure, there are signs that you can look for. On this chart you see that the stock price has its highest peak after point A, and then drops again to point B. The price of the stock at point B is lower than the last trough and almost as low as the trough before that. For many traders, they would take this as a sell signal because the price of the stock is struggling to rise past its last peak. After point B, the stock price rises again, and you wait. If the stock drops again and reaches point B then this is the place where you will decide to sell.

Whether you decide to use this sell signal, or you decide to continue to wait, understanding these sell signal signals will give you a better picture of what other traders on the market are doing. You may see a high volume of sales of that stock after the price dips below this selling point, which might cause it to dip further. This is an example of why technical analysis and market psychology go hand and hand. The attitude of the market will be reflected in the price of the stock as well as the volume at which it's being traded. Anticipating what other traders are doing will give you a leg up when you are competing on the stock market.

Recall that short sellers make their money on bearish markets by selling high and buying low. This means that they will be watching for reversals when the stock market is on a downward trend because they want to buy at the lowest point, they possibly can in order to make the biggest margin. If they pay back their broker too early, then they will miss out on the potential profits from waiting until the price drops further. Just as traders will use sell signals on a bull market, short sellers will look for signals on a bear market. Those signals will look similar, but the movements will be in the opposite direction. Below is an example of a reversal signal in a bear market; the kind a short sell might look for.

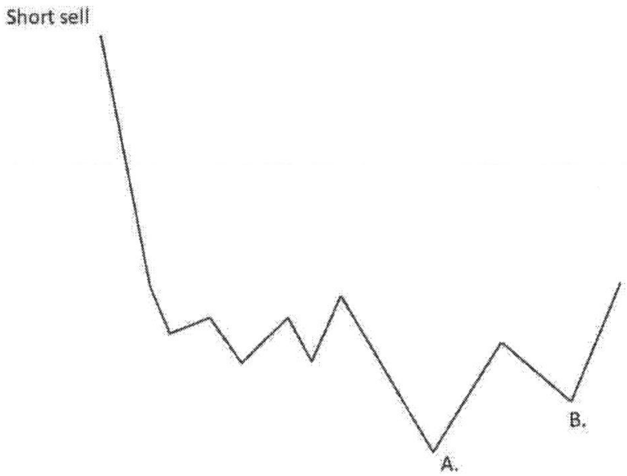

The market drops significantly, and at a very fast rate from where you short sold the stock. You want to maximize your profits though, and the stock might continue to drop so you will wait until you are as close to the floor of the bear market as you can get. The absolute lowest point in the trough as far as we know is at point A. You see that the price moves up again after point A and then does a small reversal and heads back down to point B. For many short-sellers, point B would be a sell signal because the price of the stock failed to drop lower than the lowest trough, which means that the bearish movement might be starting to lose some steam.

Again, there is no way to know with absolute certainty what will happen after point B. It could go down quite a bit further. But, if you are trying to anticipate the attitude of the market then B could be a signal to bullish traders that it's a good time to buy the stock, which means that the price of the stock might continue to rise. Remember to keep track of the volume so that you can try to distinguish noise from reversals.

This type of bearish reversal indicator can also be applied when you are looking to buy a stock, and you want to purchase it at its lowest price. You would wait through a bear market and continue watching to buy right before the trend reverses. So, buy signals and sell signals are very similar; after all the goal is to anticipate the moment when the market turns around and the trajectory changes. In these instances, low relative volumes around the peaks and troughs will give you a clearer picture of whether or not the reversal has any significant power behind it.

The most important thing about technical analysis is the belief that the movements in the stock market aren't completely random. Although there is a degree of randomness, which is why it takes time to learn, there are patterns and traders can learn from those patterns in order to improve their profits. A pattern is when a movement or a series of movement repeat themselves. If you looked at the picture of the stock market over long period of time, you'd see that it moves in cycles. It moves up slowly for a long period of time and then crashes for a while before repeating the process again. Stock traders often use the adage; "what goes up must come down". This is completely true, and the stock market has always followed this pattern. The difficult part of trading, though, knows *when* it will go up or down. Technical analysts are constantly trying to study patterns in order to determine the answer to that question.

Remember that the Dow Theory believes that the stock market is perfectly efficient, which means that the price of a stock will always consider every market factor and it will always reflect the true value of that stock. But there are many traders and investors out there who believe that isn't the case, and they build their entire trading strategies around theories that go against certain tenets of Dow Theory. In fact, there is good evidence that enforces the idea that stocks can be overvalued or undervalued, depending on market factors.

For example, if a certain company is gaining a lot of notoriety, then the price of that stock will likely increase. People will start to see it as more and more valuable, and the price of the stock will reflect that increase in value people have perceived. This can cause a stock to be overvalued, though. This type of overvaluing can be what causes bubbles to form; the value of a stock gets so inflated, and at some point, the bubbles bursts and the value of the stock drops. Afterward, it may take quite a bit of time for the stock to rise back to value before the bubble popped.

On the other hand, it's not unusual for a stock to be undervalued. It might be overlooked by the market even though its dividends and projected growth are solid. A tech company that has made a lot of headlines, promising to bring tourists to Mars in the next ten years will probably pull more investors than a waste management company, even if their fundamentals are the same. As a savvy investor, you shouldn't be afraid to dig a little deeper to try and find stocks like this that are overlooked by other investors. That's why it's important to have a solid understand of fundamental analysis before you start swing trading. It will help you make a more informed decision on what types of stocks you want to choose.

Dow Theory may not apply to all situations, but it's important to understand the concepts if you are trading with a certain psychological strategy in mind. In many cases, you are more focused on what other traders are doing and how the market is moving in patterns, rather than with the actual fundamentals of a company. This can be just as important as fundamentals if you're a swing trader or a day trader through. Oftentimes the upward and downward movements you are hoping for are caused by the market's reaction as well as psychological

The challenge of technical analysis is choosing which indicators work the best for you as a trader. Most technical analysis is a mixture of market psychology and statistics, so not all strategies will work all the time. Traders may rely solely on technical analysis and find success with that approach. Other traders may find that fundamental analysis is the most important tool they have because of the strategies they use. The type of strategies you use and the indicators that you pick will depend on your approach to swing trading. The type of companies and the sector you choose will also play a role because different indicators will be important in different industries.

While only using technical analysis might cause you to overlook the fundamentals of certain companies, fundamental analysis may not always give you a complete picture either. If you only use fundamental analysis, then you would miss an opportunity to study the market psychology and to interpret patterns in the movement of stock prices. If you want to be a dynamic swing trader, then you should have some understanding of both types of analysis. One type of analysis won't give you every relevant indicator. Skilled swing traders will review the fundamentals of a company to make their own evaluation of its health, and then they will take what they know and examine the movement of that stock up until now.

When you choose a stock, you will have to decide which type of strategy will work best with that given stock. Maybe you have a strategy in mind, so you will choose your stock by looking to see if the characteristics of the stock will fit with your strategy. In technical analysis, you will be looking for stocks with certain degrees of volatility so that you can study the historical trends of that stock. Oftentimes day traders will look for stocks based on their movements and the current environment in the stock market rather than on the characteristics of the company. They want to capitalize on the small reversals and adjustments rather than a company that has fundamentals.

If you're using fundamental analysis, then the fundamentals will depend on the length of time that you are willing to hold on to that stock, or whether you want to short sell it or hold it for a long bullish trend. If you want to get on board with a stock that has been hyped up, and you think eventually the stock will have a bubble effect, then you'll be interested in different fundamentals than if you wanted to buy a stock and hold on to it long-term.

If you aren't fixed on a strategy, then choose a company that interests you that you don't mind researching. Read about how current events are impacting the share price of that company, and how the company is performing in the current economy. Decide the strategy you would like to use based on your research and continue to monitor the company's health and progress. If you wanted to buy a business, then think about the economy that the business is trying to survive in. What types of external factors will help or put pressure on that company?

So how can you use technical analysis? The first thing that might want to know is how these types of graphs can be accessed, and how you can keep track of these movements and their volume in real-time. There are several good financial websites that will update you on the stock market in real-time. Most of these websites use the same type of chart. Financial websites tend to be a little bit more detailed than typical line graphs like the ones shown above. Although the financial sites will use a graph that is very similar, there are added elements which show more details about the movements of the stock prices.

The most common type of chart employed by swing traders and day traders is called a candlestick chart. Candlestick charts get their name from their appearance, which looks like candles with wicks coming out at either end. The length of the wicks and the length of the candlestick are certain indicators about the movement of that stocks price. Each candlestick represents a set amount of time, depending on how close you are looking. You can look at candlestick charts that represent a day, a week, or longer. You can look at charts where each candlestick represents the movement of the price of that stock on a given day. The characteristics of these charts will be identical whether you are trading stock indexes, forex, or commodities.

The image below is an example of a candlestick chart. In this chart, black candlesticks represent a decrease while white candlesticks represent an increase. Other charts may come in red and green, with green meaning an increase and red meaning a decrease. As you can see, the basic shape of the candlestick chart is like the shape of the line graphs we viewed earlier. The candlestick chart follows the flow of a line graph but it's broken down into segments which reveal more information about the price movement.

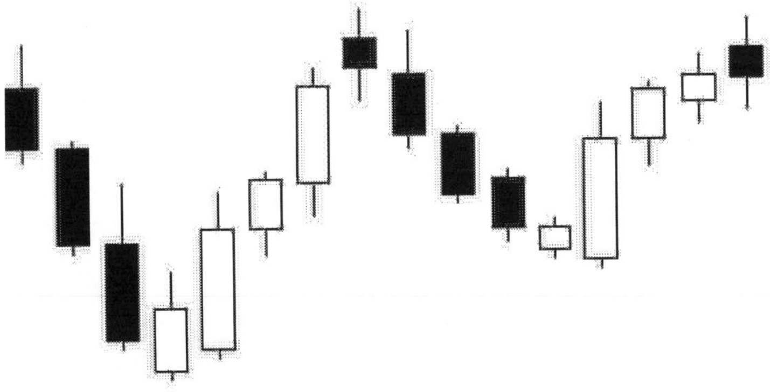

A candlestick chart is a dynamic tool because in one place we can tell a few things about a stock. If we want to break our chart into a day-by-day pieces, then the candlestick can tell us the price of the stock when the market opened, the highest price that the stock reached during that trading day, the lowest price of the stock at the trading day, and the price of the stock when the day closed. The bottom wick is used to show the lowest price of the day and the tops wick stretches up to the highest price of that stock during the same period. The body of the candle follows the wick depending on where it closed throughout the day. If the top of the candle has no wick, then the price of the stock closed at its highest price for the day. If the bottom of the candle has no wick, then it closed at its lowest point for the day.

So, from one chart you can see not only the price of a stock but how it moved throughout the day and through the days preceding. Being able to read a candlestick chart will help you have a clearer picture of the trend that this stock is moving on, and how the market perceives the stock.

When you are trading on the stock market, then you will either take the position of a buyer or a seller. If you haven't decided on what position you'd like to choose, then you exist somewhere in the middle. The stock market works because at any given time there should be buyers and sellers available who are constantly impacting the supply and demand of a stock. The candlestick chart illustrates the movement caused by these two opposing forces; the buyers and sellers. Throughout the day, if there were more buyers than sellers, then the body of the candle will be high and have a short top wick. If there were people trying to offload the stock, and the supply of the stock increased while willing buyers decreased then the candle will have a long body and a short bottom wick.

Remember that technical analysis is all about identifying trends and patterns. In Dow Theory, we talked about how traders look for certain buy and sell signals based on the volume and trajectory of a stock. A candlestick chart will be your best friend in providing you with the information needed to identify the buy and sell points. Remember to keep an eye on the volume of a stock, because trends need to be confirmed by volume even when you are looking at a candlestick chart.

Just as there are technical trends to be identified on a line graph, there are certain patterns that may appear in candlestick charts. The appearance of certain candlesticks in sequence with one another or the frequency of certain types of candlesticks may be indicative of certain movements or trends. The longer a candle is, the more movement there has been in the stocks price.

If the candlestick is long as has a shorter wick on top then the trend for the day was bullish, the meaning it was moving up. If the candlestick is long but the wick on the bottom is short, then the stock price has a bearish trend. Use the volume of the stock to decide whether these movements are noise or if there is a good indication of a trend.

Again, technical patterns on the stock market are not reliable all the time. It's important to emphasize that if this were true, then it would be too easy to predict where the market would go next. If the patterns were always consistent and readable, then trading would be easy money because you could always predict the outcome of a trend. On the other hand, there are some very common candlestick patterns that appear quite frequently. They may not always result in the exact same outcome. Just like all the other indicators we have talked about, these patterns are another indicator that you would use to reinforce your confidence in a position. No indicator is proof by itself, but if the technical indicators and the fundamental indicators match one another then your position will at least be educated and informed.

Candlestick patterns can infer one of two outcomes; they may be a sign that the current trend will continue, or they may be a sign that the trend is about to change or reverse. The type of trend the candlestick predicts depends on the order and shape in which the candlesticks appear.

The following candlestick is a type of reversal that occurs when the market goes from bearish to bullish. In this pattern, there are three black downward-moving candlesticks. The third black candlestick shows that the stock closes very close to its low point. The next day, the stock opens lower than it closed the day before, but it overcomes the last downward candlestick. If you see this pattern during a bearish market, then it is usually a very good sign that the trend is reversing. In most cases this trend will be an accurate prediction of a reversal. This pattern is known as the **three-line strike**.

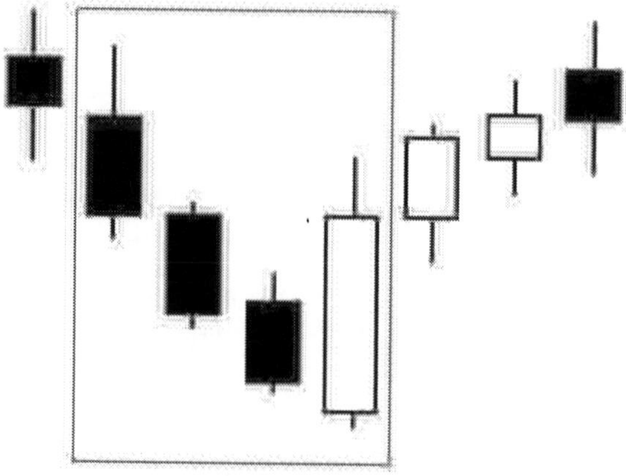

The candlestick pattern in the following picture will usually occur after a peak high. Notice the significant gap between the first two black bars. This means that the stock opened at a price which was significantly lower than the price from the day before. You can see that in this pattern there is an abrupt drop in value that happened after the trading day closed. This type of gap could form outside of trading hours as the result of some piece of news about a company that impacts its stock negatively. Maybe the company released a financial report that wasn't very promising, or the evening news reported a recall on one of their products. This pattern is a very good sign that the price of the stock will continue downward. This pattern is known as two black gapping.

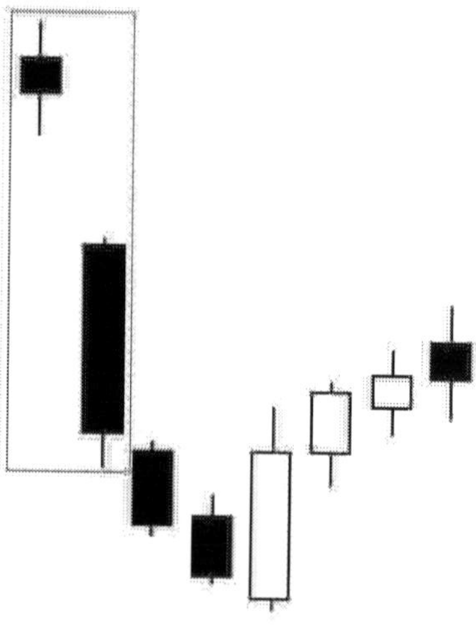

The next candlestick pattern also occurs at the end of a peak, as a bearish reversal pattern. This pattern is denoted by three black candlesticks dropping after a peak. This many consecutive days of significant price drops is a sign that this bearish trend will only continue. Traders will see this and lose confidence in the stock, exiting their positions and further exacerbating and continuing the drop. Most of the time, if you see this candlestick pattern then you can predict with confidence that this trend is going to stick and the stock will remain bearish for some time. This candlestick trend is called three black crows.

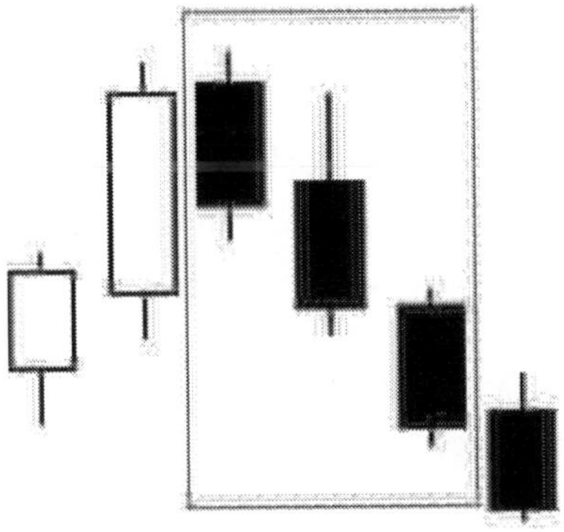

The three black crows are a bearish reversal pattern, there is an opposite reversal pattern which signifies the end of a bearish trend. The following picture shows the end of a bearish pattern followed by three consecutive days of prices trending upwards. Both of these reversal patterns tell us something about the momentum of the stock, and how trader confidence is growing as the pattern continues. In this case, we can have confidence that this bullish trend will continue on a bullish pattern. The downward momentum pattern is called three black crows, while this upward momentum pattern is called three white soldiers.

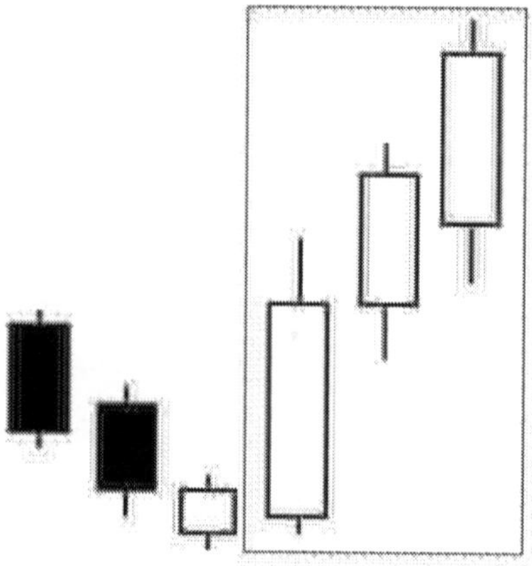

In the next candlestick pattern, the stock price is on an upward trend as denoted by the white candlesticks for the first two days. The following day, traders anticipate the trend will continue so the stock opens at a higher price. In this case, though, the momentum on the upward trend slows down significantly after the price increase and actually goes down by the end of the day. The decrease in trader confidence creates another downward gap on the following day. Usually, this candlestick pattern is an indication that the stock has peaked and will likely not go higher. The failure of the stock to keep its momentum may actually cause it to drop even further in the coming days. This candlestick pattern is called the evening star.

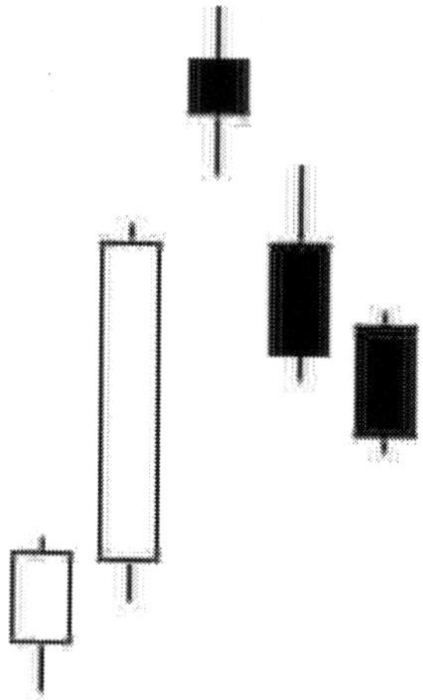

The evening star usually scares investors away because it causes them to anticipate a new downtrend. On the opposite end of the cycle, we have a pattern known as a morning star. The morning star appears at the end of a bearish trend. The morning star is a sign of new hope that inspires investors and gives them confidence after a downward cycle. As you can see in the following picture, the downward trend continues for a while but fails to maintain its momentum at the bottom of the trough. While the morning star alone isn't enough to confirm a reversal, it might inspire the beginning stages of a bullish cycle as traders begin to take positions again as confidence grows.

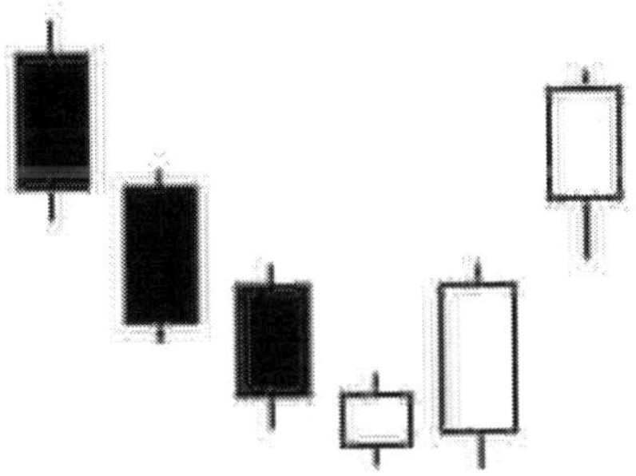

While not all candlestick patterns will be a sure sign on their own, you can combine what you know about these technical patterns with what is happening in the market. While patterns do occur, the market also has enough randomness to keep it from being completely predictable. That doesn't mean there aren't recognizable characteristics of certain trends that are worth taking note of. Being able to recognize these patterns won't be the single answer to trading successfully, but its another tool which you can add to your fundamental analysis and market research to give you a better understanding of the stock market.

Remember that the most important thing you can learn from a candlestick chart is the perception that the market has about a given stock. The movement of a candlestick chart gives us more information than just the change of the stocks price. At any given time, you are not the only trader who is watching stock and trying to anticipate the next move. Millions of other traders are doing the same thing that you're doing; trying to guess what will happen next. If you know how to read a candlestick chart and you can interpret the market psychology correctly, then you'll be in a better position to act on a position.

The tricky thing about the stock market is the way this collective mindset among traders can influence that actual outcome. If a popular analyst puts out a statement that says the price of a stock will go down, and you'd be wise to exit your position on that stock, then you might see a high volume of people selling that stock the next day. The collective psychology of traders does influence the way the prices move. When we talk about trader or investor confidence, we are referring to a collective willingness among traders to start buying a stock. Usually, this collective confidence will spread among other investors, and the belief in a future trend among many traders will make the trend more likely.

This isn't always the case though, and that's a fortunate thing because we make the most money when we see something that the rest of the market doesn't. Short sellers make money when they bet against a company. You make money on a bullish stock when you buy it low, believing that it will soon be worth much more. The fact that traders will often bet in different directions is what makes the stock market so challenging, but what opens the door to profits.

Chapter 4: The Swing Trader

With some understanding of technical analysis and fundamental analysis, you will already be ahead of most beginner traders when you enter your first trade. Beyond the research you can do, there are a handful of other aspects of trading that often get overlooked but that will become obvious over time. These things fall into the category of "stuff you wish someone had told you when you started swing trading". Luckily, this book is here to help.

Swing trading is like a test that requires constant studying a revision. You should treat it like an important test or an important paper that requires good research. If you research effectively, then you will profit. If you get lazy with your research, then you might miss obvious signs that would have led you to make a different decision in the first place.

On the flip side of that, don't get slowed down by trying to find a position that ticks all boxes of a perfect bet. You should be detailed with your research, but ultimately there are some trades where you will need to trust your gut above all else. This is a skill that is developed over time, and so you will get better at it. But you won't be able to analyze every technical and fundamental element on every trader.

This is where things like organization and good record keeping come in to play. As you enter more and more positions, you will notice certain indicators that will match your mindset and your strategy better than others. Sure, there are no indicators that are 100% foolproof, so don't try to look for those either. But your mindset and the type of trading you engage in will make some indicators more important than others. As you learn to trade more efficiently, you will know which indicators to look for right away based on the characteristics of a certain company. Don't forget about all the other indicators, but in some instances, there are certain indicators which she is highlighted about the others. If things don't line up with your strategy, don't force yourself to take a position just for the sake of trading. Start out with fewer, smaller trades and slowly expand your trading as you learn and practice. Stay organized and focused and eventually it will come together.

If you choose to participate in swing trading over other types of trading, then you are probably most interested in the time frame that swings trading presents. You are more flexible than both a day trader and a long-term position investor. If things are going well, you don't have to remove yourself from a position the way a day trader will. If things are going poorly then you don't have to ride out the roller-coaster cycles the way a position investor has to. Your advantage over the long-term investor is to seek opportunities that look good at that moment, rather than keeping your capital tied up in long term prospects.

In addition to these advantages you are also susceptible to risks that are unique to a swing trader. Because you hold your position longer than a day trader, the effects of a bad trade will be drawn out and may result in higher losses. The day trader can respond to any movements or price changes because all their positions last less time than a day. A swing trader is more likely to hold a position overnight. Even though the stock market closes, the price of stocks can change after hours. If this happens then you are stuck holding your position whether that position is a good one or not.

Remember that the stock market represents shares in companies that operate and exist outside of the stock market. Business news and company developments don't turn off for the day just because the stock market closes. A company could put out a press release that significantly affects the price of stock even after the market has already closed, leaving investors nervously sitting on their hands until the market opens again. Examples of events that could shape stock price after hours include secondary offerings and financial releases. You will have to be aware of the impact these could have on your position.

When a company issues stock, it usually doesn't release all the available shares at once. The company will hold on to a certain number of shares in the case it needs to generate capital in the future. By selling more shares later, the company will generate extra cash. This is common if a public traded company is trying to expand a product line or invest in a new development. By introducing a secondary offering at the right time, the company can get cash on hand fast.

If you're a shareholder though, the secondary offering may damage your portfolio. We've established that the price of a stock is the result of interactions between supply and demand. When a company releases a secondary offering, then the supply of the stocks will increase. An increase in the supply of something typically results in a decrease in price to find the equilibrium price point between supply and demand.

The impact of a secondary offering will depend on the position you've taken as well as the number of shares released. Sometimes the secondary offering won't be large enough to impact the price of the stock in any significant way. A small increase in the percentage of shares available may not make a big difference. But if the secondary offering is quite large then it can significantly devalue your position.

The problem is, you can't anticipate a secondary offering because companies won't announce it ahead of time. Sometimes you think you have found a good position and the company will announce a secondary offering out of nowhere. But, its an added element to be aware of if you keep a good eye on the fundamentals of your company. If a company is struggling to bring in revenue, but they are talking about expanding certain lines of their business then this company is more likely to make a secondary offering. Again, there is no way to know for sure but there are warning signs that lay in the fundamentals of a company, and now you know to keep your eyes peeled.

The next thing to watch for is financial releases or statements about the company's earnings. The good thing about these is that the company will announce them ahead of time, so you can plan around them. They always happen after the market is always closed but they still impact the way your position opens the following day. If the company announces their revenue and they are showing signs of growth, then you'll be happy you were holding a position in that stock. If the company announces stagnant growth or a decline in growth, then the results of that announcement will be reflected in the price of the stock on the following day. You can either see this as an opportunity or avoid holding positions during financial announcements, depending on your confidence in the company. Either way it's something that's worth knowing about if you plan on becoming a swing trader.

You should pay close attention to what analysts say about a stock, before and after you buy it. What they predict may come true but more importantly, what they predict may encourage certain movements among investors. They may also make predications after the market closes that will affect the value of your positions on the following day. This could either be a benefit to you or it could hurt your portfolio; keep yourself updated on what the analysts are saying so you don't wake up to any surprises when the market opens.

Chapter 5: Strategies for Swing Traders

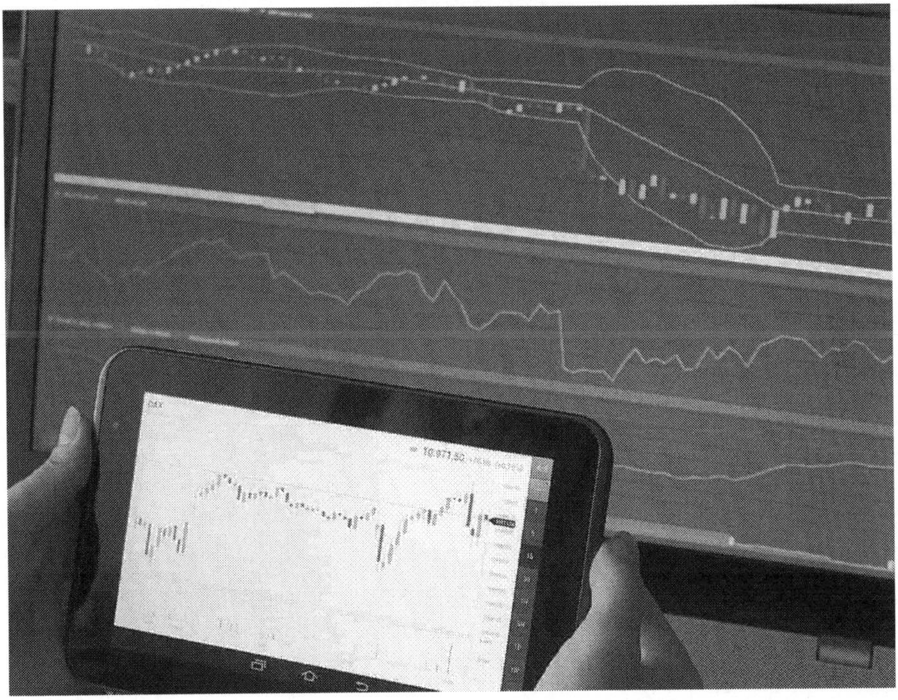

You've probably been reading this book and wondering at what point we will start to talk about swing trading strategies. After all, you are probably most interested in the actual strategies that you can apply to make money swing trading. You can see though, that there is a lot to learn before you can start to understand the strategies that people use to swing trade. The market has many factors at play, and you need to understand the tools used to assess companies and their technical movements. You won't be able to use the same strategy in every situation, so knowing how to read the market is the first step before learning strategy.

The indicators that you are looking for will depend on the type of strategy you are using, so pay close attention to the fundamental characteristics of companies and you'll start to recognize similarities amongst different opportunities.

The first step is to make a habit of mining for opportunities. There are a lot of fascinating economic and business journals available on the internet that you can peruse for information about current events and finance news. You never know how you will identify your next opportunity. An article about energy companies in Texas may inspire you to research energy contracts in the American Southwest, and which companies to watch for. An article in a tech news magazine might send you on a hunt for publicly traded companies developing a certain type of computer hardware. If it intrigues you, then let yourself be drawn in for further research. The important thing is to spend a little time each day reading and identifying possible opportunities. Once you've noticed an opportunity, dig a little deeper and review the company's involved and check out their fundamentals. How have these companies been performing? Is it worth taking a position?

You can do this research by looking at the market sector by sector. Find indexes that represent different sectors you are interested in and check up with them every day. It's good to have a relatively broad field of interests from which you can identify options. One sector might be ripe with opportunities while another sector lags on the same day. Being able to switch gears and focus on the place where opportunities are happening will make you a more effective and well-rounded trader.

The type of strategy you use will also affect what characteristics you'll be looking for. If you are willing to take on a little more risk and you want to try swing trading, then you will be looking for stocks that show signs of a moving downwards. With the uptick rule, you will have to find stocks that are moving up now, but you have reason to believe that they will continue to drop in the future.

If you want to buy a stock and hang on to it and make a profit, then you'll be looking for stocks or sectors that are healthy and have continued and consistent growth. The earlier you enter a position, the better. Look out for signs of reversals as both a short seller and a bull trader. The sooner you enter a position after a true reversal, the more you can earn.

Remember the tenet of Dow Theory that states that the average of all the stocks in the index should confirm each other. You may just take a position on one or two stocks, but its good to have a picture of the entire sector. This will tell you whether you will be swimming upstream or downstream. It's OK to swim upstream as long as you feel like you have a compelling reason.

When you have identified a stock that balances risk and reward ratio, decide what price you'd like to buy-in. This will require some research into the fundamentals of a company so you can evaluate whether you are overpaying or underpaying.

One strategy that you can employ as a swing trader is known as gap trading. In the last chapter, we discussed gaps that can open between trading days. A gap is when there is a significant difference between the closing price of a stock today, and the opening price of that stock tomorrow. As a swing trader, you can try and take advantage of these gaps by anticipating that gap and choosing a favorable position. There are instances when the gap could go against you; like with a secondary offering or a bad financial report. But there are just as many instances when you can try to predict a gap.

Swing traders have an advantage over day traders because they can use this gap. Day traders are also less susceptible to the risk that the gap creates. Depending on your outlook and your strategy, you may see the gap as either a good thing or a bad thing. Unfortunately, with gap trading, you don't have much control if the stock price moves against your position. You just must wait for the market to open the next day in order to react.

Gaps could open in several ways. A company could release a statement of earnings, and as a result, the price of the stock could drop or go up significantly in a short amount of time. Unfortunately, it's hard to anticipate a company's earnings report in order to make an educated guess on a good position. Most investors consider it to be too risky to play the gap on an earnings report because it's too easy for there to be a surprise when the company releases its statement.

Another way to take advantage of a gap is by researching companies that are developing new technologies. This type of stock can be very volatile, with attitudes changing swiftly about the predicted success or failure of the product.

The volatility could be an opportunity for the swing trader if they timed it right. Just be aware of the way the market can respond to an announcement about new technology. The stock price may shoot up to unprecedented levels as a result but often, things will settle down shortly after. Knowing how to time a position during a product announcement will be a major factor in whether you stand to make any money.

Remember; not all products succeed either. Sometimes a new product can hurt the company, in the long run, more than it helps them in the short run. Imagine an automotive company that announces the release of a new model. For a while, the model could increase anticipated earnings and investors might flock to the company. But the first model of the car might have more issues than expected, and the safety rating may be lower than normal. Remember that Dow Theory says that every action results in a reaction on the market. A product that performs poorly can do just as much harm as a product that performs well. Keep track of the progress of the companies in your portfolio, and make sure you time your positions well.

Another way a swing trader can ride a trend is to seek industries that are experiencing booms. Look for industries that are 'trendy'. Right now, the marijuana industry is experiencing a major boom and investors who recognized the possibilities of this trend early are enjoying a growing portfolio. With the legalization of Marijuana in Canada and many states in the US, there are new companies popping up all over as demand for the product is growing. Eventually, there could be a bubble once the expansion adjusts. But trends like these present opportunities for swing traders. Whether or not you decide to invest in the marijuana industry, its an example of a rideable trend. Who knows how it could play out?

These opportunities that exist in trends don't come around too often, and a swing trader must be patient in order to identify them. Usually, though, all one needs to do to find out about these trends is read the newspaper. Trends come and go and the window for making a real profit is limited. But if you're patient then there will always be another trend around the corner. The trick is to keep your ears to the wind so that you know when an opportunity has arrived.

Just like any swing trading strategy, a lot of it comes down to timing. A good example of a famous trend is the dotcom bubble in the 90s and early 2000s. A lot of people made big off the rise in internet technologies and computer companies. Eventually, though, the trend took a major dip and there were just as many losers from the dot-com trend as there were winners. Just remember that the stock market works in cycles and patterns, and these patterns often repeat themselves. Monitor your positions and stay up to date on news cycles.

When it comes to deciding on a position, timing is important. This means not only timing your exit but also timing your entry. It's better to be patient and wait for a good opportunity to buy when the stock price is low than to try and rush in out of impatience.

Before you open a position decide how much you are willing to pay. This is important because when you have a target price you can calculate exactly what you are risking before you even take on a position. Again, it's better to figure this out before you even take the position. Once you've determined an entry point then you must be patient. Wait for the price of the stock to match your ideal price. If it doesn't, then move on. Never forget that being a good trader requires discipline, which includes knowing when you should take an opportunity and when you should look at other options.

There are ways to track the price or set entry points without the need to constantly monitor the market. For example, a lot of brokerages offer alert services where you can receive notifications when the price of a stock has reached a predetermined target. You decide on an entry point and go about your day, then you receive a notification from your broker. You can even give them a limit order, which tells your broker to buy the stock for you once it hits that target. These notifications are also available for sale targets, so your broker can let you know when the stock has reached that target. They can even sell it automatically for you.

You've read about setting an exit point by now, and how sometimes you'd like to leave some flexibility in case the stock price continues to move in your favor. One way to do this is by not exiting your position all at once. Let's say you a buy a stock and the price of that stock has risen beyond your exit point and it is still moving. You want to preserve some of your earnings, but you are also curious about how high the stock might go. You take to exit your position with only a portion of your money while leaving the rest in. You slowly withdraw your position in increments, but you maintain some percentage of your position until you are completely ready to withdraw. This technique is called scaling out.

Chapter 6: Protecting Your Capital

There is no way around it; if you want to get involved in swing trading then you will have to put up some of your hard-earned money, risking it in the hopes that you make a profit. In order to play on the stock market, you have got to be willing to take some risks. If you are totally risk-averse, then swing trading isn't for you. It's healthy to be afraid of risk. You never want to lose your money, even if you're willing to put up with some risk. The trick to being a successful trader knows how to evaluate risk levels. When is the risk too high, and when should you cut your losses?

Before you even open an account, you should take time to consider how much risk you are willing to take. You should never put money in the stock market that you can't afford to lose. If you have a bad trade and your portfolio takes a hit, there are still bills to be paid and mouths to feed. Assess how much money you are willing to put into your account when you are first starting.

There are dozens of strategies and tools to help you make money on the stock market, and we've already discussed many of them in this book. There are just as many strategies which are crucial to minimizing risk and minimizing losses. Before you even begin a trade, you should establish an exit point so that when a trade results in a loss, you keep the loss to a minimum. After all, the money you lose is less money you will have to invest with later.

One of the most challenging aspects of investing in the psychology of defeat. You did your research, chose a stock, and decided on a position. After using some of your cash to pay for that position you began to see that the stock market moved against you. You were confident about your bet, but now as the market moves you are losing money. It could turn around, maybe you should wait it out. But if you wait, then you might just lose even more money. If you continue to wait your losses have only really occurred 'on paper'. But once you exit a position on a loss, you are making that loss real. When you finally decide to exit, you exit the position with less money than you started. If you keep waiting though, the market could continue to move against you and your stubbornness will only make it worse.

It's one of the most difficult parts of being a trader, acknowledging that you were wrong and backing out and moving on. In order to combat this, you must be disciplined and create an exit strategy for yourself. This means setting a stop-loss point where you commit to exiting before the trade even begins. If you buy a stock at x amount, deciding that if the stock price drops so many percentage points below x then you will cut your losses and leave the position.

If you start swing trading after reading this book and you stick with it, then there is no doubt that will incur a loss at some point. It's a part of swing trading that you should accept before you begin. If you accept this now, then you are more likely to take a step back and recognize when you decided on a bad position. But in the heat of the moment, the frustration of a loss might take over and you may find yourself struggling with what to do.

Most traders will set a stop loss point that is 6-8% below the price they bought the stock for. Choosing a stop loss point between 6-8% is ideal because it's not a huge amount to lose. If you lose 6-8% of your invested capital in a bad position, it's not hard to make that amount back on a good trade. If you let the loss become much more than that, you will have a hard time gaining that money back. You'll have to have an even more profitable trade in the future in order to just get back to where you started. I often choose 6-8% as a stop loss point because I am confident that I can make that amount back with just a few successful trades. The key is to keep your losses low enough so that you can keep trading and make that money back.

It can be difficult to force yourself to stick with the stop-loss plan. Being a good trader requires a cool, disciplined head especially in times of a loss. If you have these personality traits then you are more likely to keep your head down when things aren't going well and stick with your original plan, which means you'll be in a better position to trade again later and hopefully have profitable trades in the future. Remember that this is what makes swing trading advantageous for a beginning trader. While things may unfold quickly for a day trader, things move slower when you are swing trading.

The other question to ask before you enter a position is how much you can make, and how much can I lose. If I see an opportunity to make $100 that requires me to take a position that costs $200, then this position isn't worth it because I'm risking twice as much money as I can make. Most trades will consider the risks compared to potential rewards when picking up a new position. For any type of trader, you should only take positions where the inverse is true. If you have the potential to make twice as much as you stand to lose, then this is a better bet and the risk is more worth it.

Evaluating the risk of any given trade is the first thing any trader should do before taking a position. How volatile is the price of the stock you are taking a position on? Volatility is the frequency at which the stock moves up and down, and it can be a good indication of the risk involved with investing in that stock. If a stock has a lot of upward and downward movement then there is the potential that this stock may result in profits, but it also comes with a higher degree of risk. The more volatile a stock is, the higher the risk associated with trading that stock.

If you choose a position, and things are working in your favor, then you will need to consider how long to ride the trend in order to maximize the profit you make on that position. If you buy a stock and the price keeps rising, how long should you hold onto it before you sell? You might choose a target for your profit but get cold feet and back out before the stock price hits that level, fearing that if you wait too long then you will miss out on what you've already gained. After all, when the stock price is moving in a favorable direction for your position, you have only made money 'on paper' until you exit the position.

So, you should pick a target to exit, even on a positive trade. You should stick with your plans and choose your stop-loss and exit points carefully. But in the case of an exit point on a profitable trade, there is, of course, more flexibility. If you are willing to keep monitoring the stock and continuously reevaluate then you can be more flexible with your exit target. If you have a good reason to believe that the stock will continue to go up beyond the exit point you've chosen, then you should plan to ride it. Just be ready to exit the position quickly, and make sure you're able to stay close to a chart.

Remember that in these moments a lot of the decision comes down to our fundamental and technical indicators. This means that you must stay up to date with the goings-on of a company whose stock you've chosen a position on, and you should be able to read a candlestick chart to look for signs that the market perception of that stock is about to change. Anticipating the moves of other traders will help you decide when you think a trend is about to reverse, and when it's a good time to exit.

The last major part of managing risk involves knowing how much you should stake in a certain position. We've already talked about managing the risk/reward ratio on a potential position. But what percentage of your total capital should you stake on any one position? It's generally a bad idea to risk your entire capital by putting all your money in one position. This is a key part of diversification. Not putting all your eggs in one basket is the golden rule of trading and the most important part of managing risk.

It's true of swing trading that some of your trades will make you a profit, and some trades will end in a loss. So, it makes sense that diversification is the best way to making a profit overall on the aggregate of all your positions.

Most investors choose to use what is known as the one percent rule. You should never put more than 1% of your total account on any single position. If I had an account with $100,000 then I should never risk more than $1000 on any one position. Unfortunately, following this rule can be very difficult if your investment capital is much smaller. If you only have $5,000 in your account, then you can only put $50 on any one trade. So obviously this rule will be easier for traders with larger accounts.

Sometimes a trader may feel especially confident about a potential opportunity that they've identified. They might decide that in a certain case, it's worth it to break their own rules. It can be easy for investors to get caught in this trap, thinking that they've found a path to easy money and as a result they put more than they should have into one position. But the market often goes against what we expect. There is always the chance that something that appeared to be a sure bet turns out to be a lemon. The overconfidence that easy money could be had results in heavy losses.

Always remember that risk is a factor in every position. A wise investor will try to mitigate the damage from risk, rather than avoid it altogether. But a major distinction between traders who fail and traders who succeed is the fact that successful traders have a better understanding of the risks at play in the market. A seasoned trader will rarely break the rules as a result of overconfidence.

Being a profitable trader is not about hitting it big on investments where you outwit the market and discover some massive untapped opportunity. That idea may get popularized in movies like The Big Short, where traders made a fortune off one good position. This type of opportunity is actually very rare. Good traders are people who can manage many smaller positions at once and who have a higher number of profitable trades than trades resulting in a loss. A caveat to that is knowing how to minimize the damage when you do incur a loss and doing their homework to study the market and find several good opportunities at once.

Something that helps many successful traders is keeping a detailed record of all the trades you participate in. It not only will help you keep your position straight in your mind, but it will also give you something to refer to. You'll be able to see what worked and what didn't. If you can keep an organized and detailed record of your trades, then you can iron out your strategies with different types of stocks.

For every trade I participate in, I will take note of several things. If I rely on fundamentals to identify opportunities with certain stocks, I will make a record of which stock I was studying and what the fundamentals looked like when I took my position. I'll probably even make a note of technical details and the performance of the stock throughout the time that I held my position; opening and closing prices, as well as the trading volume of the stock that I held.

You may pick stocks for a variety of reasons. The reasons may be purely formulaic; you choose a stock based on certain fundamental indicators or based on the technical characteristics of the stocks price movement. Whatever means you use to choose a stock; you will be making a bet on that stock's future performance. So, for every stock you take a position on, you should record why you chose the position you did in addition to the performance of the stock. Did it match your expectations? If the stock didn't perform in the way that you expected, were there factors that you overlooked that would have affected your decision to take on a certain position? Do you believe there were any external or internal factors which affected your success on this trade? If there were external or internal factors, what were they?

Over time you will begin to get a feel for what indicators matter the most, and which ones fit the best with your strategy. If you keep a record of your trades, then you might notice patterns with certain kinds of stocks or certain fundamentals. The best education for a trader experiences, so you should try to get the most out of your experience by paying close attention to the factors which affect the success of your trades.

Of course, your trade journal should also include a record of which trades were successful and which trades were not, as well as your profits. How much did you pay for a position, and at what price did you exit the position? You'll start to see what your success record is. If you want to be a profitable trader, then you need to have more successful trades than trades that resulted in a loss.

The best day traders will be organized and detailed. Remember, this is real money you are investing in. Like treating stock as if you were buying the whole business, you should approach trading as if it is a serious job. It requires diligence and clear thinking as well as an organized and rational approach to your decision-making process. The better your research is, and the better your records are, the more likely you will be to learn and improve as a trader.

If you maintain an organized and logical manner of trading, then you are less likely to succumb to the stress that is associated with trading. Trading requires you to think on your feet and make intuitive decisions with limited information about the perceived outcomes. If you are organized and diligent then it will be easier to make these decisions with confidence, rather than in a state of stress.

While you must be able to accept the risk, you should go into every trade with the intention of making money on that trade. You should never enter a trade with a reckless you-only-live-once type strategy. You might make a good profit on one or two trades if you use this method, but most of the time you will lose because you didn't do your research, or you were overconfident in a position.

The stress from potential or real losses and the quick thinking that is required of a trader can make it easy to burn out in this job. People who thrive under pressure are more inclined to succeed and stick with it because they will accept the job for what it is and make decisions without dwelling too much on fear or doubt. There is risk, and some fear of risk is healthy. You should never accept risk blindly or just for the sake of taking a risk. The risk should serve a purpose or have some potential for a positive outcome.

Conclusion

With the information you've gained from this book, you are hopefully interested in starting your own account and beginning the process of researching your own trade opportunities. By now you have some foundation from which to do your research as well as a clearer picture of what to expect when choosing a broker and entering your first position.

The research required to be a successful swing trader won't stop when you finish reading this book. Every trade you enter will require another round of reading and studying so that you can choose a position with confidence. Remember what good research consists of; look at the fundamentals of a stock and the history of its performance over time.

Decide if you want to choose a strategy based on the stock or the other way around.

Keep your efforts simple at first, take your time to learn how the market works. As you gain experience your trades will go smoother and you will learn what works and what doesn't. Keep a record of how your trades go. If you continue to swing trade, then over time you will participate in a lot of trades and hold a lot of positions. To learn from them effectively you have got to take notes ad keep track of your progress. You will learn faster if you keep a record.

The amazing thing about trading and competing in the stock market is the sheer number of opportunities available. At any given time, there are new profitable positions that are waiting to be discovered. If you genuinely enjoy reading about new companies and current events, then it will be easier to identify opportunities as they appear.

The other advantage you have currently as a swing trader is the vast network of information available to you. Your stock research is no longer limited to what you can find in a public library and keeping track of the stock market in real-time doesn't require you to be attached to a landline phone. The trends that are hard to reach are more available. Imagine trying to find promising new companies to invest in before the age of the internet. You would have to hear about stock opportunities through sheer luck or knowing the right person.

Now anyone can have access to the information. This means that the market is a lot more competitive, but it also means that there are a lot more opportunities. The internet also provides endless resources to learn strategies and hear what analysts are saying. At the end of the day, take a lot of the noise with a grain of salt. The money you are risking is your own, and you should be leery of the way that certain analysts' opinion can be regarded as fact. Use the information to learn, but always fall back on your own research and intuition at the end of the day.

If you can learn how to trade profitably then you'll be able to enjoy the fruits of a rewarding job. Maybe you will decide to trade more actively and become a day trader. There is nothing wrong with maintaining a balance and swing trading in addition to your normal job. Be honest with yourself about the needs of your lifestyle, and whether your personality is a good match for that kind of path.

Whichever way you choose; whether you decide to continue swing trading or day trading, you'll gain the additional freedom that comes with being your own boss and making money independently for yourself. This is the main reason why people choose to get involved in swing trading; the added flexibility it can offer your life. But, just like any job, it requires work and dedication. Don't be frustrated with yourself if you don't see results right away. Don't think of yourself as a failure or a bad trader if you have a few bad trades. It happens to all of us when we first begin down this path, and it's a part of the learning experience.

If you are still nervous about the prospect of risking your hard-earned money on the stock market, there are other ways for you to gain practice and experience as a trader without risking your money.

Investopedia hosts a stock market simulator that is free to use and available online. When you sign up, the simulator gives you $100,000 of virtual money to use for trading securities. The simulator tracks real stocks from the New York Stock Exchange and all the major stock indexes. The simulator is updated every fifteen minutes so that you are essentially trading in real-time with the stock market simulator.

The simulator even considers the fees charged by brokers, as well as the commissions. When you trade regularly, whether, with real money or virtual money, you will have to keep track of how these fees are affecting your margins. The fees charged by brokers will affect your decision making, as they will always be a factor in the profitability of your trades. The stock market simulator will give you practice in managing these fees.

The only thing missing from the stock simulator is the psychological challenge of dealing with real risk. You will never know how it feels to truly manage risk until you are trading with real money. The main advantage of using a stock trading simulator is that you will be learning the mechanics of trading. This is just as important to be a good trader, and stock market simulators are something you should look into if you are interested in gaining some free experience.

So, if you have a hunch about a company or you can feel the air changing in the stock market but you don't have the capital to invest right now, you can use a stock market simulator to test your theories and learn in the meantime. Learning how to manage trades will give you confidence when it comes to putting your real money to work.

The more you practice and prepare to start swing trading with real money, the more likely you will be to succeed. The reality of swing trading is this; most will fail to make any profits, or they will quit before they have any success. Swing trading is difficult and competitive. You will be in a much better position to succeed if you can continue to research and learn, practicing and solidifying strategies.

You should be constantly reading about the economy and the stock market. Publications like The Economist, the Wall Street Journal and MarketView will be good resources for learning how economic news and developments will impact the performance of the stock market. They will give you a place to start your research on identifying opportunities in the current market conditions. Current events will steer investor confidence and subsequently the movements of stock prices. Even if you don't open an account right away, get in the habit of keeping up with current events and financial news.

Remember that the best way to find opportunities is to research stocks and sectors that you already have a personal interest in. The knowledge you have already is a useful tool for staying ahead of the market. If you have an interest in cars, then you'll probably enjoy reading about automotive companies; what new car models are being introduced and how do you think they will perform? If you have an interest in computers and tech; what types of technology have you read about that you think could be groundbreaking? Out of all the new companies producing these technologies, which ones have the most promising fundamentals, and are more likely to succeed? If you approach to research this way, then you'll no doubt find opportunities for stocks to trade and invest with.

With all of this in mind, I hope that it is clear to you at least that swing trading is not a passive or easy way to make extra money. You must do your research. But if you find sectors that interest you, and you have a natural interest in current events and a keen eye for opportunities then you will be better equipped to succeed.

Take what you learned from this book and continue to build on it. Swing trading is a challenging prospect with many risks. But if you maintain a disciplined strategy it also has its rewards; better financial freedom, independent income, and the ability to control your own schedule to name a few. If you continue to learn then you are more likely to succeed in this ever-changing world of opportunities.

Stock Trading for Beginners

An Easy Guide to the Stock Market with the Trading Strategy to Achieve Financial Freedom. You Will Find Inside the A-Z Glossary to All Technical Terms Used

Written by:

Nathan Real

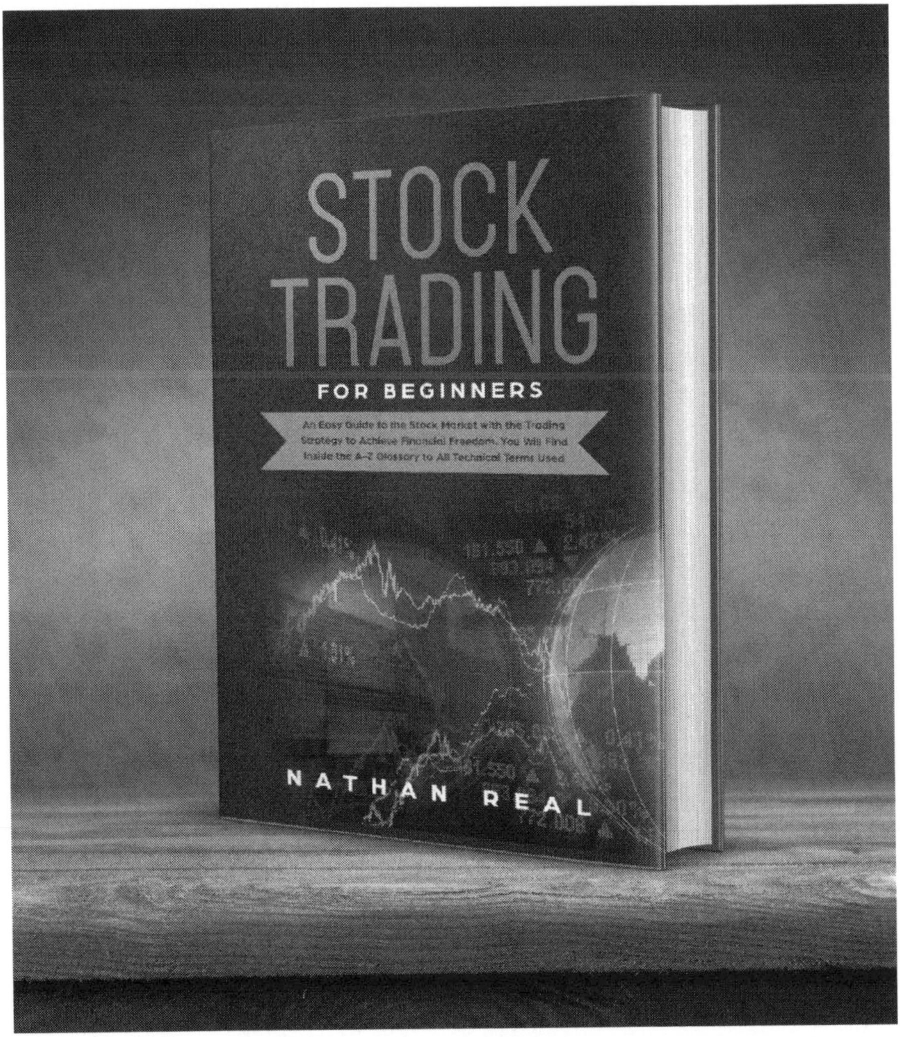
STOCK
TRADING
FOR BEGINNERS
NATHAN REAL

Introduction

Congratulations on purchasing *Stock Trading for Beginners* and thank you for doing so.

There are plenty of books on this subject on the market, thanks again for choosing this one! Every effort was made to ensure it is full of as much useful information as possible. Please enjoy!

VIPS Cafeteria, Velázquez street in Madrid, Autumn 2007. In front of me, is a book whose title invites action: 'Move your money and get rich,' by Aitor Zárate. After leafing through its pages I decide to buy it. Six hours later, my body was the same; however, my mind had transformed. The slap of reality after reading it was of such magnitude that the next day, I started to discover what day trading was and how I could do it.

I researched, studied, and prepared my best. Even today, I am a partner and friend of the author of the book that changed my life. Despite this, in the initial stage of the inevitable "intoxication," I would have liked to have a book like the one you now hold—direct, brief, practical, with little theory and a lot of decision; everything that is needed for intraday operations.

I currently manage my assets as I dreamed there in 2007. I fight twenty hours a month (yes, right, hours) in the most volatile financial markets in the world, and I can say that I am rich (both, in time and money). The key is not to earn more money, but to earn it better. Everything costs more than it seems at first but setting the goal of living day trading or intraday trading is real and accessible. Concepts must be assimilated - here they are detailed -, acquire a minimum skill, live the forced period of simulation and the subsequent jump to the real market. All this with substantial doses of humility and mental control.

On the benefits associated with the life of a day trader that obtains benefits month by month, I can hardly specify that they do not imagine. You become a nobleman, an aristocrat, a person who contemplates from the window how the system and a frantic environment engulfs victims day after day. The victims are the people who crave the freedom of day trading but do not want to give up their security (e.g., a payroll), preferring to live with the hope that everything will improve and that one day they will try.

I am an expert in marketing, but it has not made me richer or freer. This has been achieved by day trading. As a marketing expert, I got some recognition: teaching at ESADE Business School and being a freak in my old jobs. As a trader, I have reinvented myself as a free man who enjoys the present by drawing a happy future for his environment. As a marketer, they made decisions for me, but, as a day trader, that is a part of the past.

Undoubtedly, I have been right, but I have also made great mistakes. I give a good account of them here. I suggest you accept this week of intraday trading. You cannot get caught up in what you do to the point of losing curiosity. Flee from the comfortable terrain where you live and see that there are few things as stimulating as day trading. But, do remember that everything has a cost: challenging you in day trading will lead you to some failure.

You make mistakes, you learn, you make fewer mistakes, you gain confidence, and the cycle continues. The consequence of trying is failure and triumph. They are inseparable. If you want to succeed, you have to accept the risk of failure. However, it is worth it because the prize is very succulent: the day trader enjoys an independence that is difficult to explain, and the most surprising thing is that it is available to thousands of people who still do not know it.

And, that's because?

There are good reasons such as the ease of access to the markets via the Internet, the total regulation and transparency of these, the low commissions of the brokers and the minimal fixed costs necessary to start. If we also add that the capital needed to start operating is low, that it is not necessary to employ anyone, that you can choose your own hours of work based on your family reality and the market where you operate, that you can work from any place, that today there is a wide range of training and that even the inescapable period of simulation is compatible if you have a job, I find no reason for not trying it from today itself.

Others Paved the Way

Thanks to traders like Josef Ajram and his ability to explain our activity, being an intraday speculator is more bearable today. Ajram's popularity and its presence in the media have demystified the figure of the day trader, which was upset and subject to unrealistic prejudices until now. Not all traders are greedy beings, as we are caricatured, nor are we useless for society. On the contrary, many of us dedicate a large part of our wealth - in time and money - to helping the community through volunteering work, working for many inaccessible places and people, etc. So, whenever you get a chance, do thank my friend Josef for the excellent image that renders intraday trading as a positive thing.

Chapter 1 – What Is Day Trading or Intraday Speculation?

The work of a day trader, the one with the lowest risk that exists as I will explain later, is to open purchase or sell positions in financial assets—stocks, futures, currencies, options—closing those positions on the same day and generating benefits for their difference. This action can be performed on one or multiple occasions, always within the same day or session. The day traders are not investors; they do not want to make projections for weeks or months of what will happen. They operate at the moment, opening and closing operations in minutes, and do not aspire to be always right. They only intend to take advantage of the most probable and most favorable movements. If nothing is presented, then put your hands in your pockets and wait.

But day trading is not as simple as it seems. One must have concentration, audacity, self-control; in short, all that is already assumed, but it is more important that one has ... I don't know how to explain it, but here I go—one must be both a mathematician and a poet. As if poetry were a science or mathematics an art.

In the beginning, day trading was accessible to large financial corporations and investment banks, since only they had access to these market transactions and their data in real-time. But thanks to the Internet and the technology in the transmission of information, currently a trader from a small town has the same direct and immediate access to the markets as any Tokyo investment bank, Chicago or the City of London.

A day trader must choose the market in which to operate, know their conditions and schedules, as well as the existing disadvantages and the benefits of directing their talent there. As intraday traders it will be irrelevant that the chosen market is in bullish effervescence or suffering a crack; If we have chosen it, it is because it has enough volatility to make things happen every day, with the aim of "pinching it" and taking our little piece of the profit. Day trading is not an investment, it is speculation, and it serves to obtain a benefit, based exclusively on price variations over time, that is, we will go to bed knowing if the day has provided an increase or decrease in balance in our account.

The biggest advantage of a day trader is that it can make positive operations both if the market goes up—buying an asset to sell later as if the market is falling—selling a "borrowed" asset that it does not own to buy it at a lower price and make a difference This situation is called slang as being "long" or "Short", respectively. I insist, being "short" means betting because the index, the stock, the currency, etc. will fall so that we will earn money if that asset actually falls and we will lose money if instead, it goes up. Remember that being "short" does not imply a greater risk than being "long" and waiting for our asset to revalue.

Because we want to make a profit, first we need to predict the direction of the market. For this, we use the technical analysis that reports valuable real-time market information and even the current psychological situation of buyers and sellers.

As I indicated at the beginning, day trading is the most democratic profession—everything depends on you, you cannot blame anyone (one hundred percent "meritocracy"). It is also the safest in the world, knowing from the first moment what will be our maximum percentage of daily, weekly, and monthly loss thanks to monetary management. Unfortunately, an entrepreneur or businessman is unable to calculate it, risks much more—fixed costs, employees, depreciation, defaults, stock breaks, thefts, products or services that are not to the client's liking, abusive fees, and taxes—and also suffers from Leon schedules.

The potential of day trading to put money in your pocket is unlimited. Now, 90 percent of the people who operate lose the total money they invested in the first six months. If they operate again, they lose the total money again within a year. Most people who speculate on financial assets lose everything. The fact that the earning potential is so high attracts the best minds in the world, but it is a zero-sum game. This means that what we earn we take away from another, and vice versa. You have to be smarter than thousands of your opponents.

Unfortunately, there is no market for amateurs in which you can practice with lower-level traders, so when you start operating, you are struggling with very prepared people and institutions, with resources, money, and experience that you do not have now.

But calm down! You can trade and earn money on day trading, and there is evidence to prove it. You can learn it because everything is technique, discipline, and control over emotions. However, to achieve this, we must follow the stages of learning day trading without skipping any steps, one of them being the mandatory simulation period.

We must remember that there is enough in the markets to meet the needs of all traders, but not to satisfy their greed. Avoiding greed will be one of our greatest tasks. Not wanting to become a millionaire the first year, neither the second nor the third, in fact, it should not even be an objective per se. In any case, everything has its time and stages, and controlling greed increases the chances of living intraday trading and changing a life.

Market Choice

To perform an excellent day trading, we must operate in markets that meet certain characteristics. Both the futures market and the forex meet all the requirements that I consider relevant for this. They must be very liquid and transparent markets, in which it is possible to operate electronically with them, that allow them to enter "shortly" and that possess products that allow leverage.

As for liquidity, it is understood that a counterparty must be found at the moment in which we are interested. Both forex and futures are very liquid and can absorb contracts at any time without being unchanged. Also, prefer a transparent market and by that, I mean the confidence of knowing, at any time, what price we have achieved in our operations, etc.. An opaque market hides that information and does not explain why we have given the order to buy 700 and have served us 703. We need to launch the purchase and sale orders ourselves, from our home, or from a spa, when we are interested, without having to meditate with other people or intermediaries. We press a button, and our orders are launched instantly.

We need to be able to operate "short" because otherwise, we would advance to the limp leg. A day trader needs to have the opportunity to win whether the market goes up or down. And last but not least, leverage, which means in the case of futures that with a small amount of money, you own a very large underlying. For example, with a deposit of $ 5,000, we can own a contract worth $ 50,000. Leverage carries great advantages but also great risks. A highly leveraged trader obtains benefits far superior to the ordinary if everything goes as expected, but in the same way that he earns money easily, he can lose it very quickly and on some occasions, it can lead to large losses and even the disappearance of capital.

Futures

Future markets consist of the execution of contracts for the purchase or sale of financial assets, indices, currencies, stocks or certain matters at a future date, agreeing on the price, quantity and expiration date.

They were born in the nineteenth century with the aim of protecting producers of raw materials in a market characterized by times of concentration of supply of harvest and by very variable prices throughout the year, which left the work attractive.

There are currently two figures that participate in the futures market, those that do so to protect themselves from risk in an activity subject to high price variations, and those investors and speculators who assume the risk with the prospect of obtaining future benefits.

Futures are traded in regulated and supervised markets that record, offset and liquidate, open positions and whose regulatory body acts as a buyer before the selling member and as a seller before the buying member. There are many futures contracts, and we know that a trader can operate today on almost anything, from copper to coffee, from stock indexes to silver, or from pigs to palladium.

The main futures markets are the Mini Dow (YM), the Mini S & P500 (ES), the Mini Nasdaq (NQ) and the Mini Russell (ER), the mini gold contract (YG), the future of the American bond at thirty years (ZB), the future of the euro (EC), oil (CL) and mini oil (QM). The letters in parentheses represent the symbol or ticker that is used to get your quote.

It should be remembered that when we buy or sell a futures contract, we are not physically buying anything. It is simply a way of participating in the price movement of the market in question. As for this price movement, if we have bought—we have become "long"—with a contract in the future of the mini S & P500, for example, and a point moves, that is, from 1,652.75 to 1,653.75. This translates into $ 50 profit in our broker account. The same movement for the Nasdaq mini would represent 20 dollars of profit and five dollars in the mini Dow. Therefore, if we bought three contracts of the mini S & P500 and captured a two-point movement, it would be a benefit of $ 300 ($ 50 x 2 points x 3 contracts).

To buy a futures contract, we will need between 2,500 and about $ 5,000 in our broker account. This money is called the guarantee, or margin in English. There are brokers that require less guarantee to buy a futures contract. There are those that require only $ 400 per contract, which raises the level of leverage, such as the advantages and dangers that we already mentioned.

I recommend operating with a contract for every $ 10,000 in the account. In this way, the oscillations in the account are not so large, and you can operate with a cool head. If we reduce leverage and operate with a contract for every $ 30,000, we will earn money and never be anxious about the possible loss. In fact, I recommend starting to operate with only one contract. As a rookie trader, we will make mistakes, and a mistake with a contract is less dramatic than a mistake with six or more contracts.

Finally, indicate that index futures have four maturities per year, which expire on the third Friday of the months of March, June, September, and December. This from an intraday operator's perspective should not worry us as much, but we are obliged to know it. Personally, I would like to tell you that in the beginning, I operated in the futures of the mini S & P500—the Ferrari of the futures, a volatile and complicated market for a new trader. Today, however, I recommend many traders to start operating the mini Dow (YM) by having advantages such as higher fork and lower intensity. It is assumed that a novice chess player will not want to compete with Gari Kaspárov but with some provincial champion. Well, the same goes for day trading. We must gain confidence little by little and wait for the great challenges.

FOREX

The forex, short for the term Foreign Exchange, is a global and decentralized market in which currencies are traded. Currency or forex speculation is the largest market in the world, born with the objective of facilitating the monetary flow derived from international trade. The liquidity of only one day in the forex market is equivalent to a whole month on Wall Street. There are studies that indicate that there are daily transactions in the forex market for a value of four billion dollars, most of them due to the sale of financial assets for speculation.

The foreign exchange market is unique due to the volume of transactions, the extreme liquidity of the market, the large number and variety of its "actors" and their geographical dispersion. The forex market moves continuously from ten o'clock on Sunday night until ten o'clock on Friday night. It runs for twenty-four hours of each day of the week, exactly like the futures market.

Large international banks provide the foreign exchange market with a purchase price (bid) and a sale price (offer). The spread is the difference between these prices and is normally constituted as the remuneration to the entity for its intermediary role between those who buy and those who sell using its channels. In general, the spread in the most traded currencies is only 1-3 pips or basis points or even 0. For example, if the purchase price on a EUR / USD quote is 1,3300 while the price of the sale is set at 1.3302, you can clearly identify the two spread points that we will pay the broker.

The moments of greatest volatility that we will find in the forex coincide with the opening of the main stock exchanges in the world—London, New York, and Tokyo—although the forex is not directly linked to the nature of these trading centers. First, they open the Asian markets, then the European ones, and finally, the Americans. Permanent access to markets allows the advantage of a rapid response capacity to economic or political events that have an effect on it.

Fluctuations in exchange rates are generally caused by both real monetary flows and exchange expectations due to fluctuations in economic variables such as GDP growth, inflation, interest rates, budgets, and trade deficit or surplus. The important news is often published on scheduled dates so that all the investors have access to the same news at the same time. Among the factors that affect the exchange rate are economic factors (trade deficits, inflation, interest rate differences, public deficits, etc.), political factors, which can affect monetary policy, and, finally, the market psychology, that is, rumors, expectations, etc.

In the forex, currencies are traded at crosses. The most-traded are EUR/USD (Euro/Dollar), USD/JPY (Dollar/Yen) and GBP/USD (Pound/Dollar). In 2010, the US dollar intervened in 89 percent of transactions, followed by the euro (37 percent), the yen (20 percent) and the pound sterling (17 percent). Although the negotiation with euros has grown considerably since its creation in January 1999, the foreign exchange market is still focused on the US dollar.

The main operators in the forex market are financial institutions, which participate in the market in a speculative, hedging, or acting on behalf of a client basis. Any international economic transaction—from a transfer to the purchase of foreign shares—implies the previous passage through the foreign exchange market to carry out the purchase and sale of the foreign exchange necessary to carry out the main operation.

Central banks, which operate in foreign currency markets to control the money supply, inflation and/or interest rates of their country's currency, often impose exchange rates and even use their international reserves to stabilize the market. The expectation or rumor of a central bank intervention may be sufficient to alter the value of a currency. And finally, we, the private investors, through intermediaries (brokers) who are in charge of providing us with forex account management services.

Nowadays it can be assured with total veracity that the currency exchange market (FOREX or FX) is the other Ferrari of the financial markets and houses a greater projection of growth in the modern financial world, given its decentralized location as it operates as a global electronic network of banks, financial institutions, and individual operators, all dedicated to buying or selling currencies by virtue of their volatile exchange ratio. It is a transparent market that is, sometimes, and thanks to central banks, very predictive. In addition, it adapts perfectly to the risk management strategy and can operate with the minimum number of lots. The guarantees are small and the commissions low. When used under a well-weighted leverage system, it allows a trader with little capital to achieve succulent results. In short, forex stands out today as the ideal market for the professional trader.

Chapter 2 – Is Day Trading for Me?

Absolutely yes, if you work for someone else, unless you like it and feel totally involved in your current job, you have a position with freedom and ability to choose, have the full support of the management and you trust your responsibility and also feel that your performance contributes to the success of the business. In these cases, the work of others is so stimulating that it is worthwhile to pause or not to embark on trading. In the rest of the cases, the answer is yes.

Loss

If we make springs from the autumns, winter will always be far away.
– Carlos Rodríguez

The loss is overlapped to day trading like the nail to the meat. The day trader loses on many days and maybe on even more days than he earns. The key is that when we lose, "we file our nails," and when we win, "we take the whole arm." Therefore, whoever ventures to play with defined rules systems, and no matter what strategy he finally follows, the best advice he can follow is to always limit his losses. We can be attentive for twenty days and always limit the loss, but just one day of carelessness is enough, to lower our guard so that we are out of play and assuming excessive losses.

If we follow the recommendations of the SEC, the Securities and Exchange Commission (http://www.sec.gov/ investor/pubs/daytips.htm), nobody in their right mind would be interested in this discipline, but for this, we have our most faithful ally, the stop loss Thursday. Let's follow it. Let's pamper it, never underestimate it and our glory days in intraday speculation will come. Looking back and seeing the mistakes of past trades will not help much. Regrets are always late. They mean pure failure.

We hustle to bite the dust, eat the "I never ...", endure a few "I told you so" and fall again and again, for which it is an essential requirement to have risen on many other occasions. Complaining is a waste of time, and we must remember that what makes us grow is error, defeat. Most traders would rather not have suffered that moment, but at the same time, we all confess that it has made us better.

I am sure that we will live bad days and losses in day trading, but let's ask ourselves: "Bad day? Insurance?". In 1976, Ronald Wayne sold 10 percent of Apple for $ 800; today that 10 percent is worth 88,065,210,000 dollars. That is having a bad day, ours is something rectifiable, and we should not fear to assume small losses.

The people who live from day trading are privileged. However, the price we have to pay for it is high, since any carelessness, lack of concentration, or emotional imbalance can disrupt our dream and work well done. The bad days are the painful and inevitable initial experiences that allow us to realize how beautiful but also risky it is to live from this activity.

Technical Analysis

Technical analysis allows us to study the market, through the use of graphics, in order to predict future trends in price. Knowing how to interpret the graphics is essential for anyone who wants to survive in the world of financial markets. This study is vital to our interests; however, we must use it as what it is, a tool, and not an absolute truth.

The technical analysis does not guarantee anything, the graphs indicate what has happened but unfortunately not what will happen. What it does allow us is to identify bullish, bearish, or lateral movements, that is, to find trends that turn out to be large allies of the day trader. "The trend is your friend," is a maxim of intraday speculators and forgetting one of the biggest causes of capital loss. Going against a trend, looking for a price change is one of the best ways to lose your shirt.

Interpreting the graphics thanks to technical analysis, allows us to define the most appropriate time to buy or sell our assets and determine the entry and exit price. The market has memory and repeats the patterns, always stopping in the same places where it already did at other times. Magic? Sometimes it seems.

One of the principles of technical analysis dictates that "the price discounts everything," which means that all the elements that affect the market - political, economic, social, psychological, or of any other nature - are already evidenced in the price. This reflects changes in the balance between supply and demand. We should know that when demand exceeds supply, the price goes up, while when supply exceeds demand, the price goes down.

We use this knowledge and invest in it, concluding that if the price increases, it is because demand exceeds supply, while if price falls, it is because supply exceeds demand as you can see, the graphics do not move to free will. As day traders, we are not interested in knowing or analyzing the fundamental factors that cause the changes, but we limit ourselves to analyzing the consequences of the changes, that is, the price.

When preparing for the operation, we will have to "draw" or "graph" the market to know its critical points. For this, we need to have the following concepts very present:

Supports and Resistances

Support is a price level below the current one, in which the buying force is expected to exceed the sales force, so a bearish momentum will be slowed, and therefore, the price will pick up. Normally, support corresponds to a minimum previously reached. Resistance is the opposite concept. It is a price above the current one in which the sales force will exceed that of purchase, ending the bullish momentum, and therefore the price will recede. Resistances are commonly identified in a graph as previous highs reached by the price. The supports and resistances are considered stronger the more times they have been tested without the price being able to exceed the level they indicate. When support is crossed downwards, it becomes resistance and, in turn, when a resistance is crossed upwards, it becomes support.

Trends

The trend is the market direction. The price is characterized by a zigzagging movement, with the appearance of successive waves with their respective ridges and valleys. The direction of these ridges and valleys is what constitutes the trend of the market, either upward, downward or the usual lateral movements, also called periods without a trend.

Trends and Channel Lines

An upward trend line is a straight line that joins the successive lows of an uptrend, and therefore, increases its value as it extends to the right. A downward trend line is a straight line that joins successive highs within a downward trend, so its value decreases as it moves to the right.

The channel line is a line parallel to the trend line that is drawn from the other side of the graph. For a bullish channel, the channel line would be drawn parallel to the trend line, through successive highs. In a downtrend, it would be the reverse. This set is simply called the ascending or descending channel.

In summary, the technical analysis is based on the investigation of two variables: price and time. However, to obtain an optimal analysis result, it is not enough to select a time frame. The results will improve if we combine different time frames. We should not limit ourselves in the analysis of a single time frame as the basis for our trading decisions; We will always take a look at other frames. In this way, we will maintain a vision of the whole and know in which state of the trend our asset is.

Graphical Representations of the Market

These are figures that represent both the current market price and a series of data: opening prices, closing prices, volumes, maximum and minimum values, etc. The graphs arise from the need to give image and projection to such evolution. We will use these figures to standardize the data, represent them, synthesize them, and display the relevant information with a simple glance.

There are different ways of representing the price and therefore representing the market: linear charts, bar charts, candlestick charts, rank charts, dot and figure charts, etc. As we see, a whole universe of alternatives, although in this work we will focus only on the Japanese candles or candlestick.

The graphs reflect in their drawing both prices and time. We will have to define the period of the graph, which will be the general drawing that describes the evolution in the chosen period of time, and the interval or frequency, which will be each of the units whose sequence forms the global evolution and that in an isolated way describe the evolution summarized in that particular interval. We call this unit candle.

When we select a candlestick chart, for example of a period of one day with an interval of fifteen minutes, we will be shown the evolution of the value throughout that day using for this a sequence of candles where each one offers us, by itself alone and schematically, the price variation every fifteen minutes.

The references that the graphic will use to give us the information will be the price and the time. On the «Y» axis it will indicate prices, and on the «X» axis, time. Looking at the period, the "X" axis will tell us the price range where the market has moved, being able to define the supports and resistances of the day, define trends, find some chartist figure or guideline. If we look at the time, we can know what the maximum and the minimum moments are, when these maximum or minimum moments have been reached, when the trend broke or perhaps other patterns that the market shows us.

Japanese Candles or Candlesticks

Before moving forward, we must clarify that the plotters allow you to customize the color, stroke, and thickness of the candles to the taste of the day trader. The standard marks that the red or black color will represent bearish candles and green or white bullish candles.

At the time of drawing the candle the interval is indifferent; only the negotiated prices in that time range matter, so that the following candles could be drawn after sixty minutes or only three and the prices that mark summarize the price variation in that time.

If the candle is black or red, what it is telling us is that the market in that fraction of time has gone down. If instead, the candle is white or green, it is indicating that the market, at that time, has risen. The color of the candle is not defined until the end of that fraction of time. It is very common to open at a price, start to rise and therefore dye white, and after reaching a maximum, fall below the opening price and close there, so the candle, once the price goes down below the opening point, it will start to turn black.

The information provided by a candle that covers one day will also give us for candles of smaller intervals, you just have to understand that proportionally it is the same information, but for operational purposes, they do not have the same importance. We must look for that graph whose period and frequency are consistent with our investment term. As day traders, we must give greater importance to candles of small intervals since our term to speculate will end at the most at the end of the session. If instead, we were medium-long term investors, the information about the candles drawn should be about periods of four hours, day or week, since information about, for example, five minutes, would not give us relevant information.

In spite of this, the candles and the graphs of greater intervals cannot be ignored for day trading, since they show us the general behavior of the market, and in addition it can give the circumstance of being operating in a price range whose route is approaching the immediate surroundings of an important long-term support or resistance, and it may happen that in our small interval graph we have no record. Ignoring this support or resistance can cause us a loss and, however, knowing its existence can give us an opportunity.

Heik in Ashi Candles

The heik candles in ashi are a modification of the Japanese candles that try to make the information of a graphic arrive with less distortion, drawing clearer trends and patterns. In the candle charts, each candle shows four different data: the opening, closing, maximum, and minimum prices. In addition, each candle is independent and has no relation to the previous candle. But in the heik, in that way, the candles are different, and each one is calculated and traced using information from the previous candle.

In my personal operation, and in the hundreds of traders, it has been a step forward and a release of confusing noise and information. In his favor also say that it works just as well regardless of the timeframe.

The heik candles in ashi are calculated like this:

Closing price: the closing price on a heik candle in ashi is the average of the opening, closing, high and low prices.

Opening price: the opening price on a heik candle in ashi is the average of the opening and closing price of the previous candle.

Maximum: the maximum in a heik candle in ashi is chosen from among the high, opening, and closing prices, the one with the highest value.

Minimum: the minimum in a heik candle in ashi is chosen from among the high, opening, and closing prices, the one with the lowest value.

In short, they are weighted candles where the aim is not to show the opening and closing, but above all, to easily show the trend. The openings will always appear at the midpoint of the previous candle, which makes it easier to represent the trend with greater rigor. It is the only graphic that, in addition to giving us information, generates both input and output signals and serves to tell us mainly when we have a good position.

As you can see, the absence of a lower shadow in the bulls and large body is a clear sign of a strong tendency; conversely, in the case of the downtrend, as you have checked that the heik candles in ashi favor the permanence in the position, we do not leave before the end of a trend.

Most Common Chart Figures

Chartism is based on visually perceiving repetitive patterns in price and assigning them meaning. We are talking about the famous shoulder-head-shoulder figures, triple floors, double ceilings, flags, and rectangles, among others. The simpler the patterns, the more reliable they are. The more complex its structure, the less the reliability. Detecting a double floor is something that within the subjective nature of Chartism is what it offers the most degree of objectivity. However, a shoulder-head-shoulder offers a greater degree of subjectivity, since the distance from the shoulders, the height of the head or the neckline is more difficult elements to abstract than a simple double-floor pattern.

Trend Change Figures

We can divide the chart formations into two large blocks: trend change figures or trend consolidation figures. For all of them, it is necessary to bear in mind that, the greater its breadth of prices and its duration, the more important its consequences may be. The most common trend change figures are:

Double roof: It is characterized by the existence of two maximums of a similar amount, although minimum variations are admitted. When this fact occurs immediately after an upward trend, it indicates that we are most likely facing a change in trend. It appears in bull markets, and at the time it ends implies a downward corrective phase. It is one of the most common and highly reliable figures. Once the figure is produced, the subsequent fall with which we will find is at least equal to the distance that existed between the floor line and the ceiling.

Double floor: The figure is formed by two minimums, which act as resistance with an intermediate point that separates them. When the point that separated them is exceeded after the second minimum, an upward movement of equal height to the intermediate ceiling will begin with a high probability and appears in bear markets. Once it ends, it implies a period of bullish correction, and it is a very common figure and at the same time highly reliable.

Shoulder-head-shoulder: It is one of the main figures of change from upward to downward trend. This figure is made up of three maxima: the first and the last (called shoulders) at a similar level and that of the center (called the head) clearly higher. If we join the minimums that separate the shoulders from the head, we will have the valley line. Ideally, it should have a slightly bullish slope. Failing that, be horizontal but never with a clearly bearish inclination. When the price falls below that line, the formation is triggered with a downward target equal to the height that separates the valley line from the maximum of the head.

Shoulder-head-shoulder inverted: It is a figure very similar to the previous one, with the proviso that in this case, the figure is formed in bear market trends. It is, therefore, a figure of change of tendency from bearish to bullish. However, it is not a common figure, although its reliability as in normal shoulder-head-shoulder is high. The figure is composed of three minimums: the first and the last (called shoulders) at a similar level and that of the center (called head) clearly lower. If we join the minimums that separate the shoulders from the head, we will have the valley line. Ideally, it should have a slightly downward or horizontal slope but never with a clearly upward slope. When the price rises above the valley line, the formation is triggered with an upward objective equal to the height that separates the valley line from the minimum of the head.

Consolidation Figures

The most common trend consolidation figures are:

Triangles: it is a consolidation figure, so it does not produce trend changes, but indicates a break. It is a common figure. It is characterized by an evolution of the price of the value in which the maximums are becoming lower and the minimums becoming higher. If we come from a bullish situation, and the cut occurs in the downtrend line, then the figure is bullish consolidation. If the cut occurs in the bullish guideline, then the figure is from a shift from a bullish trend to a bearish trend. For a triangle to be considered as such, at least four points of contact are needed (two maximums and two minimums). The cut must occur before 2/3 of the length of the triangle. Its length is the distance from the vertex to the projection on the bisector of the first point of contact.

Flag: the figure is very similar to a channel but very narrow and short. This channel must have a tendency contrary to the sense of the existing trend. So if the trend is bullish, the flag will have a downward inclination; and if the trend is bullish, the flag will have an upward tilt. This figure usually appears after a very abrupt price evolution, so that the price rests on the flag for a very short period of time to subsequently evolve with similar momentum as it initially had.

Rectangle: It is a trend consolidation figure, being quite reliable and a very common figure. During its formation, the price moves between a support and a resistance, requiring at least four contact points: two maximums (of the same level) and two minimums (of the same level). The evolution of the volume during its formation decreases while the figure is being formed and increases at the time of cutting. With regard to the target price once the formation is broken, it is expected to reach a line parallel to the rectangle separated from it by equal distance to the amplitude of the rectangle, the distance between the support line and resistance.

Indicators

As we have seen, price is the axis on which we must mark our intraday strategy to address the market and "pinch" it in favor of our interests. However, the indicators represent for the day trader a valuable source of information and validation against the operation and its open positions. All of us, to a greater or lesser extent, use them and sometimes even abuse them, seeking in them the absolute truth or certainty that nobody and nothing can give us. The market will always do what it wants, all parameters and indicators are late and sometimes fail, so blindly trusting them can be a big mistake. In addition, a day trader must make quick decisions, and having many indicators will make the decision more complex. Simplicity should be a maxim in our activity, saturating us with information will not give us better results, so it is best to focus on two or three aspects that we consider more reliable and try to extract the most from them.

Despite these warnings, I insist that it will always be better to have these indicators and establish rules based on numerical parameters than to have nothing and trust the impression that a graphic gives us. We must take care that they are not excessively redundant and use them in several time frames.

I usually apply the principle of the Ock ham knife in my intraday operation, that is, if all things being equal, a graph with its indicators transfers the same pattern and input and output signals as another, the one that informs me of the simplest explanation is usually the chosen one, and the second, inevitably rejected and forgotten. If two systems work more or less the same, we must always keep the simplest.

The indicators that are now displayed are supplied by all the graphing programs on the market, making their application affordable and convenient.

MACD

The MACD (Moving Average Convergence Divergence) is an indicator that allows us to know when a trend starts or ends. For this, this convergence-divergence indicator of moving averages uses two lines: that of the indicator itself (that of the MACD) and that of its moving average (Sign), and it is the crossing of both that provides us with the purchase signals or sale.

Its formula is:

MACD = ema (cot. 26) - ema (cot. 12)

Sign = ema (MACD 9)

This means that we will have to calculate the exponential moving average of the last 26 value quotes and subtract the exponential moving average of the last 12 sessions, resulting in the MACD. And to calculate the second line, that of the Sign, we just have to calculate the exponential moving average of the last nine sessions of the MACD.

The buy and sell signals are produced in the cuts of the two lines (MACD and Sign), so that when the MACD line cuts upwards to that of the Sign a buy signal is generated. As long as the line continues above the Sign, the position must be a buyer. At the moment when the MACD line cuts down to that of the Sign, a sales signal is created, being the selling position while it is below.

Before acting, wait for the signals to be confirmed. And for this, we will also have to apply the analysis of graphs to that of the MACD, studying what are its overbought and oversold areas, taking into account that the MACD always moves above or below 0, so that above the value begins to be overbought and below, oversold. If shortly after cutting the MACD the Sign up (buy signal) at the same time cuts a downtrend or resistance, we will have a confirmation of the buy signal. On the contrary, if the MACD gives a sell signal when cutting down the Sign, and at the same time it breaks a support or an upward trend, we will be before the confirmation of that sales signal.

As for the divergences, we must know that they will be bullish when the minimum prices are getting lower, but on the contrary, the MACD minimums are getting higher. In this case, we will meet a purchase signal.

On the contrary, we are faced with a bearish divergence when the maximum prices are getting higher and, nevertheless, the MACD maximums are getting lower, thus showing a signal that will be for sale.

RSI

The RSI (Relative Strength Index) is an indicator that measures the force with which supply and demand action in a moment of time. It is an oscillator when expressed by percentages. Its mathematical formula is as follows:

RSI = 100 – (100 /(1+RS))

First RS = Average Gain / Average Loss

Average Gain = Total Gain / n

Average Loss = Total Loss / n

Smoothed RS = [[(Previous Average Gain x 13) + Current Gain] / 14] /

[[(Previous Average Loss x 13) + Current Loss] x 14]

Where n is the number of sessions we are going to study, which will generally be 14 sessions; RS is the result of dividing the average increase that has occurred in the sessions that have risen (within those n sessions) between the average decrease produced in the sessions in which it has been lowered (within those n sessions).

The RSI is one of the easiest indicators to read. It offers two types of signals: oversold and overbought. The value that reflects the formula will always be between 0 and 100. A value of 50 would mean that supply and demand are matched, while a value greater than 70 reveals that the demand for securities presses higher, would be overbought and the value is more likely to bounce and lower its price. Conversely, if it were close to 30, it would be oversold and the likelihood of its price bouncing increases.

Bullish divergences, as in the MACD, occur when the minimum prices are lower and, however, the minimums of the same period of the RSI are bullish, showing us a buy signal. The bears, when there are increasingly high highs in the price and lowering highs of the RSI.

Moving Averages

We can define a moving average as the sum of a set of data and its division by the amount of data added. Moving averages soften the price curves, reducing the strong variations it presents due to volatility. They make it visually easier to show the trend that an asset is leading. Unfortunately, it is not an indicator that anticipates changes in trends, but it is an excellent support instrument for decision making.

There are mainly three types of means: the simple average, the weighted average, and the exponential average. We will highlight the first and the last. The simple moving average (SMA) is the average value of N closing prices of an asset. Being the most used, some of the great criticisms of this moving average is that it gives the same weight to all data and that it only takes into account the data of the period it covers.

We must bear in mind that the longer the period, the more smoothing and the slower reaction to the price action. On the contrary, if the period of the moving average is very short, many false signals will be produced. If the period is very long, the signals are generated quite late.

Using two moving averages of different time-spaces is very useful to confirm trend changes and evaluate the continuity and possible price correction. The exponential moving average (EMA), like the SMA, offers a smoothed correlation between price action and the passage of time. The difference is that the calculation of the exponential moving average gives more importance to the latest data obtained during a given period. Therefore, the last values have more weight in the final result than the first values of the calculation period; that is, we will have a faster reaction to recent changes in the price behavior.

Since a day trader needs to have fast information, a short period EMA will be the best (I use the 18), although it is usual to use a set of moving averages with different calculation periods, that is, a moving average of a long period that provides us with the general dominant trend in the market and a short-term moving average that provides us with information on the price behavior in a more current way and gives us a good entry point, if possible, in the direction of the main trend.

If we inquire more about moving averages, we will often read the term "crossing of averages" as a critical point of entry into the market. This consists of entering long when the moving average of the shortest period crosses from below upwards a moving average of the longest period. The signal to enter short will be when the moving average of the shortest period crosses a moving average of the longest period from top to bottom.

Thanks to José Luis Cárpatos, and his indispensable lions against gazelles, I discovered the reliable use of moving averages as supports and resistances, acting as barriers where the price has difficulties to continue. It is common for the price to approach a moving average over and over again and the higher the number of times the price approaches the moving average, the greater the strength of the support or resistance, increasing the probability of a bounce up in case of support or down in case of resistance. A flat moving average indicates that a phase has been reached in which prices have been consolidated and have created underlying support or resistance.

Fibonacci

We cannot stop to comment on the life of the Italian mathematician Leonardo de Pisa but his discovery: the succession of Fibonacci and its application to intraday trading. As we know, prices tend to move laterally or in trends that can be bullish or bearish. In the event that one of these trends has shown signs of exhaustion, we must consider the possibility of a setback, that is, a movement in the opposite direction of the trend.

Fibonacci retracements refer to the possibility that the price recedes a portion of the original movement, and finds support or resistance levels at the levels established by the Fibonacci numbers before continuing in the previous direction. These levels are constructed by drawing a trend line between the extreme points of the movement in question and applying the key percentages of 38 percent, 50 percent and 62 percent to the vertical distance.

Despite the seduction and magic of these numbers, we must combine Fibonacci levels with other indicators and price patterns before making a decision to enter the market.

Chapter 3 – Operational Requirements for Day Trading

In order to operate in the financial markets doing intraday, we need a graphing platform that allows us to analyze price movements in a comfortable and complete way, according to our investment system. We need a broker that mediates between us and the market and that executes the orders that we indicate with pinpoint accuracy and a news portal that informs us of the milestones and news that happen.

Graphing or Technical Analysis Programs

There are many graphing platforms. I have been working with Visual Chart since my beginnings, and although there is an innumerable offer with different prices and benefits, I remain faithful to the Spanish graphic designer. The benefits that we must demand from any plotter are, at a minimum, the security in the representation of the price, stability, rapid update of the quotes, versatility in the use of the indicators, access to historical and a reasonable price.

Brokers

At the moment there is so much offer of brokers that we can get lost in choosing the best one. The broker is the financial intermediary in our operations; that is, it is the intermediary between buyers and sellers. Therefore it is vital that it be good.

We must choose a broker that has a lot of net worth because of the greater the capital of the firm, the greater the protection of its funds. If you are a solid and respectable broker, you will have hundreds of employees who can assist us 24 hours a day. Customer service is very important because it will help us solve any possible incidents we may have. It is advisable to find a broker that solves them as quickly as possible, which does not hinder the withdrawal of funds, that do not have many complaints from other investors.

The broker must be regulated by a competent National Futures Association (NFA) in the United States, the Financial Services Authority (FSA) in the

United Kingdom or the National Stock Market Commission (CNMV) in Spain. Avoid brokers that are in tax havens. Brokers in Europe, Canada, Hong Kong, and Australia have adequate regulations, and capital requirements are high. If your broker is in an underdeveloped country, current regulations and guarantees may not be appropriate.

We must also pay attention to the leverage it allows. This can help us obtain considerable benefits, but it can also cause us huge losses. Some brokers offer a leverage of 100: 1, which means that for every dollar in your account, you can borrow and use up to € 100. You have to take into account the leverage it offers, as this can be a great ally. It must provide us with real-time information and good graphic tools—despite the fact that we have an independent graphic designer—that facilitates decision making.

It is necessary that the broker has a free demo (paper trading), which operates in real-time since it will be essential in the mandatory simulation period. In this way, it allows us to practice and learn with fictitious or real money the system of speculation that we implant.

In the event that we decide to trade forex, we must always do so through a broker that is ECN (Electronics Communications Network), and never with a market maker.

The Market Maker

First, it is a mere intermediary that seeks compensation for your operation, charging a commission for it; while the second is who gives us the counterpart, that is, operates against us and there have been "rare" cases with this type of broker. Do not forget that the market maker covers the position with other operations or does not cover it so that it assumes the opposite risk to yours. That is if we win, the market maker loses, which generates a conflict of interest.

In short, a broker is a commission agent who does not have to know about investments and who in fact does not know, who is engaged in executing operations on our own or that of a financial institution and who charges for it (be careful, some even twenty times more than others).

They live on commissions, not that you win or lose. If you do a few operations and earn a lot of money, you are not a good customer for them. Look for a broker that does not belong to any bank and preferably from an Anglo-Saxon country, with low commissions and that has a good platform to operate in any market in the world in "long" and "short" positions. And above all, avoid choosing a broker that offers you a welcome gift, a discount or a credit account, since this is a clear warning sign, to be before a "Second B" and we want to play in "First."

Since my inception, I operate with Interactive Brokers, and I have not yet found anyone to beat him.

Newspaper

The influence of macroeconomic data is very important in intraday operations. This information comes out almost every day and news about the state of both the US economy and the rest of the world is published. The data will have more or less impact according to the different situations, but there are some that are always important. The influence of this data in the market can change a trend. Volatility tends to increase before publication, and many traders close positions before data and open them right after publication.

For our good work, we must have a news portal that anticipates these references and alerts us of the degree of relevance to be prevented. If you can afford the news of Reuters Financial perfect, otherwise, try with free information websites like www.bloomberg.com/markets/economic-calendar/ or http://investing.com/economiccalendar/ that measure the degree of importance of the news and report your possible correlation. It also has an interesting real-time alert service under subscription.

Finally, indicate that operating the relevant news intraday is something that only an experienced trader with great skill in this guillotine time should do.

Material Requirements

Sometimes, people associate the day trading activity with the operating rooms of the large hedge funds that have eight to ten screens per position, special keyboards to enter orders, advanced graphing programs, and the classic braces, ties Hermès and gummed hair. Reality is far enough.

The truth is that at the least, you will need a fast and reliable internet connection, and a computer dedicated to the plotter and to launch the orders to the broker. The number of screens you need depends on the markets in which you operate and your personal preferences. There are traders that operate with three or four screens, but there are also others that do everything from a laptop, and even the most daring ones that do everything from their iPad. Of course, the latter is not recommended, but none of it will make the difference between winning or losing.

You must feel comfortable. Have a clean workspace and where you see all the graphics and events that, in the short period of time in which you operate, arise. Avoid having unnecessary distractions on your work table. Do try to have an ergonomic chair. All this does not make you a better trader, but it helps. Be very careful with the weapon of mass distraction, for example – the mobile, totally expendable while operating. I only find its usefulness in the event that we run out of electric power at home, and we had to close our position from the application of the broker on the mobile - almost all brokers have their own. As you can see, something unusual, and that should not be a problem if we operate with protection stops.

Trades Control Sheet

You will also need the computer, portable or similar, to attend in the simulation period (Sunday) and reflect all the trades you are doing. Checking your results in a notebook - virtual or not - trading is essential. In it, and throughout the months, a decrease in errors and a growth in successes should be reflected. In day trading, as in life, one advances, stagnates or recedes; It is unbearably real. In the resources section, you can find a couple of trades tracking files that I use, courtesy of my friends Maitane Zárate and Saturnino Merayo.

Types of Inputs and Stops

One of the concepts that we should have been clearer is when doing intraday trading are the types of orders and how to adapt our circumstances at any time to enter or exit the market, always in the most advantageous way for our interests.

We must master this field until it becomes a mechanical act like when we drive a car and change gears. Obviously, each platform or broker is a different "car," but in all of them, there are the most common types of orders described here.

Market order: It is used to buy or sell an instrument at the highest possible speed at the price that can be obtained in the market. The order is executed entirely at the best possible price, always, of course, that there is a counterpart.

Limited orders: We set a maximum price for our purchase orders and a minimum for sales orders. In this way, the operation will always be carried out at a price set by us. They are usually the most common orders and are used to buy or sell an instrument when the price goes up/down to a certain level, that is, to buy below the current price or sell above it. We must not forget that if a limited purchase order is introduced at a higher price than the market, the order will be executed immediately at the price of the offer on the market, as it is a better price for the buyer than the one entered in the market order, immediately becoming a market order.

An order limited to one price may only be executed at a lower price (if it is a purchase order) or higher (if it is a sale order) than the current one.

Stop: A stop is a market order to buy or sell an asset when the price we have specified is reached or crossed. We use them to limit losses in case of adverse market movements. They can also be used to collect benefits in winning positions.

Dynamic stop: A dynamic stop allows us to establish a stop price that will move quickly with the price of the asset, as long as the movement is in our favor and respects the distance in percentage or basic points that we have established when defining the order. If the contract goes up, the dynamic stop will move, always respecting the initial distance indicated in the initial operation. If instead, the market turns against us, the stop will be anchored in the original price to protect us with it.

Bracket orders: it is my favorite and possibly the most complete order. The first purchase or sale order is sent to the market. After the execution of this first order, a limited profit target and a stop order are sent to the market. When one of them has been executed, the remaining order will be canceled. It is an order designed to help limit the risk of loss and in turn, collect the benefits.

Speculation Systems

We must start from the basis that the most important part of an intraday speculation system is the trader himself. If we are not "fine," we can already have the best system ever created that our trading will not go as it should. That said, mention that the systems that behave better in the long term are the simplest. The more complicated our system, the more variables we will be introducing and more possibilities will exist that we have optimized it uselessly, ceasing to function as soon as an unexpected event occurs.

There are certain pillars that every winning system must contemplate as is the capital, since the more is available in the broker's account, the easier it will be to obtain the necessary benefit to live doing day trading. Operating with more capital means operating with less risk. Forgetting, therefore, wanting to make a great fortune with accounts of 20,000 euros or similar, this can only be done with a large account.

Market entry is another key to the speculation system. There is not and will not be a system that yields a percentage of successes of one hundred percent, so we must develop the mental strength necessary to use only ours, not to be tempted to resort to others, and to refine our input technique, since using others at the same time will decrease our percentage of successes.

The exit, the great forgotten and probably the most critical point of the system. We are obsessed with finding the entry point, but it will be the exit point that will give us the success of the operation. If we do not want to leave manually, we will have to resort to profit stops, dynamic stops, or bracket orders. Letting go of the benefit of a winning operation is an art, and as such, it involves study, discipline, preparation and a few hundred "I should have stayed a little longer" or "pity, I had a fantastic operation, and I didn't close."

The stop loss and its fulfillment in which royal decree is the last of the pillars of the system. Avoid the "mental stops" that with the hope of "I will return my operation to the point of entry" make us lose more of the account; Therefore, they must be executed automatically. Placing the stop closer to the entry point does not mean fewer losses but more risk that a violent market movement will sweep our stop. Placing the stop loss is a matter of experience rather than technique.

Therefore, if you want to have the opportunity to live doing day trading, you must create a system that respects these laws and follows it closely, with no feelings involved. It should be remembered that the most difficult thing about a speculation system is not to create the rules but to follow them; That is where the difference lies. It is the line that separates professionals from those who are not.

If one is new in the art of speculation, the ideal is to apply other trader systems, as long as they respect our parameters, monetary management (Friday), they have been designed for the market we operate and also adapt to our profile of trader I still use two systems: one for forex and one for the mini S & P500 and mini Nasdaq, both of two excellent traders. The first one for forex is from the American John F. Carter, author among others of Dominate the trading. The second, from an excellent Spanish trader, Diego Gómez, author of the ozonotimes.com blog.

Mr. Carter designed a system called "the boxes," which consists of discovering situations in which a market rests before preparing for the next push, either up or down. We will look for a period of horizontal consolidation with at least two tests in maximums and two tests in minima. Once we have these two tests, what we will look for is to buy in an upside-down break of the box, or sell in a downward break. The time frame is usually five and fifteen minutes. The objective in these operations is the width of the box. "Carter's boxes" are a system of operations in moments of inertia, although we will not know that there is a box until the price marks the fourth test and returns to the center of the box. Once we have drawn a box on our plotter, we introduce two orders. We introduce a purchase stop a tick above the maximum of the box, and we introduce a sale stop a tick below the minimum of the box. It does not matter in which direction the market breaks, as we will be there waiting with the order ready to execute.

Let's imagine the sales stop skips. The purchase stop automatically becomes my stop loss, and we place the limited profit below the order, exactly the width measured by the box.

Imagine a "Carter box" with two supports and resistors. Once the price passes the supports, the short entry is activated, with the stop at the height of the resistance and as a first objective the width of the box. Once this goal is exceeded, we let the rest of our position run with a dynamic stop.

The general rule for the Carter box system dictates that if we have to ask ourselves if there really is a box on the chart, then there is no box on the chart. Once the boxes are formed, they are quite evident. Personally, to say that every morning when I wake up, the first thing I do is see if during the night - from the opening of Tokyo at 02.00 until 08.00 which opens Frankfurt— the EUR and USD have drawn a box. If not, that day, I do not usually operate the forex, but otherwise, I prepare my stop orders, and I get ready to see how they are executed. He usually does so with a really surprising success rate.

Returning to the general lines of intraday speculation systems, these will be more useful the more we manage to focus some master lines on a given market situation. By its very nature, intraday is best done in very liquid markets, where the negotiated volume allows us to enter and exit very quickly, always finding a counterpart and minimizing the slippage in the execution of orders.

Both the S & P500 and Nasdaq mini futures, both US indices, fit the description and are among the most traded in the world. The intraday operation allows specializing in specific market situations, in which to take advantage of specific behaviors and conditions, as for example, the opening of the market, at which time volatility is triggered and movements are very fast and of a generally greater range. To work on the Ozone Openings of the mini S & P500 and the mini Nasdaq, I first certify that the market is in trend, checking that in the daytime dimension, any classic indicator, such as the MACD, ADX or RSI point out trend unequivocally. Then, in a ten-minute chart, I await the opening of the market, starting at 3.30 pm Spanish time. I use a graphic of heik candles in ashi. The conditions to operate are simple: the same indicator that we have used during the day should set the trend, and the price should be on the same side of an average of 20 - it can be simple or exponential, according to tastes -

than that trend. If this is the case, the input signal is the first sign opposite the trend, the entry point is the maximum of that candle in the bullish case, and the stop is the minimum of the signal candle. In a bearish case, the entrance will be the minimum of the signal candle, and the stop is its maximum. The profit target is about two or three points, depending on the market volatility, which can be measured, for example, with the ATR, and give us an idea that a reasonable objective is 1/5 of the daily ATR.

Stop Loss

One of the questions I most frequently face is: "Good, but where do I put the stop loss?" My most common answer is that the best site to position the stop loss is that level that if reached would make us rethink the entire entry strategy again. However, there is evidence that without stop loss, it is not possible to calculate the profitability/risk of the operation and that we will not be able to propose a correct monetary management. Without stop loss, there is no professional trading, and there is adrenaline, chance, luck, and betting. We must understand that the market moves; it is not static, so our stop loss should not be either. We will move the stop based on technical and non-emotional criteria. Sometimes it is time to keep the stop. Sometimes it's time to move it. The analysis tells us when and the monetary management will tell us how much.

The further we stop the stop loss, the more money we can lose; The closer we get, the easier it is for us to stay out of play early. Everything that is not being passed means falling short, and vice versa. With the stop loss, we will quickly cut the losses. This does not mean that fast is the same as before time. It means that it serves to distinguish when we have succeeded and when not. We must place it at the point that shows the evidence of our error without ever meaning to lose a percentage greater than 0.5 percent of our capital. The stop loss must keep a balance with the objective to be achieved, but it will be the graph that gives us its best location. We must observe the candles and look at their shape and how they connect with their neighbors, if they are long or short, if there are jumps between them or tend to overlap each other, if they tend to have more body than shadow, if they form slowly and Predictable way, if the price makes many feints and deceptions or advances without hesitation. This type of observation is what allows us to decide if the price can go back to a certain point without losing the objective we are interested in achieving. Often, the best position for stop loss is support or prior resistance. These zones usually divide exchange zones and, if they are broken, the price trend is likely to change direction.

Before positioning our stop loss, it is also convenient to see the graph in different time spaces. Being day traders, the dimensions we use most are 1, 3, 5, 10 or 15 and 60 minutes, so we must observe the movement in all of them, in addition to seeing the general direction of the price in the day chart. This is important as we will avoid cheating. What seems to us a clear upward momentum in the one-minute chart can be an obvious setback in the five-minute chart. On a few occasions, we will be sure of the location of our stop, but these are the uncertainties and difficulties of day trading. In addition, and as if that were not enough, we will always want to enter the market at the beginning of a movement and exit when it is sold out. We will not be able to capture one hundred percent of the movement, but the stop loss should help us catch as much as possible, protecting the accumulated gains thanks to moving the stop loss as our operation progresses positively.

In short, it is very difficult to assist the trader in the position that his stop loss must put. The essential thing is to put it on and, in the event that it jumps, the monetary management that we have set is respected. The traders erred in infinite occasions; the important thing is that these errors do not suppose a definitive goodbye.

Monetary Management

Monetary management serves to maximize profits when they occur, minimize losses - which occur! - and know the maximum number of contracts we can use, although we will never put them on the market. Monetary management is the mathematics of trading and, therefore, one of the most boring and least understood by most traders. However, it will be responsible for our account to grow in geometric progression, or the cause, on the contrary, of a rapid and painful ruin.

Therefore, money management or monetary management is a mathematical algorithm that decides how much we will risk in the next operation, depending on the available capital. Many well-known authors establish the following relationship between trading and monetary management: before taking a position we are traders, and when we are already in the market, we stop being traders and become monetary and risk managers.

Monetary management must be independent of the system we apply, as well as the market in which we are operating since what we need is a series of operations with the net result of each of them. This is the information that monetary management uses, and it doesn't matter if they come from the mini S & P500 or the forex. Monetary management offers us to improve our risk-return ratio, in which profitability is measured by the net return generated by our system and the risk by our maximum DrawDown or maximum percentage of daily loss.

I am in favor of never making more than three entries in the market a day. The first one will be with a third of what our monetary management formula throws. If in the first market entry the stop skips, in the second we must enter with half of the contracts; and if we lose again, in the third and last, with fewer contracts yet. On the contrary, while we are winning, we will continue with the same number of contracts as in the first of our tickets.

This is the formula I use to operate the future of the mini S & P500:

Numerator: Capital that we have multiplied by the maximum loss in percentage that I am willing to assume per day (maximum 2 percent).

Denominator: Maximum loss in dollars that I can suffer (100 dollars since I place a 2-point stop).

Result: maximum number of contracts that you could place per day.

Example:

$ 45,000 x 2% / 100 = 9 contracts per day.

We would enter the market with a third of our monetary management, that is, three contracts. In the event that the operation is unsuccessful and there is a possibility of re-entering, there will only be two contracts with which we could operate. In the event that we also skip the stop and see another opportunity to enter the market, the last entry would be with a contract. In this way and in the case of a disastrous day like the one exposed with three consecutive stops, our maximum loss has not exceeded 2 percent of the total capital as we had set. On the contrary, if we get the first entry right, we can continue to operate with three contracts, so that we will protect our benefits when the losing streak comes and let them run on the winning streaks.

If you are a novel trader, monetary management must be very strict, even lowering 1 percent of our capital if it is less stressful. Remember the importance of operating in a market tailored to our account.

In the forex, I use the following monetary formula: I never lose more than 0.5 percent of my capital per trade, and I never do more than two failed operations a day. Under this simple premise, I place the stop loss, looking for a profit potential three times higher than my stop. I use a lot (100 k) for every 20,000 euros.

Simple truth? Well, it has taken me a lot of time and money to mark it and, above all, respect it.

When we face the market and start making numbers, we realize the importance of starting the operation on the right foot. Mistakes at the beginning are paid much more expensive; Let's see why. Suppose we start from an initial capital of 20,000 euros and, after a month of trading in the markets, we have lost 2,000 euros or 10 percent. To return to the starting point we will have to generate 2,000 euros, but now we start from 18,000 euros and not 20,000 euros as at the initial moment, so to recover the lost 10 percent, we will have to be able to generate 11 percent. If the loss is 20 percent, we need to generate 25 percent and so on. Therefore it is vital not to rush, operating in the real market only when you have a simulated experience, with a minimum number of trades and the speculation system we are going to use has been collated. Otherwise, the risk of asymmetric leverage will be our inseparable travel companion.

Goals

Every successful trader sets a goal and a time limit to achieve it. We will do the same under a prism of prudence. The answer to the question "Why more?" It can lead us to full happiness as day traders. Plausible objectives will help our operation. If we think more is better, we will never be satisfied.

One of the great attractions of day trading is to make money quickly. However, that should not be the only objective; We must worry about doing good operations and forget about the profit/loss that is at stake since it is the formula to make money consistently and improve our skills day by day. Rookie traders often ask how much money you can earn a year by trading intraday; They look for a figure that serves as a reference, a magic figure on which to base the decision to leave a monotonous job and achieve financial independence. This is not, however, the right question. What we have to ask ourselves is: "How much money will I lose until I learn to trade and create a winning trading strategy?" I insist because it is important: the objective of the trader is to make good operations, and the money must be in the background because if we make good operations, the money will come without us noticing.

The maximum objective of losses must be kept in mind. As monetary management indicates, we should not allow losses in a day that exceed 2 percent of the capital, and we will set a maximum of 6 percent of monthly losses. This means that if we move forward in a month and exceed that limit of loss with respect to our capital, we must stop the operation, check the system, make an analysis of the reasons for errors and check our psychotrading.

As for the profit objective for novice day traders, in training period or returning to operation after some lapse or bump, it is 1 point on average per day per contract, that is, 50 dollars if we talk about the future of the mini S & P500 and we operate with only one contract. They always reply that it is a pyrrhic and unambitious goal. My answer is that it is "on average," that is, there will be days that we will earn 5 points and others that we lose 4. The important thing is to add 20 points per contract per month (the months usually have between 18 and 22 days of operation).

We must not ignore what a miserable point per day per contract can do for us over the years. Not rushing to make large numbers is one of the greatest guarantees when it comes to intraday trading. Example of operation at one point per contract in the mini S & P500 (operating 11 months per year):

Starting from a capital of $ 20,000, operating eleven months a year with a slight leverage and looking for a point of half a day per contract, the fifth year we will start with a figure of 174,000 dollars, which would allow us to have an excellent return on capital. What is the problem? That many traders seek to make $ 174,000 the first or second year, leveraging excessively and seeking in their intraday operations 3 or 4 points on average per contract, and end up losing money by having an excessive target and an excess of greed.

The objectives should not be difficult, should be realistic and be adapted to each person's knowledge, and capital. This does not mean that they should not be ambitious, but above all, the goals should be possible. Earning $ 50 / day is a goal available to any trader. Let's start with that goal. More intense challenges will come. Until then, let's take the pressure off. There are hundreds of traders better than us, with more experience, larger accounts, there are hundreds of Hegde Fund traders, investment banks, large corporations, institutional investors, pension funds. We are small and live to take advantage of the small but innumerable opportunities of 1 point a day offered by the market.

Chapter 4 – Mistakes, Errors, and Enemies of the Day Trader

- Operate with positions higher than the capacity of your broker account. For a new trader, excessive leverage poses a danger of death to his account.
- Focus on the result or major objective—that which achieves your financial independence—rather than on skill and the search for patterns. A fiasco that ends most traders at first exchange.
- Pay too much attention to the opinions of others. The recommendations are free; the losses are ours. Listen to the opinions of another, if you think so, but take them like that, as opinions.
- The convenient thing is to analyze the markets and their values from their own information and perspectives. Because if everything goes wrong, the one in the recommendations will tell you some milonga and you will keep the hole in your pocket.
- The impatience. We must think trade a trade, point to point. Identify yourself with Rafael Nadal. He can't win Roland Garros without missing any ball, game, or even set. He goes slowly like us in day trading, thinking of him in the next ball and us in the next operation. Everything arrives, Rafa will win the tournament, and we will reach the goals, but neither will do it in a single set.
- Don't be afraid to ask for help. Most traders are afraid to ask for help and, when they finally decide to do so, they don't insist enough, or it's too late. Big mistake. I have lived the experience in my flesh and other day traders whose problems were easy to tackle and solve. The intraday operation seen from outside by another trader reveals behaviors or errors that the subject itself can ignore. Do not hesitate to ask for help. In the worst case, you already have it the "no."
- You have high expectations and are unaware of the link between those expectations and how frustrated a trader can feel. Every time

something is expected to be in a certain way, and it is not, it is suffered. On the other hand, when we part with expectations, we are free. Holding on means more pressure and not doing more relaxed trading.

- Compare with other traders and their results instead of measuring with respect to our objectives. Looking over the rearview mirror - the losses and/or past mistakes - and on the sides - other traders - is not a guarantee of improvement but quite the opposite, as it usually undermines our confidence.

- Security addiction. We live surrounded by control, surveillance cameras, lawyers, "guaranteed" investments, health insurance, civil liability, life and death, antivirus, armored doors ... and much more of measures that give us a false sense of security. Well, in day trading you travel naked, nothing protects you except common sense, uncertainty is the only companion, and you travel without companion insurance. Bad luck or good, depending on how you look at it.

- Avoid inflation. The hidden enemy of most people who read this book. If you keep money in the bank, without getting an amount that exceeds the effect of inflation, you're heading for ruin. A slow death, relatively painless because you still see the same amount of money, but with a decrease in purchasing power year after year.

- To think that a good day of day trading is only if we have earned money. The reality is that if you have followed good practices, executed the orders well, and respected your monetary management, you have had a good day of trading, regardless of the final result.

- Ignore that the market is never wrong; it is we who misunderstand it. Either we lose our ego, or we will lose our money.

- Underestimate the market. Stupidity, carelessness, or a simple attack of pride can empty the account of the broker won over the months.

- Going out to the real market with little training, with an untested speculation system or with little experience in managing the broker and its platform. The rush to go to the real market can be disastrous for our interests.

- Think that you have discovered the Holy Grail of market indicators. All oscillators and indicators can help us, but the trader is the most important "piece" in the intraday speculation puzzle.
- Operate in more than five or six markets. No one prohibits this practice, but common sense suggests that you only venture once you have mastered the chosen market. Operating in seventeen markets makes no sense. Maximum four.
- Try to recover the money the way it has been lost. What has led us to lose money? Operate for others, skip the stop, have no patience, risky monetary management ...? Well, to return to the path of positive operations—not recovering lost money, that has already left—we must do the opposite.
- Do not relativize. Will this error/stop loss matter in a year? Has anyone died? Well, that is not worth having a hard time for a simple mistake. If you follow your system, put the stops, and respect your monetary management, you can get carried away by these two simple rules:

    1) Do not suffer from small things.

    2) Complying with the rules, in day trading everything is small.

- Do not define the objectives. We must hope for the best and prepare for the worst. The objectives must be written. The more detailed, the better. There are no unattainable goals but unrealistic dates.
- Sinning late for mistakes and not assuming them. We are able to convince ourselves that there are still possibilities, long after accumulated evidence convinced anyone that the operation is a disaster.
- Fall in love with our market tickets. Do not keep losing operations, because you can re-enter and stop being so. Do not convert a market

entry into a swing trading entry—entries that do not close on the day, which can be days, weeks, months, and even years.

- Take failed operations to bed. I initially took three: the wrong operations of days gone by, those of the present day and those that were to come. Avoid it.
- Operate as a team. Trading is a solitary game, and the orders you place on the market should not be by consensus but by your own criteria. Trust your talent and forget Skype traders. In day trading, Excel is more useful than Skype.
- Look for market turns. Play as an intraday prophet. Intuition is good and necessary but in moderate doses.
- Do not return to the paper trading or broker simulator when it takes a few consecutive bad days. It is obvious, but the ego usually prevents it. Do not underestimate the importance of simulated trading to gain confidence and analyze the causes of our mistake.
- Do not ask yourself every day after the operation: "What did I do well today? What did I do well in this operation? What mistakes did I not make? What did I do better this week than the last?" These answers show us what works best and, consequently, what we should focus on.
- Forgetting that the objective the first year is not to live on trading, but to keep the account, minimize losses, and refine your trading system.
- Obvious intuition. In trading, there is a strong intuitive component, in which market information is scarce, and the time factor is fundamental. Intuition not only tells us what and how, but also when. Developing intuition will cost us a few stops but once developed, it will let us know when it is time to pay special attention.
- Always operate. Let's be good, bad, tired, colds, etc. Don't underestimate the value of doing nothing. If you are not centered or do not look good, turn off the screen and do not operate. There are more days than pilgrimages.

- Impulsive operations. They are as exciting as they are dangerous. They were the reason for my lousy start in the world of trading. Although we are intraday operators, we must be patient. Not everything happens in the first minute of operation.

- Forget that we will not be able to be in all market movements so you should not overwhelm us if we miss an opportunity. How many operations and trend movements will we lose in the next years of operation? One thousand? Eight thousand? Patience, and remember that in day trading we must be good snipers and not some gunmen. Launching into the market with the feeling of "I'm losing this trend movement, and I'm stopping winning" is the prelude to an ominous operation.

- Focus on profit and not skill. When you have a series of bad days, instead of operating for benefits, you operate to avoid losing money. Focusing on the result interferes with our operations and paradoxically distances us from the objective.

- Feeling scared when we earn 1 percent on our capital, which precipitates us to sell the operation outrageously. And, on the contrary, losing that same percentage and feeling hopeful and not closing, making our winning operations ridiculous with respect to the losers.

- Do not remember that no one sells us the step to success in day trading. Opportunities abound and await those who believe in themselves; they prepare and adopt positive attitudes. We must distance ourselves from spoilers. Being pessimistic is as comfortable as it is dangerous.

Chapter 5 – Psycho Trading

We enter the final stretch of the week, and it is time to address another fundamental aspect for a successful day trader: emotion management. Nothing brings us closer or further away from the success in day trading than self-control and how we react to the various scenarios that occur in intraday trading. Trading affects our psychology as much as psychology affects our trading. The market has an advantage over us, and it is that it has no emotion—quite the opposite of us, who experience states of euphoria, fear, panic, greed, anguish, among others.

Day trading is a game that involves two risks: the decrease in the capital contributed and the loss of self-confidence. The loss of money in the first shipments is insured and the second risk, too. Now, it is true that money is recovering little by little, and that trust requires daily training that will make us stronger and thanks to which, we will avoid both risks.

No one can do this psychological training for us. Other day traders can trace our system, habits, and way of operating, but what they cannot copy are the emotions we live and how we manage them. Those experiences are inviolable. My friend and trader Enrique Díaz Valdecantos says: "Do not worry about the result of the operation, worry about how you will face the emotion when it appears because it almost always appears."

Living on day trading is not a simple purpose to achieve. When we see the bulls from the barrier, we have the impression that we can "take a pass" without too much effort. But when you have to deal, in this case with the market, you quickly notice that it is not so easy. And it is not easy because we usually approach this discipline with a rational mind.

Psycho trading represents 70 percent of the success in our operations, leaving 20 percent to the monetary management and 10 percent to the speculation system. This means that the lack of emotional control is what separates the vast majority of day traders from the desired consistency, and, as a consequence, of their economic benefits. To win in day trading, you must first win yourself. Emotions end with one. We remember all the lost opportunities, and those memories devour us inside. In this frantic process of making trading decisions, keeping a cool head is vital. Emotions must be controlled, the information processed correctly, and the market position is taken. This allows us to earn points. This sounds easy, but it is not. If day trading were simple, it would not generate so much satisfaction.

The market will surprise us by not acting rationally. If we don't want to be surprised, it is best not to expect anything from him. You cannot be confused if you admit that you don't know what the market is going to do. He can only miss those who have set a pattern in his mind about his behavior. When you think you know all the answers, the market changes all your questions, as tragic as magical. Many times I hear predictions like the following: «If the price touches this resistance, it will bounce, and we will make a profit. If it were that easy, everyone would earn money.

The majority of successful day traders admit that we earn money by executing our trading plan. We don't try to guess where the price will go. We don't know what the market will do, and to some extent, we don't care. That "coldness" takes a while and a few euros to arrive since it is normal at the beginning that we sabotage ourselves, that we make a series of systematic mistakes. Sometimes, we do not get the trade thought, and we keep trying and failing. In others, we lose and enter with double the amount to recover the loss, we lose again and double again; At this point, we are already so neurotic and lost that we look like some walking dead in front of the screens. The opposite is also the case; we have a couple of great days, we believe Tom Cruise, so we increase the risk, make impossible entries and, in the end, we end the previous earnings.

As you can see, most mistakes have an emotional condition, since almost all day traders know their system perfectly and usually respect monetary management. However, the barriers to anxiety, impatience, divination, greed, fear, panic, doubts, or tiredness are more difficult to lift. Day trading bares our limits and skills, showing us who we are. When you operate, it's you alone; you don't depend on anyone just for yourself. At that moment you realize that you don't fight the market, you do it against you. Our main enemy is under our skin, we compete against our fears, doubts, insecurities, limiting beliefs, negativity, greed, pride, anxiety, expectations, frustrations, envies, etc. In short, you fight against your ego. As my trader, friend and coach German

Antelo argue: "The ego will seek at all times to take control of the situation to get rid of the operation and bring out the worst of us for its own aggrandizement. This battle is lost one hundred percent of the time. Our only advantage is that we can decide what to lose, whether the ego or the money. You choose the travel companion".

Day trading is a journey in which you will live inscrutable stages. You start with the expectation of seeing in your own flesh what is what they have told us that makes life more exciting and that makes money and, above all, time. After a start in which we focus on systems and know in detail the keys to the market, we move forward for a few months in a state of euphoric results. The operation in simulated means that we will soon have a command of the operation, because, in simulated operations, there are no risks and the emotions generated by winning and losing money does not come out. This state advances in some cases to the point of overtraining and subsequent relaxation. It seems that we were born for day trading. The excellent days follow one another, and we decide that it is time to move on to the real one.

The real step is a critical moment; emotions accelerate, we begin to doubt whether to enter the market or wait, we are afraid of the stop skips, we rush, etc. In short, we panicked at something that was exactly the same as a week ago, but now our profit and loss account varies. Faced with the first losses of both capital and confidence, there are states of anxiety, of doubts about our capabilities, of disbelief in the face of what was yesterday a state of flux with the market and today is an unbeatable storm. As a consequence, many abandon what looked like a day's flower. Those who manage to "get their heads" by force of constancy, effort and control over their abilities are true survivors, who with daily effort will achieve, in their time, the desired consistency that allows, despite having bad days, to recover the euphoric dream to live comfortably from intraday trading and be rich in time.

For all this, emotional control is one of the bases of our success as traders. We should not underestimate it, or spend less time than we spend designing our speculation system or our monetary management operation. Working our emotional control will improve the results of our operations. The main reason for not making money is in our lack of discipline, planning, and psycho trading. The powerful trading industry knows this and tries to solve our problems, outside of ourselves, leading us to the search for the Holy Grail, the last indicator or system. Let's not fool ourselves by these siren songs and learn to control our emotions.

For novice traders, the only problem they address when they start in the world of day trading is finding ways to make money easy and fast. Once the first setbacks come, they discover that trading can become the most daunting experience they have faced. The trader must learn to think in terms of probabilities and must trust himself. Traders who trust their own possibilities and do what we must do without hesitation, they are the ones who become winners. The greater your confidence, the easier it will be to execute your operations.

Intelligence and good market analysis will undoubtedly contribute to success, but they are not the definitive factors that separate the consistent winners from everyone else. Winners have achieved attitudes that allow them to remain disciplined, focused, and, above all, with confidence despite adverse market conditions.

Another reason that warns about inequality between novice traders, with poor emotional management and the winners is that the former has a low perception of the meaning of taking risks in the way in which the successful trader does so. The best not only assume the risk but have also learned to accept and appropriate that risk. They can put an operation without the slightest hint of hesitation or conflict, and just as freely admit that it is not working. They can lose and not feel emotional discomfort.

Once you learn to accept the risk, the market will not be able to generate information that can be defined or interpreted as painful. If the information generated by the market does not have the potential to cause emotional pain, there is nothing to avoid. The best traders are not afraid. The difficult and crude reality of day trading is that each operation has an uncertain result. More market analysis is not the way to consistent results since it will not solve the problems created by lack of trust, lack of discipline, or poor concentration.

Finally, when we reach a state of mind in which we accept the risk, we also eliminate the tendency to rationalize, doubt and expect the market to "give us your money" or "save" us from a painful drawdown.

At this point, we already know that the market has no rules, but in order to perform day trading, we will need them: rules to guide our minds and our behavior. Create a set of rules and submit to them without resisting. The need for these rules makes sense, but it is difficult to generate the motivation to create them. If we are also successful people in another discipline away from day trading, it will cost us more to understand its operation. In life, we develop skills and knowledge so that external factors act according to what we want, and thus achieve objectives. The problem is that none of these techniques work against the market since it does not respond to any control. Therefore, instead of controlling our environment, we must learn to control ourselves, so that we always behave in a way that is positive for our own interests.

Our goal should be to learn to think like a consistent and successful day trader, managing emotions in favor of operation without fear and without fear of making mistakes. There lies much of the success, the absence of the effects of fear and recklessness when doing our trading. This feature allows us to achieve permanent results. Once the fear is gone, there will be no reason to make mistakes and, consequently, practically disappear from our operation.

Another factor to be developed is moderation. We must counteract the negative effects of the euphoria that lurks after a series of good days. For a day trader, winning is extremely dangerous if you have not learned to control the enthusiasm and to burn off the days with positive results.

The consistency we seek is in our mind, not in the information that the market throws. Instead of learning to think like intraday speculators, most concentrate on thinking how you can make more money learning about the market. It sounds topical, but the attitude generally produces better results than the analysis or technique.

Interestingly, most traders are closer to the right way of thinking when they first operate, since they start with an unrealistic concept of the dangers of day trading. This lack of fear translates into a carefree state of mind in which there is no fear and acts and reacts instinctively. You don't think about studying alternatives or the possibility of the consequences we can suffer. It operates and is in the present moment, and the right is done, which turns out to be exactly the right thing.

Few traders reach this level of operation, because they do not overcome the fear of making a mistake. Those who do not fear the consequences enter a state of flow in which they find themselves. Once we rethink the market rationally or consciously, we are expelled from this state. Although we cannot force ourselves to enter this state of flow, since it is a mental state that one cannot voluntarily reach, we can configure the type of mental conditions that are most conducive to experiencing it, through a positive winning attitude.

As day traders, we must establish a carefree mental state, which will be an essential component for our success. When we are confident and free from fears and worries, it is easy to have a series of winning trades, because we will find ourselves in a state of mind where we will have what we need to make it seem obvious. It's almost as if the market yells at us when to buy and when to sell, and we need little analysis. Unfortunately, a positive attitude, together with a good analytical ability, can never prevent a day trader from losing operations. The markets are so unpredictable and erratic that it is crazy to consider the possibility that any trader will always be right. That only happens in dreams and in movies.

In short, why is psychotrading so easy to explain and so complicated to implement? I think my friend and trader Lorenzo Gianninoni explains it very well in his blog: "Trading is not being right or not, it is a pure probability." If we do not understand and accept that, we should not move on. Same employer, same situation, same everything, and nobody knows how that trade will end. Why is it so difficult to accept that? Because we need to change our mentality and nobody wants to change. We don't like to change!

Simulation Period

The task of the simulation period or paper trading is to reproduce the trading in the closest possible way to real trading. Once we have learned how the futures, the forex or the market that we are going to operate work, we know how to read the graphics, we know the monetary management that we must apply and the psychological aspects that we will support, it is time to translate it under our live trading plan but without the collateral damage produced by day trading. It's time to start feeling trader and operate in simulation.

Obviously, the first time we can make purchases and test sales, to see how the simulator works. But once we know how it works, we must stop launching random operations and become serious. Please, let's stay with this idea: the only difference we must admit between operating in real or virtual is that if we operate in real, we send our orders to the broker; and if we operate in virtual, we send them to the simulator. Most of the novels mistakenly think that speculating is basically issuing orders, being very far from reality. Speculating is preparing for an emotional roller coaster. It consists of developing strategies, usually on a technical analysis of graphics, and executing them with iron discipline; apply rigorous monetary management and document each and every operation as they are carried out; analyze the parameters that characterize our results and adapt to the market and ourselves constantly.

As you can see, if we take it seriously and practice to really learn, there is no better tool than a simulator. This will save us money and dislikes as long as we don't make the mistake of thinking that, by spending a while throwing random orders, we will learn to speculate. We have to work with the simulator, not play with it. The simulator allows us all the freedom in the world, but we must discipline it. Whether we have just arrived at day trading or if we are going through a period of poor results, the period of practice in simulation is mandatory, but with one condition: we must do it as if we were living in it, with the rigor of a professional. Otherwise, we will not learn anything.

Despite all the praises in favor of the simulation period, it should also be clarified that for many courses and sessions we do we will never get enough mastery in day trading if we do not put all the practice into real and risk our money. On the other hand, in simulated, we cannot practice one hundred percent the mental aspect, which is the most important. Another milestone to keep in mind is that we must contemplate that our simulated experience includes a variety of cycles and market conditions; otherwise, our trading will not be complete.

Taxation

Until 2012, capital gains from the sale of shares, currencies, futures, or capital gains from the sale of an investment fund were taxed by being integrated into the savings base of the IRPF scheme.

They did this by applying a fixed rate, which was 21 percent for the first 6,000 euros; 25 percent if capital gains were between 6,000 euros and 24,000 euros; and 27 percent from 24,000 euros. All this, regardless of the period in which the capital gain was generated. That is, it did not differentiate between more than one year and less than one year. So for our activity, in which the goodwill is generated in less than a year, and even in less than a day, if you materialized short-term goodwill, the corresponding flat rate for the savings base was applied.

However, with the new taxation of 2013, the "fiscal hell" that Spain has become today, thanks to a new package of measures that have increased the tax burden on capital gains, makes the surpluses generated in a period less than one year are integrated into the general base. What does this mean? Well, the following progressive scale is applied to the earnings generated in day trading: between 24 and 17,707.20 euros, a 24.75 percent retention will be applied; from here to 33,007.20 euros, 30 percent; and up to 53,407.20 euros, 40 percent. For day traders that generate capital gains of up to 120,000 euros, 175,000 euros, and 300,000 euros, the rates rise to 47 percent, 49 percent, 51 percent. To all this, we must add the regional sections if you reside in any of the communities that apply them, the most bleeding being Catalonia, which applies 56 percent to incomes exceeding 300,000 euros.

Chapter 6 – Trading Plan

Not all successful traders have a trading diary, but all those who carefully carry out a trading diary become operators consistent with the passage of time.

Preparing a trading diary will serve as a decisive tool for the improvement of our operations. The objective is both to correct our weaknesses in the operation and to discard inefficient strategies. In addition, it will help us to know our emotional state, and we can tackle the problems when they exist.

Every day we will complete our diary and, if we do, we have little to worry about, since it is one of the best self-control tools that exist, you learn a lot about yourself by filling it out and reviewing it at the end of the week. In most cases, you are prepared to win but not to be a winner. Making a trading diary in which you identify "game" patterns brings you closer to this goal.

We must create a diary with certain characteristics, that is, it must be easy to fill out, with very understandable and relevant information. It is not about repeating or duplicating the information already contained in the broker. Also, you have to be honest. It is no use to make up our results, quite the opposite; it would be a waste of time - although it would reflect an obvious emotional lack. When they ask me for advice on how to prepare a trading diary, I usually suggest that the interested party watch an episode of Supernanny: Rocío Ramos-Paúl—one of the many celebrities who would be an excellent day trader—assesses the child's attitude and immediately develops an action plan on some cards to improve their discipline or behavior. Well, a trading plan should look alike, even if you don't have to hang the card in our trading room. This plan is carried out when we need to modify, reduce, or increase some behavior or conduct, in our case of intraday operations. As in Supernanny, parents—that is, we traders—have to be consistent and systematic, that is, review the points and actions every day since we commit to the child (or our operation). The result is always surprising, as both the children and our operations improve.

Making a trading diary is essential if we still operate with the simulator account and also if we do it with our real broker account. It is simple if we use the newspaper with military discipline and write down the results every day.

We should also note our emotions in the operation, and we will build a habit that will lead us to be a responsible and judicious operator.

The newspaper will offer us relevant details of our operations as well as the projection that we have of profit or loss with each trade. A ratio that once settled will reflect our ability.

As for what we should write down daily in our diary, this should consist of an analysis of the success and/or failure of each operation from the point of view of the technical analysis and of the indicators that have had an impact on the performance of the operation. An analysis of the monetary management of each operation as well as the global one of the day. An analysis from the point of view of psychotrading and other factors that may have been relevant in daily operations. We must remember that nothing we reflect will make sense if it is not evaluated afterward. The idea is that we get to build a newspaper with an important sample of operations in a period of months, obtaining information about the effectiveness or not of our trading strategy. We will write down everything we deem necessary, from this will be issues that we will solve to improve our operation. What tactic works best for me when entering? In which time frame can I earn more? Have I rushed in or out? Should I have entered before, should I have expected more to do so? Should I have kept my position open? Should I have closed it before? What should I do to improve? Where could my position have increased?

After this, we should draw at least two conclusions: what makes us lose—that is, mistakes and weaknesses. And, on the other hand, what makes us win? The successes and our strengths. With this information, we can develop a code of guidelines that will be very beneficial for our intraday trading. We must never abandon the good practice of writing the newspaper and consulting our history, since the principles we extract will adapt to the way we operate, becoming our trading system. This system to succeed must adapt to us, to our personality, and not vice versa; That is why a system that works for another day trader does not work for us, and vice versa.

Once we establish the habit of using the newspaper as a guide, we will observe in a blunt way what are the areas of trading where we lack knowledge or skills. In addition, it will also reflect what strategies we should modify or abandon.

The newspaper will help us operate with prudence, judgment, and responsibility, avoiding losing money in an absurd way in each of the stages we go through as day traders.

Therefore, remember that nothing, absolutely nothing, will give us more information about our operations than the analysis of our operations history and the monitoring of it through our trading diary. Each one will elaborate according to their way of seeing and understanding day trading, but in the end, everyone should reflect the information necessary to improve our operations. Let's not lose sight of the objective. Let's face everything that comes up, don't let good or bad operations divert us from the road. We must concentrate, that is, to do the right thing at all times, never to change our "game plan" detailed in the newspaper. Let's be disciplined and not be tempted to play a pointless market or take a stop. How easy it is to write it and how stubborn we must be to apply it!

Chapter 7 – Frequently Asked Questions

A few questions you ask yourself when you start investing in the stock market (with their answers)

When you start to be interested in investing in the stock market and realize all the possibilities it offers, you may be tempted to start investing immediately to put your money to work as soon as possible. However, it is just at that moment when a lot of unanswered questions appear in your head that can fill you with doubts, fears, and insecurities.

As I have also gone through this initial moment and I have been overwhelmed by a lot of questions that I did not know how to solve, today I want to answer a few of those questions that you inevitably ask yourself when you start investing in the stock market. This will help save you time, energy, and money and will not let doubts get the better of you.

These are the questions that you will surely be asking yourself:

- Is investing in the stock market not risky?
- What happens if the stock goes down a lot?
- How much money do I need to invest?
- What profitability can I get?
- What stock should I buy?
- How many companies should I have in my portfolio?
- What is the best time to invest?
- When do I have to sell my shares?
- Experts say it's time to buy/sell, do I listen to them?
- I already have a full-time job; won't this take me too long?

These were the most common questions that disturbed me when I started investing in the stock market, so now I want to give you the answers that cost me time and effort to find. So take a seat, get comfortable, and let your investment path make it a little easier.

No. 1. Isn't investing in the stock market too risky?

Investing does not have to be risky if you know what you are doing, and investing in the stock market is no exception. There is a false belief that in the stock market, you get rich overnight or you lose everything in a few hours. But this is nothing but a false product of Hollywood and other urban legends.

It is like driving a car, in which case, there will always be the risk of an accident. However, you can minimize it in many ways, such as learning to drive, using safety features, avoiding going out on the road in extreme weather conditions, and driving at a moderate speed.

In the same way, when investing, there will always is the risk of not earning all the money you expected or even losing a part of it. However, you can do many things to reduce that risk to a minimum, such as learning to invest, using a large margin of safety, avoiding buying your shares when they are expensive and not getting carried away by the high speed of the market.

Just as using common sense you can reduce the risk of having a road accident and enjoy the benefits of traveling comfortably in your car, the same common sense can help you reduce the risk of your investments so you don't have to give up the benefits that these can give you.

No. 2. What happens if the stock goes down a lot?

Well, instead of worrying about the vast majority of people, you should be happy to buy more shares at lower prices, which will reduce the risk of your investments and increase profitability.

Do you want to exceed the average profitability of the market while assuming a lower risk? Well, you can only get it if you buy at lower than average prices, and that only happens when the stock market goes down a lot.

You must be aware that to get good investments you must wait for the exchange to fall sufficiently to be able to buy shares of good companies cheap enough to enjoy a good return via dividends and/or the subsequent price increase that will eventually happen.

In the beginning, this idea can be a bit shocking because it goes against what most people think, but over time you will realize that it is the big drops in the stock market that can change your life for the better.

No. 3. How much money do I need to invest?

Well, very little, really. One of the advantages of the exchange over other types of assets is that it allows you to invest virtually any amount of money. Remember that you can invest the amount that suits you best at all times because the market has great flexibility to adapt to your pocket.

So do not worry if you do not have much money right now since small amounts will be more than enough to gain experience and train you to be prepared the day you have much more money available to invest.

In fact, if you are in the initial stage of your investment career, I encourage you to start with modest amounts, since in this first stage your goal should not be to achieve the highest profitability, but to gain experience and the best possible training.

No. 4. What profitability can I get?

This is one of the questions that will get your attention the most. After all, you want to invest in making money, so you want to know how much you can get. Well, the answer will depend on your ability, the type of investment you decide to follow, and the market conditions you find.

To have a reference, the one considered by some to be the best investor in history, Warren Buffett, who is among the ten richest people in the world, has achieved an average annual compound return slightly higher than 23% for more than forty years.

Remember that your profitability will not be the same every year, but will vary depending on the circumstances offered by the Exchange. However, doing things minimally well will have very good years, good years, regular years, and avoid bad years, so your average annual return will be good.

In my opinion, if you want to invest in dividends to generate income without having to do anything else, aspire to an average of 5% net annual as it is a good starting point to go up to over 10% over the course of the year.

No 5. What shares should I buy?

Knowing what shares to buy is an important part of your investment routine. The answer will depend on the objectives you have and what investment philosophy you follow. I have always looked for companies that have a long-term sustainable competitive advantage that allows them to obtain higher than average returns in a sustained manner over time, increasing income and benefits in the long term and nothing or very little debt.

In addition, I want them to have a dividend policy that allows me to enjoy a growing dividend over the years, which means that the return via dividends of that investment also increases over time.

No. 6. How many companies should I have in my portfolio?

As you discover good businesses to invest in, you will begin to wonder how many different companies you should have in your portfolio. For me, the answer to this question is very simple: those that make you feel comfortable.

Some people need to be thirty, forty or more, while others feel totally calm about eight, ten, or twelve.

It will also depend on the number of good companies you have found and their quality since if you have only found six, it is absurd to buy additional ones that you do not like or do not know just because you want more. Doing this would increase the risk of your portfolio and decrease their profitability, so it is better that you focus on the companies that you have analyzed and that you really like.

No. 7. What is the best time to invest?

The best time to invest is when the prices of the shares you want to buy are cheap. So you can buy more shares with the same money or the same shares with less money.

Therefore, the best time to invest usually occurs after a large decline in the stock market, since the widespread fear of the majority makes good business actions.

There are many people who invest whenever they have some money available, so they put their money to work immediately. Others invest a similar amount periodically, thus avoiding concentrating purchases at certain times.

My opinion is that you accumulate available cash to invest while waiting for the madness of others to offer you the actions you like at the right prices to get the return you want.

Yes, you will miss some opportunities, but you will make sure that your money ends up working hard enough for you, which is what you want to achieve.

No. 8. When do I have to sell my shares?

Well, it will depend on your goals and your investment philosophy. If you practice Value Investing or Investment in Value, you will want to sell your shares when they are overvalued and no longer offer you any safety margin.

If you invest in dividends to earn income without worrying about doing anything else, the best time to sell your shares will never be.

No. 9. Experts say it's time to buy/sell, do I listen to them?

Neither yes nor no. And this means? It means that you must be able to make your own investment decisions without relying on the opinions of others, including the supposed experts.

Everyone is free to express their opinions. Taking them into account can sometimes be useful, and sometimes it only helps you to generate more indecision. Experts tend to have many followers and to have many followers, they must say things that most of them feel good and are to their liking.

Therefore, the majority of experts will agree with the majority's opinion, since if they are wrong in a pack it will be "market thing," but if they go against the flock and they are wrong, it will be "their fault."

By the way, I am talking about that majority that has no patience, that buys the most popular shares when everyone is doing it, and that ends up selling them months or years later much cheaper to those who did know how to wait.

Does this mean that you cannot find good experts to trust? Not necessarily. However, why allocate time, money, and energy in trying to guess or discover good experts to tell you what to do if you can devote that same effort in learning to make your own decisions?

So my recommendation is that you don't pay attention to them or stop doing it, but focus on spending your time finding your own investments.

No. 10. I already have a full-time job; won't this take me too long?

One of your main goals in learning to invest will surely be to earn independent income from your work, that is, no matter what you do with your time. Therefore, it is about having assets that work for you, not about having a second job.

Thus, it is an activity fully compatible with a full-time job and any other type of activity you do. It doesn't matter if you are an entrepreneur, multi-employed or self-employed, once your investments are underway, they will require very little time.

After all, that's the grace of putting your money to work for you, isn't it?

Chapter 8 – Some Last Tips

1. It doesn't matter if you don't win but don't skip the rules!
2. Once you win, touch the money. The numbers that appear in your broker are real. Withdraw a minimum of 25 percent of the profit per year. Withdrawing benefits is the best way to protect them.
3. Operate only according to what the graphics tell you, your system and instinct. Get away from the phrase "you are always ready."
4. Practice, practice, and practice. Accumulate hours of simulated trading before going to real.
5. Eliminate any distractions that separate you from the path to your goal.
6. Set a daily, weekly, and monthly profit target. Do the same for losses.
7. Do not enter the market by entering. Do not overwork. There is always a better time to do it. Wait for it to mature. There are always a couple of good opportunities a day to reach the goal.
8. When you are with earnings, do not close because the price reaches support, resistance, or because you are earning a lot. Let the market take you out, or you'll never get spectacular profits. It takes a lot of temperament to do this, so much so that you are only able to do so by turning off the computer.
9. Take care of your pre and postoperative habits. These may be the ones that make you earn money.
10. Your experience in day trading must include a variety of market cycles; otherwise, we will not know how to navigate in troubled waters or in desperate calm.
11. Losing is stigmatized in our society; it looks like something bad. In day trading, no. It is lost almost every day. When you start trading, making mistakes is inevitable. When you are an experienced trader, making mistakes is also inevitable, so don't despair, you go into a game that will be full of mistakes. The error makes us fall, but learning lifts us up. We are losers who enjoy their time, their money, and their life. The key? When we lose we "file our nails," and when we win, "we take half an arm." Remember that losing or failing is part of our activity.

12. Instead of thinking that we are going to cover ourselves with the next operation, let's think that it can go wrong, which allows us to focus on protecting ourselves from losses.
13. Trading is a game that can absorb a person's life, so it is very important to relativize and turn off screens when you play. What is the point of leaving a job of ten hours a day to be in your house like many in front of the screens?
14. Include a person in your trading plan. Your spouse, boyfriend, best friend, coach, etc. Perform an "accountability" before a third person that is far from the operative. He is a tool of great value. If you have had problems, look for a trusted person or friend to tutor your evolution. Committing to improve and measure that change adds a plus of motivation. Once everything returns to its course, try and make a monthly accountability to a third party, it will be a great ally to measure the monitoring and development of objectives. In my case, this person is my wife, and there are nights I don't have dinner.
15. Do not operate if it is bad, that is, if you have the feeling that you are operating because something is missing, craved or needed, to cover dissatisfaction, for spite of the market or to give you a "lesson," etc. These behaviors are very dangerous for our broker account.
16. Create a preoperative ritual that turns you into All black s. It is not necessary to do the famous "haka," but you can create a routine before starting to operate that brings the mind and body in tune for the game. In my case, and to operate the opening of the mini S & P500, I take a shower, do some stretching and prepare a coffee ristretto before 3.30 pm.
17. Adopt a system to your personality and don't innovate too much. As Emilio Durado says, only geniuses innovate. The rest belong to the average. I have adapted my systems of two successful traders to become a clone of the beast!
18. Concentration: the more your mind is concentrated, the more this one lives, the more focused it is on what it does. Concentration is the key to success in all facets of life. In day trading, everything comes down to a moment: carpe diem. The opportunity is there, and it appears every day, but you must be what you are outside the bubble of smartphones, tablets, etc. Two hours before the operation avoids

weapons of mass distraction (phone, social networks, PSP, PS3, Xbox, etc.).

19. Indicators, and more indicators. It is not necessary to do extraordinary things to obtain extraordinary results. More is less. A man with a clock knows what time it is; a man with two watches is never very sure.
20. If you have missed a rule, punish yourself! If you have been so brave to break a rule, have the courage to rebuke yourself. If you are not able to respect a stop, you better leave day trading. Without pain, without guilt, leave it now; Tomorrow will be worse.
21. Rest on Friday if you have achieved the goal during the week. Take the last week of the holiday month if you have achieved your goal in advance. Discipline yourself and keep under control the insatiable greed that you never have enough.
22. The more successful you are, the more humble and attentive you should be. Improving and making more points makes us careless. Beware of overconfidence because it is the preamble of unfortunate days.
23. When we teach another person, we feel obliged to act as promulgated. Guardianship to another more novel trader who wants to learn. Act with exemplarity, and that will benefit you, and the future day trader too.
24. Open to new strategies. I have learned more about trading strategies by reading Strategies for the success of Philip C. McGraw or How life imitates chess by Gary Kasparov than by studying several illustrious investors.
25. Never trade with borrowed money. It is ignorant. When you operate with borrowed capital, what can go wrong often goes wrong, and it is not pleasant.
26. Go step by step. At first, everything seems immediate, and the reality is that everything comes in its moment, but it doesn't have to be now. In the first month of actual operation, I thought that year I would have a Porsche 911 and pay the mortgage. Everything takes a little longer. Remember, day trading is a long journey in the desert.

27. Have you been doing day trading for three years and still have not chained good months of operation and have not achieved the desired consistency? Stand up and do an analysis. Seek help.
28. Track your worst day trading days in detail. You must know very well the patterns and behaviors that led you there, and of course, always avoid them.
29. Do not listen to music during the operation. Good music will transport you to a place where you should not be when you play your money.
30. Do not allow analytical paralysis; that is if you have conceived a good trading idea, if everything fits, you know that it is good and ingenious and you have tested it in simulated with good results, do not analyze more. The analysis involves seeing the pros, but also the crippling cons.
31. The environment where you play trading must be conditioned. Clean table, well-oriented screens, ergonomic chair, ambient light while you can, without phones, images, and inspirational books. It all adds up. Changing the physical environment of your "trading room" can cause immediate effects. Remember that you will spend time sitting so buying a good chair will be a great investment.
32. We are prepared to face the best, but what is the worst? Make an action plan before a disastrous month. Write it down, analyze the consequences and actions you will take, put it in a red envelope, seal it, and give it to a person you trust. If the drawdown or horrific month occurs, ask for it, open it, and continue without blinking the emergency plan that you have imposed.
33. Whatever they are, lower your expectations, more if you're starting. A novel trader is like Roger Federer, seventeen years old, looking forward to polishing and who will have to wait five years to win his first Grand Slam.
34. Search every day to learn from your operation. Of profits, to overcome greed and overconfidence; and of the days of losses, as an opportunity to develop resistance. Remember that learning is so easy that even a child can do it.
35. Open yourself to "trading 2.0" and the resources that social networks provide to share knowledge. If you feel strong, write your own blog;

it may even be your trading diary, although this option must be weighed well because in social networks we attend the largest exhibition of egos that humanity has known, and the criticisms are not always constructive.

36. Check your results and your trading notebook. It should reflect a decrease in errors and growth in successes. In trading, one advances, stagnates or recedes. It is unbearably real. As day traders, we make decisions based on a combination of analysis, experience, and intuition. The objective is to make us aware of this process and to improve it. We must broaden the vision and evaluate the most important consequences in our operations.
37. "Reduce your position," "Operate with fewer contracts," "Go slowly and do not want great results immediately," are usually three of the best tips for a day trader who starts his career, and for the rest too!
38. Forget the why? That is, why have I made that decision? Why has it happened to me? The best question to see more clearly is how: how can the problem not persist? Knowing your experience when you feel bad, brings lucidity to face the problems of intraday trading.
39. If we want to be happy doing intraday trading, we should not strive to increase our wealth, but rather to depart from dangerous greed.
40. And finally, learn more to win better. Do you watch TV? Do you dive through Facebook's neighbor yard? If you are Spanish, the answer will be yes. I suggest you "steal" one hour a day from those activities and dedicate them to something else. It will be 365 hours a year, or what is the same, more than nine work weeks that you can spend, for example, to improve your trading. Remember that they are good or bad, habits always produce results. In my case, I dedicate one hour a day to reading.

When you go on the path of triumph in day trading:

1. You enjoy the action much more than the retribution, although we eat thanks to the latter.
2. You convert your decisions into a royal decree.
3. You believe in your trading and also stop doubting that of others. You talk openly about your losses. Everyone has them, but many

hide them. Do not criticize other traders/systems because that does not improve yours.

4. You realize that you do not operate against the market, but against other traders and against yourself.
5. You are aware that trust does not come from always being right, but from surviving the many failed trades.
6. Sunday becomes your favorite day of the week.
7. Your eyes shine every time someone asks you: "And what do you do for a living?"
8. You like to transgress the rules except those of trading. In this society, it is very transgressive to be a day trader. As Kostolany said, you become an aristocrat, a nobleman who can freely spend his time.
9. You love your time. The more yours is, the more you value it. You are relentless with your operating time. More time on screens does not mean better results. You know that operating ten minutes is three times better than operating twenty. The less you are operating on the screens, the better.
10. You re-educate yourself and accept that fear is a necessary part of your operation. You never fear mistakes. You live with them, admit them calmly, and move on.
11. You stop doing just what you promised not to do. eye! It is very complicated in day trading.
12. You keep a trading diary. You know it stimulates self-knowledge.
13. You are disciplined in the operation. If we allow ourselves to be undisciplined in the small details, we will end up being also undisciplined in the big ones. The price of discipline is always less than the pain of regret.
14. In-laws stop looking suspiciously. A trader works on oneself, and that in-laws take time to see him. Despite this, it is better to omit the word "speculator" at home.
15. You live from trading and accumulate bad days, and trades no longer entails the loss of confidence in your possibilities. You know how to stop these emotions.
16. You experience that in trading there is no luck. You can hit one day, but at the end of the month, there is no place for luck, nor do you eat with it.

17. You finish every day, and you end it knowing that you have done what you could. If there were errors, you forget them as soon as possible because you know that tomorrow you should start lucid and serene.
18. When you stop listening: "[your name], be careful!" This will have been a refrain throughout your pilgrimage as a day trader, a sincere warning from people with good intentions but who do not understand the philosophy of trading intraday. On the other hand, now you hear: "[your name], when are we left to explain what you live for?"
19. You know that losing is part of the game and that the benefit has come with time and dominance. You are also aware that the days of losses sculpt your speculation system, improving it every day.
20. You understand that both life and day trading are uncertainties and that there are no one hundred percent reliable methods.
21. You operate with rules. These may be rules related to the size of the position, your stop level, the time of entry and exit, when operating, etc.
22. You think about the benefits in percentage and not in euros or dollars.
23. You conclude that, except in exceptional occasions, we are not mistaken to take profit. The key to the success of many day traders is that they always leave with profit and leave the last tics or dollars for others. Some of them, already millionaires, say that their formula was that "they always sold too soon."
24. Your operations reflect your convictions without allowing the perfect to become the enemy of the good. We cannot always enter the best point, but if we have to enter, we must enter.
25. You understand that it is the trading rules that help to achieve consistency.
26. Do not avoid the pain caused by bad operations. It's part of the game.
27. You have a security protocol and visualize the worst scenarios to know how you would act. For example, the connection has been dropped, I have a live operation, and I still don't have the stops set.
28. You are aware that 80 percent of the time the markets move laterally, with no tendency, so you become a "sniper" patient. We do a few operations, and this turns out to be the difference between an amateur and a "first sword."

29. You ignore your ego, your brain, your trader friend who tells you that he has done a $ 5,000 operation, etc. and you focus on your ability and on recognizing those patterns that make your account fat. Otherwise, the game gets complicated; it becomes impossible.
30. In front of the screens harmonize the three brains: the intellectual, the emotional, and the instinctive, so that the tyranny of none occurs. It takes time, but it is achieved.
31. You recognize that being a day trader means being destined to choose and make decisions in conditions of deep and painful uncertainty. Despite this, you take them.
32. You know that day trading will be stressful for the first fifty years. If it is not, or you are a virtuoso or a madman, or perhaps both.
33. You have the ability to know how to convert the path to the great goal into very affordable small steps. Thus the path becomes a rosary of small achievements, and you manage to create an attainable and positive vision of what is desired.
34. You have the mental strength, a characteristic that distinguishes the winners from the rest.
35. You try to distrust your emotions and avoid operating in states of euphoria—we let our guard down and low—our state paralyzes us.

Conclusion

Thank you for making it through to the end of *Stock Trading for Beginners*, let's hope it was informative and able to provide you with all of the tools you need to achieve your goals whatever they may be.

If you've come here, I congratulate you. All of this is what I believe in. We must learn, play, have goals, have fun, etc. We will be so little around here. No matter what day trader you want to be, you can be. We are all called to do important things, but few are convinced that we can achieve it. Beat your fears and uncertainties. You have an idea to live with meaning, being the scriptwriter of your life. What will change your life will not be knowing more, but the decisions you make and the actions you address.

If you do not undertake intraday trading activity, at least look around. I was a bum for thirty years, and you don't let life and others do the same to you. We are linked to the routine, just try to brush your teeth with your left hand so you can tell. You can continue with your daily life without changing your habits, and nothing terrible will happen, but it is very likely that nothing will happen either. Avoiding challenges is not an objective we should be proud of. In twenty years you will regret much more about the things you stopped doing than the things you did. There is no game you can win if you don't play.

Day trading opens a door for you, an opportunity that you have at your fingertips. The prize is so succulent - to be rich in time and money - that in my opinion, it is worth a try. No one of those who live from this activity long for our previous life, for something it will be.

The road is not easy, to be a day trader you need discipline, ability to analyze with yourself, have a system that allows some advantage. Here, I have explained two. Also, accept that you are solely responsible for what happens, understand that there are no magic recipes for trading; just some tips—trusting oneself and being able to get up after the inevitable turmoil that the market inflicts on you, keep a trading diary, not be afraid of a bit of bad luck—although you should not count on it. We must remember that our first and most important objective is to preserve heritage. Not losing or losing as little as possible will be the main step to start winning.

We will live situations and scenarios to which we will not have an answer, and we must accept that the mystery exists in day trading. Despite this, we always look forward to getting answers for everything. The trader with problems often endures uncertainty. Happiness in day trading comes the day you operate without fear, and that day also results. Don't get too complicated, work on what works, and that's it. Your most valuable asset is your energy, and you shouldn't waste it looking for new indicators that will give you one more tick of benefits a week—unless it becomes your passion, of course. Follow the maxim of being better than you were yesterday; that will take you to the path that everyone craves, that of wealth in time and money. Remember that when you want something with great intensity, no sacrifice is excessive.

Excellence in trading takes time, perseverance, and patience. If you apply all the principles and techniques discussed in the book, you will achieve your goal. You will fulfill your dream even though in the search you will find obstacles and you will feel stuck. Inevitably, it's normal, but that's where 80 percent usually give up and give up. But a sensible trader like you discovers that if you stand stubbornly, in the end, you take a seemingly sudden leap and move to a higher level of performance. Be patient. Wait there. Do not give up. You will get it. The principles of trading always work.

Finally, if you found this book useful in any way, a review on Amazon is always appreciated!

Glossary

The basics of options trading are always easy to understand. However, the trade involves more advanced aspects that need time and patience to learn. It is not surprising that options trading has hundreds of terminology and jargon, some of which you may never have heard about. We have come up with a comprehensive list of the terms used in the trade as a reference tool that you can use when learning more about options. Here they are:

Actions—certificates that represent a small part of the property of a company.

Anticipation—it is the act of a stock trader predicting the security market future before either buying or selling their stock.

Arbitration—operate in two or more markets at the same time to take advantage of a temporary positive fluctuation in one compensating losses of another and obtain a profit.

Asking price—an initial price at which the security can either be sold for by the investor in the security market.

Asset—an asset is what is being exchanged on markets, such as stocks, bonds, currencies, or commodities.

Assignment—this is the process of issuing an option seller or writer with an exercise notice instructing them to sell or buy 100 shares of particular equity at a stipulated amount as the strike value.

At the money—at the money option is one that has a cost that is equivalent to the value of the equity.

Automatic exercise—this refers to the process where options that are in the money are exercised automatically, if still in the money during expiration.

Base currency—the base currency is the first currency in a currency pair, and the other currency that determines the price of a currency pair is called a counterpart. Knowing the base currency is important as determining the value of the currencies (national or real) exchanged when a currency contract is negotiated. The Euro is the most used base currency against all others. The British Pound is the next in the hierarchy of currencies. The main currency pairs against the British Pound could be identified as GBP/USD, GBP/CHF, GBP/JPY, GBP/CAD. The United States dollar is the next predominant base currency. USD/CAD, USD/JPY, USD/CHF would be the normal currency pair according to the main currencies; the dollar is listed as EUR/USD and GBP/USD.

Bearish—market expectation that the value or price of an option will decline over time.

Bearish stock—a form of stock that is anticipated to decrease in value over a specific time by a stock market trader.

Bear market—when the overall prices of a market are on the decrease.

Bear spread—a spread that aims at generating profit from bearish price movements.

Bid—the price at which the market accepts to buy a specific currency pair.

Bid price—it is the highest price of securities such as stocks in the security market a dealer is willingly prepared an offer in exchange for the securities.

Bid-ask spread— the value obtained by calculating the difference between the ask and bid prices of an option.

Black Scholes pricing model—model that uses factors such as the value of the underlying security, strike price, time value, and volatility to estimate the price and profits made from options.

Bonds—it is a kind of loan that investors make to their issuers in exchange for a fixed payment (interest) every certain time; the issuer under different conditions not only pays the interest but also returns all of what was lent at the expiration of the term.

Breakeven point—the point at expiration where an option strategy returns zero profit and zero loss.

Broker—(definition 1) a person or organization that processes option contract orders on behalf of traders and investors.

Broker—(definition 2) the professional who is responsible for either buying or selling securities such as stocks for their clients.

Broker—(definition 3) the intermediary between the secondary market and investors. Through its infrastructure, people with liquidity surpluses can negotiate securities.

Brokerage—an individual or a firm responsible for arranging transactions of buying and selling securities for the sake of getting commission after the exchange is successful.

Bullish—a market state defined by the possibility of the cost rising in the future.

Bullish stock—a type of stock that is predicted to rise in value over a certain period of time by a stock trader in the security market.

Bull market—state when the overall market prices are increasing.

Bull spread—trading spread established to generate profit from bullish stock and market movements.

Buy to close order—an order generated when a trader wants to close an existing call position. This is achieved through purchasing contracts that you previously sold to other investors.

Buy to open order—this is an order that you place if you want to enter a new position of purchasing contracts.

Cable—a technique used by operators to refer to the British Pound Sterling in the exchange rate of the British Pound/US dollar. The term began to be used because the rate was originally transmitted by means of a transatlantic cable initially in the mid-1800s.

Call option—the kind of option that gives a buyer some authority to buy 100 shares for given equity at predefined prices and expiration periods.

Carrying cost—the cost incurred when using capital to buy options based on the interest received from borrowed capital.

Cash or spot—platform or live market price. The value agreement in transactions without completion period but at a certain starting price.

Cash account—one of the brokerage accounts where an investor is required to make full payments of the securities they have purchased.

Cash-settled option—an option where profits are given to the holder in terms of cash, not in the form of shares.

Central Bank—the main monetary authority of a nation, controlled by the national government. It is responsible for the issuance of the currency, for establishing monetary policy, interest rates, exchange rate policies and regulation, and supervision of the private bank's sector. The Federal Reserve is the Central Bank of the States United. Others include The European Central Bank, The Bank of England, and The Bank of Japan.

CFDs—although its exact definition is "Contract for difference" and is a financial derivative, its practical meaning is the possibility of accessing an underlying title with leverage. It sounds a bit complex, but in practical terms, it is very simple. Suppose that you are going to invest in an action that is worth $1,000 and has COP $10,000, this would only allow you to buy 10. If you did it through a CFD, the broker provides leverage by converting your COP $10,000 into COP $100,000 allowing you to buy 100 shares instead of 10. Of course, that extra leverage is not free, and you must pay interest in accessing the product.

Close—to end a trading position. Also refers to the time of the day when the market stops operating and the final option prices are determined.

Closing order—an order that you raise to end a contract that is already in existence.

Combination order—an order that comprises more than one basic order.

Contingent order—an order that allows you to set customized parameters for entering or exiting options contracts.

Contract range—the highest prices of a single contract minus its lowest prices.

Contract size—the number of share units covered by individual contracts. In options trading, the default size is 100 shares.

Conversion—it is the process by which assets or liabilities denominated in one currency are exchanged for assets or liabilities denominated in another currency.

Cost of interest financing (cost of carry)—the cost or benefit associated with the continuation of open operations from one day to another, calculated by using the short-term interest rate differential between the two currencies that make up the currency pair.

Coverage strategy—a strategy designed to reduce the risk of investments used to require options, introduce positions, short sales, or futures contracts. Coverage can help to ensure profits. The purpose is to reduce the volatility of a portfolio by reducing the risk of losses.

Covered call—a trading strategy used to make profits from existing contracts when the market is neutral.

Covered put—a trading strategy that works together with short selling to make profits from existing positions. This strategy protects your investment from short-term price increments.

Currency—it is the unit of exchange of a country issued by its government or Central Bank, whose value is basic to commercialize.

Currency option—a form option that has currency as the equity.

Commission—money you give to brokers or brokerage companies for their services.

Credit—the amount of money you get in your account for selling an option.

Cross exchange rate—the exchange rate between two currencies. It is called the cross-exchange rate because it is not common in the country where the currency pair is quoted. For example, in the United States, a GBP/CHF price would be considered as a cross-rate, while in the United Kingdom or Switzerland it would be one of the primary pairs of traded currencies.

Day trader—a person who purchases or sells securities in the security market within a single day.

Debit—the amount of money you give out when purchasing an option.

Derivative—an instrument, which obtains its value from other financial instruments. For example, options and futures.

Devaluation—decrease in the value of the currency of one country in relation to the currencies of other countries. When a country devalued its currency, imported goods become more expensive, while exports become less expensive abroad and thus more competitive.

Differential (spread)—the difference between the sale and purchase price of a currency. It is used to measure market liquidity. Smaller spreads mean higher liquidity.

Discount broker—a broker that only carries out basic order processing for options traders.

Discount option—an option that sells at a price that is less than the intrinsic value.

Dividend yield—a form of a dividend that is illustrated in form of a percentage of the present share price.

Dividends payout ratio—it is the relative amount of the total revenue that a company pays its shareholders.

Dividends—these are the returns that are paid by a company to an individual who owns shares in it.

Drawdown—it is the consecutive loss in market operations and its potential impact on the income statement generally assessed within a possibilities test or statistical analysis of the reliability of an operations system.

Early assignment—when a contract seller fulfills the requirements of the contract before its expiration period.

Early exercise—the process of closing contracts before they expire.

Earnings per share—the portion of the profit made by a firm that is allocated to each share that is outstanding in the firm's common stock.

Equity ratio—a ratio that portrays how much assets in a firm are being funded by the equity shares.

Entry orders—order executed when a specific price level is reached and/or penetrated. The execution is handled by the negotiating table and is in effect until it is canceled by the client.

Entry stop order—orders executed when the price of the coin breaks a specific level. The customer places the order considering that when the price of the coin breaks the specific level, the price will continue in that direction.

Exchange—a currency exchange is an operation that combines cash and installment transactions in the same negotiation.

Exchange trading funds—funds invested for trading in the stock exchange trade.

Exercise—buying or selling an options contract at a specific strike price and time period.

Exercise price—the price of each share at which it is sold or bought at expiration. This is another name for the strike price.

Expiration date—the date when a contract stops existing or expires.

Expiration month—the month in which expiration takes place.

Expire worthlessly—a contract that expires worthless is one that returns no profit at the expiration date.

Extrinsic value—those aspects of an options pricing that are determined by factors not related to the cost of the equity or security.

Fixed exchange rate—it is the decision of a country to immobilize the value of its currency with respect to the currency of another country, gold (or other product), or set of currencies. In practice, even fixed exchange rates can fluctuate between high and low bands, which can lead to intervention.

Foreign exchange market—the simultaneous purchase of one currency and the sale of another in an extra stock market.

Forex—it is a very controversial term since many illegal activities also use this word to explain their profitability. This is not an illegal market in the world, and many of the activities that gave rise to its restriction never invested in Forex. In this market, the different currencies of the planet are negotiated, such as USD (Dollar), EUR (Euro), GBP (Pound Sterling), JPY (Yen), etc.

Fundamental analysis—(definition 1) a method of analyzing the intrinsic value of a financial instrument in the stock market and its price value in the future.

Fundamental Analysis—(definition 2) a discipline that seeks to know and evaluate the true value of a financial instrument based on the causes that influence the composition of the price, that is, its value as a commercial profit or its value based on the expected future performance of it.

Futures—another financial derivative that allows investors to reserve a product today, providing only a small percentage of its total value. Being standard contracts, delivery dates of the products are agreed upon, where the investor will cancel the remaining percentage of the previously separated titles and receive them. Although many traders use them for speculation (which makes them extremely risky), they were originally created for hedging or coverage.

Hedge fund—this is a non-regulated private investment fund for large investors (investments that start with a minimum of 1 million dollars) specialized in high risks, short-term speculations in bonds, currencies, options of stock, and derivatives.

Hedging—(definition 1) the process of investment that seeks to minimize the risk of trading tour investments.

Hedging—(definition 2) through financial derivatives such as CFDs, futures, and options, etc. investors can secure the price of a security by making it totally immune to changes in the market price. This can be more easily illustrated in the following example:

Suppose you are an oil company and the market price of crude oil is USD100 per barrel. If the price reaches USD50, your income is reduced by half, but if you cover your production with a derivative of USD100 and the price falls to USD50, both you and your counterpart pledged to deliver and receive the production to USD100 respectively. Now if the oil reaches USD150, you will be paid USD100. As you can see, it is a way to keep the price fixed.

G7—the seven most industrialized countries in the world such as the United States, Germany, Japan, France, the United Kingdom, Canada, and Italy.

G10—the members of the G7 plus Belgium, Holland, and Sweden are an associated group that takes part in the discussions of the International Monetary Fund. Switzerland is sometimes involved.

Historical volatility—measures the volatility levels of a stock through studying past price movements over a period of time.

Horizontal spread—spread created from several contracts that feature the same strike price and different expiration dates.

Implied volatility—an estimate of the future volatility levels of underlying security based on current prices, using pricing models.

Index option—a contract on the options market whose underlying asset is not stock but an index.

In the money—contract whose stock value s more than the current cost in the case of a call position, the opposite is true for a put contract.

Inflation rate—the percentage in change of either the rise or fall of prices of securities in the stock market.

Inflation—a moment where the prices of securities can either experience a sudden rise or an impromptu fall.

Interbank rates—the rates at which large international banks exchange their currencies with other large international banks.

Interest rate—an amount of interest that is paid after a certain amount of time to a stock trader for the money they have invested in the stock market.

Interest—this is the amount of money an investor in the stock market receives in turn from the money they invest in the stocks purchased.

Intrinsic value—a contract whose equity value is higher than the strike amount.

Investor—an individual who willingly allocates their capital in the stock market to get profits in return after a certain amount of time.

Largo (long)—this is what most people are used to in the market. Buy in the hope that the price will rise after closing the transaction. If you buy at a price X, you will earn money only if the price of the asset increases, this is basically a long one.

Leg—individual positions that form up a contract comprising of several positions.

Leverage—(definition 1) the process of using options to obtain more payoffs from the options market.

Leverage—(definition 2) the amount, expressed in multiples, by which the final amount traded exceeds the real invested. It can also be referred to as a lot size in 100K equivalent to $ 100,000 dollars and the required margin is $ 1,000 dollars, the operator can perform operations 100 times the size of its capital under margin. For investors, leverage means increasing profit in value without increasing investment.

Liquidity—the ability of a market to accept large volume transactions depending on volume and activity in a market. It is the efficiency and effectiveness of prices with which positions can be operated and orders executed. A market with greater liquidity will provide more frequent price quotes as the smallest differential buying/selling.

Limit entry orders—these are orders that are executed when the price of a coin reaches (not rubbing) a specific level. The customer places the order considering after they have reached the specific level, the price will move in the opposite direction to their previous moments.

Limit order—(definition 1) an order that allows you to trade options at the specified minimum and maximum strike prices.

Limit order—(definition 2) an entry limit order for a specific position is programmed to secure the earnings of a position. An entry limit order programmed in a purchase position is a sales order. A stop-limit order remains in effect until the position is liquidated or canceled by the customer.

Limit stop order—an order that instructs positions to close when certain prices are attained.

Liquidity—the level of availability of a certain financial instrument. In other words, this is a measure of the level of ease that a certain instrument can be bought or sold without affecting the prices.

Listed option—an option that is listed on the options market.

Long bull—position to buy large volumes of coins as well as to sell them, so that an appreciation of the value is made if the market price increases.

Long position—a position that is created when you purchase a call or put contract.

Lost stop orders—an entry order related to a specific position to stop the position thus avoiding incurring additional losses. A loss stop order located in a buying position is a stop entry order to sell such position. A loss stop order remains in effect until the position is liquidated or canceled by the customer.

Margin—customers must deposit funds as collateral to cover any potential loss due to adverse price movements.

Margin account—a type of brokerage account that an investor has the choice to get cash from customers for them to purchase securities or other financial instruments.

Margin call coverage—request for additional funds or other guarantees, from a broker or negotiator, to increase the margin to a necessary level that guarantees execution in a position that has moved against the client.

Margin requirement—this is the amount of money that a trader deposits in their brokerage account to cover for naked option positions. These act as collateral for the brokerage firm to purchase or sell options on behalf of the trader.

Market bubble—a situation where prices of stocks are escalated above their actual value by traders.

Market indicators—formulas and ratios that can illustrate the gains and losses in the indexes and stocks.

Market order—(definition 1) one used to buy or sell a contract at current market prices.

Market order—(definition 2) is the order to buy or sell at the live price of the base currency.

Market stop order—the order that closes a position when certain market prices are attained.

Market size and liquidity—the ten most active traders' accounts provide the market with bid (buy) and ask (sell) prices. The bid (buy)/ask (sell) offer is the difference between the price at which a bank or a market manufacturer will sell ("ask" or "offer") and the price at which a market-manufacturer will buy ("offer") to a wholesale customer.

These offers may not apply to retail customers in banks, who will routinely mark up the difference to say 1.2100/1.2300 for transfers, or 1.2000/1.2400 for banknotes or travelers' checks.

Point prices in market manufacturers vary, but in EUR/USD, even in times of high volatility, they are generally not more than 5 pip wide (i.e., 0.0005). This difference, known as "spread," also depends on the brokerage in which it operates.

Recently, some Forex brokers have expanded the options chart and made it possible to trade with metals, indices, food, and other resources.

Moneyness—a technique used to define the correlation between equity in underlying cost and the strike amount of an option.

Morphing—the process of creating synthetic positions or transitioning from one position into another using a single order.

Naked call—it happens when a speculator sells a call option on security without ownership of that security.

One-sided market—market state when buyers are significantly more than sellers or sellers more than buyers.

Online brokers—a broker that allows you to process your orders through an online platform.

Opening order—an order used to create new options contract positions.

Options—it is another financial derivative that unlike futures and CFDs is not affected by the price movement. To access the product, you simply pay a premium, and on the expiration date, the investor decides if they stay with the underlying derivative price or market price.

Optionable stock—stock that acts as underlying security for certain options.

Options contract—a right to purchase or sell shares at specified strike prices and expiration times.

Options holder—the person who owns an options contract.

Options trader—a person who buys and sells options.

Out of the money—an option gets out of the money when the cost of the equity of the underlying security is not favorable to the trader based on the strike price. A call option can become out of the money if the value of the underlying equity is below the strike charges. On the other hand, a put option becomes out of the money when the cost of the underlying equity is higher than the strike charges.

Over-the-counter options—options that are traded over the counter and not through online exchange platforms.

Over valuing—an occurrence where a stock market trader estimates the prices of stocks to be higher than the actual value in the market.

Oscillators—oscillators are mathematical models applied to price action, based on some specific observation about market behavior. They are usually plotted below the stock chart, either as lines or histograms, and measure the strength of trends or movements in the price. When weakness in the trend is detected, it is suspected that it might be close to reversing.

Point or pip—a term used in the currency market to represent the smallest possible variation for a currency pair considered. Ex.: EUR/USD = 1,200, a fluctuation of 0.0001 equals 1 pip and for USD/JPY = 111.28, a fluctuation of 0.01 equals 1 pip.

Portfolio—a grouping of several financial assets such as currencies cash, bonds, stocks, and other cash equivalents that are owned by an individual or an organization.

Position—a clear vision of an operator to buy or sell currencies; and can also refer to the amount of currency in which an investor owns.

Pricing model—a formula that can be applied in the determination of the abstract or theoretical value of a given options contract using variables such as the underlying security, strike price, and volatility.

Premium—the amount paid to acquire an option in the options market. Premiums are often quoted as price per share.

Profit—it is the excess revenue a stock trader gets from either buying or selling stocks in the stock market.

Physical option—the kind of option that has underlying equity in the form of physical assets.

Primary market—treasuries are either public (countries) or private (companies) that issue securities for the first time before they can be traded on the stock exchanges.

Put option—an option that allows you to write or sell underlying equity at a specific strike amount and expiration times.

Realize a profit-making some profit when you close a position contact.

Realize a loss—incurring a loss when you close a position contract.

Renegotiation—when the settlement of the operation is extended to another date with the cost of this process based on the differential in the interest rates of the two currencies. A change overnight, specifically the next business day with respect to the next business day.

Retail trader—a person or an organization that is focused on investing their capital in futures, options, bonds, and stock.

Revaluation—an increase in the exchange rate of a currency established by other currencies or by gold.

Revaluation rates—the rate for any period or currency used to revalue a position or book. Rate revaluation is the rate used in the market when an operator runs an end-of-day to stabilize gains or losses on the day.

Risk—it is an unforeseen factor that can lead a stock trader to experience losses.

Scaling out—a situation in the stock market where a trader gets out of their position to either buy or sell their financial instruments.

Secondary market—once the securities have been issued by the treasuries, they can be traded on local or international exchanges. These exchanges are known as the secondary market. Some examples of them are BVC, NYSE, NASDAQ, etc.

Securities—any product negotiable in the stock market. Some examples are Stocks, Bonds, CFDs, Forex, Futures, Options, etc.

Security index—an indicator in the security market that uses statistical data to analyze the changes that are experienced in the securities market.

Sell to close order—order placed when closing a long position that is already in existence.

Sell to open order—order placed when opening a new contract position.

Settlement—when contract terms are finalized after exercising a position.

Shares—an indivisible form of capital that is used to signify a person's ownership of a certain company.

Short—some markets are deep enough to allow investors to sell products that they do not have allowing them to obtain returns from falling prices. This means when you make a short belief that the market will fall and if your hypothesis is successful, you will earn money.

Short position—the state attained when you sell contracts.

Short selling—a phenomenon where a stock market investor borrows securities that their sell later in the stock market to make a profit by buying them later.

Spread—a position made from selling several contracts belonging to the same underlying security.

Spread order—an order that instructs a broker to create a spread of several positions that are transacted simultaneously.

Stock—it is a type of security that gives individual ownership to a certain company and it is sold at a particular market price.

Stockbroker—they are those who advise investors in the purchase of securities from which they receive a commission. However, unlike traders, they do not operate in the market.

Stock market—a loose network of several traders who willingly buy and sell stocks that represent ownership of certain businesses.

Stock options—an agreement settled by the stock market investor and their broker granting the broker exclusive rights to buy or sell shares at a predetermined price.

Stock trader—an individual or a firm involved in the trading of stocks.

Stop loss—it is a highly recommended practice in the stock market that consists of defining how much you are willing to lose in an investment. In practice, it is about saying if my losses reach X percentage (I do not recommend more than 1% per operation) I close the position before it hits my account considerably.

Stop-loss point—points where a stock trader gives instruction of certain stocks to either be sold or bought when they attain a certain price in the stock market.

Stop order—an order implemented to close positions from the market when certain price parameters are attained.

Strike price—the amount of money given or received when a contract holder decides to close a contract position.

Swap—a derivative contract through which the parties involved exchange the cash flows from two different financial instruments.

Swing trader—(definition 1) a stock trader who holds their financial instruments such as stocks for a long time before they trade them.

Swing trader—(definition 2) an individual who either buys or sells securities in the market for several days or weeks to capture the gains of the market.

Synthetic position—a trade position that combines options and stocks in a single contract to emulate another option position.

Synthetic long call—a synthetic position that allows you to own calls. It entails purchasing puts as well as their related underlying assets.

Synthetic long put—a position that allows you to own puts. It entails purchasing calls then short-selling the underlying security related to the call.

Synthetic short call—a position that is similar to purchasing short calls. Entails selling stocks and selling put options associated with the stock.

Synthetic short put—a position that is similar to trading short puts. It entails purchasing stock then selling call options associated with the stock.

Synthetic short stock—this is a synthetic options position that is similar to going short on stocks. It entails writing one call contract at the money than purchasing one put option that is also at the money for the same underlying stock.

Support and resistance—the concepts of support and resistance are key pieces of the technical analysis of financial markets. Support is a price level below the current one in which the buying force is expected to exceed the sales force, so a bullish momentum will be slowed. Normally, support corresponds to a minimum previously reached.

Resistance is the opposite concept of support. It is the price zone above the current one in which the sales force will exceed that of the purchase, ending the bullish momentum, and therefore, the price will tend to recede. Resistances are commonly identified in a graph as previous highs reached by the price.

Take profit—many talks about the market going up or down; this is incorrect. The market moves down or up, that is, the market goes up and down all the time, but in a trend, a larger proportion of one prevails of these movements. Being aware that the market changes direction all the time it is prudent to take profits from time to time since its direction or tendency does not remain eternally. We call this prudent action to monetize benefits "Take Profit."

Technical analysis—(definition 1) a technique used to predict the price of financial instruments such as stocks through analyzing the historical price data of the underlying security.

Technical analysis—(definition 2) is a probability test whose result is the forecast of future price movements. It is the study of market action, mainly through the use of graphs, with the purpose of predicting future price trends.

Theoretical value—refers to the cost of an option position derived using pricing models and mathematical formulas.

Time decay—the period when the extrinsic value of an option decreases as it approaches the expiration date.

Trading plan—this is a plan that traders create to outline how they will carry out transactions on the options market. The plan always contains objectives, trading methods, and strategies to be used.

Trailing stop order—this is an order whose stop price is a percentage change from the best price ever reached by a given position.

Trader—any person who trades securities in the market with either their own money or someone else's.